THE NATIONAL CONVENTION

AS IT MET ON MONDAY, THE 4TH OF FEBRUARY, 1839,

AT THE BRITISH COFFEE HOUSE

FROM A SCARCE ENGRAVING

HISTORY OF THE
CHARTIST MOVEMENT

HISTORY OF THE

CHARTIST MOVEMENT

1837—1854

BY

R. G. GAMMAGE

ILLUSTRATED WITH NUMEROUS PORTRAITS

MERLIN PRESS
LONDON

This edition, a facsimile of the 1894 edition,
was first published by The Merlin Press Ltd.,
Sufferance Wharf, Isle of Dogs, London in 1969.
Reprinted 1976 by Whitstable Litho of Whitstable,
Kent.

ADVERTISEMENT.

THIS edition of the History of the Chartist Movement has been thoroughly revised and in many parts rewritten. It is to be regretted that the able author of the work, Mr. R. G. Gammage, did not live to perform this necessary revision, as the information he possessed would have added greatly to the value of the book. He died at Northampton in 1888, whither he had retired after spending upwards of thirty years of his later life as a medical practitioner in Sunderland.

For the valuable index which appears now for the first time, the publishers are indebted to the industry and ability of Mr. Thomas Marshall, Solicitor, Sunderland.

All the very rare portraits and views have been collected (some by loan,) from various sources, not without considerable difficulty.

INTRODUCTION.

An author who lays claim to a share of the public regard, should give a clear and definite idea of his object in the publication of any particular work, and in order that there may be no misconception of the object of the present production, it shall be stated in a few words. I have often been pained to observe that writers for or against Chartism, have been swayed rather by party bias than a regard for impartial truth, in giving vent to observations upon that movement which, whether for good or evil, has for many years commanded no little share of public attention. This is to be regretted, for it is only by rigid adherence to impartiality, that a sound and healthy opinion can possibly be formed. The purpose then of this work is to supply this obvious want. The Chartist movement has been signalized by many virtues, which it were folly to overlook, as well as unjust towards those who have borne a large share in that movement. Besides, we have no right to misrepresent, or even to pass over in contemptuous silence the opinions and actions of a large mass of our fellow creatures, be those opinions and actions right or wrong. The pursuance of such a course always recoils, and that most justly, on the heads of its authors, however influential their position. Whether Chartism be an actual truth, whether its principles will pass unscathed through the ordeal of investigation or otherwise, it must have had some important foundation for its existence, and the true politician will not hesitate to examine that foundation, in order that, if sound and good, he may be prepared with such concessions to justice as the case may require ; or if rotten and bad, that the rottenness may be pointed out and the consequent errors exploded. If Chartism has had its virtues, it is at the same time but too painfully evident that no small amount of folly has been mixed up with the movement. It has had its vices as well as its virtues, and though for those vices we shall feel disposed to make great allowance, we should be neglecting our duty to the cause of truth, were we to pass them by unnoticed, or fail to apply to them the needful correction.

Although this work will be principally a record of, rather

than a commentary upon events, and the men engaged in them, yet we shall from time to time as we proceed in our labours, make any observations which may appear to be necessary, for the historian should not be a mere recorder of the actions of men, but should also search into, examine, and give his candid opinion as to the springs of those actions, and the manner in which they have been performed.

It is possible that some of the strictures on the conduct and character of the prominent advocates of the Charter, will give rise to offence to their more devoted admirers, but to avoid this is impossible where there exists such a variety of sentiment and opinion. But although far from desiring to give unnecessary pain, I should despise myself could I stoop to flatter what appear to me to be unworthy prejudices. My object is truth, and by that truth I will stand whatever be the issue.

As the reader will perceive, brief biographical and critical notices of leading characters are interwoven with other matter, and if I mistake not, this will form not the least useful and interesting feature of the work. So far as the author is aware a distinct history of Chartism has never previously been even attempted. This is an additional justification of the present undertaking; and he hopes that his effort, however humble, will not be deemed unworthy of a place in the historical and political literature of his country.

1854   R. G. GAMMAGE.

CONTENTS.

CHAPTER XII.

CHAPTER XIII.

CHAPTER XIV.

ILLUSTRATIONS

HISTORY OF

THE CHARTIST MOVEMENT

CHAPTER I.

THE ARISTOCRACY

EVERY class in society has particular principles and prejudices
which it cherishes above all others. The Aristocracy
pride themselves on their distinction of birth, and on this distinction they found exclusive privileges which they seek to
guard with jealous care. To stand aloof from general
society, except in so far as that society contributes to their
necessities and pleasures, has ever been with them a favourite
practice. Under this phantom of superior birth they have
shielded themselves from contamination with the "inferior
orders," until the inordinate indulgence in luxuries has compelled them to an alliance with plebeian families, who, from the
active pursuits of trade and commerce, have become richer than
themselves. The downward tendency of Aristocracy in
England has been made more manifest as trade has become
more extensive ; in times when we were almost totally
independent of commerce and relied upon the produce of the
soil, as the Aristocracy held that soil in possession, their
power was almost absolute, and it was a long time even after
trade and commerce had progressed to a large extent, that
that power began sensibly to decline.

Modern civilization has, however, produced a mighty change
in the relative positions of classes. It has become an established fact that wealth is power, a power, moreover, that
threatens in its onward march to absorb all the fancied greatness of the patrician orders. Towards the close of the 18th
century this power began to assume colossal proportions.
It grew day by day, every year added immensely to its weight.
The French Revolution and the Wars of Napoleon threw the
titled class into consternation, and they were ready, like the

A

crew of a sinking ship, to grasp at any and every means to save themselves from that boiling ocean which threatened to engulf the Aristocracies of Europe.   To wage a war of exter-mination against the French Republicans appeared to them the only chance of saving themselves from an otherwise inevitable fate, and they spared no amount of blood or treasure in the prosecution of their object.   They threw themselves into the arms of the monied class.   All who possessed the sinews of war were urged to lend their aid in crushing the spirit of democratic innovation ; and the close of Napoleon's brilliant, but bloody and ambitious career, found this country saddled with a debt of between eight and £900,000,000, a burden entailed upon that and succeeding generations in return for the re-establishment of legitimacy and hereditary privilege.   Thus the nobility sought to prop up their falling power at the expense of the nation, and the monied class was the medium through which they hoped to attain their purpose.

It will not be difficult to suppose, that, as the middle class had become so necessary for sustaining the falling empire of the nobility, they would not long remain content under their exclusion from political privileges, and they soon made mani-fest their intention of sharing power with those whom they had so effectually served in the hour of need.   The legislative autho-rity had so far been almost exclusively in the hands of the patrician class who clung to it with a most tenacious grasp. The House of Peers was entirely their own, and between that and the house below, elected as it was under aristocratic pa-tronage, but little difference in reality existed ; on most points a cordial sympathy was cherished between the two bodies, who justly regarded each other as branches of the same tree.   The middle class was, however, every day rising to greater import-ance, as the result of commercial enterprise, and at last the gentle breeze, which wafted to the ears of the class above the dreaded name of reform, grew into a loud and clamorous swell, which seemed to shake the very foundation of patrician power.

The middle class, finding themselves not sufficiently power-ful alone, had invoked the aid of the labouring millions, and the two classes combined made every available spot echo and re-echo with the now popular cry of reform.   The press began to teem with speeches and articles urging the justice and ne-cessity of a more extended system of representation, and to back the loud demand, Captain Swing assumed his authority in several large and important towns ; and although some of the agents in this destructive warfare suffered the penalty of their transgressions, these proceedings only hastened the coming empire of the middle class, until at last signs of dis-

affection amongst the military enabled them to reach the goal.
Amid the burning excitement of an expectant nation the
Reform Bill, after repeated rejection, passed both Houses
and received the royal assent.   Thus was established the
Charter of the middle class.   The Aristocracy had availed
themselves of the aid of that class to crush Democracy,
little dreaming that they were contracting obligations to a
power which would ultimately crush themselves.   Thus
privileged tyranny often steps over one grave only to find
another a few paces beyond.

It was not, however, without the promise of substantial advantages that the middle class succeeded in winning the
co-operation of the masses, who were themselves looking
forward to an extension of political power, but who were too
easily turned aside from the pursuit of their object.   The
middle class persuaded them for a season to forego their
more extensive claims, in order the more effectually to secure
them ultimately.   "Aid us," said they, "in gaining the
Reform Bill, and as soon as we are enfranchised we will
make use of our power in assisting you to the attainment of
your rights."   This was the promise invariably held out to
the working class whenever they ventured to moot the
broader question of popular sovereignty.   A promise the more
readily believed because at that time an idea pervaded their
minds that the interests of the two classes were identical.
It was conjectured therefore, that the one could have no purpose in deceiving the other ; a breach of faith was never
anticipated, for they could not comprehend the object
of such a possibility.   The wide disparity in the social
position of the two classes was lost sight of altogether ;
a confused notion had taken possession of their minds that
an adjustment of taxation and a few other measures which a
middle class parliament might safely pass, was the main object
of their enterprise.   A man had therefore only to call himself
a reformer or a liberal, and indulge in a few vague generalities
upon trivial subjects, to command the sympathies of
the majority as effectually as though he were about to introduce them to the bowers of a social paradise.   Reform,
retrenchment, peace, reform of the church, corporation
reform, justice to Ireland, these were the watchwords of
the middle class patriots ; the poorer class studied but little
what all these things amounted to, but they took the good
intentions of their allies upon trust ; they looked with bewil-
dered eyes to some future amelioration of their condition the
extent of which they never gave themselves the trouble to
examine, and which, therefore, they did not understand.

The new middle class constituency gave to the reformers an immense majority in the Commons, and on that majority the hopes of the people were fixed. But a short time, however, elapsed before all their magnificent castles evaporated into that air in which they had been erected. Justice to Ireland was illustrated in a speech from the throne in which a stringent coercion bill was recommended for the relief of that suffering and injured country. Even O'Connell, the ally of the Whigs, was compelled to put his stigma on that paragraph of the royal speech, to which he applied the term "bloody," and in as plain a style he denounced his allies as "the base, brutal, and bloody Whigs." Despite, however, the powerful denunciation of the great agitator and his Irish supporters, a bill was introduced, and carried through the Legislature by sweeping majorities, the very year after the enactment of the Reform Bill.

The whig doctrine of retrenchment was soon after exemplified by the introduction of a measure to amend the 43rd of Elizabeth in regard to the relief of the poor. The framers of that measure made no disguise of their intentions. Those disciples of Malthus intimated that the object of the bill was to bring the poor to live upon a coarser sort of food ; and, in proof of this being their object, Lord Brougham contended that the ill-paid labouring classes ought to save sufficient means in their early days to support themselves in the decline of life. The sternest opponent of this new-fangled doctrine was the immortal William Cobbett, who bitterly condemned it by speech and pen, and voted on principle against every clause of the measure. There were a few others, who, in the Legislature, championed the cause of the poor, but all opposition in the House was fruitless,—the bill was enacted. In the names of reform and liberty the Parliament abolished Parochial government, and rendered the relief of the poor subservient to the dictates of a triumvirate over whom the ratepayers had not the slightest control.

The Government shortly afterwards proceeded with measures for the reform of that scandal on religion and civilization the Irish Church. Unsuccessful in their attempts they resigned office, and were succeeded by Sir Robert Peel and his party. The right hon. baronet did not for many months enjoy the sweets of office, and the Whigs were speedily reinstated, when they abandoned the very principle on which they had previously resigned. Afraid to invoke the spirit of the people Government and Parliament proceeded in their work of temporization ; and it became evident that the reformed House of Commons was powerful only for the perpetuation of evil. Such was the

Parliament to which the deluded people had looked forward with such sanguine hope.

The rotten House of Commons numbered, however, amongst its members a few who made larger professions of a leaning towards Democracy than the vast majority. At the head of this diminutive band stood John Arthur Roebuck, and joined with him were John Temple Leader, Sir William Molesworth, Colonel Thompson, Thomas Wakley, Sharman Crawford, Joseph Hume, Dr. Bowring, and Daniel O'Connell. These men, with a few others, formed the extreme section of the Commons ; and certainly, on popular questions, they often spoke with a boldness that contrasted markedly with the milk-and-water speeches of the Whigs and their supporters. The amendment of the representation they made a frequent subject of discussion, although never introducing any well digested measure embodying their object. One would bring before the House the question of the franchise, another the Ballot, a third the duration of Parliament, and a fourth the state of the property qualification.

The boldest step taken by the radical party was on the opening of the first session after the accession of Her present Majesty, by which time, however, Roebuck and others had been ousted from their seats at the general election. On the address in answer to the royal speech being moved Mr. Wakley proposed an amendment in the shape of an addition to the address. The addition represented to Her Majesty that the House would, at its earliest convenience, proceed to the consideration of measures for securing a better representation of the people by extending the elective franchise, adopting the Ballot, and shortening the duration of Parliament. Sir William Molesworth seconded the amendment. Lord John Russell, on the part of the Government, met it with the most decided opposition, and it was on that occasion that the noble lord made his celebrated declaration of finality. Sir Robert Peel also announced his resolve to oppose all further democratic changes. O'Connell ratted from his party, and voted with the Government. It is also worthy of remark that Mr., afterwards Sir Henry Ward voted for the amendment. On a division only twenty-two members, including tellers, were found in favour of reform, while the majority against it was enormous.

A little previous to that time a society was established in the metropolis under the unassuming title of the Working Men's Association. Although its name gave no indication of a political tendency its leading object was to secure for the people their fair share in the representation. So careful did the Association affect to be of the influence of the working class, that no person out of their ranks was admitted to a voice in its affairs. Persons belonging to the middle and upper classes were accepted as honorary members but nothing more. By means of meetings, banquets, and printed addresses, the Association attempted to draw the attention of the country to the subject of parliamentary reform. The finality declaration of Lord John Russell had given to the little band of parliamentary Radicals an out of doors position. They were invited to attend these meetings and banquets, which they frequently did ; and between them and the Association a connection was at length regularly formed.

A committee had been appointed, consisting partially of M.P.'s and partially of members of the Association, whose office was to mould their views into the form of a bill to be afterwards submitted to a public meeting ; which bill contained six cardinal points. The six points were :—Universal Manhood Suffrage, Annual Parliaments, Vote by Ballot, No Property Qualification, Payment of Members, and Equal Voting Districts. To this bill was given the title of *The People's Charter*. At the public meeting held to inaugurate the new movement several of the radical members attended and supported the resolutions. It is possible that they never imagined that any considerable amount of public opinion would be rallied in their favour, for exactly as that opinion grew in strength their radical sentiments declined. A slight glance at the past and present position of these men may not be uninstructive. O'Connell was the man who handed the Charter to the secretary of the Association, exclaiming as he did so, "There, Lovett, is your Charter, agitate for it, and never be content with anything less." It was not long after that time that the same man did all in his power to discredit the movement, and he continued virulent in his opposition to the day of his death. Dr. Bowring has since accepted a snug place under the Government, previous to which he had become remarkably silent as to his former principles. The once radical Mr. Ward accepted the governorship of the Ionian Islands, where he became a monster of cruelty, second only to the ever-to-be execrated Haynau himself. Sir William Molesworth has become a member of the present coalition government, and what of democracy he still retains is of the smoothest character : his rose-water speeches now contrast strangely with that energetic language which once drew forth cries of "order" in the House of Commons. John Arthur Roebuck has been for some years in search of a place, and seems—although still in Parliament—to have almost retired from public life under the weight of his vexation and disappointment. John Temple Leader speedily

HENRY HETHERINGTON

FROM A MINIATURE IN THE POSSESSION OF
EDWARD TRUELOVE, ESQ.

sank into a political nonentity and quitted the country for a more congenial clime. Wakley has retired from public life. Sharman Crawford—the most consistent of them all—was ousted at the last general election. Colonel Thompson became as eccentric as Brougham as he advanced in years and was seldom to be relied upon ; and Joseph Hume is so democratic as to indulge in tirades against the press for too strongly denouncing the proceedings of continental despots. Such are the people's champions of former days. Surely, in taking a glance at the above, there should be sufficient to teach the people that in pursuing the path of political and social elevation they must place reliance only on themselves.

A little previous to the inauguration of the movement for the Charter, the metropolitan Association had dispatched its missionaries to the country for the purpose of forming provincial associations on the model of the original. The principal deputy engaged in these preliminary operations was Henry Hetherington. Perhaps, for the success of the mission, a fitter man could not have been selected, for his name was sufficient to procure the attendance of all the leading radical reformers. Hetherington was no shining orator to move multitudes by the force of his eloquence. He possessed but few of the requisites for stirring up the passions. He was not the man for those impulsive beings upon whom solid argument is lost, but whose souls are stirred to their depths by fiery declamation ; but was rather adapted to the intelligent and thoughtful ; and it was persons of the latter description who generally composed his audience. It was not his mission to create new elements but to cement those already in existence, and these elements he found in every town he visited.

In the great battle of the unstamped press in which he bore so conspicuous a part, sustaining as he did several government prosecutions, his name became a household word amongst the members of the radical party. Possessed of indomitable courage and inflexible perseverance, defying persecution, and trampling on the Stamp Act as so much waste paper, he had earned for himself a reputation which caused the more advanced of the working class to gather round him in scores, sometimes in hundreds. His rough strong logic struck conviction into every mind, while his dry and essentially English humour, gave to it an agreeable zest. His meetings were generally held within doors : indeed, anywhere else they would, in more senses than one, have been out of place. His mission was highly successful : Associations rapidly multiplied. Sometimes, indeed, they started with no more than a dozen members, but even these grew by degrees into formidable bodies, who promised to wield no little influence in political matters. In some of the towns where these Associations were established, members of Parliament answered their communications with respect, and sometimes condescended to visit their meetings in person in order to conciliate their favour for an approaching election. The majority of members were, it is true, non-electors, but many of them belonged to the electoral class, and it was deemed not unimportant to look after these, in case of a close and doubtful contest. Nor were the non-electors thought to be so insignificant as to be worthy only of contempt. Such were the Working Men's Associations in 1838.

Although the Associations at the outset only affirmed the general principle of democratic government, no sooner was the Charter in all its details ushered into existence than a copy was transmitted to every radical association throughout the kingdom. As the leading principle had already been sanctioned, there was little difficulty in obtaining universal assent to the details which were to give practical form to that principle. The radical party had long been charged with a lack of statesmanship. Very fine theorists and assertors of undeniable abstract principles they were admitted to be, but their ability to reduce those principles to tangible shape was denied. The appearance of the Charter rendered these denials perfectly groundless. Whatever opinion might be held of the principles themselves, the document was such as might have reflected credit on the most learned of the legal profession. True it was not much interlarded with legal technicalities, and it was void of those ambiguities which have rendered our laws so uncertain, and given rise to a harvest of speculation for the lawyers ; but it was its very freedom from these that enhanced its value by making it easy of comprehension to the common mind.

The radical party had also been charged by their opponents with being lax in their notions as to the binding properties of law. The Charter, by the penalties which it proposed to inflict on the violators of its provisions, was sufficient to shew how utterly groundless was the accusation, and proved that its originators held public virtue in the very highest esteem. The Bill was unanimously adopted by the provincial Associations, but strange to relate, the men of the half-radical school began to complain that a general principle, on which all might have agreed, had been fettered with non-essential details, and they made that their excuse for holding aloof from the movement. Thus, whatever course they pursued, the poor Radicals found themselves inadequate to the task of pleasing their opponents and their half-hearted friends. If they discarded details they were charged with being mere theorists, and with not having done enough. ·Those details adopted, they were charged with having done too much. Thus it ever was—thus it ever will be—until the last knell of tyranny shall have rung. But it was not the political question alone which engaged the attention of the radical reformers. Political reforms were certainly valued because of their abstract justice, but they were also looked upon as a means of securing a better social position for the humbler classes ; and argued in this sense, the speeches of the radical orators always told with most effect. It may be doubted whether there ever was a great political movement of the people without a social origin. The chief material object of mankind is to possess the means of social enjoyment. Secure them in possession of these and small is the care they have for political abstractions. It is the existence of great social wrongs which principally teaches the masses the value of political rights. This truth has received repeated manifestations. In times of comparative prosperity there is scarce a ripple to be observed on the ocean of politics, but let that prosperity be succeeded by a period of adversity and the waves of popular discontent will roll with such impetuous force as to threaten the safety of the political fabric. The masses look on the enfranchised classes, whom they behold reposing on the couch of opulence, and contrast that opulence with the misery of their own condition. Reasoning from effect to cause there is no marvel that they arrive at the conclusion—that their exclusion from political power is the cause of our social anomalies. There might be no clear idea in their minds at the commencement of the movement for the Charter of the way in which political power was worked to their disadvantage. Still less might they be aware of the nature of those social measures which the possession of that power would enable them to apply for the improvement of their condition. That mystery, the cause of social misery, the Working Men's Association endeavoured to solve. At the bottom of their card of membership appeared the following striking words :— "The man who evades his share of useful labour diminishes the public stock of wealth, and throws his own burden upon his neighbour."

accordingly.   He   never   ventured   to   enter   upon   the
dangerous ground of logic ; had he done so there is little
doubt that he would have set all its rules at utter defiance.
His oratory, moreover, was not really so good as it appeared.
As one listened to him from the platform he seemed to cap
the climax ; it was his attitude, his voice, his gesture,
and his enthusiasm, rather than his language, which contained the summary of his power.   Occasionally, indeed,—
we must do him the justice to admit—he delivered a
grand and beautiful sentence, but only occasionally.   He
could impress his hearers with the conviction that his speeches
were from beginning to end masterpieces of eloquence ; but
the moment they appeared in black and white the sweet
illusion vanished, the charm was dissolved, the magic spell
was broken, and he appeared but little more than an ordinary
speaker.

This was the man whom the Association appointed to rouse
the slumbering energies of the masses ; and never, under
similar circumstances, were the efforts of a popular orator
crowned with more brilliant success.   Wherever he appeared
he drew forth the most enthusiastic responses.   Vincent lived
at this time in a whirlpool of pleasing excitement.   His labours
were confined principally to the Midland and Western districts of England and the South of Wales.   Occasionally he
ventured northward, but it was not there that the graceful
orator shone to the best advantage.   Northampton, Leicester,
Nottingham, Banbury, Coventry, and Birmingham in the
Midlands ; Cheltenham, Bath, Trowbridge, Bradford, Bristol,
Wootton-under-Edge, Stroud, and other places in the West ;
these were the principal theatres of his oratorical displays ;
and in some of them he wielded an influence which even a
prince might envy.   Among the Welsh his fervid declamation awakened every sympathy of the heart.   His thrilling
tones as he depicted the burning wrongs of the toiling class
fanned the passions of that excitable people into a flame
which no after prudence could allay.   So successful was he as
an agitator that even the richer class often attended his
meetings in considerable numbers from a mere love of
curiosity ; and whilst admitting his power they execrated
his principles and invoked the spirit of persecution to shorten
his career.

While the London Association was pursuing its course in
the Midlands, the West, and Wales, other parties were no less
active in the work of organization.   Political unions became
the order of the day.   There was scarcely a town or village
throughout the extensive manufacturing districts of Lancashire

Yorkshire, or Cheshire, that did not contain its muster-roll of ardent Democrats. The Unions in these districts were on a somewhat different basis from that of the Working Men's Association. As before observed the latter excluded all but working men from a voice in its affairs. Whatever the object of this rule might have been, it was based on an evil principle, the principle of class exclusion, which is as unjust when carried out by one class as by another. Democracy levels all distinctions of class and recognises man as such without regard to external circumstances. There was, however, more than a suspicion that it was not so much a jealousy of the higher orders that suggested the rule in question, as a desire to exclude from their councils certain obnoxious individuals whose influence was too much dreaded by its promoters. If such were the fact it was impossible to have pursued a course more at variance with wisdom. When a man belonging to the upper or middle ranks undertakes to advocate the cause of the poor, to throw obstacles in his path without producing a justifiable reason is regarded by the mass of men as a species of persecution, and they are sure to rally round the victim of such injustice. It might be that the Associations deemed the advocacy of certain individuals injurious to the cause, but the proper course was to show wherein these individuals were wrong, and not attempt to smother their voices by a violation of the principle of equality,— the very principle they were themselves espousing both by speech and pen.

The principal person judged to be aimed at through this proscriptive clause was one who had long previously attracted to himself a share of attention in the sister kingdom, and whose influence was beginning to be felt amongst the British working class, the renowned and eccentric Feargus O'Connor, who was able to boast of his descent from a race of Irish kings. How such a boast could be of any service in recommending him to the respect of the people has often been a puzzle, for certainly if ever men deserved to be classed among cowards and poltroons, and to meet with the scorn and derision of mankind, it must be frankly confessed by all readers of Irish history that the kings of Ireland were entitled to that distinction, and none more so than the ancestors of O'Connor.

Feargus O'Connor first came prominently before the people of Ireland in 1831. His chief mission was that of securing the return of liberal members to the House of Commons. In no part of the United Kingdom are elections contested with such virulence of party spirit as in Ireland. It requires, therefore, the extreme of energy on either side to ensure success.

O'Connor was just the man suited to the strife of an Irish election. No member of the prize ring could fight his way with more desperate energy through a crowd than could this electioneering pugilist ; and it was not alone with his fists that he was useful to his friends. A barrister by profession, and an Irishman possessed of more than an average amount of rhetorical ability, he could plead the cause of a candidate on the hustings with no little share of persuasive power. In this way he rendered essential service to O'Connell, who, for a time, received him into his grace and favour. It was impossible, however, for such elements long to remain in a state of assimilation. O'Connor enjoyed no little share of Irish popularity, as was evinced in his return for the County of Cork in 1833. O'Connell, as the leader of the Irish people, could not brook a man who was calculated to divide with him any considerable amount of power, nor could O'Connor acknowledge a superior. The words Milton puts into the mouth of the rebelious angel were strictly applicable to him : "Better to reign in hell than serve in heaven." During the time that O'Connor was in parliament he was ever at loggerheads with his chief. Let us, however, admit that it was his greater consistency that was generally the cause of their differences. O'Connell was frequently truckling to the Whigs with the view of securing place and power for his party at the expense of principle. In this policy O'Connor never agreed with the great agitator, and constantly sought to defeat his plans. This course eventually caused the two to separate, never again to be united.

When O'Connell repudiated his former friend he made a present of him to the English Radicals. By a portion of these, as we have already intimated, he was received with no great favour ; but by another portion his services were freely accepted. What assisted in gaining him a passport to their society was the fact that having sat in the House of Commons he was ousted after his last election on the ground of non-qualification by a parliamentary committee. The manu-facturing districts were the places selected by O'Connor in which to win for himself a prominent position. This was no difficult task for a man of his unbounded energy. He traversed those districts accordingly, and wherever he went a political union was the result of his exertions. When the proper time arrived the whole of these unions gave in their adhesion to the Charter.

As public opinion appeared to be growing in favour of organic reform, another important political body underwent

a re-organization.   This body had for its title the Birmingham
Political Union.   Its directing council numbered several
members who held an influential position in society.   Its
leader was Mr. Thomas Atwood, the member for the borough.
Two others were the brothers Muntz, one of whom at present
fills the post from which Atwood retired to enjoy the
sweets of private life.   Mr. Douglas, editor of the *Birmingham
Journal*, was also an active member.   Mr. Edmonds, afterwards converted into town clerk, lent it his countenance ; but
perhaps its principal spokesman was Mr. John Collins, a
working man.   Before the movement for the Charter was
inaugurated the Union had agreed upon an agitation for
Universal Suffrage, the Ballot, and Annual Parliaments ; but
seeing the tide of opinion setting in in favour of a more complete reform they were easily brought to form a part of the
swelling stream and to give a formal adhesion to the
Charter.

The counties of Northumberland and Durham were not
behind their southern brethren in the great work of reform.
The public mind had been in a measure prepared by one of
the boldest and most consistent Radicals that ever mounted
a public platform, Augustus Beaumont.   On all the
leading questions of the day that gentleman frequently
addressed numerous audiences in Newcastle and the surrounding neighbourhood.   As he promulgated the most extreme
opinions consistent with justice the Charter was not likely to
be unfavourably received.   Every day the feelings of the
people waxed stronger in favour of democratic change.   The
Radicals of the two counties formed themselves into a body
under the title of the Northern Political Union which embraced
several thousand persons.   The great mass of them belonged
to the producing class, but a considerable number
were members of the middle ranks of society, who took a very
active part in the movement.   At Carlisle the elements of
Democracy also began to unite.   Its population, one
of the poorest in the kingdom, embraced with eagerness a
movement which had for its object the elevation of the
working people.   There were leaders of talent amongst this
class ready to give direction to their efforts.

In Scotland the utmost activity began to be manifested.
The Birmingham Political Union deputed Collins to sound
the opinions of the radical party and he made an extensive
tour for that purpose.   He proclaimed the political gospel in
not less than twenty churches during his perambulations and
found matters according to his desire.   The leading politicians
appeared all ripe for a change.   Differences on points of detail

were flung to the winds. Like their brethren of Birmingham they waved all minor matters in the wish to cement their forces in one great whole. But a short time elapsed before Charter unions sprang up with amazing rapidity ; and the Radicals of Great Britain at every point now seemed united into a mighty phalanx, all equally bent on securing the one great object on which they had fixed their hopes.

The formation of political unions was only a part of the machinery necessary for carrying out a great popular movement. It would have been of little use to call the people together if no organ had existed to enforce their claims or give a record of their proceedings. It was, therefore, a matter of necessity for the radical party to establish a press through which the public might be supplied with information on all subjects relating to the common cause.

The London Working Men's Association already possessed its journal. When the law which imposed a fourpenny stamp upon newspapers was repealed, Hetherington's *Twopenny Despatch* changed its title to that of the *London Despatch,* which it retained until it ceased to exist. Its editor was a gentleman known by the name of Beaumont—a relative, we believe, of Augustus Beaumont—who conducted it with considerable ability. It was almost exclusively to political changes that the columns of this journal were devoted, although occasionally it touched upon social grievances. Its great aim was the enactment of the Charter, to which it made all other questions subservient. Its policy was that of what was called the moral force party, who disclaimed all idea of seeking a change by physical force. It sought constantly to impress upon its readers that the political emancipation of the people must be achieved by peaceful means alone. Its articles were generally of a mild persuasive tone. It never enjoyed a very extensive circulation. This journal was the organ of the Association. Another paper was launched in the borough of Leeds under the title of *The Northern Star.* Its proprietor was the popular Feargus O'Connor who had become the idol of the operatives in the manufacturing districts. Never was a journal started more opportunely. It caught and reflected the spirit of the times. It was not, however, with his own means alone that O'Connor succeeded in establishing the *Star.* Not less than £800 was subscribed in shares by his friends, without whose timely assistance it is doubtful whether he could, at that time, have ventured on the speculation. Those friends had faith in its success, and the result proved the reasonableness of their anticipations, for *The Northern Star* speedily stood at the head of the democratic journals. Its editor was the Rev. William Hill, an acute and clever but not a very agreeable writer. It was not, however, for its editorial department that it was so much valued. Two circumstances contributed to raise it in popular estimation. One of these was the popularity of O'Connor, a popularity which was largely due to the fact of his having a journal in which to record all his proceedings and to place his words and deeds in the most advantageous light. The other circumstance was, that the *Star* was regarded as the most complete record of the movement. There was not a meeting held in any part of the country, in however remote a spot, that was not reported in its columns, accompanied by all the flourishes calculated to excite an interest in the reader's mind, and to inflate the vanity of the speakers by the honourable mention of their names. Even if they had never mounted the platform before, the speeches were described and reported as eloquent, argumentative, and the like ; and were dressed up with as much care as though they were parliamentary harangues fashioned to the columns of the daily press. Thus men of very mediocre abilities appeared to people at a distance to be oracles of political wisdom. It must not be thought that these observations are intended to cast a slur on the real talent exhibited by the working class in this great movement ; for, however much that talent was exaggerated, it was more than sufficient to forbid its being despised.

It must be borne in mind that down to about this period, with the single exception of the time of the Consolidated Trades' Union, even the more enlightened of the working class had been but little accustomed to public speaking. The platform had been almost exclusively occupied by the upper and middle classes, and it could hardly be expected that the working men, deprived in a great measure of educational advantages, would become adept speakers in a day. But the dawn of the Chartist movement was quite an era in working class oratory. It gave to the humblest the opportunity of raising his voice in public meeting, an opportunity that was embraced with avidity. It is needless, perhaps, to say that these speeches, as well as the meetings to which they were addressed, were often enormously exaggerated in the *Star*, but that very exaggeration was one of the grounds of its success. Men who had never previously been accustomed to see themselves in print were flattered by the proud distinction ; and, though they sometimes experienced a difficulty in detecting their own portraits, the over done colouring of the artist was not uncongenial to their tastes. Who amongst

citizens to the rising movement, and there ensued such a display as will never be forgotten by those who witnessed the proceedings. Arrangements were entered into by the working men for holding a great aggregate meeting on the Green, a spacious piece of ground which acts as one of the lungs of Glasgow, at the bottom of which the rushing waters of the majestic Clyde sweep on. The working men got up this mighty demonstration of their numbers on the 28th of May, 1838, almost unassisted by any other class. Only one or two individuals of the middle ranks gave the movement their countenance; but no business could have been transacted with better care, or have reflected greater credit on the parties concerned. The whole arrangements bore proof of the capability of the Glasgow working class to manage their own affairs. The Birmingham Union had resolved to lend all possible influence to make the demonstration effective and commanding, and for that purpose appointed Messrs. Atwood, Douglas, Edmunds, Muntz, and Collins, to assist the Glasgow Democrats.

Before eleven o'clock the gathering masses mustered on the Green in tens of thousands, and at that hour the procession started to meet Mr. Atwood at the east end of the City, where he was expected in company with his colleagues. The numerous bodies of men walked six deep, and at a rapid pace, while the streets along the whole line were thronged by a dense crowd of human beings all eager to participate in achieving the great work of political reform. It was computed that not fewer than 200,000 of the stalwart sons of labour displayed their toil-worn faces in this gigantic gathering. Not even at the time of the Reform agitation did such immense numbers turn out of their workshops and houses to join in the rallying cry of the nation. The very heavens rang with the lively strains of music and the shouts of the enthusiastic multitude. There were forty bands of music placed at respective distances along the line of march, more than two hundred flags and banners of every size and variety, most beautiful in appearance, waved gracefully in the breeze, and added to the gaiety of the day. One of these from Strathaven was an object of great curiosity and interest from the fact that it had waved over the hardy covenanters at the battle of Drumclog, during that fierce and mighty struggle of Scotland for her religious liberties. The procession was an hour and a half in passing a given spot, and when Mr. Atwood and his colleagues made their appearance nothing could have surpassed the enthusiasm of the people. Having marched back to the Green, Mr. Turner, a member of the City Council, was voted to the chair, and the meeting was addressed by several working men in support of the various resolutions and the petition to Parliament ; after which the thanks of the vast assemblage were accorded to Mr. Atwood and the rest of the deputation, upon which that gentleman addressed the meeting as soon as the enthusiastic cheering, waving of hats, and beating of drums would allow him to proceed. He first dwelt with much force and feeling on the distressed condition of the working class, and expressed an opinion that the Reform Act had turned out to be an utter failure in securing the good of the country. He afterwards developed the plan of action agreed upon by the Birmingham Political Union. The petition was to be signed by all the Democrats throughout the country, and he calculated that there would be two or three millions of signatures. This petitioning process was to be repeated again and again should Parliament not be disposed at first to concede the popular demands ; and if after giving the Legislature a fair trial, they should still refuse, then the working men with such of the middle class as might be disposed to favour their views, should proclaim a solemn and sacred strike from every kind of labour. Not a hand was to be raised to work, but every heart, every head, and every arm was to be directed to the furtherance of the people's cause until victory smiled upon their efforts. Messrs. Edmunds, Muntz, and Douglas, all followed in a similar strain to the great delight of the meeting. None of the four gentlemen seemed disposed to pass over the obstacles, as far as they saw them, which would impede the people's path. "We have against us," exclaimed Mr. Atwood, "the whole of the Aristocracy, nine-tenths of the gentry, the great body of the Clergy, and all the pensioners, sinecurists, and bloodsuckers that feed on the vitals of the people ;" but he never seemed to contemplate the greatest obstacle of all, the newly enfranchised middle class.

Mr Murphy and Dr. Wade appeared as a deputation from the London Working Men's Association ; and the latter gentleman addressed the mighty concourse of people in a most hopeful strain. "We have," he exclaimed towards the conclusion of his speech, " sufficient physical power, but that is not necessary, for we have sufficient moral power to gain all we ask."

After the speaking had concluded, the meeting dispersed in the greatest order. Captain Millar, the city superintendent of police, acted as grand marshal on the occasion of this manifestation of public opinion, and he declared that never did he attend a meeting which was conducted in a better spirit.

This great demonstration was followed in the evening by a banquet, which was attended by about six hundred persons. Mr. Moir, tea merchant, presided ; and he was supported by Mr. Atwood, Mr. Douglas, Mr. Muntz, Mr. Collins, Mr. Edmonds, Dr. Wade, Mr. Murphy, Mr. Turner, the Rev. Mr. Edwards, and other gentlemen.   The same enthusiasm characterised the proceedings.   Every speaker seemed full of hope for the future, and all expressed a fixed and firm determination to go on with the mighty work, which they appeared to anticipate would result at no distant day in the freedom of the masses from political inequality and social misery.   The demonstration on the Green had given them fresh inspiration, and they expressed a resolve to use their strength in the cause of national liberty.

On the 27th of June, 1838, the men of the Tyne and the Wear resolved to shew their approval of the new movement by one of the most magnificent arrays of moral and numerical power ever exhibited by the masses of this country.   The gathering was announced to be holden on the Town Moor of Newcastle, a spacious piece of common ground a little to the north of the town.   Early on the morning of the appointed day crowds began to line the public thoroughfares and to manifest a deep interest in the coming demonstration.   At nine o'clock St. Nicholas' Square, an open space in front of one of the handsomest churches in Europe, began to be thronged by an excited crowd.   Processions of the trades marched from the various quarters of the town towards that spot as the centre from whence the main body was to proceed. These organized bodies of men formed lines of six deep, and were hedged in by a multitude on each side throughout the long line of procession, the extent of which was so great that when the head reached the place of meeting the rear was yet wending its way through the streets at a distance of a mile and a half from the hustings.   There were not less than fourteen bands of music in the vast procession, and, at a distance of about thirty yards from each other, along the whole line banners of the most tasteful appearance waved in the breeze.   A considerable number of these contained patriotic inscriptions from the works of Byron, of which the following are a few:—

"FREEDOM."

"When once more her hosts assemble,
    Let the tyrants only tremble ;
    Smile they at this idle threat ?
    Crimson tears may follow yet."

"HOPE."

"Methinks I hear a little bird that sings,
The people bye and bye will be the stronger."

"OUR BIRTHRIGHT."

"Freedom, such as God hath given
Unto all beneath His heaven."

"THE PAST AND THE PRESENT."

"Must we but weep o'er days more blest,
Must we but blush our fathers bled."

"THE WHIGS."

"That worse than worst of foes, the once adored
False friend, that held out freedom to mankind,
And now would chain them to the very mind."

"REVOLUTION."

"I've seen some nations, like o'er-loaded asses,
Kick off their burdens, meaning the high classes."

On another flag appeared the well-known quotation from
Burns :

"Man's inhumanity to man
Makes countless thousands mourn."

On another, also from the same author :

"The rank is but the guinea's stamp,
The man's the gowd for a' that."

There were various other inscriptions from Cowper, Goldsmith,
and others, but the larger number were original.

The whole of the procession had not reached the ground
around the hustings when Mr. Grey moved Mr. Doubleday,
a veteran champion of Democracy who had taken an active
part in all public meetings, to the chair. The Moor at that
time presented what the foes of progress would designate
"a truly awful appearance." The numbers present were
estimated at eighty thousand, and as they came on to the
ground, they manifested the warmest enthusiasm. Amid
renewed cheering the chairman proceeded to open the business
of the meeting. The good humoured expression of that
gentleman's face was well calculated to gain upon a meeting
of the masses, and perhaps no speech of the day produced a
deeper impression. We will do him the justice to insert an
extract.

"Universal Suffrage was the usage of the country up to the
middle of the reign of Henry the Sixth. Well, how was this

lost? It was in the confusion of the civil wars. The people did not know its value, and under plausible pretences the law was altered. From that time to this Englishmen had been feeling the effects of this treacherous deed. The evil crept on gradually. The country was then rich, and the common people wealthy to an extent they had no idea of. There were hardly any taxes ; and there could be none, because a parliament elected by the people took care of the people's earnings. But when this was lost all changed. The Aristocracy gradually found out that the people were too rich, and so they made laws to cure this evil. Yes, they actually made statutes to keep wages down to a certain level lest the people should get too luxurious, and the statute wages shewed the state of the country at that time. Even under these statutes the labouring man earned as much in a week as would buy a fine fat sheep, or a pretty decent lump of the carcase of an ox. They were nice times then, were they not? Could they do so now? Well, so kind were they that they not only took care that the people should not eat too much, but also that they should not dress too finely, so they made a law that no working man or artizan should wear a cloak, or hose, or vest of cloth that cost more than about twenty-four shillings of the present day per yard. Small need of such a statute now. So the thing went on. As the power and insolence of the Aristocracy increased the people were made poorer, till at last, about 1770, having fleeced England to some tune, they thought they would try and tax the American colonies. The brave Americans, however, would not stand this ; they resisted, the battle was fought, the patriots succeeded, the United States became a free Republic, and that thing called the National Debt of England, was now pushed up to the enormous sum of two hundred and fifty million pounds ; and all this to gratify the propensities of a plundering Aristocracy. Ten years after that the French Revolution broke out. The greedy Aristocracy got dreadfully alarmed. They made war upon the French people to prevent their having a good government. That iniquitous conflict went on for twenty years, and the upshot was that the people of England were loaded with eight hundred million pounds of debt, and a load of taxes unequalled in this world."

So well was the chairman's speech suited to the taste of the meeting that it was with difficulty he drew to a close ; when he did so he introduced Mr. James Ayr, a working man, who, in the course of his speech, made the following remarks :—

"He was proud of the thousands which had banded together this day, to worship at the altar of freedom. The sword of oppression hung over them, but if need should be, they would draw the sword of justice, and never return it to the scabbard till justice should be done to the wronged and outraged people of England. He had been anxiously looking round him for an aristocratic face, in order that he might tell him what he thought, but could not recognise lord this or the duke of that. No! no! They dare not meet the righteous indignation of the men of Newcastle. He would advert to a portion of the resolution which he held in his hand; it declared that they would use every means,—not every legal means, mark!—but every means for the attainment of Universal Suffrage. He could not help again alluding to the Monarchy; hitherto it had reigned for itself, but he declared before that vast assembly, and in its name, that if it did not reign for the good of the millions, it should not reign at all. The famishing and the helpless, the widow and the orphan, and future generations would depend on them for freedom--should posterity find them wanting? The interests of working men were everywhere the same, and oppressors would find that working men were about to be everywhere united. Knowledge was power, and union was strength, and in the diffusion of knowledge and the union that had now sprung up among the people, he foresaw, and that too at no distant period, the downfall of Aristocracy all over the world. They had the representative of the despot Nicholas, and of the sleek tyrant Louis Phillipe, and the representatives from all their brother tyrants, assisting to crown sovereign of a great nation a little girl who would be more usefully and properly employed at her needle ; but the people would be no longer led away by their gaudy trappings ; they would look to themselves and to their families, for if they saw the gewgaws of royalty on the one side, they would see the damnable Bastile on the other."

The above is perhaps one of the best specimens of the working class oratory of that period, and we may affirm that the diction employed would be no disgrace to any assembly. But how lamentable to see men wasting words on comparatively trivial subjects. What intelligent man of the present day regards the Monarchy as the root of the nation's grievances ? Abolish that Monarchy to-morrow, and leave the fundamental relations between capital and labour on their present footing, and you will have accomplished virtually nothing. We say not a word in favour of monarchical institutions, but why strike at the lesser evil, while you leave the greater one untouched.

Feargus O'Connor was quite at home in addressing the

vast assemblage. There was the usual promise to lead them on to death or glory. He also informed the meeting that he was the unpaid advocate of the people. But the passage of his speech which was best relished, was this in which he alluded to Lord Brougham and the new poor law :—

" Harry Brougham said they wanted no poor law as every young man ought to lay up a provision for old age, yet, while he said this with one side of his mouth, he was screwing the other side to get his retiring pension raised from £4,000 to £5,000 a year. But if the people had their rights they would not long pay his salary. Harry would go to the treasury, he would knock, but Cerberus would not open the door, he would ask ' Who is there?' and then luckless Harry would answer ' It's an ex-chancellor coming for his £1,250, a quarter's salary;' but Cerberus would say ' There have been a dozen of ye here to-day already, and there is nothing for ye,' then Harry would cry ' Oh! what will become of me! what shall I do!' and Cerberus would say ' Go into the Bastile that you have provided for the people.' Then when Lord Harry and Lady Harry went into the Bastile, the keeper would say, ' This is your ward to the right, and this, my lady, is your ward to the left; we are Malthusians here, and are afraid you would breed, therefore you must be kept asunder.' If he witnessed such a scene as this he might have some pity for Lady Brougham, but little pity would be due to Lord Harry."

While O'Connor was thus addressing the people it was impossible to control the bursts of laughter and cheering with which he was greeted. Geo. Smith, operative coachmaker, Mr Parker, also a working man, Mr. Charlton, Mr. Lowrey, and others addressed the meeting. The latter said :—

" I am glad to see the tremendous demonstration that has been made this day, despite the inducements that have been held out to the people to hold themselves back from this great meeting. Every means has been tried to keep the people at home on this momentous occasion, but they have been tried in vain. At Cookson's Alkali Works in South Shields both persuasion and threats have been resorted to, and even the military, whom the people feed and cloth, had had the audacity to march past them with their fixed bayonets; but let them be told that Englishmen too could arm, that there was a sufficiency of muskets and of men that could handle them on the banks of the Tyne, to put to flight all the men that ever entered yonder barracks."

Towards the conclusion of O'Connor's address a body

of dragoons appeared, marching from the barracks, (which were contiguous to the Moor), and defiling about a hundred paces from the meeting. When he arose a second time to address the assembly, a long line of cavalry, accompanied by a piece of cannon marched down upon the meeting on the one side, while a column of infantry slowly defiled upon the other. The people were entirely unarmed, there could not therefore have been the slightest reasonable pretext for the appearance of this military force, and its display produced the strongest feelings of indignation amongst the vast number assembled at the meeting.   From these movements of the military and the appearance of cannon there was every indication that the Moor of Newcastle was to be made a second Peterloo.   Unarmed as the people were they received the troops with a shout of defiance when O'Connor said :—

" He was deeply indignant at this daring and contemptible display ; it should be brought before the House of Commons, and he only regretted that the men around were not in a condition to reply to it in the only language it deserved, and to repel force by force. His friend Mr. Lowrey could assemble at half an hour's notice, ten thousand men in South Shields last evening to hear him (O'Connor) preach principles of liberty, therefore let the brats of Aristocracy take care lest they dared the people to assemble, and bring their arms too,—they would find there were gallant hearts and virtuous arms under a black coat as well as under a red one."

These remarks drew forth the most deafening shouts from the unarmed, but excited, and indignant multitude.   There was every effort made for gaining a pretext for slaughtering the people.   One of the officers rode his horse during the time O'Connor was speaking, against the crowd.   This act was repelled by a storm of hisses and, cries of " Off ! Off !" and one spirited young man, incensed to the last degree by such brutal and cowardly conduct pushed off the horse by force, exclaiming as he did so, " Get along you scoundrel, is it not enough for us to support you, but must we also be insulted and trampled upon !"   The chairman replied to a vote of thanks proposed by O'Connor and congratulated the people on their manly and peaceable demeanour, a demeanour which the military authorities to the very last resolved to shake, for just as the meeting was about to disperse, the troops again surrounded the people, and by displaying their force endeavoured to provoke them to resistance. Nothing but the good sense of the working class prevented bloodshed.   The conduct of the authorities would seem to justify a remark made by Bronterre O'Brien, that it is unsafe for the people to

meet in large numbers to discuss their rights without arms
in their hands to defend themselves against the attacks of
their oppressors. Everything however concluded peacefully,
the meeting separated in good humour, and thus concluded
(considering the population of the district) one of the largest
demonstrations made in favour of the Charter.

This demonstration was succeeded by another, on an
equally magnificent scale. The processions were arranged
as before, every trade contributing its separate staff, even the
most aristocratic of those bodies did not hold aloof, and the
coachmakers, who were more under the influence of the
higher orders than any other trade, because more immediately
depending on them for a livelihood, were amongst the number.
The very apprentices displayed their banner with this curious
device :—

"As the old cock crows the young one learns."

The women, all honour to their public spirit, were not behind
in the march towards Democracy; they attended the procession
in large numbers, and vied with the men in their eagerness to
listen to the fiery words of political inspiration. The meeting
was held for the purpose of electing three delegates to the
Convention. The political faith of the gentlemen selected by the
Council was such that only the most ardent friends of the movement would have endorsed their selection, but the enthusiasm
of the multitude when their names were mentioned, proved
how cordially the nominations were accepted. The names of
the three selected were Dr. John Taylor, George Julian Harney, and Robert Lowery. Dr. Taylor was one of a family of
that name whose residence, and property which was considerable, were situated in the County of Ayr. He had for some
time resided at Glasgow, where he edited a paper under the
title of the *Glasgow Liberator*, which enjoyed, however, but a
short existence, owing perhaps to more active duties requiring
the doctor's attention. He had served for a considerable time
as a surgeon in the navy, and possessed all the frankness,
generosity, and courage of the sons of Neptune. For several
years too he had resided in France, and had formed an
intimate aquaintance with the most ardent and enthusiastic
Democrats of that country; his early training rendered him
careless of consequences to himself; the society in which he
had moved, together with his naturally bold and intrepid spirit,
induced him to regard a physical revolution as the shortest
and surest path to success. Taylor was at that time in the
prime of manhood, being about thirty-four years of age ; his
personal appearance exhibited a touch of romance, and was
well calculated to produce a favourable impression. Above the

GEORGE JULIAN HARNEY
FROM A WOODCUT

middle height, and proportionately stout, with a handsome intellectual face, large brilliant dark eyes, a head of black flowing hair, parted in the middle, and hanging in long curls below his broad shoulders, in his loose sailor's dress, he looked the very personification of careless ease, and that ease was as remarkable in his oratory as in his personal appearance. He was none of your long winded prosy speakers, who seem to delight in talking chiefly because they give delight to nobody. Twenty minutes or half an hour was generally the extent of time which his speeches occupied, but during that time the words were poured forth in a clear flowing stream, without a pause that was not correct, in language of the most glowing eloquence, delivered with an air that was truly impressive, his voice though loud, pealed forth tones of the richest music ; in short, no orator possessed more completely the happiest combination of natural gifts and artistic power than Dr. John Taylor. He was moreover, free from all the little devices of the demagogue. He never sought by clap-trap to win popular applause, never made a boast of his sacrifices for the people. From any allusion he made to himself, it would scarce have been known that such a man as Dr. Taylor existed ; the glory of the cause was with him far before any glory with which he desired to invest himself. He was without a doubt, one of the most frank, honest, fearless, single-minded, and disinterested Democrats of that day.

Of George Julian Harney it is impossible for us to speak in such unqualified terms of approbation, but at the outset let us do him the justice to observe that we never for a moment doubted, as some did at that period, his ardent attachment to the cause of Democracy. Harney assumed the same carelessness of manner as his colleague, but the effort was too palpable not to be noticed by the discerning portion of his friends, to many of whom it gave pain, while it afforded a subject for ridicule to his opponents. Vanity was one of his prevailing weaknesses. Perhaps at that time he might be somewhat excused, for he was little more than past his minority, a very dangerous time of life for a man even of the strongest mind to be elevated to greatness, and Harney's mind was not one of the strongest. We do not intend to cast a slight upon his talents, for they were considerable, but many men of respectable talents fall into the mistake of supposing themselves to be greater than they really are, and from this weakness Harney was not free. There was little in the subject of our observations of the frank, open, ingenuous manner of Dr. Taylor; on the contrary, his dark piercing eyes were shaded by a rather moody brow, and were never at rest, but constantly

changing from one object to another, as though he distrusted
all around him.   About his lips there was an appearance of
strong vindictiveness, which pointed him out as a dangerous
enemy, and experience only served to prove the correctness of
the impression.   It may, however, be said of him, that to those
whom he considered his friends no man could be more warmly
or devotedly attached.   In the early part of his political life
Harney aspired to be the Marat of the English Revolution, with
whom, indeed, he was once charged with comparing himself.
His talent was best displayed when he wielded the pen ; as a
speaker he never came up to the standard of third class orators.
He would occupy a meeting for a period of two hours, but with
so much hesitancy as to make it painful for all lovers of oratory
to listen to his harangues.   In a time of calm he would never
as a speaker have succeeded in gaining a prominent position;
but that was not a time of calm,—strong words were in brisk
demand, and the masses cared for little else.   Harney had a
sufficiency to stock the political market, and he was ever
liberal in their use.   Sometimes he was extravagant to downright nonsense, but with a large number the glittering dross
passed current for pure gold.   The more knowing politicians adjudged him from that extravagance to be a spy, but
there was no ground for such a supposition.   Many a young
man of inflexible honesty has been as foolish in his day as was
George Julian Harney.

The third man differed greatly from both of the preceding.
Lowrey was a member of the working class, by trade a tailor.
Deformed in his lower extremities which were also exceedingly
weak, he suffered greatly from the nature of his occupation,
and laboured under the additional disadvantage of impaired
health.   He was rather small in stature, of a somewhat intelligent and pleasing expression of countenance, which was much
enhanced by any sudden excitement, for then his eye, usually
placid, was bright and animated.   His oratory would be
rather difficult to describe, but certainly it was far above the
common order.   His speech was slow and deliberate, but from
this very circumstance, it was instinct with much force.
His voice was not of the most musical, but his intonation
was loud, distinct, and far from disagreeable.   For solidity
and clearness of argument he excelled the majority of speakers.
Without any great effort to be logical, a vein of sound
reasoning ran through nearly all that he advanced, and
though he never reached the highest order of eloquence, it
were vain to deny that his rhetoric was pleasing, powerful,
and sometimes lofty.   His language generally was not so
extreme and decided as that of either of his colleagues, but he

was often carried away by the current of events, and his words sometimes indicated that he had no objection to their physical force doctrines. Possessing, however, in a pretty large degree, the useful faculty of caution, he chalked out for himself certain limits which he seldom overstepped. The following will perhaps give as clear an idea as anything we could adduce of his cautious reserve. Owing to the growing excitement there was a talk of the Government calling out the Militia. In one of his speeches Lowrey alluded to the subject in words to the following effect :—

" We are told it is the intention of Government to call out the Militia, and I have heard that the young men are forming themselves into clubs for the purpose of procuring substitutes. Should the Government perservere in this resolution, my advice is, not to form clubs, but to take the arms which they offer you,—how to make use of them I leave to your own judgment and discretion." The meaning of the speaker it was impossible to misunderstand, yet no one could assert that he advised his hearers to use their arms against the Government.

Such were the three men who had been selected as fit and proper persons to be proposed to the meeting as representatives to the Convention, and after a considerable time had been spent in addresses, the multitude confirmed the previous decision of the Council by voting unanimously in favour of its proposals.

The County of Durham was not a whit behind its neighbour in manifesting its attachment to the rapidly advancing movement for Democracy. Sunderland was the head-quarters of the Durham Radicals, it being the largest town in the county, and its population devoted more warmly to the cause, and better furnished with speakers than any other. There were two young men in particular who held a considerable sway over the minds of the working class. These were James Williams and George Binns, who held a kind of partnership in agitation, for the one generally assisted the other in addressing the numerous meetings which were held in various parts of the county. These two men were in temperament and disposition extremely unlike each other ; their very cast of countenance betraying a wide dissimilarity. Williams' features were rather long, but their expression was somewhat contracted, evincing a cunning which escaped the eye of the thoughtless and undiscerning, but which the experienced physiognomist could easily detect. Of logical ability Williams had a pretty fair amount, but his soundest and clearest reasoning was often so intermingled with plausible sophistry that it was sometimes difficult to distinguish the true from the false. In speech he was generally measured, slow, and deliberate, rather choosing to hesitate than to commit himself by uttering words which it might be inconvenient to hear of at a future time.   He was what might be considered a good speaker, but almost entirely intellectual. Of soul, which gives force to the true orator, he possessed but little ; without erring on the side of injustice, we will venture to affirm, that if at any time he warmed to his subject, and his feelings were aroused at their depths, that the intellect, even then, was generally master, and dictated the exact amount of passion to be displayed.

George Binns was, on the contrary, a young man in whom the soul was predominant over all.   He was also possessed of a clear and masterly intellect, but was void of the cunning and Machiavelian qualities of his colleague.   Without exaggeration he was what may be styled a handsome man. As a speaker he was free, lucid, fluent, elegant, and florid. Scarcely past his minority, at that age when in men of his stamp the soul gushes forth in every word, there was an un-mistakable ingenuousness in all he uttered ; no studying how to accommodate smooth set phrases to his audience, but a strong sense of right and duty pervading every sentence, and breathing in every word. It is curious to observe how genius sets even the most studied training at nought, demolishing the work of half a life in a single day. The parents of Binns were members of the Society of Friends, who are often very good people in their own peculiar way, but careful and assiduous in using every effort for repression of the passions. Of course, as quakers, they held the principles of the peace society, but all their care and attention failed to fashion their son to the cold and passionless maxims of their order. Being engaged in the business of drapery, they initiated him into the mysteries of the shop, but not even the minute and petty calculation of profits could crush the soul of George Binns.   There was pure metal at the bottom of his nature. So unsuited was his father's business to his tastes and inclinations, that he had scarcely attained his majority when he left it and joined Williams in the more congenial trade of printing and bookselling.   As Democracy was in the ascendant, the sale of publications having that tendency became the rage, so that the young orator was in his element, in the dissemination of that knowledge, which, quoting the poet, he often told his delighted audiences, was,

" The wing wherewith we fly to heaven."

Williams and Binns kept the County of Durham in a per-

petual state of agitation. There was scarcely a day in the
week that did not witness one or more meetings. Where
rooms were not to be obtained the broad canopy of heaven
served for a covering, and a large number of the meetings
were thus held in the open air. John Collins was on his way
from Scotland, and it was resolved to embrace the opportunity
by getting up a great out door demonstration. Two nights previous Collins had addressed a meeting at Newcastle, pre-
paratory to the first great demonstration, held on the Town
Moor. Sunderland has its Moor as well as Newcastle, and it
was determined to hold the meeting on that spot. A procession
of several thousands of persons paraded the town with bands
and banners, on one of which latter was the inscription,
" Working men are the true nobility of the Nation"; and on
another, " The union of the brave and free, it is a great and a
noble cause, a cause which ought to prosper, and must eventually
triumph." Before the business of the meeting commenced the
united bands struck up the fine old martial and patriotic air of

"Scots wha ha'e wi' Wallace bled."

Mr. James Williams presided on the occasion and in the course
of his remarks observed :—

" Six or seven years ago they had met on that ground for
the attainment of what they thought would be freedom. They
joined the middle class that were then struggling for their
rights,—they obtained for them political freedom, and they
trusted to their gratitude for assisting to secure the rights of the
great masses of the community,—they had been deceived, basely
deserted, but they now stood forward again in their own might
and majesty, and again they would triumph. He was not
ashamed that they had been deceived, he did not regret that
the people had stood forward on that occasion, it reflected upon
them the highest honour, but it reflected dishonour on those
who had now abandoned the cause of justice, and of man. He
felt assured that measures were now in progress that would
within the short space of twelve months obtain for the people
of England those rights of which they were iniquitously
deprived by an unjust and unchristian Aristocracy."

See how easily Mr. Williams fell into the common cant of
attributing the political slavery of the masses to the Aristocracy.
That the Aristocracy were opposed to their emancipation was
true enough, but the great power that now leagued with the
Aristocracy against the millions, and which was more powerful
than its brother in the cause of political proscription, was the
middle class—the class that Mr. Williams himself admitted
had obtained the support of the masses in gaining power for

itself, under the promise of securing the same power for them in return. To talk after that of being deprived of their rights by the Aristocracy was worse than nonsense. The House of Commons was responsible for any disabilities under which the mass of the people might labour, and it was chiefly composed of Middle Class representatives.

Scarcely had Mr. M'Kinny proceeded to address the meeting in support of the first resolution, when the thunder pealed, and the rain came down in a perfect deluge. As it was impossible for any person to address the meeting with effect, there was an adjournment to the Assembly Rooms, where the business was resumed. From Mr. Binns' speech we quote the following specimen of his fervid eloquence:—

"Eighteen hundred years ago the simple and sublime doctrine of equality was preached and taught and acted upon, but that doctrine had long been lost sight of, and now they saw nothing but unchristian selfishness. But the people had got one resource—a resource that had never failed them, and he trusted they would again, and he hoped it would be for the last time, draw on that resource and unite for their regeneration. The tyrants might call them the rude unwashed, they might heap upon them all the vile epithets their devilish imaginations could devise, but let them remember that they were to meet at the one Judgment seat, and take their places beside the poor. The tyrants might boast of their discipline, but the people could boast of numbers and energy. The tyrants might array their cruelty, but they, the people, would oppose their bravery; we are bound together by no selfish tie, they may boast of their Wellingtons, but we have a God."

In order to judge of the effect which these and kindred sentences produced upon the meeting Mr. Binns must have been heard. He was often interrupted by the most vociferous cheering, and at the conclusion of the sentence quoted the effect was magical. The whole meeting rose and greeted the youthful impassioned and eloquent orator with the most overwhelming applause. Mr. Collins, being a stranger, and one moreover who had been taking an active part in organising the masses, was of course the hero of the day. He stated the causes that had combined to bring him into the agitation, telling the meeting that from eight years of age until the time he joined the democratic movement he had been working for fifteen hours a day. He stated likewise that he had not quitted home till he saw twenty thousand families comprising eighty thousand or a hundred thousand individuals thrown upon charity. He could then endure it no longer, and he had come amongst the people to ascertain whether they would at length feel for themselves,

or depend on the sympathy of others. Mr. Collins continued:—
" Every interest was represented in the Legislature save
and except the interest of the people. The church, the bar, the
landed and monied interests, and all these interests flourished.
Jack says to Tom,—'Will you assist me to pass this bill for
the landed interest ? ' ' Certainly,' says Tom, 'if you will
assist me in passing the other bill for the monied interest.'
Jack attends to Tom's request, and Tom attends to Jack's,
and between them the people are victimized. If the wolf had
to legislate for the lamb, if the stork had to legislate for the
fish, they would soon put both lamb and fish in a position in
which they could most easily prey upon them. The exclusionists
said that the people were not able to choose proper representatives; that argument came with a bad grace from men who chose
a House that was ready to come to a resolution to-day and
rescind it to-morrow; but it was a falsehood,—had they not
benefit and other societies, and if any officer belonging to such
societies did not discharge his duty properly, there was always
as much intelligence found among the people as would dismiss
him from his office; but the melancholy truth was, that in many
parts men were receding in knowledge, and if they were not
fit now, they were getting worse.   He would take his
stand upon the eternal principles of right.   Suppose a man
were to make good his claim to an estate, would the judge say
that he was so ignorant he would make a bad use of it.   No !
No ! however ignorant he might be, the estate would pass into
his hands, and he would at once become fitted for a legislator."
    After Collins had concluded his speech Binns stepped forward
and said that before the resolution was put he would call upon
them to show that they were ready to go with the men of
Birmingham if necessary even to death.   The speaker was
replied to by the meeting with a tremendous burst of cheering,
after which the National Petition was unanimously adopted.
The whole meeting then turned out, with bands, and banners,
and accompanied Mr. Collins to the coach, where he took his
departure for Leeds amid the thundering applause of the vast
crowd, the bands all the time playing lively and patriotic airs.
Everything wore a joyful aspect, and the people of Sunderland
were big with hope for the speedy success of the national cause.
    The large meeting was followed in the evening by a soiree
at which Mr. Williams presided, and Messrs Binns and
Lowrey were the principal speakers, The conclusion of the
speech of the latter is worthy of insertion, as being a good
specimen of his eloquence.
    " He was a friend to Democracy, because it was the political
law of God.   He was for liberty, because it would seat justice

E   2

in her temple,—her throne was righteousness, and her altar peace. The oppressors might gnash their teeth and howl, but the fiat of their destruction had gone forth ; God had said that the oppressors would surely perish, and though their bayonets might bristle and the thunder of their artillery roar, yet liberty would look them in the face and they would shiver and be silent before her. Like the vestal fire on the altars of old,—it would never die,—it would extend from Aikos' peak to Andes' crown, and shed joy and gladness and happiness over all the human race."

The Glasgow, Newcastle, and Sunderland gatherings were quickly responded to by the democrats of the Midlands. The men of Northampton, the most central town of any considerable size in England, had resolved to shew their sympathy with the movement by holding an open air meeting to which they invited Henry Vincent. This demonstration was organised under the auspices of the Working Men's Association, and to lend it an additional interest, the first of August, 1838, was the day selected, that being the anniversary of the emancipation of the slaves. The term "emancipation" should here be understood only in a limited sense, for the men whose liberation they had agreed to celebrate by the holding of their meeting were at the very moment in a condition inferior to their own ; they were going to meet in order to denounce their own slavery to the rich, and to express a resolve to burst the shackles which held them in a state of bondage. Slavery has numerous phases, but every system which tends to place the labour, life and destinies of man at the disposal of another, deserves to be classed under that odious name.

To give the proceedings all the importance which they deemed the occasion deserved it was resolved to spare no reasonable expense in drawing the attention of the public to the meeting. Placards couched in forcible and eloquent terms announced that a procession would leave the Market Square at three o'clock, and, at that hour the Square and the avenues leading thereto presented a very animated appearance. A number of flags, made for the occasion, and bearing devices emblematical of the liberal principles, waved gracefully in the summer breeze. The members of the association appeared with tri-coloured rosettes at their breasts, and having formed into procession, the band struck up a lively air, to which the people marched forward with almost military regularity. The procession traversed the principal streets, gathering numbers as it advanced, until it reached the racecourse, the grand stand of which had been secured as the most eligible position from which the speakers could address the meeting.

This democratic gathering whether as regards talent or standing in society was not to be treated lightly. The body of the meeting belonged, of course, to the working class ; but the platform presented a tolerable sprinkling of the middle orders. As befitted a meeting which sought to raise the power and influence of the masses, a working man was called upon to preside, Mr. Joseph Wright, a journeyman shoemaker, performing the functions of that office. The chairman's introduction of the business was marked by plain, strong common sense, and a pretty good acquaintance with his subject. The existing rulers of the country came in for a fair share of his condemnation, but as if to shew the force of circumstances and the frailty of human nature, the same man shortly after entered the police force, in which he rose to distinction, and thus became an accredited servant of that very government which he had so warmly condemned. The Rev. John Jenkinson, of Kettering, was one of the speakers. His address was forcible, pointed and impressive; he took for his text the motto on the Kettering flag, "Justice to all," which subject he handled with good effect. The Rev. J. C. Meeke, Unitarian Minister, also addressed the meeting in a strain which combined sound argument with bold and manly declamation, and a farmer from the country, named Burdett, enlivened the audience with some admirable specimens of racy old English humour, which were most gratefully received.

But, of course, the lion of the day whose oration was anticipated with the most exciting interest was Henry Vincent. Nor did that gentleman disappoint the hopes and expectations that had been formed of his power to please. Just, however, as the great orator commenced his address the sky darkened. This was only the forerunner of torrents of rain. A heavy shower sometimes acts as a cooler even to an enthusiastic assembly, and the meeting began to manifest signs of wavering, but Vincent, completely protected from the cooling element by means of a huge umbrella which one of the friends held over his head, exclaimed in an encouraging tone while his face was lighted up by one of his brightest smiles, "Stand to your duty my friends, never mind a little rain," and whether from a sense of shame, or a nobler motive, the heaving mass implicitly followed his injunction. Vincent having once fairly proceeded with his discourse there was no danger of a disruption in the meeting. He rivetted the earnest attention of every soul in the assembly, he was even more than usual declamatory; the Whigs came in for some of his most pungent remarks, and he exposed to view the pretended patriotism of that faction when on the shady side of office, contrasted with their despotic leanings when safely installed in power. The contrast produced a powerful impression on the audience, as was testified by the alternate laughter and cheers with which he was greeted ; and yet, perhaps, Vincent did not give a fair and candid statement of the case, for it ought to be known that whatever the middle class might promise the people, Lord John Russell and his aristocratic friends never made a profession of attachment to Democracy. It is true that they interlarded their speeches with general remarks upon popular rights and constitutional liberty, which might mean anything that occasion required, and which, with them, never meant more than liberty for the middle class to share with the Aristocracy their despotism over the labouring millions. But as previously observed ambiguous phrases at the time too easily satisfied the masses ; into the particular meaning of those phrases they seldom enquired, so easily are men deluded by mere clap-trap generalites. At the conclusion of Vincent's address a resolution in favour of the Charter was unanimously carried.

Three other meetings were held before the orator took his departure, one on the following night in the Association room, at which he spoke in his happiest style. No man was ever more ingenious than Vincent in turning to advantage a sentence from the work of a favourite author. So entirely did he appropriate and weave it into the thread of his discourse that it was almost impossible to feel that it was other than his own. Although he might acknowledge (as he sometimes did) that the sentence was borrowed, so magnificent was the delivery of the speaker that he generally gained credit for the words as well as for their powerful utterance. He had studied in the political school of Thomas Paine, and on the night in question he finished up an apparently brilliant peroration with the following well known sentence of that republican author. " It is wrong to say that God made rich and poor, he made male and female, and he gave them the earth for their inheritance." No other man in the movement could have done equal justice to this sentiment, the splendid utterance, theatrical attitude, and the flushed and excited countenance of the speaker, brought down repeated manifestations of the most uproarious approval.

The second in-door meeting was to have been held at the Saracen's Head, one of the largest rooms in the town, and bills were posted to that effect, but certain conservative influences began to work, and on the Committee applying on the night of lecture for the keys of the room, they were politely informed that it was closed against them. To get another room was impossible, and there was no alternative but to resort to the Market Square, where a great crowd was speedily collected, all the more excited by the petty persecution which compelled them to stand in the open air, while they listened to the harangue of their favourate orator. Vincent rose that night with three-fold influence over his hearers. His countenance was truly majestic, and his declamation bolder than ever. He hurled defiance at the government and the magistrates, and compared them to the most ludicrous things in nature. Such stimulating food was exactly suited to the public palate, and it was the more highly relished on account of the seasoning with which it was so plentifully dashed.

On the following night Vincent gave his farewell lecture in the Association room on the comparative education of the various classes. In the course of his oration the higher orders were mimicked to the very life. He related how at a public meeting held to congratulate her Majesty on her accession to the throne, he a poor journeyman printer had driven the Marquis of Londonderry from the president's chair. His imitation of the grave stammering of the noble lord caused his voice to be drowned in shouts of laughter. The result of these meetings was the enrolment of four hundred members in the books of the Association. The tide of democatic progress rolled on with accelerated force, and threatened to supplant the old Whig and Tory influences. As we proceed we shall see how far this progress was a solid reality, and how far it was the mere effervescense of the moment; whatever it was in fact, there is no denying the importance attached to it by all classes. The press was compelled to notice the proceedings. The whig *Mercury* dressed itself up in "namby pamby," but the tory *Herald* while admitting Vincent's fluency of speech and tact, bespattered him unsparingly with its Billingsgate, and sought to turn into ridicule the principles he expounded and endorsed. It represented the meetings as composed of a few ragged shoemakers. The worthy editor was a clergyman. As regards the numbers attending the meetings he was guilty of deliberate falsehood, for they were all numerously attended, and that too by various classes. We cannot here avoid carrying back our thought to the commencement of the Christian era. Had his reverence lived in that age how would he have written of the founder of Christianity and His poor disciples the fishermen of Galilee? Out upon you ye venders of sacrilegious fraud ! Ye hypocritical deceivers of the credulous and confiding ! Ye jumble of lies and darkest cunning ! Ye betrayers of the great and holy principles of justice and equality taught by Him whom you have the detest-able hypocrisy to call your Master, but whose doctrines you constantly crucify between your base cringing subserviency to unjust power, and your insatiable thirst for gold!

CHAPTER III.

PROGRESS OF THE MOVEMENT.

Scarce had the echoes of the orator's voice died upon the ears of the people of Northampton, ere the Birmingham council commenced operations upon a grander scale. Birmingham, containing and surrounded by a dense manufacturing population, had been held almost omnipotent in agitation. Its Reform Bill associations had raised it into an importance enjoyed by few other towns, and it possessed the additional advantage of being led in its movements by its own members of parliament. Thomas Atwood, who, after the passing of the Reform Bill, declared that had that measure not become law, he would have marched two hundred thousand men to the Metropolis to demand its enactment, was not a man to be despised. The Council determined to convene a great district meeting, which was to assemble at Holloway Head, the scene of many a previous popular demonstration, and they worked with their accustomed assiduity to render the meeting effective and in this they succeeded to admiration.

Although we must in excited times make allowance for exaggeration, it was without doubt a vast gathering, the numbers being computed at two hundred thousand. As early as nine o'clock the streets were crowded with human beings, and presented a scene of bustle and animation. A meeting had been arranged for in the town hall, consisting of the members of the Political Union, at ten o'clock. It was densely crowded ; not a nook or corner of the vast edifice was left unoccupied. At this meeting the Council of the Union were elected for the ensuing year.

Messrs. Atwood, Salt, and Edmunds of the Political Union ; Mr. O'Connor ; Messrs. Moir and Purdie from Scotland ; Dr. Wade ; Messrs. Vincent and Hetherington from London ; Mr. Richardson from Manchester ; and Mr. Falkner from Oxford, entered the hall, amid loud cheers, while groans as loud and hearty were given for "whig tricksters and tory tyrants." Let us here notice a banner that was displayed in the hall, on

which was represented the figures of three loaves of different
sizes, but all marked at the same price. The English loaf was
the smallest, the French loaf larger, but the Russian loaf was
the largest of all.   Underneath was inscribed,

"The effects of the corn laws."

Mr. Edmunds announced that Mr. O'Connor had been
deputed to attend the meeting by six towns in Yorkshire,
Leeds and Halifax being amongst the number.   The loudest
applause followed this announcement.   Mr. Douglas produced
the financial accounts of the Union, which shewed that, notwithstanding the large outlay, the Union had nearly two
hundred pounds in hand for the purposes of agitation.   He
also informed the meeting that a deputation of ten thousand
men had just arrived from Walsall.   This announcement drew
forth a loud and unanimous cheer.   After the Council were
elected processions of the various bodies moved towards
Holloway Head.   The Birmingham division proceeded from the
Town Hall, Messrs. Collins and Pearce, who had been chosen
Marshals, leading that body on horseback.   There were six
other divisions from Wolverhampton, Walsall, Dudley, Hales-
owen, Warwick, and Studley. These various bodies marched
up several streets, all meeting at the great centre of attraction,
at which they arrived shortly after one o'clock.   The open
space at Holloway Head is in the form of an amphitheatre, and
the hustings were so placed that a large number of people
could distinctly view the speakers, and hear them at an immense
distance.   Various   trades   graced   the   great   procession,
accompanied by flags and banners, their several mottos and
devices presenting great variety of appearance.   Every advantageous position which commanded a view of the interesting
gathering was occupied at an early hour, so that before the
procession arrived there was an immense concourse of people
already assembled. The beating of the drums having announced
the arrival of their brethren, the air rang with a loud shout of
welcome.   It seemed as though the procession would never
have an end, so continuously did the moving mass keep
streaming in.   A more sublime sight than that mighty multitude in such an interesting position, it were scarcely possible to
contemplate.

Mr. Atwood was voted to the chair, and delivered a speech
quite in character with his antecedents.   He professed himself a peaceful man, and declared that he would never sanction
the commission of violence for gaining the people's object,
but as he warmed to his subject, he talked about the Legislature being unable to resist the demand of two millions of

men, which, if not speedily complied with, would result in the two millions being increased to five, and he threatened the House of Commons that this immense body of people would exercise on them a little gentle compulsion if they hesitated in conceding their rights. If petitioning was found to fail in making the necessary impression, the honourable gentleman suggested a national strike for one week, during which time not a hammer was to be wielded, nor an anvil sounded, nor a shuttle moved, throughout the country, and he told his hearers that although he would be opposed to the employment of any violence, if the people were attacked the consequences must fall on the heads of the aggressors. He told the meeting too, that if the government dared to arrest him in the execution of his peaceful purpose, a hundred thousand men would march to demand his release.

Now, however peaceful the sentiments which Mr. Atwood was desirous of impressing on his adherents, it occurs to us that at least a portion of his advice could only, if acted upon, have led to the consequences which he so much appeared to deprecate. The last mentioned prediction meant nothing short of physical force, that is supposing it to have had a meaning at all, for if his hundred thousand friends had marched in a body for the above stated purpose, and had met with a refusal there would have been no alternative but to fight it out, or beat an ignominious retreat. In the latter case, all the marching and counter marching would have been simply ridiculous, and would only have served to remind us of the facetious lines of the poet,

> " The brave old Duke of York,
> He had ten thousand men,
> He marched them up a great high hill,
> And he marched them down again."

Moreover, Mr. Atwood's plan of a cessation from labour could scarcely have ended in anything but a physical revolution. The wealthy classes could very well have afforded to dispense with labour for the short period of a week, knowing that at the end of that time the working people would have to resume labour. If stronger means to achieve success were not to be resorted to, no man should recommend a people to cease labour. A strike must either be successful or be followed by the appliance of physical force, or the whole thing result in a miserable failure, and the object of the strike be indefinitely postponed. We doubt whether Mr. Atwood was prepared to follow out the almost inevitable consequences of his own advice, but it served to produce an effect upon the mighty assemblage whom he addressed. His appeals were heartily responded to.

Indeed, no monarch ruled more absolutely than Mr. Atwood seemed to do over that immense mass of people, and O'Connor was the first to hold up his hand as willing to be one of the hundred thousand men to demand the chairman's release in case of arrest.

Mr. Scholefield, the colleague of Mr. Atwood, addressed the meeting, as did also Messrs. Muntz, Douglas, Vincent, Moir, and others.   Excepting the chairman the great lion of the day was Feargus O'Connor, and that gentleman was determined not to be behind Mr. Atwood in the strength of his language.   He recommended that when the petition was ready for presentation, five hundred thousand men should assemble in London and accompany Mr. Atwood and the petition to the House of Commons, and that they should send in a message to the House that they were waiting for an answer in the Palace Yard: but O'Connor went far beyond this. Of the staple of his speech the following quotation from Moore will give the best idea :—

> "Then onward, our green standard rearing;
> Go flesh every sword to the hilt.
> On our side is Virtue and Erin,
> On their's is the Parson and Guilt."

The quotation of these singularly inappropriate lines, (inappropriate because they were addressed exclusively to the Irish people, whereas O'Connor was appealing to an audience almost entirely English, and that too upon grievances not peculiar to any particular portion of the country but common to all) was a proof at once of his recklessness, and want of taste ; a proof which gave no promising indication of the future discretion of the great and powerful agitator.   Such a quotation indeed served to arouse the more excitable just for the moment, but for any really useful purpose nothing could have been more out of place, and it was easy to perceive that such indiscretion was laying the foundation of a schism which could be productive only of the most fatal consequences to the success of the movement.   The countenances of some of the leading men betrayed evident signs of dislike, and the meeting was scarcely over ere that dislike found vent in words, which shewed that, between them and O'Connor there was but little sympathy as to the policy which was to control the agitation ; and yet who shall say that after the remarks of the chairman, O'Connor was altogether in the wrong ; he was only explaining the too probable bearing of Mr. Atwood's advice, and, if his language was not justifiable, it at least admitted of excuse. However strong O'Connor's language, it was by no means disagreeable to the mass of those whom he addressed, while in every other respect he possessed qualifications superior to any other man present for impressing a Birmingham audience in his favour. The description by Byron of his Corsair,

"No giant frame set forth his common height,"

was not in the least applicable to him, for compared to the generality of men he was a giant indeed. Upwards of six feet in height, stout and athletic, and in spite of his opinions invested with a sort of aristocratic bearing, the sight of his person was calculated to inspire the masses with a solemn awe. So true is it that despite the march of civilisation, and the increase of respect for mental superiority, men are generally impressed with a veneration for superior physical power. O'Connor's short neck—-so short as to be imperceptible to the beholder, was the only defect in his physical appearance, and even this, so far from conveying an unfavourable impression, rather enhanced than detracted from the idea which the public entertained of the great strength of his iron frame.

O'Connor however did not depend alone upon physical strength for the involuntary respect in which he was held by the multitude. His broad massive forehead, very full in those parts where phrenologists place the organs of perception, though considerably deficient in the faculties of reflection, bore evidence, in spite of these defects, of great intellectual force. To assert that he possessed a mind solid and steady were to say too much, no man with an equal amount of intellect was ever more erratic. Had the solidity of his judgment been equal to his quickness of perception he would intellectually have been a great man, but this essential quality of greatness he lacked, hence his life presents a series of mistakes and contradictions, which, as men reflected more, lowered him in their estimation. No man in the movement was so certain of popularity as O'Connor. No man was so certain to lose it after its attainment. It was not till he proceeded to speak that the full extent of his influence was felt. This however depended greatly upon circumstances. With an indoor assembly Vincent was by far his superior. Out of doors O'Connor was the almost universal idol, for the thunder of his voice would reach the ears of the most careless, and put to silence the most noisy of his audience. At the Birmingham meeting he had no mean amount of oratorical talent with which to cope, but what was that talent when placed in competition with a man who conveyed every word in a voice that made the vault of Heaven echo with its sound, which out Stentor'd even Stentor himself. The effect was irresistible.

He eclipsed all others in the estimation of that vast and excited crowd. The strongest language was at that time the most popular. O'Connor grasped the opportunity to please, and employed it to his temporary advantage. Mr. Atwood, in speaking of his hundred thousand men gave him the starting point, and he speedily shewed how easily he could distance his honourable competitors in the race for popularity. The dislike of the Birmingham leaders to O'Connor was, however, for the present repressed ; all the resolutions were unanimously carried, and George Frederick Muntz, Philip Henry Muntz, Robert Kellie Douglas, Thomas Clutton Salt, George Edmunds, Benjamin Hadley, John Collins, and John Pearce, were elected delegates to a Convention, which was to meet in the ensuing year, to see to the proper presentation of a petition, and to advise the best measures for enforcing the claims of the Democracy. It is worthy of remark that the Birmingham meeting was attended by Tom Steele, Daniel O'Connell's intimate, who however only gave a pledge of the Irish people's attachment to three out of the six points of the Charter.

The Birmingham meeting was shortly succeeded by a Radical demonstration in the metropolis, arranged with the intention of bringing public opinion more immediately to bear upon the Legislature. The arrangements were under the superintendence of the Working Men's Association, who sought to invest the meeting with an air of authority. With that view a numerously signed requisition was presented to Sir Francis Smedley, the high bailiff of Westminster, requesting that functionary to convene the meeting. Sir Francis without hesitation acceded to the wish of the requisition, and appointed the meeting for the seventeenth of September at mid-day, and Palace Yard was to be the scene of the gathering. At the appointed time and place the meeting was accordingly held. But that it answered the sanguine hopes and expectations of the party, may be fairly doubted. In point of numbers, taking the population of the metropolis into account, it was a decided failure. They were computed at thirty thousand. When it is borne in mind that two hundred thousand had assembled at Birmingham, it will be seen at a glance how comparatively insignificant was the demonstration. It plainly evinced the small amount of interest felt by the metropolitans in political questions. Nothing affords a deeper scope for the study of the political philosopher than the wide dissimilarity between the capitals of France and England as regards the popular struggles for Democratic institutions. In the former country, Paris is

always the great centre of agitation, giving the life-like impulse
to the provincial districts.   It may, without exaggeration, be
affirmed, that in all onward movements of the people Paris
is France, for the rest of France moves at her bidding.   The
repeated Revolutions which have occurred in that country
testify to the truth of this remark.   London, on the contrary,
whenever moved, is impelled by some external power ; it is the
provinces which give a direction to her efforts, and the difficulties which thus stand in the way of the formation of a sound
and healthy public opinion, appear almost insurmountable,   It
is also worthy of observation that the majority of the leaders of
popular movements in London are men who have migrated
from the provinces, and not natives of the capital; your Cockney
is seldom a real politician.   It is true that with the necessary
means it is possible to get up a great political display, music,
banners, and equipages will warm the soul of a Cockney into
active life, and with the aid of these hundreds of thousands
may be drawn into the streets, but the majority of such people
are brought together by the mere thirst after excitement,
and would be equally gratified by a Lord Mayor's show, or a
royal procession, as by a popular political demonstration.
Without some of these attractions to turn the current of their
feelings, the natives of the metropolis are almost absorbed in
matters of business.   To turn the penny seems to be the
chief aim and object of their lives ; and this one absorbing
object excludes the consideration of matters which influence
deeply the general community, but which do not, on the
surface, appear much to affect man in his individual capacity.
The Working Men's Association had neglected to use the
only means which would have secured a large demonstration,
but in pursuing that course they acted wisely.   Public
opinion built upon mere excitement is not worth the trouble
of forming.   Founded on real intelligence, excitement may be
valuable ; without that intelligence it is worse than vanity.

What the meeting lacked in numbers it undoubtedly made
up in talent and influence.   The chair was taken at one o'clock
by the high bailiff, while around him were to be seen Mr.
Leader, M.P. for Westminster ; Mr. Dillon Browne, Member
for Mayo ; Colonel Thompson ; Feargus O'Connor ; Dr.
Wade ; Rev. W. J. Fox ; Ebenezer Elliott, the great corn
law rhymer ; Mr. Lowrey, of Newcastle ; Mr. Richardson, of
Manchester ; Mr. Duncan, of Edinburgh ; Mr. H. Williams, of
Carmarthen ; and many other gentlemen from various parts of
England and Scotland.   Mr. Coulier, from Paris, also honoured
the assembly with his presence.

Mr. Lovett was the mover of the first resolution, and he

enforced its necessity in a truly noble and manly speech, in which he urged the justice of a thorough change in the representative system.   In allusion to which he said :—

"The national petition embodied all that they wanted, because it would then be impossible for them to be agitating for one thing, and in the eleventh hour be cheated into something else.   They had been listening for six years to the proposal of taking instalments, but what had those instalments been? A rascally coercion bill for Ireland, several despotic measures for England, revolution and despotism for Canada, they wanted no more of such instalments."

Mr Hetherington was the seconder of the resolution, which was supported in a glowing speech by Ebenezer Elliott. Speaking of the richer class, the poet said :—

"Are they not every day perpetrating fresh treasons? Have they not lately deprived you of your privilege of out door relief, in the face of their own parliamentary declaration, placed, thank God, on eternal record, that they are themselves the most destructive horde of beggars that ever infested any community?   One of the darkest, saddest, bloodiest pages in history, is that which records the first acts of the first few months of the reign of Queen Victoria.   During those few months, your oppressors perpetrated in Canada atrocities which would have disgraced the reign of King Castlereagh, and which Wellington Imperator, when the time comes, will not be able to parallel ; and why were these things done? Because the Canadian Commons refused the supplies.   Now, if the Canadian Commons have no right to refuse the supplies, the British government have none.   I doubt whether there are one hundred men in London, worth twenty thousand pounds each, who do not in their hearts hate and fear every working man who is supposed to have a mind of his own.   Even in America that is true.   The Senate of the United States, representing the monied Aristocracy of that country, would at this moment, if they could, make a swindling banker dictator of America.   Yet, America has only one senate, you have two, neither of them representing you, yet making your laws, because they are all men of one sort, that is to say, all idle and all rich."

Mr. John Fraser, of Edinburgh also addressed the meeting in a warm and hopeful speech, as did also Messrs. Hartwell, Cleave, and Douglas.

Mr. Lowrey spoke in an energetic manner, and in language bold, though somewhat tinged with caution.   He recommended no recourse to violence, spoke not a word of what he would do himself, but in reference to the state of affairs said :—

" The men of the north are well organised. The men of Newcastle would dare to defend with their arms what they utter with their tongues, as the military would have learned on the coronation day had they made any attack upon the meeting. We are willing to try all moral means that are left, we are willing to try a throne, so long as it is conducive to the happiness of the people ; we are willing to have an Aristocracy, so long as they behave themselves civilly ; but we think we have a right to have a reciprocity of rights, and if not, we are prepared to go against the throne and the Aristocracy. The men of the Tyne and the Wear would not draw their swords until their enemies draw upon them, but having once put their hands to the plough they would never look back." Lowrey having found these sentiments highly relished by the meeting, supplied it with more of a similar kind, and thus concluded :—" Could things be worse than they are ? the throne is falling into contempt, the Aristocracy are held in disdain, the laws are considered as the medium whereby the rich oppress the poor, and the Church has dwindled into a political machine. Those who ought to preach humility and peace, were the most greedy of wealth, and the most tyrannical when they possessed power. Had they not seen in Ireland that the ministers of the gospel ever arrayed themselves with the sword in one hand and the bible in the other ; they had stripped poverty of its last mite ; in fact, wherever exertions had been made for the enfranchisement of the masses, or the amelioration of the people, the priests had always been found against them. He would exhort them to assert their own independence, they had a right to do it, and their rulers dared not refuse it."

Colonel Thompson was the next speaker, and came out most decidedly against the ministry, and asserted the safety of entrusting the people with power.

" Was it likely," asked the gallant Colonel, " that the people would ever do half the mischief their rulers had effected ? The people did not ask for themselves a majority, and an overbearing power, as the rich had hitherto done, and misused it most damnably. They did not seek for that, they only sought to have a fair share of influence in the councils of the country. He was one of those who had stood for triennial parliaments, but he had now come to sing a new song, and would tell them why. At the commencement of the new parliament did not the ministers profess to unite and go hand in hand with the Radicals, till the parliament had been elected for seven years, and then did they not say, now we have got you fast for seven years, we will tell you a secret which we before concealed. We always

G

were for the establishment of the agricultural preponderance.
Fifty million a year, no more reform." The gallant Colonel
was loudly cheered.

Mr. Leader spoke and cautioned the meeting against violence.
"The people must trust to themselves, and to themselves
alone, they were engaged in no child's play. They had not
undertaken an easy task, for they had to contend against the
most wealthy, the most powerful, and the most intelligent
Aristocracy that ever oppressed a community. Let them
in all their efforts bear in mind that it was by reason, by
argument, by obtaining that moral influence which the masses
must obtain, that they could eventually succeed in all things.
By at all times opposing violent counsels, by setting their faces
against violent language, and refusing to participate in
violent deeds, they would find safety and the best means
of success. Let them recollect what had occurred in
Ireland ; there, by what was called legal agitation how much
had the Irish not obtained." (cries of little or nothing,) " they
had made some progress, little enough he would grant, but let
them look at the evil effects of violence in Canada." (Mr.
Cleave : "Aye, but they were in too great a hurry.") "Then if
that were so he would beg of the people of England not to be in
too great a hurry. He would assert that they would get everything if they agitated with effect, and in the spirit of the organization that was now going on all over the country."

After the more stirring orations of Elliott and Lowrey, the
speech of Mr. Leader fell but coldly upon the great body of the
meeting, but the people were soon restored to their former
element by the introduction of the energetic and ubiquitous
O' Connor, who told them that he stood there as a representative
of forty or fifty towns in Scotland and England. His speech
was Irish throughout. Versatile, witty and occasionally
pointed, here is a good specimen :—

" The people were called pickpockets. Now, he would ask,
what difference was there between a rich pickpocket and a poor
pickpocket ? Why there was this difference, the poor man picked
the rich man's pocket to fill his belly, and the rich man picked
the poor man's belly to fill his pocket. The people had borne
oppression too long and too tamely. He had never counselled
the people to use physical force, because he felt that those
who did so were fools to their own cause, but, at
the same time, those who decried it preserved their authority
by physical force alone. What was the position in which the
working class stood? They were nature's children, and all
they wanted was nature's produce. They had been told to
stand by the old constitution. Why, that was the constitution

of tallow and wind. The people wanted the railroad constitution, the gas constitution, but they did not want Lord Melbourne and his tallow constitution ; neither did they want Lord Melbourne and his fusty laws ; what they wanted was a constitution and laws of a railroad genius, propelled by a steam power, and enlightened by the rays of gas. They wanted a legislature that had the power as well as the inclination to advance after the manner he had just pointed out. They wanted the science of legislation to advance. The people had only to shew the present House of Commons that they were determined, and its reform must take place. But still such men as Sir Robert Peel and little Johnny Russell would try to get into it, even though they got through the keyhole. But it was said the working class were dirty fellows, and that among them they could not get six hundred and fifty eight who were fit to sit in the House of Commons. Indeed ! He would soon alter that, he would pick out that number from the present meeting and the first he selected he would take down to Mr. Hawes' soap factory, then he would take them where they should reform their tailor's bills, he would next take them to the hair-dressser and perfumer, where they should be anointed with the fashionable stink ; and having done that by way of preparation, he would quickly take them into the House of Commons, when they would be the best six hundred and fifty eight that ever sat within its walls. He counselled them against all rioting, all civil war, but still, in the hearing of the House of Commons, he would say, that rather than see the people oppressed, rather than see the constitution violated, while the people were in daily want, if no other man would do so, if the constitution was violated, he would himself lead the people to death or glory." In another part of his speech O'Connor said. "They had had a slight taste of physical force in the north. A short time since some of the metropolitan police were sent down to Dewsbury, but the boys of that noble town sent them home again. His desire was to try moral force as long as possible, even to the fullest extent, but he would always have them bear in mind, that it is better to die freemen than to live slaves. Every conquest which was called honourable had been achieved by physical force, but they did not want it, because if all hands were pulling for Universal Suffrage they would soon pull down the stronghold of corruption. He hoped and trusted that out of the exercise of that judgment which belonged exclusively to the working class, a union would arise, and from that union a moral power would be created, sufficient to establish the rights of the poor man ; but if this failed, then let every man raise his arm in defence

G 2

of that which his judgment told him was justice." In the course of his speech O'Connor alluded to the fault that had been found with his quotation from Moore at the Birmingham meeting, so by way of atonement he gave them a parody on the verse, which ran as follows :

> " Then onward your black banners sweeping,
> Go stick every pen in the ink,
> On our side is suffrage that sweet thing,
> On theirs is corruption and stink."

We do not believe that any of our readers will, after a perusal of the above lines, fall into the mistake of supposing that O'Connor possessed a talent for the highest order of poetry, and it will be impossible to avoid being struck with the racy and rambling character of his oratory. From the extract it will be seen that he lacked the power of reasoning closely upon any given point, but that he possessed the faculty of jumping from one point to another, in such an agreeable way, as to please and entertain his audience to the close of his address. He was frequently interrupted during the delivery of his rhapsodies with alternate bursts of laughter and cheering, and as at Birmingham he was the idol of the vast majority.

Dillon Browne addressed the meeting as the representative of four hundred thousand Irishmen, in favour of the Charter. He was followed by R. J. Richardson of Manchester, who rivalled O'Connor in his allusion to physical force. In the course of his observations he remarked :

" That the people of Lancashire had begun to think seriously on the matter, and having read Blackstone's Commentaries on the Laws of England, they had learned that the people had a right to petition ; that failing they had a right to remonstrate, and that failing they had a right to arm in defence of their liberties. The people of Lancashire had last session laid on the table of Parliament, a petition bearing a quarter of a million signatures, and praying for a repeal of the Poor Law Amendment Act. How was the petition treated ? Why it was carried away by two gentlemen in long robes and grey wigs, and never heard of more. The people of Lancashire had therefore determined to petition no more, but would remonstrate, some said they would not remonstrate but would arm ; the people began to arm, the people were armed, he had seen the arms hanging over the mantlepieces of the poor with his own eyes. But the National Petition came in most opportunely, though the people could not have been persuaded to sign it if it had not demanded Universal Suffrage. If that petition should fail, he could not attempt to say what would be the consequence. Rifles would be loaded, that would be the next step no doubt, and he defied the power of any government, or any armed Bourbon police to put them down. It was of no use to disguise the matter, secrecy was the ruin of all things. Everything would be done openly by the people of Lancashire, and it would be done constitutionally and legally."

Mr. Duncan spoke most energetically on behalf of the Radicals of Edinburgh, and represented their fixed determination to stand by the great principles of Democracy. Dr. Wade; Mr. Reave, of Brighton; Mr. Carrier, of Trowbridge, and several other gentlemen addressed the meeting in the course of the proceedings, and on the motion of Mr. Layton of Brentford, Messrs. Cleave, Hetherington, Lovett, Vincent, Hartwell, Moore, Rogers, and Bronterre O'Brien, were unanimously elected to represent the Democrats of London in the coming convention. Thus ended the metropolitan Radical Demonstration, the meeting having lasted upwards of five hours.

We must here pause to remark, that although no open dissatisfaction was evinced at the election of the delegates, considerable discontent existed among a portion of the London Democrats. Another society had sprung into existence under the title of the Democratic Association. A young man, whom we have already named, and who was becoming well known in the radical world, was the reputed leader of that body, viz., George Julian Harney. A government prosecution, followed by a short period of imprisonment for vending the unstamped newspapers, had given him, when a boy, a political standing. Losing his parents when young, he was condemned to struggle alone along the thorny path of life, and doubtless poverty and illtreatment had much to do with the formation of his political character, and gave a bitterness to his spirit which breathed in nearly every word he uttered and every line he penned. Chosen as secretary to the Association, he composed the various addresses of that body, which were all characterised by a warm, but almost ferocious eloquence. These addresses commanded attention from their enthusiastic, fiery, and sanguinary tone. They generally finished up with an exhortation to the people to win their rights by means of an insurrection. Only by and through that terrible medium it was declared could those rights be accomplished. These documents frequently ended with the ominous words, "Universal Suffrage or Death." This party was in direct antagonism to Lovett and his moral-force associates. They boasted of having on their books the names of three thousand enrolled members, and some of them afterwards complained of the injustice of being ruled in the selection of delegates to the convention by the Working Men's Association, which they declared did not number more than four hundred members, but which had, nevertheless, put forward seven of theit own men, the eighth being O'Brien, who belonged neither to the one nor the other. The main strength of the Democratic Association lay among the distressed and starving Spitalfields weavers, who, driven by poverty to that desperate state in which endurance becomes next to impossible, were ready to listen to the speaker who promised the shortest termination to their miseries, and such a speaker was George Julian Harney. But, as before observed, there was no open schism manifested at the meeting in Palace Yard—the grumbling was limited to the select meetings of the associates.

Great as was the rising excitement in other quarters, the manufacturing counties of Lancashire and Yorkshire exceeded all others in the intensity of their agitation. In the former especially, the minds of the operative class were in a state of continual fever, the particular causes of which we will briefly point out. There had been in these districts from the first a wide-spread horror of the provisions of the new poor law. The operative looked upon the repeal of the 43rd of Elizabeth, and its substitution by the new enactment, as a cancelling of the bond which had hitherto bound them to the richer class, as the breaking of the last link in the chain of sympathy. Huge, prison-like workhouses had risen in various parts, serving to remind the poor of their coming doom. With scanty wages, in many instances insufficient to support life in a tolerable state of comfort, there was nothing before them but misery in the present, and the Bastile in the future, in which they were to be immured when the rich oppressor no longer required their services.

About the same time the police system was coming into active operation. The large towns were first burdened with this new force, but it was afterwards extended to the smaller towns and villages. This gave a considerable shock to the old English feelings of the people, who saw in the various schemes afloat a tendency to that system of centralization, which aims at the abolition of local authority.

At that time, too, the factory system was on so wretched a footing as to be monstrously oppressive to its victims. It is true that the Legislature did not entirely withold protection from the factory worker, but it was of so questionable a character as to be little better than no protection whatever. Wages were so low as to compel thousands of parents to send their children to the mills, where they were worked beyond the powers of endurance. It was with tottering limbs that the poor young creatures staggered from the factory to the cheerless home. These several grievances were fertile sources of discontent amongst the masses, and they only wanted a voice to utter their burning indignation. That voice was speedily supplied. Two men were at that time well known to the operative classes as the great denouncers of their grievances, one in Yorkshire, the other in Lancashire, and the north of Cheshire. In the former county Richard Oastler, was their champion. This sympathising friend was acting in the capacity of steward to Squire Thornhill, a gentleman of property in that county. Against the new poor law, Oastler, waged a most determined warfare. In politics he professed to be a Tory. The term conservative he abhorred, believing that it indicated a lukewarmness as to political principles, in other words that it was but a name for shufflers and gentlemen of easy political virtue, and he detested shufflers of every description. His toryism was, however, of such a nature as to embrace in its provisions a strict attention to the comforts of the poor ; " the Altar, the throne, and the cottage " was his favourite motto, and no man ever more warmly denounced the rich for their intense selfishness, and their cold neglect of the suffering class, than did the tory Oastler. But it was against the water gruel philosophers of the liberal school that his efforts were mainly directed, and these he lashed most unsparingly. He attended meeting after meeting of the operatives, at all of which he addressed his hearers in an eloquent and fiery strain. "Arm, arm, arm," was the oft repeated exhortation with which he finished up his speeches. He was styled the "king of the factory children" from his long and earnest advocacy of their cause. Amongst the working class of every grade in politics his popularity was exceedingly great for they recognised in him a man who had singleness of purpose, and that purpose the universal good. They saw that he wished for a happy combination of all classes. They might not all have faith in the potency of his measures, but the goodness of his intentions they never for a moment questioned, and the "good old king" was the title by which he was generally known.

In Lancashire the Rev. Joseph Rayner Stephens wielded the popular feeling, if possible, with a still greater power. This gentleman had been a minister in the Wesleyan Connexion, and was one of their most eloquent preachers. The slavery of this order of men is a well known fact. Without seeking to give offence to any religious sect, it may safely be asserted, that if there is a body of men in England who are in

be slung on a musket, or a bayonet, and carried through their bodies by an armed force, or by any force whatever, that was a tidy sentence, and if this meeting decided that it was contrary to law and allegiance to the sovereign—that it was altogether a violation of the constitution, and of common sense, it ought to be resisted in every legal way. It was law to think about it, and to talk about, and to put their names on paper against it, and after that to go to the Guildhall and to speak against it. And when that would not do, it was law to ask what was to be done next. And then it would be law for every man to have his firelock, his cutlass, his sword, his pair of pistols, or his pike, and for every woman to have her pair of scissors, and for every child to have its paper of pins and its box of needles, (here the orator's voice was drowned in the cheers of the meeting) and let the men with a torch in one hand and a dagger in the other, put to death any and all who attempted to sever man and wife."

In the same month Stephens addressed a meeting at Glasgow, and concluded a very eloquent speech as follows :—

" If they will not reform this, aye uproot it all, they shall have the revolution they so much dread. We shall destroy there abodes of guilt, which they have reared to violate all law and God's book. If they will not learn to act as law prescribes and God ordains, so that every man shall by his labour find comfortable food and clothing—not for himself only, but for his wife, and babes,—then we swear by the love of our brothers —by our God who made us all for happiness—by the earth He gave for our support—by the heaven He designs for those who love each other here, and by the hell which is the portion of those who, violating His book, have consigned their fellow men, the image of their God, to hunger, nakedness, and death ;we have sworn by our God, by heaven, earth, and hell, that from the East, the West, the North, and the South, we shall warp in one awful sheet of devouring flame, which no arm can resist, the manufactories of the cotton tyrants, and the places of those who raised them by rapine and murder, and founded them upon the wretchedness of the millions whom God, our God, Scotland's God created to be happy."

In a sermon preached at Ashton-under-Lyne, Stephens spoke thus feelingly and eloquently :—

" Did God make you in his own likeness ? Then there's your babe in your likeness—can you hate it ? Well, then, these little ones spring from your loins. They are brethren and sisters. They dance the green together. They twist the flowers together. They twine them in their hair. They make chains and put them round each other's necks, and girdles

H

around each others waists. They gambol at your feet upon
the floor together ; they are playmates together ; they are bed-
fellows together ; and they are schoolfellows together.   They
rise into life.   The sister and the brother, can they hate each
other ?   God has made of one blood all the nations of the earth.
We are all brethren, and He made us in this way, arranging
and constituting the human family in the manner I have just
described, in order that man should know nothing to his
fellow man, breathe nothing to his fellow man but friendship,
brotherly kindness, and charity.   Thus you see how wisely
all was arranged.   Who first broke this law?   Cain, who
slew his brother.   What said God to it ?   No sooner was
the blood of Abel shed, than the smoke of it ascended to
heaven, and went into the nostrils of Jehovah.   The voice of
it rose to heaven and went to the ears of God, and God came
down.   He went to Cain, and said unto him—Cain, where is
thy brother ?   I see him not ; he was here this morning, where
is he to-night ? where is thy brother ?   There's his house,
there's his weeping wife, there's his weeping children, but
where is he ?   And Cain answered, am I my brother's keeper ?
And God demanded of him an account ; and God demands of
every murderer an account to this day.   God says to every
murderer, whether it be the murderer of an individual, or the
murderer of a community—God says where is thy brother ?
God is saying that in Ashton to-night.   God says it to your
magistrates ; God says it to every one of those mill-owners
who have slaughtered hundreds if not thousands.   God says
to them, where is thy brother ? and God will be answered."
     In alluding to the Poor Law, he exclaimed :—
     " I will tell every man in the land, instead of drawing his
sword for that law, to draw his sword against it ; instead of
firing his musket for that law, to fire his musket against it.
Oh yes, my Lord Russell, it is too late, it is too late, it is too
late, thank God, it is too late !   Put me where you like, and
keep me there as long as you like, as long as God and my
poor body will allow you.   You may do just what you like
with me, it is too late, it is too late, it is too late ; the blood
is up, aye ! it tingles in your fingers, it is ready to spurt out
at your finger ends, and to blow the skull cap off.   Your
father's blood is up ; your mother's milk is flowing round, and
round, and round ; you are beginning to be men ; you are
beginning to be women ; you are beginning to be the offspring
of men and women ; thank God for it !   He has poured a new
language upon the people, it is too late, it is too late."   (Here
a man in the crowd, in the pure Lancashire dialect, exclaimed
to the following effect :—' Aye, it is too late ; I tumbled a

watchman out of our house this morning that came a harken-
ing ; I told him to come again and I would make him so that
he would want carrying out.') "Aye, he came into your
house did he ? He came into your house unlawfully. You
did quite right under these circumstances. If any watchman,
or any policeman, lift up your latch, you have a right to lift
the pistol off your shelf ; if he draw the bolt, you have a right
to draw the trigger. Watchmen beware ! and Lord John
Russell beware of sending policemen here to shoot the legs of
my little piecers ; so surely as they shoot the legs of my little
piecers, as they have done at Bury, so surely we will try
whether we can't take a better aim somewhere else. They
told the magistrates that they shot over the people's heads,
and hit one of the boys in the leg. Very bad marksmen
indeed !"

Of such as the above were the speeches and sermons of
Stephens generally composed. His action and gesticulation
were always suited to his language. Pointing to a monster
mill he would exclaim : " You see ·yonder factory with its
towering chimney, every brick in that factory is cemented with
the blood of women and little children." On another occasion
he said : " If the rights of the poor are trampled under
foot, then down with the throne, down with the Aristocracy,
down with the bishops, down with the clergy, burn the Church,
down with all rank, all title, and all dignity." It will require
very little stretch of the imagination to conceive, that although
both Stephens and Oastler declared that they were not Democrats in politics, they were nevertheless paving the way for any
scheme which had for its object the destruction of the rich
man's power over the people. The Charter had that object,
and the poor looked forward to it as to the guiding star of all
their hopes of future good.

Manchester being the great centre of the Lancashire agitation as well as the most populous town in the distrct, it was
resolved to hold a meeting there, which from the greatness of
its numbers, and the sternness of its determination, would be
calculated to give an impetus to the National Movement, and
produce an impression upon the governing classes. With
these objects, committees in the various towns set themselves
earnestly to work to organise a demonstration of their numbers
and their strength. The meeting was fixed to take place on
Monday, September 25th, and on that day the whole district
seemed alive and stirring to make the mighty gathering
worthy of themselves and their cause. There was scarcely a
town or village anywhere around the neighbourhood of
Manchester, that did not contribute its share to the immense

aggregate of human beings.   Stream upon stream of the
mighty masses poured forth towards the spot which was to
witness their determined patriotism.   Although the meeting
was not announced to take place before one o'clock, crowds
of people lined the streets by break of day.   As early as nine
o'clock the processions of people from the country marched
into the town.   The extent of the meeting may be tolerably
well guessed from the fact that at least twenty bands of music
played in the procession, and two hundred flags and banners
fluttered in the soft breeze, with every variety of radical
mottoes and devices.   On one splendid banner was a picture
of the Peterloo massacre, on which were inscribed the words:
"Murder demands justice!"   On another was a device not
very classical, but of a more humorous kind, viz., "More
pigs and less parsons!"   On a third appeared a death's head
and cross bones, and a hand grasping a dagger, with the
interrogative inscription: "Oh tyrants! will you force us to
this?"   Others contained devices explanatory of the principles
of the Charter; but a large number were of a threatening
character, and perhaps did as much to cause consternation as
the speeches of the most fiery orator; for those devices were
chosen in the moments of deliberation, and the deliberate
threat of vengeance is generally more terrifying than words
dropped in the heat of a speaker's enthusiasm, and brought
forth by the cheers of a crowd.   Stern were the countenances
of the men in that vast assemblage.   Their haggard emaciated
features bore evidence of suffering, and were more than
sufficient to excuse wrath at the conduct of their oppressors.
The pale wrinkled cheek, the sunken eye, and the stooping
attenuated frame, were standing witnesses against a system
which forced the many to labour in order that the few might
enjoy.   Such were the continually increasing numbers, that
although the first procession left the committee room as early
as ten o'clock, it was one o'clock before the various bodies had
arrived at the place of meeting.   There were not less than
twenty thousand from Oldham and its immediate vicinity.
The several processions now formed into a dense and compact
mass were estimated by the reporter for the *Morning
Advertiser* at not less than three hundred thousand persons.
The meeting for convenience was held in a hollow space in
the centre of the Moor, to give to the greatest possible
number a view of the speakers who were to address them.
The banners were held at suitable distances from each other
on rising spots of ground, and presented a most beautiful and
animated appearance.   Stephens and O'Connor arrived
together in a carriage-and-four, and were greeted with such

hearty bursts of cheering as were seldom heard even among the excitable people of the manufacturing districts, and as the different speakers mounted the spacious hustings they were greeted with renewed shouts of applause. It was amid a deafening burst of cheering that John Fielden, the member for Oldham, was voted to the chair. A few of the observations contained in his opening speech may not be inappropriate :—

" I am one of those who think that life, liberty, and happiness, ought to be chiefly studied by the representatives of the people, and that the comfort and safety of the people ought to be consulted in preference to accumulated property. I am not the only person in England who entertains such opinions, nor am I singular in those sentiments with reference to the statesmen and politicians of other countries. The wisest men that as a body ever existed—the founders of the American Republic—stated that very same opinion, and in all their essays and speeches promulgated precisely similar doctrines. Poverty, I contend, ought not to be a barrier against the exercise of the elective franchise, and as to the ignorance of the people, which it is alleged should prevail against the right of voting, I should like to compare the working men of England with the representatives in the House of Commons. If the Parliament was composed of working men, they would not have suspended the laws and constitution of the country, and have passed a Coercion Bill for Ireland. If the Parliament was composed of poor men, they would not have passed the new Poor Law Amendment Act, but they would have first secured to the working class fair remunerative wages. If we had a House of Commons composed of working men, they would not have voted sixty thousand pounds for the London police, and then sent them to annoy and disturb the inhabitants in the remotest districts in the kingdom. If we had a House of Commons composed of working men, they would not repeal the Malt Tax one day, and on the next day, at the bidding of the Chancellor of the Exchequer, withdraw that repeal; they would not be long before a repeal of the Corn Laws would be effected by them."

Hodgetts moved a resolution in favour of the Charter. In the course of his remarks he made allusion to the Peterloo massacre. For a considerable time the vast multitude evinced great sensation at this allusion ; nothing, indeed, ever excites a Lancashire audience like the name of Peterloo. Stephens, although no Radical, seconded the resolution, but it was several minutes before the loud cheers of the people would allow him to proceed. He made a characteristic speech, and told the meeting that they had not come there for speaking, for their minds were already made up, but they had come there to demonstrate their will, and to show their strength. O'Connor followed Stephens with one of his usual speeches. He accused the Whigs of treason, and called upon all who were of that opinion to hold up their hands, when the immense concourse of people appeared unanimous in their decision. The meeting was afterwards addressed by Mr. Fitton, from Brighton ; Mr. Halliday, from Oldham ; Messrs. Douglas, Collins, and Pearce, from Birmingham ; Mr. Lowery, from Newcastle ; and Mr. Duffy, from London ; besides several local speakers. Mr. Wheeler moved the following getlemen as delegates to represent that meeting in the Convention :—Dr. Fletcher, for Bury ; the Rev. J. R. Stephens, for Ashton ; Mr. Taylor, for Rochdale ; and Mr. Bronterre O'Brien, for the town of Manchester, Mr. Nightingale, Mr. Richardson, Mr. Cobbett, and Mr. Roe, were the other four. The whole of the gentlemen proposed were unanimously elected, when the mover said :—

" He trusted that they would support the delegates through all their precarious duty, and protect them, and if the rascally Whigs dared to lay a hand on them, and the people submitted to the interference, they would deserve to live only what they were, fit objects to be slaves."

Notwithstanding that during the latter period of the meeting the rain poured in torrents, it seemed to produce no impression on that enthusiastic and excited throng. The dense mass seemed welded together, and were so intent on their object that nothing could turn them aside from the path they had chosen. The meeting was peaceable in the extreme, and at its conclusion no religious assembly could have dispersed in a more orderly manner. So general was the participation in the enormous gathering that the workshops and factories throughout the district were generally closed. The manufacturers saw so evidently the bent of the working class, that they deemed the opening of the factories would be useless, and, like wise men, they complied with the general desire for a cessation on that day from all labour, excepting the work of political and social redemption. The influence which Mr. Fielden's presence had given to the meeting was a subject of congratulation amongst the Democrats. That gentleman was known as the successor to the principles and honours of the immortal Cobbett, and was deservedly popular for the warm and unceasing interest he had taken in the fate of the industrial millions. No man, according to his powers, had been a more strenuous opponent of the new Poor Law ; and against the police system he had taken an equally decided

stand ; but what most gained for him the heartfelt affection of
the working class, was the position which he, a rich manufacturer, had taken as the unqualified denouncer of factory
oppression.   There was scarcely a measure which he was not
prepared to adopt in order to protect the people from the
grasping cottonocracy.   A Ten Hours' Bill was the object of
his constant advocacy, and it was he who succeeded at last
in carrying that measure through the Legislature.   Our own
opinion of all such measures as the Ten Hours' Bill, good as
they are in themselves, is, that they are inadequate to the
accomplishment of the end desired.   They leave untouched the
causes of the people's misery, and those causes remaining, the
effects are certain to continue, though it may be for a time in
a somewhat mitigated form.   But our opinion of the measure
itself, does not blind us to the worth of the man who, standing
apart from the generality of his class, ventures in whatever
way to plead the claims of suffering humanity against wealth
and power.   Fielden too, had shown himself to be something
more than a mere factory reformer ; he had everywhere
declared himself to be the advocate of universal suffrage.   He
did not merely profess himself willing to protect the people
against oppression, but by striving to arm them with the vote,
he manifested a desire to give them the opportunity of protect-
ing themselves.   In this he proved himself to be something
better than a mere humanity-monger, aping philanthropy for
the purpose of catching at a little popularity.   As a speaker,
he was far from being effective ; his sincerity, rather
than his oratory, gave him force.   He was ever earnest,
disdaining to strive after mere effect, but courageously plodd-
ing on in his own humble and unpretending way towards the
attainment of his object.   He has now gone to the tomb of his
fathers ; peace rest his ashes ! The sun has seldom shone over
a better man than John Fielden.

As the South of Lancashire had held its great aggregate
meeting, the West of Yorkshire was resolved not to be far
behind its neighbours, and Peep Green was the spot selected
on which to hoist the standard of Democracy.   This celebrated
place is situate on the road between Leeds and Huddersfield,
and is the most central and available spot for that immense
cluster of towns which form so large a part of the Western
division of the county. The meeting was appointed to be held
on the 15th of October.   Though scarcely equal to the Lancashire meeting, it was nevertheless a noble gathering ; the
numbers were estimated at two hundred and fifty thousand.
As at Kersall Moor, there was no lack of music, flags and
banners, to give spirit to the proceedings.   Bands attended

from Leeds, Bradford, Halifax, Huddersfield, Dewsbury, and all the towns within convenient distance of the place of meeting; and as one after the other they marched upon the Green, the appearance of the various bodies, with all their paraphernalia, was most imposing. In addition to O'Connor and other gentlemen from a distance, the radical talent of the West Riding was present on the occasion. O'Connor was to have a high honour conferred upon him by being appointed as the representative of that vast meeting, not in the Parliament of the rich, but in that Convention where he would be a man of far greater distinction. The cheers with which he was hailed as he mounted the hustings were tremendous; the air echoed with the ringing shouts of the mighty multitude, than which nothing could be more inspiring to the object on whom they were bestowed. Noise was O'Connor's proper element; even in disapprobation it was sweeter to him than the calmness of indifference: but there was no disapprobation at the West Riding demonstration, for

"All went merry as a marriage bell."

The enthusiasm of the meeting drew from him one of his most vigorous speeches. No man varied more in the tone of his address. At one time his speech was almost entirely a string of the wildest declamation; but there were occasions when he could be calm and truly eloquent, and on these occasions he took those who had never been previously accustomed to listen to him by surprise—they only having read of him as the ranting demagogue O'Connor. But the West Riding meeting found him not in his calmer mood; everything was calculated to work up a sanguine man to a state of excitement, while the favour with which he was received led him into the too oft repeated error of talking about himself, instead of directing the attention of the people to subjects of more vital importance. His colleagues were Lawrence Pitkeithly, a merchant of Huddersfield, and William Rider, a working man. The former was a man of a benevolent turn of mind, somewhat of the Cobbett school of politics; a speaker whose earnestness, rather than his oratory, made him popular. About Rider there was nothing of the orator, he was as plain in speech as in personal appearance; indeed, he appeared to regard talking as mere child's play. Belonging to the extreme physical force school, he deemed all moral means of agitation, beyond what was necessary to marshal the democratic forces, as mere waste of time. The three candidates addressed the meeting, O'Connor speaking at considerable length and with great effect; and after several other gentlemen had favoured the people with their views, the vast assemblage dispersed with the same good order as marked all the meetings of that period. In the meantime many of the larger towns proceeded to the election of their delegates, irrespective of those elected at the aggregate gatherings, while in others the same delegates were chosen several times over by their respective constituencies. The large and populous town of Bolton elected Messrs. Carpenter and Warden as its delegates, while the Democrats of Preston made choice of Richard Marsden, a working man, drawn from among the very poorest of his class, and who was the fitting representative of misery. Perhaps of all the men elected there was not one more sincere in purpose than Marsden ; he belonged to the extreme school of Harvey and Rider, and seemed ready to adopt the most forcible measures in order to effect the object of his wishes. As a factory operative he had suffered the utmost extreme, short of death, in the shape of poverty and oppression, and this had rendered him desperate as to consequences, but there was nothing in the nature of Richard Marsden which savoured of ferocity. As a private man he would not have crushed a worm. Whoever looked into his mild blue eyes, and gazed upon his placid open countenance, was forced to conclude that in his breast at least there flowed abundantly the milk of human kindness. If that milk was at times converted into gall it was from his contemplation of the burning wrongs of his class. In conversation he was benevolent and unassuming ; as a speaker his language was marked by deep pathos, and his voice was as pathetic as his words. As the destitute condition of the toiling millions pressed upon his mind, his language became proportionately forcible and strong, but even his worst words of hatred to despotism were breathed in a tone of love for humanity, which nothing on earth could render harsh. Many years of cruel and painful suffering had forced upon him the conviction that there was but one road out of the vortex of misery, and that road was only to be reached through a river of blood. Doubtless it was often painful to his humane and generous nature to labour incessantly under this terrible conviction ; but even that conviction reigned supreme and irresistible, and every day's experience seemed only to fix it more firmly in his mind. Shall we blame him for this state of feeling ? Before we do so let us at least place ourselves in his position. Let us suppose ourselves thrown idle and destitute upon the world by the merciless mandate of a factory lord, simply for cherishing the conviction that man was not doomed by a bountiful Creator to a life of misery, and that such misery is attributable only to the injustice of his fellow. Let us further suppose a beloved wife and lisping children depending on us for bread, while we are utterly unable to supply their wants; that this fact does not apply to ourselves alone, but also to thousands, aye, tens of thousands of our class; that we behold this oppression and misery so far from diminishing, increasing with the resistless march of time, and that in addition to these things, we mark a fixed determination on the part of the oppressor to maintain and continue the horrid scourge. When we have imagined all this, let us ask ourselves honestly whether, under such fearful circumstances, we should have been more gentle or pacific than Richard Marsden, and if we mistake not, candour will compel us to answer in the negative.

The Democrats of Bradford elected Peter Bussey as their delegate. Bussey was the landlord of a beerhouse in that town, which was a favourite resort of numbers of the radical party. He was a happy specimen of the burly Old English publican; his uncouth manner rendered him an especial favourite of the Bradford Democrats, who regarded his bluntness as a proof of his genuine honesty. Without any desire to detract from the character of Bussey, we may remark that this is not an unexceptionable criterion by which to judge humanity. There is an affectation of coarseness as well as of refinement, and it is sometimes the worse affectation of the two. The speeches of the Bradford delegate always smacked of physical force, and he was pretty often complimented by O'Connor for the bravery of his language. Ashton-under-Lyne and its vicinity also elected its delegate. This was done originally, as the reader will have observed, on Kersall Moor, but events transpired in the affairs of Stephens, which we shall by and by have occasion to notice, that led to the retirement of that gentlemen from his post, and a substitute was therefore appointed in his place. The agitation had not long commenced when a young man stepped into the political arena who was destined at no distant day to play an important part in the movement. The name of this gentleman was Peter Murray M'Douall. The subject of our notice was the son of parents who occupied a middle station in society, and who educated him for the medical profession. Newton Stewart, in the West of Scotland, was the town in which he first saw the light, but while young he removed to Ramsbottom, a small town near Bury, in Lancashire, at which place he enjoyed a pretty extensive practice in his profession. Up to the time that the agitation commenced his circumstances in life were good, and he had every prospect of rising to distinction. Joined to a good constitution he had the advantage of youth on his side, being not more than 24 years of age. In stature

M'Douall was rather short, but possessed a straight and well-erected frame ; in personal appearance he was decidedly handsome ; his general features were extremely prepossessing ; his mouth was small but well formed, void of any unpleasant compression of the lips, his face rather inclined to the oval ; his eyes were full, and in moments of excitement sparkling and fiery ; his brow was moderately high, very full and broad, and his eyebrows dark and finely pencilled; his hair which was light, approaching to sandy (although a government description once stated it to be black), was parted in the centre and hung in long graceful curls behind his ears, and his whole appearance was highly interesting. The Doctor was of an ardent fiery temperament, and though naturally possessing strong reflective powers, was impulsive to the last degree, and by no means deficient in the quality of courage. That he entered the movement from a generous regard to the people's welfare, and a thorough conviction of the justice of their cause, there is very little reason to doubt, for he sacrificed a lucrative profession, and devoted whatever means he possessed to the furtherance of the cause in which he embarked. He was first introduced to the people at a public meeting in the town of Bury by his friend Dr. Fletcher who was already engaged in the same cause. Those who witnessed M'Douall's first effort at public speaking had little hopes of his success in that department. Like many other young speakers he suffered terribly from nervous excitement, which rendered it extremely difficult for him to proceed. Those, however, who judged of his ultimate success by the failure of his first attempt were agreeably disappointed, for M'Douall became one of the most powerful and graceful speakers in the movement. A short time sufficed to dispel the nervous fear which marked the commencement of his public career. He ceased to stammer, and his words were uttered with the boldness and force of a practised orator. When Stephens declined the honour of sitting in the Convention, he and M'Douall were on intimate terms, and he recommended M'Douall to the people of Ashton, who elected him with unanimous consent. Sheffield elected William Gill, a working man ; Mr. Deegan, another working man, was appointed for New Mills ; the county of Durham was represented by Mr. Knox ; Marylebone, the pet district of the Aristocracy, elected its separate delegate in the person of William Cardo, a shoemaker, while the extensive and populous district of the Staffordshire Potteries chose an old veteran worker named John Richards, or Daddy Richards, as he was more familiarly termed, to be the exponent of its wishes. Wigan, one of the poorest and most miserable towns in England, was represented by Mr. Fenny.

The midland town of Leicester elected an old gentleman named Smart, while the Democrats of Loughboro' sent J. Skevington, another veteran in the Radical cause, to represent them.   The agitation had even aroused the spirit of Democracy in the fashionable town of Brighton, where a Mr. Osborne was elected to the Convention.   Nottingham, famous in the annals of agitation, secured the services of the Rev. Dr. Wade. The worthy doctor had for many years been a favourite with the Radical party.   The active part he performed at the time of the Consolidated Trades' Union ; the warm sympathy he manifested on behalf of the Dorchester labourers, and the interest he always took in anything that related to the working class, had gained for him their general confidence and esteem, which was doubtless enhanced by the curious fact that he was a clergyman of the Established Church.   Oldham was represented by a Mr. Mills, while the Democrats of the large commercial emporium of Liverpool honoured two gentlemen named Whittle and Smith with their confidence.   The Radicals of Reading—never very numerous—sent to the Convention a delegate of the name of Tite.

The West of England also proceeded in the work of delegation.   Vincent had perfectly aroused the Democratic feeling in that quarter.   Bristol elected to the Convention a member of the London Democratic Association, an associate of Julian Harney's, Mr. C. H. Neesom. He was a man past the middle age of life, and had been mixed up in Radical movements for many years. Neesom possessed no large amount of talent, or breadth of views, but the extreme language he employed was his passport to popularity.   He made no secret of his prepossession in favour of a physical revolution, and it was this which secured him the favour of the Bristolians.

The Radicals of the aristocratic city of Bath were represented by Mr. Mealing, one of their own citizens, while William Carrier was elected for Trowbridge and Bradford, at a public meeting at which thirty thousand persons, from various parts of Somerset and Wilts, were said to be present.

The Democrats of Wales chose two delegates to represent them in the Convention ; the first of these was a tradesman and magistrate by the name of Frost, whose residence was at Newport, in the county of Monmouth ; and who was chosen for the southern part of the Principality. Vincent was the first public lecturer who was invited to that district, and he found an enthusiastic population ready to receive him.   The Welsh are a people almost as implusive as the Irish.   History affirms the gallant spirit of this people in their maintenance of a distinct nationality.   This spirit continues to some extent even to the

JOHN FROST

FROM AN ENGRAVING BY W. READ
AFTER AN ORIGINAL PAINTING

present hour, for considerable numbers refuse to recognise the English language, and cling to their native tongue with the strongest devotion. This spirit of nationality is often condemned as evincing a narrowness of mind, and as being opposed to that spirit of universality which is of a world-wide application. Nothing can be more unjust than such reflections. Undoubtedly it will be a glorious day when a universal spirit of brotherhood shall cement all the nations of the earth into one community, with one heart, one mind, one interest ; but this universal spirit must be the result of mutual understanding and not of conquest, for the spirit of love can never be the offspring of brutal force. The history of the world is the history of conquests, and of the moulding of many nations into one by the ruthless and lustful hand of power, not for the interest of mankind, but for the wicked gratification of despots. Wales was overcome by the power of the sword, and it is the knowledge of this injustice which even now rankles in the minds of many of its people, and induces them to cling with devotion to all which serves to remind them of the glory of their past.

This impulsive people received Vincent with open arms. He was just the man to rouse all the keener emotions of the masses, whose condition was none of the best, and it was not long before a spark of fire ran from breast to breast, which threatened to ignite into an inextinguishable flame. On his visit to Newport, John Frost received Vincent with all the hospitality which marks the Welsh character, and he embraced the principles advocated by the youthful orator in a disinterested spirit worthy of the days of chivalry, and all his family were as enthusiastic in the cause as himself. His position as a tradesman and a magistrate gave him an extraordinary influence over the poor people, who looked to him as a sort of Moses who was to lead them into the promised land of liberty and plenty.

There is an order of men who are democratic by nature ; who, place them in whatever sphere you will, instinctively incline towards the side of justice and humanity. John Frost was a man of this stamp. Justice with him was more than a sentiment it predominated over all. No effort of distorted reason could possibly have conquered the strong sense of right which was manifested in his every act. It was no wonder, then, that he embraced a movement which had for its object the elevation of the masses. Of a deeply religious, though not a fanatical turn of mind, he looked upon God as the universal father, and mankind as brothers, whose rights should be equally respected and secured from invasion. In short, John

Frost really and truly loved the people, and they loved him in return, and awarded him that confidence which, despite whatever appearances to the contrary, he never betrayed.

Charles Jones, of Welshpool, was the person elected by the Democrats of North Wales as their representative. The parents of Mr. Jones had destined him for the Church, and he was educated in accordance with that view ; but just as they were about to accomplish their object, he threw himself heart and soul into the movement, and frustrated all their designs. For this act of insubordination he was utterly discarded by his family connections, and thrown for the means of existence on the justice of his party. Unfortunate man ! Jones was no extemporaneous speaker. All the speeches he ever made were first written and committed to memory. His language was powerful and in the best taste ; popular without being vulgar. His delivery was forcible and good, and his voice exceedingly impressive. In person he was tall and commanding, with a bold profile, dark flashing eyes, and curly raven hair ; but so irascible in temper as often to wound even his best friends. The difficulties of his position doubtless contributed to this irascibility.

Scotland was not behind in contributing its quota of delegates. The Democrats of Edinburgh were represented in the person of W. Villiers Tankey, the son of a member of the last Irish parliament, who voted on every occasion against the act which brought about the legislative union of the two countries. Mr. Mair was delegated by the masses of Glasgow to represent them in the People's Parliament, while the Radicals of the land of Burns appointed Hugh Craig Bailie, of Kilmarnock, to give expression to their sentiments. Mr. Burns was elected for the large manufacturing town of Dundee ; and Messrs. Duncan, Halley, and Matthew, served for Dumfermline, Paisley, and some other places in Scotland. There remains still one man at present to notice, and as we must do so at some length, we will here conclude the present chapter.

BRONTERRE O'BRIEN

FROM A MEDALLION IN THE POSSESSION OF
WILLIAM TOWNSHEND, ESQ.

CHAPTER IV.

JAMES BRONTERRE O'BRIEN.

At the period of which we write there was one man who wielded more of the real democratic mind than any other man in the movement; and who, with the single exception of O'Connor, was also more generally popular. Yet this man had been but little accustomed to the labours and honours of the platform. It was through the medium of the press that his influence had been principally felt. The name of the gentleman alluded to was James Bronterre O'Brien, a native of the sister country, as his name would seem to indicate. The father of Mr. O'Brien was for many years an extensive wine and spirit merchant, as well as tobacco manufacturer, in the county of Longford. His son was born in 1805, consequently, at the commencement of the Chartist Movement, he was about 33 years of age. The genius of O'Brien manifested itself in very early life. Before completing his tenth year he had made the study of several languages, in which he attained considerable proficiency. In consequence of the stoppage of several firms in the city of Dublin his father failed in business, and going shortly after to the West Indies with the view of mending his broken fortune, he was overtaken by illness, which terminated his life. He was left now, like Byron, to the sole care of his surviving parent, and she resolved on educating her son for one of the learned professions. Naturally inclined to study, and applying himself incessantly to the acquisition of knowledge, he mastered with great rapidity the Latin, Greek, French, and Italian languages, and conquered with brilliant success the mathematical and other sciences. He also exhibited great aptitude for composition in poetry and prose. The late Lowell Edgeworth, brother of the celebrated authoress of that name, became acquainted with the promising qualities of this youthful scholar, and, taking a delight in making educational experiments, he intimated to the mother of O'Brien his desire that her son should join the Edgeworth Town School, an establishment which was conducted on the Monitor system of teaching,

which Mr. Edgeworth believed to be the best plan of helping
his more advanced students in completing their education.
O'Brien had not been long at this school before he became
principal of the twenty-one monitors of the establishment, in
which capacity he had the teaching of the more advanced
classes.   Miss Edgeworth was a frequent visitor at her
brother's, and on one occasion she presented O'Brien with a
handsome copy of Pope's works, as a reward of his superior
merit.   Sir Walter Scott, on the occasion of a visit to the
school, was so struck with his singular talents and acquirements, that he presented him with a silver pencil case as a
mark of his admiration, and he received from the same consideration, subsequent presents from other eminent persons.
Having remained at the above named establishment for several
years, he removed to Dublin and entered the University of
that city, where he reaped high academic honours during his
undergraduate course, and before he left the University, he had
taken the degree of B.A.   Shortly afterwards he entered himself
as a student of King's Inn, from whence he removed to Gray's
Inn, London, at which places he was qualifying himself for the
bar ; but just as O'Brien was advancing towards the goal which
had been selected for him to reach, he became acquainted with
Cobbett, Hunt, and other leading reformers, and that acquaintance led to his introduction to the world of politics.   From
that hour he was doomed to an incessant struggle against the
institutions of what is called society.   It was by Mr. Hunt
that O'Brien was first introduced to the British public, which
introduction took place at a meeting held in London, we believe,
in the year 1830.   Mr. Hunt informed the meeting that it was his
pleasure that day to introduce to them a young gentleman of
great abilities, whose sympathies were entirely with the people,
and who he believed would prove a valuable accession to their
cause'; and, in his own blunt way, he exclaimed to O'Brien,
"Come up my man, and speak for yourself."   Like many
others who are about entering upon public life, the young
speaker had some difficulty in conquering his diffidence, as he
rose in a tremour to address the meeting ; but from his first
effort it was easy to foresee the fact, that at no distant day
O'Brien would exercise a powerful influence over the minds of
the working class.   When the battle of the unstamped press
had commenced, Mr. Hetherington perceived the advantage
that would accrue to the cause by securing O'Brien as a
writer, and he accordingly became the editor of *The Poor Man's
Guardian*, a journal which proclaimed itself to be published in
defiance of law, to try the power of right against might, and
it was through this journal that the worth of O'Brien, as a

public writer, became known and appreciated. He also contributed powerful articles to *The Twopenny Despatch*, *The People's Conservative*, *The Destructive*, and other papers. The immense excitement which those papers caused will be well remembered by the politicans of that period. The Government tried every available means to put them down ; not so much from a consideration of revenue, as from a fear of the progress of the doctrines they enunciated. In 1836 O'Brien made further progress in democratic literature by the publication of a translated work entitled, *Buonarotti's History of Babeuf's Conspiracy for Equality*. O'Brien held that all the previous so-called historians of the French Revolution were little better than mere denouncers, and that while they held out to the world's admiration the greatest enemies of society, they equally blackened and traduced the character of the people's best, most humane, and enlightened friends. He regarded Buonarotti's work as well calculated to throw a light upon the men and events of that important period, and his acquaintance with the French language enabled him to render as perfect a translation as it was possible to give. The work is prefaced with an introduction by the translator, in which the conduct of the higher and middle classes of France is powerfully and vigorously denounced. In some parts of the work there are copious notes, explanatory of what may appear obscure in the writer, and occasionally correcting his views. When we state that Buonarotti's History received the praise even of the tory *Quarterly Review*, the reader will form no mean opinion either of his credit as a historian, or his ability as a writer. Shortly after the publication of this work, O'Brien paid a visit to Paris, partly, we believe, for the purpose of collecting information which should enable him to write a true and faithful life of Robespierre, whose character he conceived had been most foully and shamelessly belied. It was the very malignancy of his defamers that first suggested to the mind of O'Brien that Robespierre was a man the exact reverse of all that historians had recorded of his character, and he resolved, if possible, to sift the matter to the bottom. It was in the following way that O'Brien reasoned on the subject with himself : " The very men who have written on the character of Robespierre belong to the very class whose monopolies and usurpations it was his mission to destroy. Those classes had been guilty of precisely the same crimes which they sought to fasten upon their victim. As it was manifestly their intent to shield themselves from obloquy, it was equally their interest to blacken the character of their antagonist, whose virtues, if known and contrasted with their own manifold crimes, would have stood against them as a constant reproach." He held, therefore, that the more virtuous Robespierre really was, the more they would naturally seek to stamp his character with infamy. It was not long before a volume of the Life of Robespierre was issued from the press, and it certainly was one of the most masterly productions of the kind that had ever been given to the world. In this work he endeavoured to show that the subject of it, so far from being the character he had generally been described, was one of the most enlightened, humane, and virtuous reformers that ever lived. A bolder step could not possibly have been taken by a public writer. It was directly flying in the face of an almost universal and strongly-established opinion,—in the face apparently of all sterling truths. Let us here present a summary of Robespierre's bad qualities, as given by his enemies, and then we may form a tolerable idea of the amount of courage that was required to enable a man to write in his defence.

Montgaillard, Mountgoye, and Desodoards, all French writers, set forth that Robespierre was "ignorant, ugly, grim, sombre, malignant, vulgar, lascivious, brutal, envious, a hater of journalists, a second Omar against literature, a barbarous proscriber of the arts and sciences, a murderer of his enemies, an assassin of his friends, a bachelor only because the chastity of marriage did not suit his taste for libertinism, a seducer of his host's daughter, a filthy beast that finished his daily orgies of lust and the guillotine by a nocturnal debauch amongst common prostitutes." Here was certainly a very pretty character of the man who had taken so prominent a part in the French Revolution, and it required a bold man to enter on the perilous task of defending a man thus assailed. But that task O'Brien undertook, in defiance of all the prejudice which would naturally be excited against such a proceeding ; and he brought a mass of evidence forward, sufficient to stagger the faith of all impartial men in the truthfulness of those pretended historians. It had been asserted that Robespierre was naturally cruel, and that he manifested that cruelty in particular instances at a very early period of his life. O'Brien shows by counter testimony the falsity of such charges, and that Robespierre was gifted with far more than an ordinary share of humane and generous feeling. The charges of ignorance and vulgarity he is equally successful in refuting ; and by the productions of his early genius, attested by some of the first scholars in France, he proved that Robespierre was a man not only of great original powers of mind, but that the language in which he clothed his thoughts was of a highly refined and classical character, and that all his acts had gone to prove that he was in the truest sense of the term, the warm, energetic, and untiring friend of justice and humanity. That O'Brien did not, in writing this work, seek to impose upon the world the mere creation of his own fancy, there is not only a sufficient body of evidence to prove in the work itself, but Lamartine, the applauder of the Girondists (Robespierre's bitterest enemies), abundantly testifies. That great writer, in his famous *History of the Girondists*, tells his readers that Robespierre was perhaps the only man who from the first comprehended the end of the Revolution. He also bears testimony to the greatness and universality of his views, and he relates frequent instances of his humanity and his horror of bloodshed ; showing to all who will take the trouble to read and compare, that where Robespierre sanctioned the destruction of human life, he was compelled to that course by stern and imperious necessity.

Previous to the commencement of the agitation for the Charter, O'Brien, as a public writer, had taken a course very unfashionable at that period amongst politicians. He was something more than a mere political declaimer. Not that he undervalued political reforms ; he showed, on the contrary, how abortive must be the efforts of the people for their social emancipation, so long as all legislative authority remained in the hands of the oppressors. But he also comprehended and endeavoured to explain to his readers, that the highest amount of political influence would never be of the slightest utility in enabling them to burst the bonds of social misery, unless they understood the true basis of society ; and he sought to trace our great fundamental evils to two monster sources, viz., landlordism and usury, in all their multifarious shapes and forms. Up to that time there may be said to have existed only two classes of social economists ; the one side contending for what is called the rights of property, without any regard to the claims of industry ; and the other side, who, like Robert Owen, were for striking at the root of all private property, by substituting for it community of possessions. It is true that there was a thin party of the school of Oastler, but their claims on behalf of labour were those of benevolence rather than of fundamental right. Between the two first named classes it was the mission of O'Brien to steer, and while repudiating the pretensions of the former, he showed the absurdity of the latter in seeking to force a crude and undigested theory upon society. But he was not a mere fault-finder, for he sought to reconcile the rights of private property with the most complete justice to the labouring class. His plans at that time were not so complete as they were rendered in later years, but the principle indicated was set forth in the numerous emanations from his powerful pen.

Although other men had taken upon themselves the initiation of the movement for the Charter, it was the writings of O'Brien that laid the foundation for that movement, and his great share in the work was acknowledged as soon as the agitation had fairly set in. Although not seeking to attract public notice to himself, he now began to be sought by the people, for whom he had so long and so ardently laboured. As soon as the holding of a Convention became settled, he was invited by no fewer than thirteen constituencies to represent them in that assembly. The whole of these invitations he at first respectfully declined. With some of these constituencies refusal was, however, utterly vain, for they persisted in electing him even against his expressed wishes. Amongst these were London, Manchester, Stockport, Norwich, Leigh, and the Isle of Wight. These decided manifestations of confidence overcame his scruples, and he consented to accept the post of delegate. A few words on the personal appearance and qualifications of O'Brien must conclude the present notice. In stature he was considerably above the middle size, of fine figure, though rather inclined to the stooping posture of the profound student. His general features were often adjudged to be handsome, though we have sometimes heard expressed an opinion to the contrary. This difference of judgment might in some measure depend upon the mood in which their authors beheld the object of their remarks. Viewed while unpleasant thoughts were agitating his mind, he was certainly not the most prepossessing of men, but under the influence of pleasant sensations, there was no man more fascinating than O'Brien. His lofty, broad, and massive brow, showed him to be a man of extraordinary mental ability, while that portion of his head where phrenologists have fixed benevolence, was of unusual development. It is not too much to say, that of all the democratic leaders who figured at the commencement of the Chartist movement, he was undoubtedly the man with the greatest breadth of mind. In the Chartist ranks he was universally known as the schoolmaster, a title bestowed on him by O'Connor. His veriest foes bore testimony to the greatness of his intellect. The *Weekly Chronicle* was one of the papers that heaped upon him the most unmeasured abuse, but in the same article it described him as a man having more in his little finger than all the other Chartist leaders put together.

As an orator, O'Brien stood alone in the peculiarity of his style. We have known some go so far as to assert that he was destitute of the qualifications necessary to the orator. There was never a sorrier mistake. True, he spoke not in the flowing style of Vincent, nor in the rapid declamatory strain of O'Connor, nor were his addresses always marked by the measured deliberateness of Lowery ; but he combined in a measure the advantages of all three. When reasoning a point he was deliberate to admiration. No other speaker was capable of rising to such a height, or of so impressing an audience with the strength and intensity of his feelings, while no orator could outrival him in action and flexibility of voice. In handling the weapon of satire, he enjoyed an immeasurable superiority over all his compeers. There was no flippancy in his wit. It was grand and solid—solid as logic itself, and fell with an equal weight. No man could so easily mould reason, satire, or declamation into one compact body, or hurl the triple weapon at the head of an antagonist with more terrible force. He always enjoyed, too, the happy facility of adapting himself to the comprehension of his audience. An orator may generally be better judged by the effect he produces than by any other standard, and taking this criterion in the case of O'Brien, his oratory must be pronounced of the first order; for when in health and spirits, and favoured by a numerous audience, his principal difficulty was not that of exciting his hearers to a sympathy with his sentiments, but it consisted in keeping down the tumultuous applause with which he was greeted. Let it be stated, too, that at the time of which we write, he detained his audiences longer than any other public speaker. Three hours was about the usual time he occupied a meeting ; but he sometimes spoke for four, and even five hours, rivetting the attention of his audience to the close of his address. We can have no hesitation in pronouncing the opinion, that a man who was possessed of such capabilities, was an orator of no ordinary power, and that he must have been a master, not only of words, but of ideas.

While the Democrats of London, the Midlands, and the North, were urging forward with constantly accelerated speed their demands for the People's Charter, those of the West, as before intimated, were anything but sparing in their efforts to swell the cry. For this sweeping parliamentary reform, Vincent was every day assembling the people in their thousands. Bristol, Bath, Cheltenham, Trowbridge, Bradford, and other places were kept in a state of constant excitement by the arduous exertions of this celebrated orator, to whose popularity in these districts it was scarcely possible to affix a limit. The ladies appeared even more enthusiastic in their attachment to the great movement than the men. They formed themselves into radical associations, in which hundreds of names were enrolled. Doubtless the fascinating personal qualities of Vincent had their share in rousing the patriotism of these fair

Democrats, for, as before remarked, that gentleman was with the sex an universal favourite. The women Democrats of Bath were in the habit of holding meetings, at all of which Vincent was the honoured guest. To show their appreciation of his services, they entered into a subscription, with which they purchased a valuable gold watch. This testimonial was presented to him at a public meeting, on which occasion he excelled himself, by the graceful terms in which he acknowledged the pretty compliment. As a proof of the amount of spirit which animated the ladies of that fashionable, beautiful, and romantic city, it need but be mentioned, that on its being known that Vincent was to honour them with a visit, they engaged the Hartshill Gardens, situate about a mile from the city, in which four thousand of them assembled to give him welcome, while vast numbers were unable to gain admittance, every available spot being occupied. A somewhat amusing incident occurred at this gathering. It had been agreed upon by the ladies, that with the exception of the favoured Vincent, not one of the masculine gender was to be admitted to witness the proceedings. It so happened, however, that notwithstanding this prohibition, a member of the rougher sex, with a curiosity which might have been excused in one of the gentle fair, by ensconcing himself in female attire gained admission to the gardens. The trick was, however, speedily discovered, and almost as speedily communicated to the meeting, who in the best possible humour buffeted the intruder from their presence. Mrs. Bolwell, the wife of one of the leading Radicals of Bath, occupied the chair, and Mr. Vincent addressed the assembly at great length. The proceedings in the garden being at an end, he harangued the persons outside who were not able to gain admission, amid the waving of handkerchiefs and other demonstrations of the delight of his fair hearers.

The meeting which was held at Bath to elect a delegate to the Convention was most numerously attended. It was estimated that fifteen thousand persons were assembled together. In addition to Vincent and the other speakers, the meeting was favoured with the presence of Colonel William Napier, who addressed the congregated thousands on behalf of Universal Suffrage. The gallant Colonel was, however, deeply offended during the proceedings. Vincent, in the course of his speech alluded to the parties who placed themselves in opposition to the people, and observed that they, the people, were kept down by knaves. " Lord John Russell was a knave, Harry Brougham was a knave, the Duke of Wellington was a knave." The Colonel, stepping forward, exclaimed:

"I deny that. The Duke of Wellington is no knave; he fought for his country nobly, bravely, honourably, and he is no knave." Vincent rejoined : "I say that any man, be he a Russell, a Wellington, or a Napier, who denies me the right to vote, is a knave." The Colonel expressed the opinion that such language as the speaker had that day uttered was calculated to injure the cause. With the exception of this little incident, everything passed off in the greatest harmony.

The largest demonstration of the Western Counties took place on the 30th September, 1838, on Trowle Common, a spot of ground situate between Trowbridge and Bradford. Two numerous processions started from these towns ; one from the former place was not less than three-quarters of a mile in length. Before the procession started from Trowbridge, a young lady, on behalf of the single ladies of the town presented Mr. Vincent with a silk scarf, and the married ladies paid a similar compliment to Mr. Carrier. The two bodies from Trowbridge and Bradford met each other at the Common, and as soon as the recognition was made, they rent the air with the most enthusiastic shouts of applause. It was calculated that thirty thousand people swore fealty that day to the popular cause. When we reflect on the comparative meagreness of the population of this district, we cannot but be struck with the amount of excitement which it must have taken to draw together such an immense concourse of persons. The fact is that Vincent had completely fired the minds of the masses, and several men of talent emulated his example, volunteering their services as public speakers, and devoting their energies to the cause. Among the number was W. P. Roberts, a solicitor of Bath, and cousin to the then Lord Chief Justice Sir Nicholas Tyndal. From Vincent's first visit to Bath, Roberts took him by the hand, made him his most intimate friend, and shared the dangers and the honours of his struggles. A young chemist of Trowbridge, by the name of Potts, an enthusiastic Democrat, performed his share of the labour, devoting himself to the cause with all the zeal and intrepidity of youth. William Carrier, the same man who figured at the Palace Yard meeting, a working man, but the best of all the local speakers, also lent his aid to pro-pagate its principles. Whatever might, at the outset of his career, have been the moral force sentiments of Vincent, all his speeches now assumed more or less a physical force tend-ency. He spoke of the speedy victory of the people in the most encouraging terms. He attended large and excited meetings of the Democrats of Bristol on Brandon Hill. On one occasion he went to the meeting on a white charger, and dealt out the most unmeasured invectives against the Government, and presaged their speedy downfall.   At Trowbridge, the "loyal" portion of the public became daily more alarmed at their apparent imminent danger.   Potts was so open in his physical force predilections as to decorate his window with a formidable array of bullets, which he had sufficient boldness to label as "tory pills."   Vincent was so fully engaged in this quarter, that for some considerable time he could not spare a single day to devote to any other part of the country.   His services were in constant demand, and the more he worked the stronger and more frequent did those demands become.

While Glasgow, Newcastle, Birmingham, London, Manchester, and Peep Green were the theatres of the monster aggregate meetings, other places were no less active in disseminating the principles of the Charter.   The town and villages around Newcastle were as enthusiastically devoted to the movement as the Democrats of that noble town.   On the 10th of October, the people of the little seaport town of Blyth turned out to the number of a thousand, and were addressed by Messrs. Arkle, Hepburn, Brown, Bird, Smith, and Lowrey. The utmost enthusiasm was manifested, and the people present pledged their devotion to the Charter.   At the village of Usworth, an equally enthusiastic meeting was held, where the persons assembled were addressed by Mr. Hammond the chairman, and Messrs. Thomason, Smith, and Devyr ; at the conclusion of which they formed a branch of the Northern Political Union.   At Greenside, a village on the southern side of the Tyne, the people met in the open air to the number of two thousand men, with a large number of women. A splendid band from Winlaton was in attendance.   Mr Foster the chairman, and a deputation from Newcastle addressed the meeting.   Everything passed off in the highest spirit, and at the conclusion a procession accompanied the Newcastle deputation on the road to Winlaton where a meeting was to be held on the same evening.   The theatre had been taken for the latter meeting, but the place was utterly inadequate to hold the assembled thousands, and an adjournment to the open air became necessary.   Mr. Summerside occupied the chair, and the meeting was addressed by Messrs. Alder, Smith, Parker, Thomason, Charlton, and Cockburn.   Throughout the entire proceedings the utmost enthusiasm animated the assembly. At Carlisle the same spirit pervaded the masses.   In August a public meeting in favour of the movement was held in the Town Hall, a building capable of holding a thousand persons, which was literally crammed, while nearly the same number remained outside unable to secure admission.   Messrs. Hall,

Hanson, Barnes, Baird, McKenzie, Barr, and Lawrence were the speakers. There was not a dissenting voice from the resolutions proposed, and it was announced that the union numbered one thousand two hundred persons. In Scotland, Aberdeen, Dumfries, Dundee, and the majority of the Lowland towns, large and small, were actively engaged in the agitation. At Aberdeen a large meeting was held, at which Mr. Duncan spoke at great length, giving in the course of his speech some clever hits at the clergy. "The Tories (said Mr. Duncan) are all religious men. They talk much about religion. They want more new churches, and more stupid blockheads for ministers, and each parson, for telling the truth (query), is to have a bond on the exchequer. The tory parsons are our modern Pharisees; they make long prayers; they pray at the corners of the streets, but devour widows' houses. It is thus that the Gospel of Jesus Christ is abused. The tyrant pays the priest, and the priest deludes the people for the sake of the tyrant. We pay twelve million to support our men of war, and have not an enemy in all the world. Twenty-five thousand bayonets are required to protect the Gospel of Jesus Christ in Ireland. Are you content to tolerate such a state of things?" The interrogation of the speaker was responded to by loud cheering, and cries of 'no, never!' At Dumfries the meeting was held on the Corbelly Hill, in a field belonging to Provost Shortridge. There were several banners displayed on the brow of the hill. Messrs Campbell, Knight, and Wardrop addressed the assembled thousands, and the meeting unanimously expressed a firm resolve to stand by the principles of the Charter.

At the great commercial town of Liverpool thousands of persons assembled on the 25th of September in the Old Infirmary yard. The rain poured in torrents during the entire time of the meeting, but Messrs. Goodfellow, Robinson, Edmunds, O'Connor, Murray, Cobbett, Collins, Lowery and others managed by their eloquence to keep the crowd in good spirits, and the resolutions were unanimously adopted. This was followed by a large public dinner in the evening, after which the speakers entertained the company till twelve o'clock, the utmost order and harmony reigning throughout.

Even in the government town of Devonport, the spirit of Democracy was not asleep. A meeting was held in a room which held two thousand persons, but the crowd was so great as to compel an adjournment to the open air, where the *Sun* acknowledged that four thousand persons were present, and expressed its surprise at the fact. The warmest enthusiasm was manifested by the meeting. At Sheffield the Democrats

L

appeared to emulate the spirit of Ebenezer Elliott, as displayed at the Palace Yard meeting. They met on the 25th of September to the number of twenty thousand. The great corn-law rhymer occupied the chair, and the meeting was addressed by Gill, Buchanan, and other talented speakers. The whole of the proceedings passed off with the greatest glee. On the 30th of September, the Radicals of Brighton made an immense demonstration of their numbers. Feargus O'Connor was the great lion of the day, and the meeting displayed a perfect rage of enthusiasm. At the city of Coventry a large out-door demonstration attested the feelings of the people in favour of the Charter, while in the county of Northampton, Long Buckley, Kettering, Daventry, Wellingboro, and several villages held their meetings and subscribed to the principles which were taking such a general hold on the public mind. At the little town of Kettering there were not less than three hundred members in the Radical Association. In the East the Democrats of Ipswich held a large public meeting, at which the petition was unanimously adopted. At Birmingham the radical ladies formed themselves into a union. The utmost spirit was displayed at their meetings. At one meeting of this body, held in the beginning of September, the chairwoman stated that one thousand three hundred had already joined the union. She likewise stated that for a long time past she had omitted that part of the grace which thanked God for His good creatures, as very few good creatures made their appearance on her table. At this meeting ten pounds was voted out of the funds to the coming Convention. A week after another meeting of the same body was held, at which Mr. Collins introduced James Ayr, from Newcastle, who adverted in strong terms to the subject of the new Poor Law. He told the assembled hundreds that " so hostile was he to its provisions, that he felt no difficulty in swearing before them, as he had done elsewhere, that if the overseers under that Act should at any time attempt to separate him from his wife they should carry the law into operation over his lifeless corpse." This sentiment was vehemently cheered by the fair assembly.

The Birmingham Political Union was resolved to try the public spirit of Kidderminster, and Messrs. Muntz, Douglas, and others attended a public meeting for that purpose. A hustings was erected in the open air. The meeting was large, but there was considerable confusion in consequence of some drunken middle-class scamps taking possession of the hustings before the deputation arrived. These " respectable " noodles constantly interrupted the proceedings. They were well drubbed by the speakers, but, as may be judged, with very little effect upon themselves, although the body of the meeting entirely sympathized with the deputation. At Birmingham the Political Union continued to hold its meetings weekly. O'Connor was often their guest. At one of these gatherings he announced that he was no longer the leader of the people, but a follower of Messrs. Atwood and Fielden. He was told in reply that the Union recognized no leadership, but would unite with all who would work honestly and earnestly for the common cause. Through all the manufacturing districts, even in the smallest villages, meetings were now continually on the increase, and many of the agricultural villages were in a state of agitation. Men and women enrolled in the ranks by thousands, and their devotion to the Charter was becoming deeper every day.

The forces of the Democrats had not long been mustered to declare their adhesion to the People's Charter ere manifest signs of division began to appear in the camp. The bone of contention was the nature of the means to be employed for the attainment of their common object, for upon the object itself there were no visible signs of disunion. The cause of the Charter was, however, espoused by advocates of two different schools. The first consisted of those who contended that the people's rights must be secured by moral means alone. The other was composed of the more determined, who could not conceive that the ruling class would bow to anything short of physical force, and who generally made use of threats in the course of their various speeches. O'Connor was looked upon as the leader of the latter party, for, although he professed a desire to try all moral means before any other was resorted to, his language was generally of so physical a tendency, and he was so much in the habit of bestowing the favour of his countenance on the most violent of his party, that his few weak moral force professions were regarded as nothing more than the remaining remnants of his prudence, to be cast aside whenever circumstances might favour a bolder policy. We intimated that the speech of O'Connor at Birmingham produced a feeling of dissatisfaction among the moral force reformers, which, however, was for the moment smothered. But that smothering it was impossible to continue long, the policy of the physical force party being every day more clearly developed. The time came at last for the blow to be struck. The tocsin of alarm was sounded in three quarters, London, Birmingham, and Edinburgh. In the first, the Working Men's Association were the parties to throw down the gauntlet to the physical force party. In the second, the Council of the Political Union took upon themselves to condemn the line of policy in question; and, in the third, a public meeting was made the medium through which the physical force advocates were sought to be silenced. Now of all men living O'Connor was the last to be put down by his moral force opponents without a struggle, and in accordance with his determination, he summoned the Democrats of Birmingham together, and announced himself ready to defend his policy. A meeting was accordingly held, when he entered into an elaborate defence of his conduct, and concluded by moving a resolution in accordance with his speech, which resolution finished up with an expression of confidence in himself. His opponents presented themselves, but notwithstanding their wealth and former influence, O'Connor was more than a match for them, and he succeeded in carrying his resolution by an overwhelming majority. In Edinburgh the moral force party was more successful. A public meeting was held on the Calton Hill, at which John Fraser, who at the London demonstration spoke so warmly in praise of O'Connor, Abraham Duncan, and the Rev. Patrick Brewster of Paisley, were the principal speakers. While all these gentlemen professed an attachment to peaceful agitation, the language of some of them was anything but peaceful towards their opponents. Brewster dealt out no measured invective, and talked of sweeping the field clear of the Oastlers, the Stephens',—"he would not say the Feargus O'Connors, for he believed that Feargus O'Connor, with all his delinquencies, was an honest man." The resolutions were all carried, but it was pretty clear that the majority of the Edinburgh Radicals looked upon the proceedings with no just favour, for whereas the meeting at which the Charter was first adopted in that city was attended by fifteen thousand persons, only five thousand met to express their dissent from the physical force policy of O'Connor. The last named gentleman replied to his assailants through the columns of the *Northern Star*, in a characteristic style, half flattering, half condemnatory. Fraser he lauded in the highest terms, while he tried to settle Duncan by relating that the first time he saw his face he enquired his name, and on his being informed that it was Abraham Duncan, he rejoined, "beware of that man, for he is not to be trusted." He drew his deduction from Abraham's physiognomy, although he did not profess himself to be much acquainted with that science. Brewster, the most clever, learned, and popular man of the three, he dealt with in a singularly off-hand manner. Addressing them all three, he said, "Fraser, I love you; Duncan, I thank you; Brewster, I don't know you," thus reducing the latter to the smallest significance. It is but right to observe that shortly after Duncan was praised most warmly in the pages of the same *Northern Star* in which the above opinion appeared.

Anything more unfortunate than this division could scarcely have occured. It was indirectly playing the game into the hands of the common enemy, by each of the two sections weakening and destroying the power of the other. We believe these discussions of moral and physical force were, generally speaking, a mere waste of time. We look upon the two kinds of force to be inseparably linked. In political matters, unquestionably so. Governments are necessarily institutions of force, moral to a certain extent, but beyond that extent, physical. A government without physical force would be simply no government at all. We will suppose a government of the very best kind to be established, executing laws which had been enacted by common consent. So far it would be strictly moral in the exercise of its power ; but a law is of little avail unless there exists a physical power for its enforcement, for without such physical power a small minority may turn refractory, and refuse to obey that law in the enactment of which all have had an equal voice ; in which case the just interests of the general community must succumb to the selfish and exclusive interests of the few. The law, then, should always be supported by a power physical in its nature, but founded on the moral opinion of the people, for without this it is a dead letter. If, on the other hand, a government rules in defiance of the will of the majority, it necessarily rules by force alone. Let that majority manifest a resolve to bring about a change in the system of government ; the usurping class, who in their greedy love of exclusive power evince their contempt of moral force can never be moved but by the knowledge that such moral force is backed by another kind of force stronger than itself. We might challenge the history of the world to show that any government on earth, of an exclusive character, was ever moved to the abdication of its usurped functions except by physical force or the fear of it. Where that force is not used, the usurping class invariably feel the danger of its approach before they concede one iota to the claims of popular justice. At the same time it is undeniable, that to talk about using physical force against a government to a people who have not shown themselves to be prepared for its use by even the smallest sacrifice, is not only to do no good to a popular movement, but to sink it in immeasurable contempt. For a people, unprepared to make smaller sacrifices, will never be prepared to make the larger one of life. Hence all threats of physical force should be avoided in every case, until the people are imbued with a sound knowledge of their political and social rights. When so prepared, should their oppressors refuse to concede their claims, they will want but little admonishing, for the law of self-preservation will tell them what to do, and they will implicitly obey its voice. The war words of the moral and physical force reformers waxed warm on both sides ; it did not, however, for a time, detract seriously from the power of the movement. Each party agitated in its own particular way, and a considerable time elapsed before the split began materially to operate to the weakness and injury of the radical party, but that weakness and injury came at last.

CHAPTER V.

From the time that England had enjoyed anything like a settled constitution, bad as that constitution was, petitioning had been always regarded as the legal right of her inhabitants, and both moral and physical force advocates of the Charter agreed in the propriety of a petition, in which was to be embodied an abstract of the people's claims.   In obedience to the general desire the Council of the Birmingham Union applied itself to the task of drawing up a document for that purpose. This document will, doubtless, be interesting, as the first petition of the United Chartists, and under such an impression we introduce it to our readers.

" *To the Honourable the Commons of Great Britain and Ireland,
in Parliament assembled, the Petition of the undersigned, their
suffering countrymen,*

" HUMBLY SHEWETH,—

" That we, your petitioners, dwell in a land whose merchants are noted for their enterprise, whose manufacturers are very skilful, and whose workmen are proverbial for their industry. The land itself is goodly, the soil rich, and the temperature wholesome.   It is abundantly furnished with the materials of commerce and trade.   It   has   numerous   and   convenient harbours.   In facility of internal communication it exceeds all others.   For three and twenty years we have enjoyed a profound peace.   Yet, with all the elements of national prosperity, and   with   every   disposition   and   capacity   to   take advantage of them, we find ourselves overwhelmed with public and private suffering.   We are bowed down under a load of taxes, which, notwithstanding, fall greatly short of the wants of our rulers.   Our traders are trembling on the verge of bankruptcy ; our workmen are starving.   Capital brings no profit, and labour no remuneration.   The home of the artificer is desolate, and the warehouse of the pawnbroker is full.   The workhouse is crowded, and the manufactory is deserted.   We have looked on every side ; we have searched diligently in order to find out the causes of distress so sore and so long continued. We can discover none in nature or in Providence. Heaven has dealt graciously by the people, nor have the people abused its grace, but the foolishness of our rulers has made the goodness of God of none effect. The energies of a mighty kingdom have been wasted in building up the power of selfish and ignorant men, and its resources squandered for their aggrandisement. The good of a part has been advanced at the sacrifice of the good of the nation. The few have governed for the interest of the few, while the interests of the many have been sottishly neglected, or insolently and tyrannously trampled upon. It was the fond expectation of the friends of the people that a remedy for the greater part, if not for the whole of their grievances, would be found in the Reform Act of 1832. They regarded that Act as a wise means to a worthy end, as the machinery of an improved legislation, where the will of the masses would be at length potential. They have been bitterly and basely deceived. The fruit which looked so fair to the eye, has turned to dust and ashes when gathered. The Reform Act has effected a transfer of power from one domineering faction to another, and left the people as helpless as before. Our slavery has been exchanged for an apprenticeship to liberty, which has aggravated the painful feelings of our social degradation, by adding to them the sickening of still deferred hope. We come before your honourable house to tell you, with all humility, that this state of things must not be permitted to continue. That it cannot long continue, without very seriously endangering the stability of the throne, and the peace of the kingdom, and that if, by God's help, and all lawful and constitutional appliances, an end can be put to it, we are fully resolved that it shall speedily come to an end. We tell your honourable house, that the capital of the master must no longer be deprived of its due profit ; that the labour of the workman must no longer be deprived of its due reward. That the laws which make food dear, and the laws which make money scarce, must be abolished. That taxation must be made to fall on property, not on industry. That the good of the many, as it is the only legitimate end, so must it be the sole study of the government. As a preliminary essential to these and other requisite changes—as the means by which alone the interests of the people can be effectually vindicated and secured, we demand that those interests be confided to the keeping of the people. When the State calls for defenders, when it calls for money, no consideration of poverty or ignorance can be pleaded in refusal or delay of the call. Required, as we are universally, to support and obey the laws,

nature and reason entitle us to demand that in the making of
the laws the universal voice shall be implicitly listened to.
We perform the duties of freemen ; we must have the privileges
of freemen.   Therefore, we demand universal suffrage.   The
suffrage, to be exempt from the corruption of the wealthy and
the violence of the powerful, must be secret.   The assertion
of our right necessarily involves the power of our uncontrolled
exercise.   We ask for the reality of a good, not for its
semblance, therefore we demand the ballot.   The connection
between the representatives and the people, to be beneficial,
must be intimate.   The legislative and constituent powers, for
correction and for instruction, ought to be brought into
frequent contact.   Errors which are comparatively light,
when susceptible of a speedy popular remedy, may produce
the most disastrous effects when permitted to grow inveterate
through years of compulsory endurance.   To public safety,
as well as public confidence, frequent elections are essential.
Therefore, we demand annual parliaments.   With power to
choose, and freedom in choosing, the range of our choice must
be unrestricted.   We are compelled, by the existing laws, to
take for our representatives men who are incapable of
appreciating our difficulties, or have little sympathy with them ;
merchants who have retired from trade and no longer feel its
harrassings ; proprietors of land who are alike ignorant of its
evils and its cure ; lawyers by whom the notoriety of the senate is
courted only as a means of obtaining notice in the courts.
The labours of a representative who is sedulous in the discharge
of his duty are numerous and burdensome.   It is neither just,
nor reasonable, nor safe, that they should continue to be
gratuitously rendered.   We demand that in the future election
of members of your honourable house, the approbation of the
constituency shall be the sole qualification, and that to every
representative so chosen, shall be assigned out of the public
taxes, a fair and adequate remuneration for the time which he
is called upon to devote to the public service.   The management of this mighty kingdom has hitherto been a subject for
contending factions to try their selfish experiments upon.
We have felt the consequences in our sorrowful experience.
Short glimmerings of uncertain enjoyment, swallowed up by
long and dark seasons of suffering.   If the self-government
of the people should not remove their distresses, it will, at
least, remove their repinings.   Universal suffrage will, and it
alone can, bring true and lasting peace to the nation ; we
firmly believe that it will also bring prosperity.   May it therefore please your honourable house, to take this our petition
into your most serious consideration, and to use your utmost

endeavours, by all constitutional means, to have a law passed, granting to every male of lawful age, sane mind, and unconvicted of crime, the right of voting for members of parliament, and directing all future elections of members of parliament to be in the way of secret ballot, and ordaining that the duration of parliament, so chosen, shall in no case exceed one year, and abolishing all property qualifications in the members, and providing for their due remuneration while in attendance on their parliamentary duties.

"And your petitioners shall ever pray."

It will be perceived that only five out of the six points of the Charter, were embodied in the petition. Whether this was an oversight we know not. Probably its framers regarded equal representation (the point omitted) as a necessary part of universal suffrage, and regarded therefore the mention of it as unnecessary. This petition received the sanction of the Chartist body throughout Great Britain. As we have before seen, Mr. Atwood was in expectation of two or three million of signatures being appended. Although all sections of the Democracy agreed in the propriety of petitioning, they did so from various motives. The moral force reformers endeavoured to persuade themselves that such a step would have considerable weight with the Legislature. Some were sanguine enough to believe that the prayer of the petition would be immediately granted in deference to public opinion. On the other hand, the physical force men had not the slightest hope of such success, and they signed it only in order to give the Legislature another opportunity of showing its contempt of public rights, so as thoroughly to convince the people how futile were all such efforts for achieving their object. They declared, moreover, that it was the very last petition they would ever condescend to sign ; and that if its prayer were refused, there would remain nothing to be done, but to wage a " war to the knife," against the corrupt House of Commons and the classes by whom it was elected and supported. Others there were who wavered between the two extremes, who had not implicit faith in the Legislature conceding the popular demands, but who, at the same time, were not thoroughly persuaded that the demands would be rejected, and who thought that at least there could be nothing lost by making the trial. O'Brien, in all his speeches and writings, advised the people to sign the petition ; but he plainly told them that if they were not prepared to back their signatures with something still more powerful, they would never produce the slightest effect. From these various motives all sections of the radical party resolved to sign. It was agreed to transmit the petition with its signatures to the Convention, in order that the whole might be properly inspected by that body, and re-committed to the care of Messrs. Atwood and Fielden for presentation to the House of Commons.

The unfortunate split which had taken place on the questions of moral and physical force by no means deterred the general body from pushing forward for the support of the Convention. At the Birmingham demonstration, a resolution had been come to for collecting a national subscription, the details of which were entrusted to the delegates appointed by the meeting, and these delegates arranged such details accordingly. They advised that every town should be divided into districts, and collectors appointed for each division, who should canvass the public for subscriptions. They fixed the sum of £2 10s. for every thousand of the population, and the sum of sixpence as the lowest amount to be subscribed by an individual. The first Monday in October, 1838, was the day appointed for the commencement of the subscription all over the kingdom. When the amount subscribed should reach £5, it was to be transmitted to Messrs. Prescott, Grate, and Co., Bankers, London, and entered in the names of George Frederick Muntz, Philip. Henry Muntz, and Robert Kellie Douglas. It was agreed that the personal expenses of the delegates should be defrayed by their respective constituencies ; but it was clear that there would be other and numerous expenses, such as rent of room, correspondence, payment of missionaries, &c. Soon after the time appointed the working committees were in active motion. To carry out the resolution of a fixed amount for a certain number of the population was, however, found to be impracticable, for in some districts the Radicals were much stronger in numbers than in others, and it was only the radical portion of the public that could be expected to subscribe. There was great earnestness displayed in the collection of this fund. Men devoted themselves after the performance of their labour, night after night, to the furtherance of the work, and submitted good-humouredly to every sort of reply to their solicitations. They placed a considerable amount at the disposal of the Convention, so that when, after his resignation, one of the treasurers furnished his report, it was found that more than £1,700 had been subscribed, which after defraying all expenses up to that time, left a balance in hand of nearly £700. It will be seen, then, that at the time in question there was spirit sufficient to support the delegates in making a vigorous effort for the cause they had undertaken to espouse.

The meetings had continued to engage, for a considerable time, the attention of all classes and parties, without any

M 2

interference on the part of the Government. Stephens, in particular, was holding forth every day to crowded and excited audiences, whom he addressed in the most terrific language ; terrific to the propertied class, but extremely gratifying to the miserable thousands to whom it was addressed. While depicting their wretched condition, he even went the length of pointing their attention to the well stored larders and cellars of the rich, telling his hearers, in terms perfectly free from obscurity, that if they were deprived of the necessaries and comforts to which their labour justly entitled them, it was no crime, but in strict accordance with the moral law, to take those necessaries and comforts from the superabundance of their oppressors. This doctrine he enforced by repeated appeals to Scripture, and cited the eighth commandment in support of his position. He set forth that the command "not steal," was equally incumbent and binding on all, and endeavoured to show that in the work of plunder the rich were the aggressors, in having by legal forms robbed the poor of the fruits of their honest industry. He argued from this, that to take from those classes their ill-gotten and superfluous wealth, was nothing more than an act of moral justice and righteous resumption of their own. Indeed, he held that to allow the rich to retain possession of that wealth, which they had so unjustly wrung from their impoverished slaves, was to sanction the worst of rebellion against God, and treason against humanity. A large portion of the press noticed these and similar harangues, and held that the Government was responsible for permitting the meetings to go on. These attacks upon the Government for its apathy were reiterated week after week, and had the effect of at length drawing forth a declaration from Lord John Russell upon the subject. In September, 1838, his lordship was invited to dine with the civic authorities of Liverpool, and in the course of his address he made the following observations :—

" He would not, before such a party, wander into the field of politics ; but there was one topic connected with his own department, upon which he might be allowed to dwell for a few moments. He alluded to the public meetings which were now in the course of being held in various parts of the country. There were some, perhaps, who would put down such meetings ; but such was not his opinion, nor that of the Government with which he acted. He thought the people had a right to meet. If they had no grievances, common sense would speedily come to the rescue and put an end to those meetings. *It was not from free discussion, it was not from the unchecked declaration of public opinion that governments had anything to fear. There was fear when men were driven by force to secret combinations. There was the fear, there was the danger, and not in free discussion."*

This declaration was held to be decisive as to the intentions of the Government. There could have been no more direct encouragement given by a statesman to the continuance of the agitation. The press, however, continued to launch forth its invectives against the Government, whom it accused of cowardice, and of being the abettors of sedition. Some portion of the "glorious fourth estate" asserted that it was more guilty of risking and periling the peace of society, than the agitators themselves. Other portions held that it could not interfere without condemning its own past acts, seeing that it was by the selfsame means of agitation that it had lifted itself into place and power. For a time, however, the meetings were allowed to continue without interruption, although the incitement to Government prosecution became stronger every day. Let us pause here to make a few remarks upon the responsibility of governments. The victims of persecution are but too apt to blame governments for all their acts against the liberty of the subject. In numerous, if not in the vast majority of instances, the burden of censure is made to rest upon the shoulders of parties who are but secondary actors in the drama. So far, at least, as this country is concerned, however bad a government may be, it is but the representative of a power greater than itself. No cabinet could exist for a single week in opposition to the will of the House of Commons. The House of Commons could not exist without the sanction of the electoral body, *i.e.,* the landlords and capitalists, which latter are at the bottom of all laws and institutions ; are in fact the real and only rulers of society, and who give the government to understand precisely how it shall act, either directly or by implication. The parliament, the local authorities, and the press, are the instruments through which the will of these classes is made known, and the press invariably sounds the first note of alarm. Now, in the case just cited, we clearly see that the Government of itself had no disposition to interfere, and if it afterwards abandoned its resolution, it did not do so until incessantly urged, entreated, and threatened, by a power on which it depended for its very existence. We have no desire to hold up our governments to admiration ; at the best they are bad and despotic enough ; but they are in most cases only the creatures of a power above themselves, and the man who would teach the contrary is holding a veil to blind the mental optics of society. From the very outset of the movement the press unloosed the vials of its wrath. That wrath it at first attempted to conceal under the cover of contempt ; but as the popular cause increased in power, it threw the cover aside, and represented the principles of the Charter as naturally tending to the reign of robbery and spoliation, and to the unloosing of all the bonds which bind together human society. These observations are necessary, in order that real reformers may see the power with which they have to grapple, and thus be prepared to give battle to their oppressors, instead of directing their wordy batteries against mere tools and subordinates.

In the autumn of 1838 the meetings began to assume a formidable character. It was inconvenient to hold repeated assemblages of the people by day. Their means of living were too circumscribed to admit of their voluntarily subjecting themselves to loss of time. Now and again it might be very well for them to assemble in their myriads, as at Kersall Moor ; but it was an experiment which would not often bear repetition. There were no rooms to be obtained capable of holding the dense crowds who were every day more anxious to express their hatred of the existing system, and the Town Halls were almost always refused. There is a way out of every difficulty, and a project speedily suggested itself to the minds of the leading men which would make them independent of all halls and places for in-door meetings. They suggested the holding of meetings by torch-light, as being better suited to the people's convenience, both as regards time and expense. The expedient was but little sooner suggested than adopted, and for a short period the factory districts presented a series of such imposing popular demonstrations, as were perhaps never witnessed in any previous agitation. Bolton, Stockport, Ashton, Hyde, Staleybridge, Leigh, and various other places, large and small, were the scenes of these magnificent gatherings. At the whole of them the working people met in their thousands and tens of thousands to swear devotion to the common cause. It is almost impossible to imagine the excitement caused by these manifestations. To form an adequate idea of the public feeling, it was necessary to be an eye witness of the proceedings. The people did not go singly to the place of meeting, but met in a body at a starting point, from whence, at a given time, they issued in huge numbers, formed into procession, traversing the principal streets, making the heavens echo with the thunder of their cheers on recognizing the idols of their worship in the men who were to address them, and sending forth volleys of the most hideous groans on passing the office of some hostile newspaper, or the house of some obnoxious magistrate or employer. The banners containing the more formidable devices, viewed by the red light of the glaring torches, presented a scene of awful grandeur. The death's heads represented on some of them grinned like ghostly spectres, and served to remind many a mammon-worshipper of his expected doom. The uncouth appearance of thousands of artizans who had not time from leaving the factory to go home and attend to the ordinary duties of cleanliness, and whose faces were therefore begrimed with sweat and dirt, added to the strange aspect of the scene. The processions were frequently of immense length, sometimes containing as many as fifty thousand people; and along the whole line there blazed a stream of light, illuminating the lofty sky, like the reflection from a large city in a general conflagration. The meetings themselves were of a still more terrific character. The very appearance of such a vast number of blazing torches only seemed more effectually to inflame the minds alike of speaker and hearers. O'Connor, Stephens, and M'Douall were frequent attendants at the torch-light meetings, and their language was almost unrestrained by any motives of prudence. Incitements to the use of arms formed the staple of the speeches of the two latter gentlemen. O'Connor, in nearly every speech, went so far as to name the day when the Charter was to become law, and usually finished up by a declaration that if it were not granted by the 29th of September, the Legislature should have Michælmas goose on the 30th. Stephens did not hesitate to declare that the ruling class were nothing better than a gang of murderers, whose blood was required to satisfy the demands of public justice.

Among other torch-light meetings held about this time, there was one that took place in the town of Hyde, at which the Rev. Mr. Stephens was the orator of the evening. The 14th of November was the night of meeting. No less than fifteen thousand persons walked in the procession, which was headed by a band of music, and a large number of banners were to be seen in the blazing light. On one of these was Stephens' favourite device,

" For children and wife, we'll war to the knife !"
On another, the scriptural quotation, " He that hath no sword, let him sell his garment and buy one." A third bore the inscription, "Ashton demands universal suffrage or universal vengeance !" Another banner showed the words, " Remember the bloody deeds of Peterloo !" While a fifth bore the ominous inscription, " Tyrants, believe and tremble !" There were a large number of red caps of liberty carried upon poles, and, at intervals, the loud reports from pistols announced the fact that persons in the meeting were armed. When the

procession drew up to the place of meeting, Stephens began to address the crowd. He announced that he had that day attended several meetings, and that the people were all of one mind, determined to have their right. He said that at Bolton the magistrates had waited upon the military authorities, requesting their attendance at a public meeting. That the officer guaranteed it in case the civil power was not sufficient. "But," said Stephens, "I had a friend in the barracks who assured me that if the soldiers had been called out there was not one of them that would have acted." Let us pause in our narrative to ask, was Mr. Stephens simple enough to believe every random assertion about the determination of the military not to use their arms against the people? If he was, he was simple indeed. We have, in our time, heard scores of similar assertions, but always felt bound to receive them with great caution. We have, in many instances, been told by military men, that in case of the rising of the people, the soldiers would turn round and assist them. It is possible that some of the persons who were thus communicative were in the full belief of what they uttered. It is also possible that in some instances they had good grounds for their assertions; but what is more probable is, that in the vast majority of cases they had no grounds whatever, and it might be that they were employed for the purpose of diffusing false reports of the sympathies of the soldiers in order to incite to a premature outbreak, in which the imperfectly armed and the imperfectly disciplined people would be shot down, in the very quarter from whence sympathy and aid might be expected to come. At all events, it is dangerous for a people to trust to assistance from men who are in the pay of their enemies, for where there is one chance in their favour, there are ten against them. The truth is, that a people who determine on a revolution should never rely on extraneous assistance from any quarter. They should never venture on so hazardous an experiment unless they are persuaded that they have sufficient strength and power of their own to accomplish their ends. With such a power, the military may turn round upon their masters (for soldiers in such cases almost invariably go with the strongest), but without such a power, all promises of military sympathy should be regarded with extreme distrust, if not positive disbelief. Stephens went on to say that the burial and other clubs in the district were applying their funds to the purchase of arms. In alluding to the factory system, he said that the right or title of Mr. Howard's mill, was written in letters of blood on every brick and stone in that factory; and, speaking again of physical force, he advised his hearers to get a large carving knife, which would do very well to cut a rasher of bacon, or run the man through who opposed them. Stephens asked them, towards the conclusion of his speech, if they were ready, and if they were armed ; which was responded to by two or three shots. " Is that all?" he asked, and was answered by a volley of shots. He proceeded, however, to test the meeting further, and he called upon all who meant to buy arms to hold up their hands, when a forest of hands were exhibited, and again there was a loud firing of arms. After telling them to procure guns, pistols, swords, pikes, or anything that would tell sharper tales than their tongues, he said, " I see it is all right, and I wish you good night."

The intense misery suffered by the people rendered such language as that of Stephens extremely palatable. Indeed, nothing in the English tongue was too strong or inflammatory for those hard-worked, ill-fed, sons of toil. A recommendation tó moral force would have been laughed to scorn ; it was only the most determined appeals that met with a favourable response, and these were in almost every instance responded to, not only by the loud thunder of their myriad voices, but as we have seen, by the discharge of firearms, and also by the brandishing of pikes, numbers of which were taken to the meetings as an earnest of their fearful resolve to resort to the last resource of an injured people in the vindication of their claims. Meanwhile the upper and middle classes were organizing the means of resistance to those demands. The Government encouraged them in their undertaking, and offered to supply them with all the munitions of war, if they would form themselves into clubs for the protection of life and property, and several clubs were accordingly formed. As a general rule, however, these classes preferred trusting their safety to armed and disciplined troops, to encountering the peril of their own defence. In consequence of the government offer, a resolution was brought forward by R. G. Gammage, in the Northampton Working Men's Association, instructing their secretary to apply to the Secretary of State for two thousand stand of arms, ammunition, &c., for themselves and friends, so as to enable them to defend their lives and properties against all assailants. The resolution was unanimously adopted amid loud applause, and numerous other bodies of Chartists adopted similar resolutions. It is perhaps unnecessary to add, that although some of these communications were duly answered, in not a solitary instance did the Home Secretary return a favourable reply to these applications. It was only the lives and properties of the rich that were deemed worthy of protection ; and yet we have seen, as in the case of the great Newcastle meeting, that

N

the working class had their lives endangered by the presence of a military force, to obstruct them in the peaceful exercise of a constitutional right, and all the redress obtained, was the simple assurance of the Government that there was no intention on the part of the authorities to interfere with the meetings. Was it any wonder that such gross injustice tended to convince the poorer class that nothing but force could wrest from their oppressors their rights?

The large and numerous torch-light meetings had assumed an attitude so alarming to the upper and middle classes generally, and the representations made to the Government were of so significant a character, that it was left without any alternative but either to strike a decisive blow at those assemblages, or to acknowledge its incapability. It was scarcely to be expected that it would do the latter, for that would have been tantamount to an abdication of its functions; a step which no government will take until driven to the very last extremity, and it did not conceive that such an extremity had arrived. In a short time, therefore, a proclamation from the Queen appeared on the walls of every town, in which it was set forth that the torch-light meetings were illegal, and that all persons attending the same would be held amenable to the laws. To say that the appearance of the proclamation was the cause of great excitement, were to convey a very inadequate idea of the state of popular feeling. That feeling had been worked up to such a feverish state, that a sort of delirium now seized upon the people, and thousands expressed their determination to trample the proclamation under foot, and set the Government at defiance. O'Connor recommended, through the medium of the *Northern Star*, the abandonment of the torch-light meetings, which, if persisted in, might seriously damage the cause. On the other hand, the rage of Stephens knew scarcely any bounds. He denounced the proclamation as an insult to the oppressed people, and at variance with the constitution, and declared that it was entirely destitute of the force of law. From that time, however, the said meetings were virtually abandoned, no others being held but such as had been previously announced. It was not to be expected that the Government would stop here, and the issuing of the proclamation was speedily followed by a warrant of arrest against the Rev. J. R. Stephens, and three separate cases of attending illegal meetings and using seditious language were preferred against him. He was arrested, and underwent an examination before the magistrates of Manchester. The excitement previously existing was increased to an alarming degree; as soon as the news reached the public ear, it became the universal theme of conversation.

Men, women, and children lined the streets of the manufacturing towns throughout that immense and populous district. Two sentiments alone appeared to animate the breasts of the toiling class, viz., profound and burning indignation at the conduct of the authorities, and the deepest and most ardent sympathy with the object of their persecution. There was not a word of enquiry as to how far Stephens had been prudent in his career of agitation ; it was enough for them that he had always been their friend. In him they saw the denouncer bold of their manifold wrongs, and the persevering, earnest, eloquent advocate of their plundered rights ; and it is not too much to say that they worshipped him with a most religious devotion. On the day appointed for his examination, every street leading to the court house was literally besieged, so eager were the masses to gain a sight, and learn the fate, of the man they loved. His appearance was the signal for tumult upon tumult of applause. The air was literally rent with the deafening shouts that reverberated along the streets, and appeared to shake every building to its very foundation. We know not what must have been the feelings of the object of all this enthusiasm, as he bent beneath the tumults of a people's applause ; but judging him by the ordinary feelings of human nature, we cannot be wrong in assuming that he felt that hour to be the proudest—we were going to add the happiest—of his life. But sweet as is the grateful approbation of an excited people, there is sometimes attached to it no insignificant consequences. Stephens had gathered around him the popular feeling, but what human being could predict whither that feeling would lead either its possessors or himself? The man who wields the sympathy of a multitude of his fellow creatures, incurs a grand but fearful responsibility ; and while the cheers of that multitude may give rise to sensations of pleasure, a feeling of awe will sometimes steal over the senses, to check the gushing flood of joy.

It was amid the breathless silence of the magistrates' court that the examination of Stephens was introduced. A number of witnesses were called on behalf of the prosecution, the delivery of whose evidence lasted a considerable time. And now the moment came for testing the dignity and courage of the defendant, who was asked whether he had any observations to address to the court in answer to the charges brought against him. Now, the question is, what was the proper course for Stephens to pursue? He had the honour of being the first man on whom the Government sought to wreak the vengeance of the law for his participation in the new movement. He had, therefore, not only his own personal dignity, but the dignity of the cause also to support. In our opinion, a firm and modest silence was the most calculated to win respect for both. Not so thought Mr. Stephens, for he proceeded to deliver himself of a long rambling harangue conceived in the worst possible taste. It was alike destitute of clearness and point, and could only involve his case in worse confusion. He did not, it is true, as yet flinch from the avowal of his previous sentiments; but his very attempt to influence the magistrates in his favour, was something like showing—though perhaps obscurely—the " white feather." He knew, or should have known, that the body of evidence before the magistrates was sufficient to warrant them, according to law and custom, in committing him for trial, and nothing that he might possibly allege could influence them to a contrary course. His conduct, therefore, was at the least unwise, and it stripped him, in the estimation of reflecting men, of that dignity which otherwise he might have maintained. He should have waited until opportunity had afforded him the means of addressing a superior court, by which time he could have collected and arranged his materials into order. He chose a different course, and showed himself to be little better than a mere babbler. As might have been anticipated, Stephens was committed for trial, but was held to bail, himself in £1,000, and two sureties in £500 each, for his appearance at the assizes. During the progress of the examination the utmost excitement reigned among the multitude outside the court. As a matter of course there were all sorts of conjectures amongst so vast and excited a crowd of people. The noise and tumult ran to such a fearful height, that at times during the proceedings the magistrates became dreadfully alarmed, and more undignified than Stephens himself. They even went so far in the extremity of their fear, as to solicit O'Connor—who was in the court watching the proceedings—to go and try his influence in quelling the disorder. O'Connor replied that the application was a strange one; but doubtless proud of the office which they were so anxious, for their own sake, to assign him as preserver of the peace, he complied with the request, and went to a window, where he was no sooner recognised than he was hailed with tumults of applause. He waved his hand in token of silence, and with a truly wonderful facility he calmed down the boiling passions of that infuriated multitude. The mighty mass in one minute became cool as prudence itself, and then he essayed to address them, urging them not to sully their glorious cause by an act of rashness, and promising to see justice done to the object of their adoration. The calmness, however, was but temporary, and was soon succeeded by an excitement equal to that by which it was preceded. In the evening O'Connor addressed a crowded assemblage in Manchester, on the events of the day. He promised, in the most encouraging terms, a speedy victory of the people over their oppressors. With respect to Stephens, he spoke of the love and veneration he felt for that gentleman in the warmest strain, and then alluded to the probable result of his trial. He said Oastler had predicted that Stephens would be transported, but that was impossible, for it was not a transportable offence. If, however, the tyrants should so far strain their authority as to transport him, his (Stephens') menacled limbs should never pass to the transport ship but over his (O'Connor's) lifeless body. It need not be said that this declaration drew thundering plaudits from the meeting. As will be easily imagined the enthusiasm was almost boundless, and it was difficult to judge which was the more popular of the two idols, Stephens or O'Connor.

As may be easily imagined the excitement occasioned by the arrest of Stephens was not confined to the neighbourhood of Manchester, but was participated in by the Democrats in every part of the country where the standard of the Charter had been hoisted. Throughout Yorkshire the feeling of the working class was intense. In the Midlands the sensation although not so general was most profound. In the West large meetings were held at which resolutions were passed denouncing the proceedings of the Government. At Bristol, Vincent addressed the people on Brandon Hill, and proposed a resolution of sympathy with Stephens, strongly denunciatory of his persecutors, which was carried amid deafening acclamations. On the following Saturday the *Northern Star* appeared nearly full of these resolutions. The reverend gentleman became more popular than ever. Numerous letters reached him from districts far and wide, breathing sympathy, promising support, and containing warm invitations to favour their authors with a personal visit. Committees for his defence were formed in every town and village where his sentiments had penetrated ; and notwithstanding the collection of the national subscription was going on at the same time, a fund was started and multiplied every day, so that before the time announced for his trial, not far short of £2,000 was raised for the Stephens' Fund alone ; subscribed, too, almost exclusively by the working class. Stephens still continued to address the people in speeches and sermons (generally confining himself to the latter), every week. A report of them appeared in the *Northern Star*, and they were afterwards issued in a separate form, under the title of the " Political Pulpit." These sermons were eagerly bought up, and in numbers of towns groups of people assembled on the Sunday to hear them read. As they listened to the reading of his impassioned appeals, their sympathy for Stephens increased the public curiosity as to the result of his trial.

As soon as the middle class manufacturers perceived that the people were earnest in their movement for the suffrage, they strained every nerve to draw them aside from the pursuit of their object. They knew that the Charter meant, if rightly understood, an end to the reign of social monopoly, and they turned anti-monopolists themselves. The only monopoly, however, which engaged the attention of these "friends of the people," was that of the landlords. They described the corn laws as the one great source of the social misery of the working-class, and the repeal of those laws as the panacea for all their ills. They urged how important it was that the people should join them in their demand for that repeal, even in preference to their agitation for the Charter. They had no objection to the Charter, not they, it was their right. In the abstract, all its provisions were very good, but it was not the time. The friends of the Charter in the House of Commons were but few, and, for the present, it stood not the slightest chance of success ; whereas, the corn law repealers in Parliament were numerous, and backed by the intelligence of the working class, they would soon become omnipotent. The bait did not, however, take so easily as perhaps these gentlemen had anticipated. They relied for the main part of their strength on the manufacturing districts, and in those districts a strong and decided public opinion had set in against them. The outraged feelings of the operative classes enabled the Chartist leaders to thwart the corn law repealers in nearly every effort that they made. They were brave enough in the outset to appeal to the public sympathy, but they speedily found how little of that was in their favour. The reasons given by various men amongst the Chartist body for not going with the League widely differed. With a very large number it was a detestation of the social tyranny exercised by manufacturers, which led them to believe that anything coming from such a quarter was not likely to be very favourable to their interests. The party of the Working Men's Association took a different ground. They admitted the desirability of getting rid of the corn laws, but they at the same time contended that so long as the Legislature remained upon its present footing, to attempt to get those laws repealed was hopeless ; or, at all events, that it would take an amount of agitation to effect that object equal to what would obtain the Charter ; the result of which, when gained, would be not only to repeal the corn laws, but every other law which was based on injustice to the community. They contended, moreover, that the middle class had never thought of corn law repeal until they saw a determination on the part of the masses to gain political power for themselves. That if they really desired the object they professed to have in view, it was easy for them to accomplish their wishes, inasmuch as the majority of the House of Commons was elected by the middle class and their subordinates ; and they declared that they looked with extreme suspicion on a class of men who sought to steal away the attention of the public from the greater, in order to fix it on a comparatively trivial object. There was, however, another party, and by far the largest, who contended that Free Trade under the existing arrangements of society, so far from being beneficial, would rather prove injurious to the producing class. At the head of this school stood James Bronterre O'Brien, and following in his train was Feargus O'Connor, and a majority of the most influential men of the movement. The way in which O'Brien viewed the question may be stated in a few words. He had but little sympathy with the class of landlords whom he looked upon as the hereditary enemies of society. But there was another class whom he regarded with greater dread, viz., the great monied class, which had risen to immense importance, and whose power was on the increase. He saw in that class a multitude of persons who were living on fixed incomes. The natural tendency of Free Trade, the economists themselves admitted, would be to cheapen commodities, and O'Brien argued that this would enable the usurer, the tax eater, the parson, and all other classes whose incomes were fixed, to command, with the same amount of money, an increase of those commodities, just in proportion to their cheapness, and in that proportion their incomes would thus be virtually raised. He contended then, that if those parties, without any additional service rendered by them to society, were thus enabled to command a larger share of wealth, they could obtain it only at the expense of others, those others being the labouring class, who are the source of all the wealth produced. O'Brien also took into account the state of the private debtor and creditor interests, showing that debts had been contracted under the restrictive system while prices were high, and money consequently low in value, which would have to be paid under the free trade system, when prices should become low, and the value of money would consequently be enhanced. He had no objection then to the principles of Free Trade as such ; but he contended, that in order to make Free Trade honest for all classes, there ought at the same time to be an equitable adjustment between the public and private debtor and creditor, and that all public officials should have their incomes reduced, as otherwise the non-producing class would rob the producers to exactly the amount of difference in the prices of all that they consumed.   As before observed, those of the Chartist leaders who possessed the largest share of influence, generally fell in with these views, and wherever the Free Traders appeared, O'Connor, O'Brien, and others met them on the platform, showed them the hollowness of their pretensions, and in every case carried public opinion against them.   O'Brien not only assailed them by speech, but he wrote in the pages of the *Operative* some of the most powerful articles that ever flowed from his masterly pen, in which he laid bare the selfishness of their schemes, and launched at them all the logic, wit, and denunciation that his great talents afforded.   Since the enactment of Sir Robert Peel's measures in 1846, O'Brien's views may have appeared to many to be falsified.   Upon that subject we shall take occasion to comment in a future part of this work.

The result of the Chartist opposition to the Free Traders drove those agitators into holes and corners.   All that the Chartists had claimed to do at their public meetings, was simply to discuss the differences between them.   Discussion with the Chartists was not, however, what those men wanted. With the landlords they would have had no objection to discuss, because the ground taken by that class was not so tenable ; but whenever a Chartist appeared to debate the question with them upon terms of general interest, they manifested as much alarm as though a bombshell had dropped amongst them ; and in order to stifle debate, they ticketted all their meetings, so as to exclude the Chartists from taking any part in their proceedings.   If a solitary individual of that party chanced to be admitted, and rose to express his dissent, the tools of these peaceful agitators generally treated him to physical force.   Sometimes, however, even when they had taken the utmost precautions, the Chartists obtained possession of their tickets, and carried the vote against them.   We do not by any means approve of this policy.   If a select party meet to debate or advance a question, we should no more think of intruding ourselves upon them against their wishes, than we should think of breaking in upon the privacy of a domestic circle.   It is only when the public is fairly and openly appealed to, that we believe opposition to be justifiable ; and under such circumstances, we should even assert the right of all men to the free expression of their opinions, and maintain it, if expedient, even by physical force.

WILLIAM LOVETT

FROM A WOODCUT

CHAPTER VI.

Throughout the winter of 1838-9, the agitation for the Charter, so far from slackening, proceeded with rapid strides. If the Chartists were defeated in one plan, another was speedily adopted for the forwarding of their object. The authorities, by forbidding the torch-light meetings, and by the arrest of the most popular men in the manufacturing districts, had aimed a severe blow at the movement ; but still, the utmost activity pervaded the body. Out-door meetings in the day, and in-door assemblies in the evening, were frequently held, and the speeches abated not a jot in their accustomed vigour. The various committees worked with redoubled assiduity. Convention Fund and Defence Fund proceeded each to the satisfaction of the most ardent, and all eyes now looked forward to the assembling of that body, which, in the absence of an extended parliamentary representation, was to speak the feelings, the thoughts, and the sentiments of the political helots of society. On the 4th of February, the delegates met in the Metropolis ; their first meeting was held at the British Coffee House, Cockspur-street ; but, two days after, they removed to Bolt Court, Fleet-street, where a commodious room had been fitted up for their accommodation. On the delegates assembling in London, they were honoured by the Democrats with a public dinner in the spacious room at White Conduit House. O'Connor, Frost, and many other leading men, were the speakers of the day. The former, notwithstanding his almost iron constitution, had laboured so hard in the agitation, that he appeared in very delicate health ; the usual flush on his countenance had given way to a sickly paleness, and fears were entertained that his constitution was breaking down ; but the energetic advocate of democracy, though never ceasing to work, speedily recovered his wonted vigour. The mention of a circumstance in relation to Mr. Frost will not here be out of place. That gentleman, as before observed, had, at an early period of the movement. joined the people in their demands.

The consequence was a letter from Lord John Russell rebuking him as a magistrate for the part he was acting. Mr. Frost replied to his lordship most suitably, denying his right to interfere with his (Frost's) political opinions. His spirited reply drew forth a croaking epistle from the minister, in which he assured Frost that he had not the slightest desire to coerce him. In short, Lord John ate his own previous words most completely. At the dinner in question Mr. Frost took occasion to allude to the subject of this correspondence, and remarked that if the government took his name off the list of magistrates, the people would speedily restore it. The minister, on seeing this speech in print, immediately wrote to the magistrate to know if his speech was correctly reported, and on receiving an answer in the affirmative, Mr. Frost was at once deprived of the commission of the peace. The utmost enthusiasm was manifested by the White Conduit House assembly, as the various delegates delivered themselves of eloquent and spirited addresses. From what has been stated in preceding chapters, it may be readily supposed that when the Convention met it did not turn out to be a perfectly harmonious body. Most of the Scotch, London, and Birmingham delegates, as well as some others belonged to the moral force school. The majority, however, held more or less the doctrines of physical force. Baillie Craig, delegate for Ayrshire, was appointed chairman, and William Lovett received the post of secretary. The mere formal business having been arranged, the differences amongst the members were soon made manifest. The gentlemen of the Cobbet school were of opinion that the body should be nothing more than a petition Convention, and that after the presentation of the national petition their mission should cease. The vast majority were, however, of the contrary opinion. Moral and physical force men generally agreed that the people would expect something more at their hands. That after the promises which had been made, and the hopes that had been excited, there was no alternative but to resort to ulterior measures of some sort, in case the prayer of the petition was rejected. Cobbett's resolution were therefore negatived, as unworthy of a body assembled for the avowed purpose of gaining the rights of the people. After this decision, the Cobbett party figured but little in the Convention.

While one small section endeavoured to prevent the Convention from doing anything in the shape of ulterior measures, another section, equally small, sought to urge it forward with railroad velocity ; the latter was the party of Julian Harney. These men affected to believe (some of them doubtless did believe) that the people were ready to take their rights without delay, and they accused the majority of the Convention of cowardice and imbecility, because they did not at once take the initiative in a physical revolution. A public meeting was convened by the more ardent Democrats for the purpose of giving an impulse to that body. At that meeting, Harney, Ryder, and Marsden figured as speakers, and spoke in most unreserved terms of the preparedness of the people, and the tardy proceedings of the Convention ; and a resolution was passed to the effect that universal suffrage might be carried in the short period of two months if the Convention did its duty. To aid them in the dissemination of their views, the ultra physical force section established a periodical under the title of the *London Democrat*, in which Julian Harney was the principal writer. It was ably and eloquently conducted, and the general tenor of its articles was to urge onward the revolution, which its writers professed to believe was near at hand. Harney attended a meeting in the open air at Smithfield, and appeared on the platform wearing a red cap of liberty, in imitation of the patriots in the French Revolution. He announced his readiness to fight, and strongly censured those who by their inaction were marring the cause of the people, by damping their ardour, and destroying their efforts for emancipation.

The proceedings of Harney and his friends were not lost sight of by the Convention. W. Villiers Sankey brought forward a motion disapproving of those members who were injuring the cause by making use of French terms and wearing French emblems. The conduct of Harney in particular was called in question, and many of the members expressed their indignation at the foolish course he was pursuing ; but most of them were opposed to taking any steps in the matter, and the motion was, after some discussion, abandoned.

The Convention proceeded to more useful work than the discussion of these trivialities. They appointed missionaries to scour the country, and address meetings, with a view to the further enlightenment of the people on the question of their rights. A large portion of its funds were devoted to this useful purpose. Some of their best orators were despatched to the country ; but the error was committed of sending them nearly all to those districts that were already in the agitation, instead of opening up fresh ground in the more unenlightened parts, where the masses were still as ignorant of their rights as though those rights had never existed.

Although the extreme section of the Convention received but little countenance from that body, yet the majority were more disposed to the advocacy of physical force than otherwise, as was evidenced by their speeches at the various meetings they addressed. They were somewhat prompted to this course by the large amount of discontent evinced by the working-class, especially in the manufacturing districts ; a discontent brought about by the most poignant distress, and unrelieved by any hope of amelioration. That state of distress was frequently made the subject of discussion. On one occasion, Marsden, the Preston delegate, alluded to it, and exposed it in a speech which appeared in the newspapers, and which caused a sensation of horror wherever it was read. In illustration of the effects of the factory system he instanced the case of his own family, and stated that his wife and children had been utterly destitute of the means of existence. That, with an infant at her breast, his wife was without food, and became so reduced in consequence of her privations that when her babe sought the natural nourishment which its mother should have afforded, instead of that nourishment, it drew from her nothing but her own blood. This statement was afterwards confirmed to the writer of the present history by Mrs Marsden herself. Is there any wonder that her husband, naturally a humane man, should be anxious to resort to any and every means, to put an end to a system which conduced to such horrible results ? The greater wonder is, that any man could be an eye witness to such social atrocities, without being stung by them to utter madness.

The differences between the various sections in the Convention still continued, more or less, to engross the attention of that body. At last an event occurred which led to a disruption in the ranks. On the 11th of March, 1839, a crowded meeting was held at the Crown and Anchor, and was addressed by Messrs. Frost, O'Connor, Harney, and others. Mr. Frost occupied the chair. Most of the speeches delivered on the occasion were couched in the strongest language. All the speakers urged the people to be prepared for the approaching struggle, and the meeting by its enthusiastic cheers endorsed the sentiments of the speakers. When the speeches appeared in print they created an immense sensation. The hostile portion of the press alluded to them in reproachful terms, and speedily after, Messrs. Salt, Hadley, and Douglas tendered their resignation as members of the Convention. This act led to very different feelings. The friends of those gentlemen approved the step they had taken, but those friends were few. The vast majority of the Chartist body condemned them, and the term " traitor" was levelled at them almost throughout the country. The Democrats of Birmingham speedily elected Messrs. Brown, Powell, and Donaldson to fill the vacant seats ; but it is needless to say that the secession was productive of injurious consequences, which were soon manifested in the growing weakness of the Birmingham Political Union. Early in May, Messrs. Cobbett, Wade, Matthews, and Rogers, seceded from the Convention. Other delegates were elected, but every such secession was productive of weakness in the Chartist forces, and tended gradually to thin their ranks. Still there was an immense excitement going on, more especially in the larger towns, and all the meetings were very numerously attended.

At length the Convention found itself in such a position that it was bound to take decisive steps in order to bring matters to a crisis. One of its most influential and popular members, Henry Vincent, had been arrested by the authorities of Newport, and there was every probability that other arrests would soon be made, and the ranks of the Convention be made thinner than ever. For the purpose then of testing the people, Lovett, the secretary, drew up a number of propositions to be submitted to them at public meetings. These meetings were appointed to be held simultaneously, on Whit-Monday, and it was arranged that, with the exception of a committee which should remain at head quarters, the various members should distribute themselves over the country, so as to be present at as many of the meetings as it might be possible for them to attend. The excitement growing stronger every day, the Convention at last, following out a suggestion of Mr Atwood's at the commencement of the agitation, resolved on adjourning from London to Birmingham. It was thought that this step would give it additional power, as it would be surrounded by a dense population enthusiastic in the national cause. On the 13th of May the Convention accordingly adjourned to Birmingham.

The propositions which the Convention agreed to submit to their constituents, were such, that if followed out by an intelligent people determined to have their rights, could hardly fail to ensure success. The principal of them were, a run on the banks for gold ; abstinence from all excisable articles ; exclusive dealing ; arming ; and an universal cessation of labour. These propositions underwent considerable discussion. Julian Harney denounced the proposition for abstinence from excisable articles as savouring of humbug. He was rebuked by R. J. Richardson, who replied that they had that day witnessed a specimen of the evils of intemperance in language, which ought to teach them the value of temperance in other respects. Harney appeared to think that nothing but the most extreme measures were of the slightest value. He was for moving towards the object by the speediest means, and he seldom, if ever, stopped to calculate the cost.   As the Convention had decided on submitting ulterior measures to the people, they did perfectly right in putting forward moral means, and in testing them as to the amount of sacrifice they were prepared to make before resorting to more forcible measures.   It might serve very well for men who wanted a reputation for bravery to deal out high sounding phrases about death, glory, and the like ; but no body of men have a right to organize an insurrection in a country, unless fully satisfied that the people are so prepared as to hold victory in their very grasp ; and a conviction of such preparedness should be founded on better evidence than their attendance at public meetings, and cheering in the moment of excitement the most violent and inflammatory orator.   A people prepared to sacrifice their lives will never, in this country at least, object to the smaller sacrifice of their appetites; and, if not prepared for the latter, there is the strongest presumptive evidence, that they are but little prepared for the former.   A run on the banks for gold, abstinence from excisable articles, and exclusive dealing, if generally adopted, would have given evidence of the people's resolution ; and they would have done something more, for while they would have crippled the enemy in his vital part, they would have put the people in possession of those means which would have enabled them to resort, if necessary, to stronger measures, such as a cessation of labour, and in case of an attack by their enemies, to the self-defence of freemen.   There is, however, an order of men who set themselves up for leaders of the people who never seem happy but in extremes. Incapable of, or disdaining to reason from cause to effect, they either cannot or will not see that certain preparatives are necessary before a people can be in a position to defy their rulers.   These men are generally the biggest talkers, making up by bluster and balderdash what they lack in reason and intelligence.   In times of strong excitement, fanned as that excitement is by the bitterness of suffering, men of this description too often command public confidence in preference to others with far superior qualifications, but who are too conscientious and intelligent to sacrifice a people to either selfishness or folly.

As previously observed, the Convention having resolved to submit ulterior measures, did right in first testing the moral resolution of the people ; but it would have done still better had it never submitted ulterior measures of any kind until it had completely prepared the masses for their exercise, by the wider diffusion of political and social knowledge.   Before ulterior measures are ever recommended there should always be a tolerable certainly of their adoption, or the trial is a mere waste of time and strength. The means which up to that time had been taken for enlightening the people were comparatively trifling. Public meetings, so far as certain districts were concerned, had certainly been numerous enough ; but something more than public meetings was required. The people would have been ·better with less of platform oratory, and more of book knowledge, a fact which seemed to be overlooked by the vast majority of their leaders, in whose estimation mere talk appeared to be the most necessary thing for bringing up their minds to the desired standard ; and in large portions of the country the people had been left without instruction, either from the platform or the press. Ulterior measures, therefore, however under other circumstances desirable, should not, in the above case, have been even mooted ; because, so far from there being any prospect of their general adoption, there was the moral certainty that when the hour arrived both those measures and their proposers would be abandoned by all, with the exception of a comparative few of the most hearty and enthusiastic, who would be sacrificed to the ignorance and supineness of the mass. The Convention, however, determined otherwise. They were certainly placed in a peculiar position. When men have once overstepped the bounds of prudence they are often compelled to a course not the wisest in order to prevent themselves from sinking into contempt. Such was the position of the Convention. Large promises had been made to the people on the one hand, and threats had been dealt out to their rulers on the other, and those who made them sought to maintain their credit. They determined, however, not to proceed without some degree of caution, and the simultaneous meetings were made the medium through which they questioned the people as to how far they were prepared to assert their rights.

As was anticipated very numerous gatherings were held in all the great centres of agitation. The Convention anticipated the possibility of an interference with these meetings on the part of the authorities. It was evident that a blow at the Chartists was in course of preparation, for a large number of the London police had been introduced into Birmingham, that town not then being blessed with a similiar force of its own. The magistrates had signified their intention of putting down the meetings held in the Bull Ring and other parts of the town. There was no disturbance at any of these meetings previous to the introduction of the police, but when that force appeared, it received the execrations of the people assembled, and nothing but the influence of Bronterre O'Brien, Dr. Taylor, and other talented members of the Convention, prevented a

collision, before the adjournment of that body for the simultaneous meetings.

In the Convention sitting of the 16th of May, O'Connor
alluded to the carrying of arms to meetings, strongly denouncing the practice, which Lord John Russell had declared in the
House of Commons to be illegal, and he recommended his
friend, O'Brien, to draw up a resolution on the subject, for
adoption by the Convention, as a recommendation to the
people attending the meetings about to take place. On the
next day O'Brien accordingly brought forward a series of
resolutions, as follows :—

" 1st.—That peace, law, and order, shall continue to be the
motto of this Convention, so long as our oppressors shall act
in the spirit of peace, law, and order towards the people ; but
should our enemies substitute war for peace, or attempt to
suppress our lawful and orderly agitation by lawless violence,
we shall deem it to be the sacred duty of the people, to meet
force with force, and repel assassination by justifiable homicide.

" 2nd.—That in accordance with the foregoing resolution,
the Convention do employ only legal and peaceable means in
the prosecution of the great and righteous objects of the
present movement. Being also desirous that no handle should
be afforded to the enemy for traducing our motives, or employing armed force against the people, we hereby recommend the
Chartists who may attend the approaching simultaneous
meetings, to avoid carrying staves, pikes, pistols, or any other
offensive weapons about their persons. We recommend them
to proceed to the ground sober, orderly, and unarmed. As
also to treat as enemies of the cause any person or persons
who may exhibit such weapons, or who by any other act of
folly or wickedness, should provoke a breach of the peace.

" 3rd.—That the marshals and other officers who may have
charge of the arrangements for the simultaneous meetings,
are particularly requested to use every means in their power
to give effect to the recommendation embodied in the preceding
resolution. We also recommend that the aforesaid officers
do in all cases consult with the local authorities before the
meetings take place.

" 4th.—That in case our oppressors in the middle and upper
ranks should instigate the authorities to assail the people
with armed force, in contravention of the existing laws of the
realm, the said oppressors in the upper and middle ranks
shall be held responsible in person and property for any
detriment that may result to the people from such atrocious
instigation."

When these resolutions had been passed, and other business

transacted, the Convention adjourned to the 1st of July. The most formidable of all the demonstrations held about this time was the demonstration on Kersall Moor. It is impossible to correctly ascertain the numbers at such immense gatherings. The *Northern Star* set the number down at half-a-million. This was, however, highly improbable, even in that extensive and densely populated district ; but undoubtedly it was the largest gathering that ever took place on that spot, and it will be remembered that the *Morning Advertiser* computed the numbers attending a former meeting at 300,000. The military, commanded by Colonel Wemyss, were present at the meeting, but the strictest order was maintained throughout. Next in importance was perhaps the West Riding meeting, held on Peep Green, when 200,000 persons assembled, who were addressed by O'Connor, O'Brien, James Taylor, Mills, Pitkeithly and Bussey, of the Convention ; besides Messrs. Dickenson, Thornton, Vevers, White, Ashton, Arran, Hoey, Crabtree, and many other local speakers. The Earl of Harewood, Lord Lieutenant, had been requested to convene the meeting, which, however, his lordship declined to do, and instead caused a proclamation to be posted warning the people against attending illegal meetings, and cautioning all publicans against selling beer or spirituous liquors on the spot. A display of physical force was made in the shape of yeomanry, pensioners, military, and special constables, but everything passed off peaceably. At this meeting, William Ryder, who had previously declared that there were not eight honest members in the Convention, resigned his seat as delegate for the West Riding. The meeting before separating passed a vote of thanks to the magistrates for preventing liquors being sold upon the ground. Although the language used upon the occasion by the principal speakers was such as did not bring them into collision with the law, yet much of it was bold and striking. O'Connor, in alluding to the relative position of the people and their rulers, observed :—

" By the constitution of this country, the Queen may act illegally as well as the working man. But it is, in my opinion, more criminal in the Queen to act unconstitutionally, than in the people to act illegally. Do the magistrates think of putting down our meeting by acts of violence ? I for one think they do, and should we be attacked to-day, come what will, life, death, or victory, I am determined no house shall cover my head to-night. I am quite ready to subscribe to the doctrine of Mr. Vevers, to stand by the law, and not to give our tyrants the slightest advantage in attacking us in sections; but should they employ force against us, I am for repelling attack by attack."

O'Brien's speech was full of valuable matter, bearing on the condition of the various classes. Towards the conclusion of his speech, he said:—

"At the next general election we must have Chartists as our representatives, and when they have been elected by a show of hands, we must insist on having a formal return to that effect made by the returning officer. We shall thus have a parliament legally chosen under the Queen's writ, and we shall then soon show our tyrants the difference between a parliament nominated by nine or ten millions, and one elected by three or four hundred thousand monopolists. The people's parliament will meet at Birmingham, and then it may be necessary that 500,000 of their constituents should proceed thither, to protect them in the discharge of their legislative duties, and when they are all thus assembled, then I will tell you what I mean to do, but not till then. I will not make a step further until I am stronger than both the law and the constitution. You support the whole tribe of landholders, fundholders, and 2,000,000 of menials and kept mistresses, together with 100,000 prostitutes in London alone. Why should you not have institutions to make these people get their living honestly? Universal suffrage would at once put the remedy within your grasp. The National Debt has been nearly doubled since the peace. Rents have increased from 4,000,000 to 40,000,000 since the reign of James the second. One hundred pounds stock is worth three times as much as in 1815. Shall we not then, seeing all this, at length say to those traitors and robbers, 'thus far shall you go, and no further.' The National Petition will be a notice to quit, and they will very shortly be served with a process of ejectment. I will now conclude by earnestly entreating you to co-operate with the General Convention, and above all things to avoid premature and partial outbreaks. For myself, wherever I may be, and whatever may become of me,—and I understand there is a warrant out against me,—I shall to my latest breath advocate the principle, that the people ought only to be governed by the people themselves."

Some persons may find it hard to reconcile with fact O'Brien's statement that the National Debt had nearly doubled since the time of peace, but it had done so ; not in the nominal amount, but through the lowering in price of the products of labour, principally caused by our juggling monetary system, which enabled the national creditor to command so much more of the products of industry.

At Liverpool, a meeting of about 15,000 persons was held in Queen's-square, which was attended by Dr. Fletcher of the Convention, who was received with great enthusiasm. A faction was organized to disturb and upset the meeting, but to no effect. A person moved an amendment to the resolution, which fell to the ground for want of a seconder. Several working men addressed the meeting, and the best spirit prevailed ; but, as will be seen, the numbers, though large, were not equal to those attending the meetings in the manufacturing districts. Newcastle-upon-Tyne did not in the least shrink from its former character. A meeting was held on the Town Moor, which was attended by no less than 100,000 persons. Processions and bands came from a distance of twenty miles around. More than one hundred banners waved along the line of procession. Messrs. Ayr, Charlton, Cook, Blakey, Devyr, Cockburn, and others were the local speakers, and Messrs. Duncan, Harney, Knox, Lowrey, and Dr. Taylor attended from the Convention. Duncan said :—

" I hope the hired moral assassins, the scoundrel minions of a tyrant government, those vile police spies who have been sent down from London, and who are now among you, will have brains enough to report correctly, and tell Lord John—what I would tell him to his teeth—that he shall no longer trifle with a nation's rights ; and tell him, too, that it was not the mere voice of a working man which spoke, but that the cheers of tens of thousands responded to the sentiment. Tens of thousands of men in our land are now in such misery, that even a field of battle and a death of pain present no terrors to them. It is of little use prophesying in these times ; but I may be allowed to predict, that the next time you meet in such numbers here, it will be to pass very different resolutions, and that your conduct will be that of a people united in one solemn determination either to see their country free, or perish in one common conflagration."

Lowery said :—

" He was for peace, law, and order ; but he would have no peace with oppression and injustice. He would battle with that system which robbed the poor of their wages, and left their homes desolate. He would not admit that to be law, that was for the rich, and against the poor. Nor would he call that order which gave one man £10,000 as pay for doing nothing, while the working man could only get ten shillings per week. That was disorder and robbery. Their enemies said they had nothing to lose. Why they had produced everything, and if they had got nothing some one must have robbed them most infamously."

At the above meeting there was no interference of the military as at the first great demonstration, and everything passed off with the utmost unanimity.

At Carlisle, the people of that neighbourhood met on the Sands to the number of ten thousand. Messrs. Hanson, Bowman, and others spoke in favour of the resolution, as did also Dr. Taylor, Julian Harney, Duncan, and Knox, who were all received with enthusiastic cheers.

At Sunderland, the men of North Durham met on the Town Moor. The various bodies of men came marching in from many miles around, with their respective leaders at their head. Great was the excitement as procession after procession poured its eager masses into the town. The great body of the people consisted of hardy colliers, who evinced the most determined spirit. There were not less than 50,000 present at the meeting, in spite of proclamations, swearing in of special constables, and other hostile displays. James Williams presided ; and in addition to a numerous staff of local speakers, Messrs. Duncan and Knox addressed the vast assembly.

At London, the Chartists assembled on Kennington Common in considerable numbers, and were presided over by James Watson, the radical bookseller. Messrs. Wall, Cameron, Le Blond, Ackerley, Moor, and others were the speakers.

At Bath, the Chartists of that district met in an open field. There were about 6,000 present ; a number comparatively small, owing to the course taken by the authorities, who used every kind of intimidation. So great was the terrorism exercised by those functionaries, that it was with the greatest difficulty a place was secured for the meeting ; and even when obtained, the whereabouts was obliged to be kept somewhat secret, lest the owner should be intimidated, and withdraw his assent. Proclamations, specials, and military, were the order of the day, but the Chartists acted with the greatest caution. Messrs. Bartlett, Bolwell, Metcalfe, and Young, and also Messrs Neesom and Mealing of the Convention, addressed the assembled thousands, who cheered them enthusiastically. After the meeting the Chartists walked into the city, where they met a troop of hussars, whom they saluted with a cheer, which was returned by the military with a move of the hand. The Welsh were not a whit behind the English in demonstrating their attachment to the cause. The various bodies met at Blackwood, Monmouthshire, being a central place for the two counties of Monmouth and Glamorgan. Large masses poured in from all the neighbouring towns and villages, and numbered in the aggregate from 400,000 to 500,000 persons. Mr. Jones, a working man, presided. Several speakers addressed the meeting in Welsh. The chief speaker was their delegate, Frost, who was received with every demonstration of the most cordial esteem and affection. He had become very popular throughout the country, and had been invited to several of the English demonstrations. The imprisonment of Vincent, however, demanded his presence in Wales, and in accordance with his naturally humane disposition, he preferred remaining there, and attending to his case. The men of the above two counties had requested the Lord Lieutenant to call the meeting, but that functionary, like many others, refused.

At Hull, the Victoria Rooms were densely packed by an enthusiastic audience; the Town Hall having been refused by the Mayor, though requested to grant it by 220 householders. Messrs. Burns and Hartwell, of the Convention, were the principal speakers.

At Preston, the Chartists met in the Orchard, an open space of ground, after walking in procession with bands and banners through the principal streets. Messrs. Hatton, Stagg, Bird, and Murphy addressed the people, as well as Richards of the Convention.

At Northampton, the Chartists assembled in the Market-square—one of the prettiest in England—to testify their devotion to Democracy. John Robins, a warm hearted son of toil, was the chairman, who in his opening speech alluded to the swearing in of specials, calling out of pensioners, and other silly proceedings of the authorities. Mr. Leatherland, of Kettering, author of " Base oppressors leave your slumbers ;" Messrs. Elmer, Wilmot, Bayley, Joseph Jones, and Robertson, each addressed the audience, as well as Messrs. Collins and Jones, members of the Convention, and the former was appointed delegate for the county to that body. Exclusive of the West Riding demonstration, the people of Bradford marched in procession to Hartshead Moor with numerous banners. One of them excited great attention ; it was a picture of Marcus practising on an infant his plan of painless extinction. The meeting was immense, and the spirit most enthusiastic. Bussey was the principal speaker. The Democrats of Sheffield presented a requisition to the Master Cutler, but he refused to call a meeting, and they convened the people together in Paradise-square, who assembled to the number of 15,000, with bands and banners. A large procession came also from Rotherham. Messrs. O'Connor, Bussey, Mills, and Taylor of the Convention, were expected, but were unavoidably absent. Mr. Wolstonholme presided, and Messrs. Gill, Foden, Barker, Chatterton, Lawson, Lingard, and Turner addressed the meeting. Gill read a letter from O'Connor, assigning as a reason for non-attendance, that the Magistrates of the West Riding having issued a proclamation against the demonstration there, it was necessary for him to be on the spot to give the people his advice. Gill alluded to the threatened establishment of a rural police in the following pithy sentences:—

" He considered the very idea of a rural police an insult to the country. If they were prepared to submit to it, let them do so; for himself he would do his duty, and resist it to the death. If the country was of his opinion, the whole population would rise against this atrocious plan, and Lord John Russell's head would be placed where his lordship had said the heads of certain individuals should be placed. He must inform them that Lord John had written a book on the constitution of this country, in which was stated, that those who conspired against the liberties of the people, merited to have their heads stuck on Temple Bar. Now he thought the rural police was intended to crush the liberties of the people, and that the head of Lord John Russell should therefore be stuck there at once."

At South Shields, a meeting was held in the Market-place, which was attended by 15,000 persons. Julian Harney was expected to attend, but in consequence of some delay in the train, did not arrive in time. Messrs. Byrne and Gray, in the absence of Harney, addressed the people, who cheered them enthusiastically.

At the little town of Leigh the people assembled to the number of 10,000, although the meeting was a spontaneous one, being called together merely from it being observed that Dr. Taylor and Messrs. Warden and Fenny were walking in the town. These gentlemen addressed the meeting, which was worked up to a pitch of almost frantic enthusiasm. At Penrith, Cockermouth, Wigton, Dalston, Carlisle, and other places, Julian Harney addressed large and enthusiastic gatherings. At some of these, he was presented by the women Chartists with testimonials of their esteem.

At Glasgow, a nightly gathering took place on the Green. The *True Scotsman* estimated the numbers at 130,000. Notwithstanding the unfavourable state of the weather, the vast multitude stood to their posts, and displayed the warmest enthusiasm. Moir, the Glasgow delegate, presided. The local speakers were Messrs. Gillespie, McKay, Hamilton, Paterson, Rodgers, Andrew, Ross, and several others; and Messrs. Collins, Frost, Richardson, O'Brien, Dr. Taylor, Bussey, and Lowrey, were present on behalf of the Convention. Frost, addressing the people, said :—

" The advice I have given to my countrymen in Wales, is the same as I will give you now. They are determined to hold by the law, and I have advised them to hold this opinion, that they who break the law make themselves amenable to it. The members of the Convention have never yet broken the law, nor are they likely to do so ; and, therefore, if they are attempted to be laid hold of by the Government, we are determined to lay hold of some of the leading men in the country, as hostages for the safety of the Convention. If your enemies do as James the second did, it will then be our duty to see that those who break the law shall not do so with impunity."

The meeting responded to these sentiments by a loud burst of cheering.

Richardson, in alluding to the run on the banks, said :—

" He did not advise them to make a run upon these banks, nor to make any alarm in the country; but he advised them to look sharply after what they had in these savings' banks. To advise a run upon the banks was illegal; to advise them to embarrass the Government in money matters was illegal; but to advise them to look after their own was perfectly legal, and just, and reasonable. He would say to them, do not go to the savings banks, because it might chance that they would get their money, and the people of Manchester would get none ; but let us know when you are ready, and we will all go together. Only give us a fair start. If the Government had not the people's hard cash to trust to, the army would be disbanded, and the navy laid up in dock. Would they believe, that when they were going to deposit their twelve shillings in those banks that that twelve shillings went to buy a musket for the army, or that a shilling went to purchase ball cartridges for these muskets? He did not advise them to take that help from the Government, but he did not think that they would be so foolish as to lend a man a stick, and ask him to thrash them."

The speech of Richardson—the sarcastic tendency of which was seen through by the meeting—was alternately hailed with bursts of laughter and applause.

O'Brien, alluding to the Chartist policy to be pursued at the next election, said :—

"He would not give a fig for all their clamouring and clapping of hands, unless the people were prepared to do something effective. Their present House of Commons did not represent them; it represented the fellows who live by profits, who live by usury. It also represented a rascally crew of attornies, bishops and parsons, pawnbrokers and stock-jobbers. It represented men who had no interest in the welfare of the country. The stockjobber had the same interest in the public calamity as the pawnbroker had in private distress. It also represented military officers, and it was a fact that about

2,000 brothel-keepers in London had votes. Nobody would dare to say that the representatives returned by them (the people) at public meetings, called for the purpose by royal authority, should not be the real representatives of the country. At any rate, it was their business to act in that way, and to do that in spite of Whigs or Tories. He would take the opportunity of telling them the character which their enemies gave of one another. The Whigs said the Tories were guilty of perjury; nay, Daniel O'Connell declared that every man of them had been guilty of perjury, of the most atrocious perjury, and that he could prove it. That was the character of one side of the House. The rascals did not dare to deny the charge, because they knew that it was the truth; but they replied, the Whigs had been guilty of more perjury, and that they were endangering Queen Victoria's throne. They had attacked property, and the attack would proceed from one kind of property to another; therefore they said, you Whigs are traitors as well as perjurers. The Whigs never said that the Tories should not have votes because of their perjury, but they denied them (the people) who were not guilty of any crime. They gave votes to the perjurers, and the Tories were equally willing to give votes to traitors as well as perjurers. When they had elected their 300 or 400 delegates at the poll, they could meet at Manchester or Birmingham and when they were there, he would give them his head for a red herring if he did not point out a new mode of petitioning. He would require stout able fellows to back them, and to stand by Queen Victoria as their lawful and constitutional sovereign, in defiance of both Whigs and Tories. The Government never told him any of its secrets, neither would he tell them his secret, the new mode of petition-ing, until he found himself in such a position that it mattered not whether they knew his secret or not. The meetings of the Convention were strictly legal. He never advised the people to violate the law, not that he cared a fig for it, but that he had a precious regard for his own carcase, and for the bodies of working men. The ancient constitutional law of England said that the polls should be counted, and that the candidate who should have the greatest number of polls should be declared duly elected. Now the word poll meant their heads, and he was sure that it would take a pretty long time to count all their polls, but he believed they would all be counted on the side of justice and equality. The plan he had sketched for them was a safe one, and possessed a number of advantages. When their delegates met, if they found them-selves very weak they would go on petitioning. Having the power over the law, it would then matter little whether they broke it or not."

During the time that O'Brien delivered his speech, of which the above is but a faint outline, the effect produced on the meeting it were almost impossible to exaggerate. At nearly every sentence the speaker drew forth a burst of laughter or cheering, or both, according to the nature of his remark, and the style in which it was delivered.

Dr. Taylor said:—

"They did not require his opinions on the principles they were contending for. As to the resolution they had just heard read, he had always said that exclusive dealing was one of the best plans to bring their enemies to their feet. And if they chalked up the doors on each side of the streets, and marked every shopkeeper who would not assist them to gain their freedom, they would soon bring them to think that the working class were fit for the exercise of the franchise. And as the music of the pennies—the only music the shopkeeper loves to hear—ceased, and the boxes become empty, he might be brought to acknowledge the right of the people to be represented. If they acted on this plan, and put it into immediate execution, that alone would secure the Charter, and their committee had only to set up a shop, and they would find plenty of rivals on every side of them on the chartist principle."

Dr. Taylor was loudly applauded throughout his address.

Bussey said:—

"There was no sympathy existing between the classes; it was entirely a question of pounds, shillings, and pence. Gold was the God of the shopkeepers; and if the way to an Englishman's head was through his belly, he believed the way to a middle class man's head was through his pockets. It was high time for them to come forward and take a part in the struggle, and if they refused, all that he could say was, there was more honesty in doing a good turn to a friend, than to an enemy, and he advised them to go invariably to the man who would assist them to gain their rights."

Lowrey said:—

"He asked them, were they prepared to fulfil their pledges? There were no idle pledges. No man should utter that with his tongue which he would not execute with his arm. They would not then allow the Convention to wear a fool's cap on its head, but prove that they were the sons of the men who had left their homes, and taken to the mountains with their broadswords by their sides. They could not be afraid; they had truth and justice on their side; and though they might not talk with grammatical accuracy, they could point out hypocrisy —they could prove that their opponents were the men who

Q

broke the commandments, and violated God's humanity. They might ask them, what they had done with the millions of money they had taken from the people? And the clergy who talked about the ignorance of the people might be asked, why did they allow children of twelve and fourteen years of age to vote in matters affecting their eternal concerns, and yet refuse the youth of twenty-one a voice in the making of the laws by which he is governed? He would ask them why they give the people a certificate for heaven, and yet refuse them a certificate for earth? What blasphemy and mockery of religion to say that God shall call men to account, and yet they will be told they were too ignorant for the franchise—they could not know right from wrong."

Such is a sample of the meetings which were held in various parts of the country. It was in vain that proclamations in many cases declared the meetings to be illegal; they were held despite proclamations, and all the displays of force made by the ruling classes:—and that, not in a few instances, but in every town and village throughout Great Britain, wherever the voice of Democracy could find an echo. While, however, meetings were going on in other parts without any interruption —except such as we have noticed above,—in Birmingham the proceedings of the authorities were of a more significant character. Two of the leaders, named Brown and Fussell— the first a member of the Convention—had addressed numerous meetings in the Bull Ring and other places, and for the speeches thus addressed to the people they were arrested, and underwent an examination before the magistrates. These arrests took place just before the time for the simultaneous meetings, and were probably made with a view to intimidation. We are the more inclined to suspect this, from the fact that much of the evidence given against Brown referred to meetings he had addressed two months previously. This, too, was the heavier part of the evidence, and that which referred to meetings of a later date was of a comparatively trivial character. The magistrates appeared at this time resolved on striking a blow at the Birmingham meetings. Some of those magistrates were renegade Chartists; and it is a fact that renegades almost invariably act with the greatest virulence toward their former associates. Brown and Fussell were both committed for trial; and although working men, bail was demanded for Brown to the amount of £800, and for Fussell to the amount of £400. Fussell was bailed immediately; but Brown's bail not being forthcoming, he was removed to Warwick guarded by dragoons, and cheered by thousands of people who were assembled outside awaiting the decision of the court. Stephens too, was about this time sermonizing in London, to which place he had been specially invited.   He addressed large audiences on Primrose Hill and Kennington Common, and his denunciation of the rulers of the land, for their adherence to the Poor Law, was as stern and decisive as ever.

The simultaneous meetings being at an end, the Convention re-assembled at Birmingham, according to appointment, on Monday, July 1st.   The first subject which engaged the attention of that body was the removal of itself to London. Moir gave notice of a motion urging the necessity of such removal.   O'Connor gave notice of an amendment, thanking the men of Birmingham for the reception given to the Convention, and declaring that they would continue their sittings in that town.   The subject of a National Defence Fund was then brought forward, and O'Connor announced that with a view to that object, he had addressed public meetings in Newcastle, Carlisle, Edinburgh, South Shields, Sheffield, Mansfield, Nottingham, Loughboro', and other important towns.   He also stated that he had opened a subscription at the *Northern Star* office, which he had led with the sum of £20.   He then said that they ought to advise the people as to their right of possessing arms, and gave an account of a trial before the magistrates at Mansfield, in which he had attended to prosecute several shopkeepers, who had been training and drilling with arms, which had been supplied them by the Duke of Portland, and in which case the magistrates decided in favour of the shopkeepers.   He also alluded to the state of Birmingham, and informed the Convention that three hundred special constables had been sworn in that very day.   This led to a discussion on the propriety of the people continuing their meetings in the Bull Ring. Lovett, Neesom, Craig, O'Connor, and several other members expressed their views, and it was at length unanimously agreed, that in order to deprive the magistrates of all excuse for interfering with their proceedings, it would be better for them to walk in procession through the streets, and hold their meetings outside the town.

The Convention was now applied to for assistance for thirteen men who had been arrested for training and drilling at Newtown, and a committee of thirteen was appointed to consider the application.   It was announced that £50 had been collected for the defence fund at Newport, Pontypool, and the neighbourhood.   £100 had been subscribed in Merthyr Tydvil alone. This was a proof of the strong devotion of the working class in Wales, for although among the poorest, these sums were almost entirely subscribed by them.

On Tuesday, Moir brought forward his motion for the removal of the Convention to London, and urged the critical position of the Government as a reason for such removal. He thought the Convention ought to be on the spot, to avail itself of any embarrassment in which the Government might be placed. He quoted from the *Sun* paper a statement, showing that from the 20th to the 26th of June, 49,090 ounces of silver bars, 247,344 ounces of silver coin, 11,750 ounces of gold coin, and 6,570 ounces of gold in bars, had been lately sent out of the country. He thought it was questionable whether the Bank of England was able to pay eighteenpence in the pound. This, he stated, was his reason for wishing to remove their sittings to London. Deegan seconded the motion. O'Connor then moved an amendment, curious enough when contrasted with his speech against the motion. He said there had been occurrences taking place nightly that demanded them to remain in Birmingham, and in no place could the Convention protest and guard against danger better than in the spot where it was taking place. He then moved that the Convention should proceed to London on Monday next. Messrs. Fletcher, Craig, and Pitkeithly supported Moir. Dr. Taylor and Cardo supported the amendment. Thirteen voted for the amendment, and ten for the motion. Bussey moved that the Convention remain in Birmingham until the country's reply to the manifesto had been received. This motion was negatived,—Messrs. Fletcher, Richards, O'Connor, Cardo, and others speaking against it. Lovett said he did not see the advantage of being near the Bank, as was urged by Moir. They could convert the paper money into gold by merely stating their wish to their constituents to do so. Their fiat would be obeyed just as well as though it were to come from London ; and besides, if they removed, he thought it would show an indecision of character, and that they did not deliberately consider their plans previous to adopting them. Surely if it was necessary to come to Birmingham at all, it was necessary to stay longer than they had as yet done. It was ultimately agreed that the Convention should meet in London on Wednesday week. The delegates then reported the result of their mission; and as their statements are necessary to enable us to form a clear judgment of the movement, and of the men engaged in it, we feel bound to give a digest of those statements.

Craig reported that the people of Ayrshire were willing to obey the legal and constitutional orders of the Convention. Deegan reported that at public meetings at Leicester, Nottingham, Derby, and Sutton in Ashfield, the manifesto was adopted with surprising unanimity. Dr. Fletcher said that the Kersall Moor and Liverpool meetings promised to support the Convention. Cardo said he had been to Cornwall, where the people were in the greatest ignorance respecting politics; that the miners were getting but five shillings per week, and were all in favour of the manifesto, which they were determined to carry out. That at Penzance the people were withdrawing their money from the savings' banks, and the town was like a fair. There were two clergymen standing on the steps of the bank, urging them not to withdraw their money; but it only caused the greater anxiety to get their money into their own hands. They could get nothing but Bank of England notes; and he felt assured that steps might be taken that would cause a great run upon the banks in Cornwall. Dean reported that at Chichester, at an open air meeting, the people were quite anxious to carry the ulterior measures. Neesom reported that he had attended meetings near Bath and Stroud; also at Bristol and Cheltenham, and in Wiltshire, Somersetshire, and Leicestershire, and that the men were looking forward for them to adopt the ulterior measures, and were not disposed to wait long for them. Frost stated that a policeman at Bath, upon having a cutlass given him, asked what it was for; and upon being told said, that he would not take up arms against his countrymen, and as a proof of the feelings of the magistrates with respect to them, that man was in the police force at the present time.

O'Connor stated that he had attended three meetings, one at Kersall Moor, one at Peep Green, and the other at Birmingham; and at the three meetings above a million of persons were present, who were determined to carry universal suffrage, morally if they could, but physically if they could not without it. He believed that they were in the last stage of agitation; the first stage was the creation of public opinion— the second was the organization of public opinion—and the third was the direction of public opinion. They had created it, and its organization was nearly completed, but he would not be for directing it until they could irresistibly direct it. He was firmly convinced that they were now in a position to take a bolder stand than they had hitherto been able to do. They now stood in such a commanding position, that they could say to the Whigs, you must give us universal suffrage, or we will take it. That was really the position in which the people stood, and they might expect that a return would soon be made to them.

Dr. Taylor had attended large meetings at Carlisle, Newcastle, Penrith, Leigh, and several other places, and gratifying results had been obtained. Donaldson reported that at Stourbridge, Lye Waste, and Dudley, he had attended meetings. The people desired a missionary to be sent amongst them. They were determined not long to endure such misery, and were only waiting the orders of the Convention to know how to act. Marsden said, that at Newtown they found it impossible to hold a meeting, the place was filled with military, and the secretary of the Association had been arrested, and if they still cried " Peace, peace," the effect would be the total destruction of the cause. At Lancaster, Burnley, Chorley, and other places where he visited, the questions of the Convention were all answered affirmatively. Moir said that he had attended from twenty to thirty meetings, at which there were large numbers present, ready to obey the Convention in all that was legal and constitutional. Hartwell announced that in the neighbourhoods of Hull and Scarborough, there were great accessions of strength to the radical cause daily. Burns stated that Hartwell had omitted to mention that they even found policemen members of the Radical Association, and actively engaged in collecting the subscription. Richards said he had attended meetings in Cheshire, and there the people were thoroughly determined to take ample vengeance on their oppressors, if their grievances were not redressed very speedily. Collins reported that he had attended various meetings at Greenock, Bannockburn, Alloa, Dunfermline, Montrose, Dundee, Perth, Edinburgh, and other places, and with the exception of Dunfermline, he never saw such spirit manifested in the course of his life. Such were the principal reports given in by the delegates, and on the strength of these reports, the Convention proceeded on the following day to the discussion of ulterior measures.

The first motion on the subject was made by Cardo, and seconded by O'Connor, for a committee to ascertain the best means of changing Bank of England notes into gold, when Messrs. Moir, James Taylor, Bussey, Cardo, and Fletcher were appointed for that purpose. Dr. Taylor then moved that an address to the country be prepared and issued immediately, calling upon the people to withdraw their money from the banks, to run for gold, to commence exclusive dealing, to give up all excisable luxuries, and to use their constitutional privilege of arming as speedily as possible. O'Connor was also the seconder of this motion, and observed that they were there not merely to attend to the presentation of the petition, but to carry the Charter, and he was convinced that until they had a sacred holiday they should never have universal suffrage. The Convention was now the only constituted authority in the country, and he thought they should not press the power which was in their hands too suddenly upon the people. It had now gained a great importance in the country, and it would not be well to hazard a general defeat by gaining a sectional triumph. Craig had no instructions from his constituents to urge the ulterior measures. Bussey moved that the Convention recommend to the public the necessity of acting upon the manifesto on the 15th of July, 1839, which was seconded by Cardo, who thought a run upon the banks would be quite sufficient to bring on the general holiday. Dr. Fletcher thought a general holiday would be the best plan for carrying their views into effect, which a run on the banks would be sufficient to cause. Dr. M'Douall stated that the people of Ashton had adopted the plan of providing themselves with arms. He wished the sacred month to be adopted as speedily as possible, and as July was a celebrated month for revolution and reformation, he would recommend July, for they had a good harvest before them which they could reap. Warden supported the resolution of Bussey, because he thought that a national holiday was tantamount to a national insurrection. Collins gave his strenuous support to the original motion. Brown, who had been liberated on bail, expressed his pleasure at being present to support the motion of Bussey. Lovett agreed with Dr. Taylor's motion. At the same time, he could not help entertaining the opinion of Bussey and others, that a holiday, or sacred month, would be found to be the only effectual remedy for the sufferings of the people; but while he entertained that opinion, he was for testing the House of Commons respecting the motion of Mr. Atwood regarding the Charter. Previous to recommending so solemn and serious a thing as a sacred month, he thought that some provision should be made for the people before they were ordered to retire from their labours. He thought it would be better to appoint a committee of ten or a dozen, to devise the best possible plan for carrying out the sacred month. And also, he thought that one great means of effecting the holiday would be, to select a few trades whose cessation from labour would cause all other trades to leave off work, and they should form a provisional fund to support them. That would be a good test of public opinion; for if the people would not subscribe one shilling or sixpence a-week against such a time, he should much doubt whether they would leave off working themselves. He therefore thought it advisable to carry Dr. Taylor's motion, and then to appoint a committee for the objects he had stated. Dr. Fletcher suggested that the people should be called upon to support the measures named in the resolution, and if the

Charter was not carried by the 20th of July, that there should be an entire cessation from labour. Frost agreed with a sacred month being held, but he did not think they were prepared to give advice to the people of England to act upon it. Richards said the mere mention of a run on the banks had caused people in the north of Staffordshire, and the south of Cheshire, to withdraw their monies. The manifesto had caused great excitement in the Potteries, where exclusive dealing was a very powerful engine. They were ready to adopt the sacred month if the Convention ordered, but would rather have a few weeks for preparation. Messrs. Neesom and Marsden strongly urged the fixing of a day. Moir thought the time had not arrived for ceasing from labour, the Charter not yet having been rejected by the Commons. While he would recommend a run upon the banks, he was opposed to any day being fixed for the sacred month to commence, it not appearing that they could do so with safety. Lovett said a division was to take place on the Charter on the 12th instant, and the 1st of August might be a proper time to consider the matter. Dr. Taylor recommended that they should see how the Charter was disposed of on the 12th, and then they could meet on the 13th to fix the day for the sacred month to commence. Hartwell's constituents were for a run on the banks, but he was not instructed to vote for any particular day in reference to the sacred month, till it was known how the Charter was disposed of on the 12th. Woodhouse thought that previous to the holiday, if exclusive dealing, a run upon the banks, and abstinence from all excisable articles, were to be carried into effect, they would be equally beneficial. Dr. Taylor would add to his motion, "and that the members of the Convention meet on the 13th of July, for the purpose of appointing a day when the sacred month shall commence, if the Charter has not previously become the law of the land." Dean had been instructed by his constituents to vote for immediately fixing a day for the holiday to commence, for many of them were in a state of starvation. The masters of mills in Ashton and the neighbourhood, had stated that they would either reduce the wages of their workpeople, and run their mills three or four days a week, or they would close the mills for a whole month. He felt convinced that if a day was not named, the people would come to a collision with the authorities. Pitkeithly would have them remember that if the people made a struggle when unprepared to sustain it, they would only rivet their chains the faster. It was their duty to do all they possibly could that appeared most essential for the safety and progress of the cause, and they had all chances in their favour if they did not act with indiscretion, for the Government was sinking lower and lower every day, while the people were rising in their dignity; and if they were only a few days beforehand with any measure, it would very likely put them twenty years back.   Dr. Fletcher said that at the meetings he had attended, the people did not attach so much importance to any of the points of the manifesto, as they did to the run upon the banks, and the national sacred holiday.   Collins said if they adopted a part of the ulterior measures, it would be a guarantee that they were prepared to carry out the others, if it should be necessary to do so, and they should gain the confidence of the people more than if they fixed a day rashly, and injured their cause.   Smart was decidedly of opinion that they should not come to a hasty decision in the matter; and the motion of Dr. Taylor in its amended form, met with his hearty and thorough concurrence. Stowe's constituents were ready to back the Convention by keeping the holiday, or by adopting any other of the ulterior measures which they might order; and he further stated, that many sick and secret societies which had funds in the savings' and other banks, had begun to withdraw their money.   Deegan's opinion, as that of his constituents', was for leaving the holiday out of the question, and to recommend the other parts of the manifesto for the adoption of the country.   Dr. M'Douall was authorised by the colliers of Stockport to state that as a body they were prepared to defend the Convention, and to follow their orders; and further, that they were prepared to do it with something in their hands.   Bussey withdrew his amendment, and Dr. Taylor's motion was carried unanimously.

On glancing over the preceding sketch of the debates, one cannot but be struck with the rash and foolish conduct of the vast majority of the Convention.   It is evident, from the reports, that however great was the spirit in favour of the Charter, there was no general inclination for the sacred month. In many instances there was a decided opinion against it.   In some others, there was only a general resolution of support to the Convention.   A third part were ready to strike if the resolution to do so became generally adopted.   The majority of the most important districts were by no means cordially in its favour, and in most instances, the resolution to strike was adopted in the effervescence of public meetings, under very exciting influences.   Those meetings were no test of the calm and deliberate opinions of the persons attending them.   A large portion of the members appeared to feel this; but not brave enough to stand against the taunt of cowardice, with all their doubts of the practicability of a sacred month, they stultified themselves by voting for a motion, the latter part of which actually pledged them—not to further consider the propriety of fixing, but actually to fix a day for the strike to commence if the Charter was not received with favour by the House of Commons on the 12th of July. And notwithstanding the diversity of opinion that existed amongst both the members and their constituencies, there was not one member of the Convention to oppose Dr. Taylor's motion as amended, although that motion actually bound them to the sacred month. The want of due reflection on the part of some of the members was remarkably striking. For instance, one urged the necessity of the strike, because the employers were talking of shutting up their mills for a month. Why, the strike was the very thing that those employers wanted. We fancy, too, that we see the laugh of the enemy, as he read that speech of Burns, who reminded his colleague, Hartwell, of his having omitted to state in his report, that at Hull the very police had joined the Association, and were actively engaged in collecting the subscription. Why, no policeman would have been allowed to collect for a single week after the fact became known to the authorities, unless the man was acting as the tool of those authorities, for the purpose of supplying them with information of what was going forward. So easily are clever but inexperienced men duped in periods of excitement.

JOHN COLLINS
FROM A SCARCE ENGRAVING

CHAPTER VII.

As intimated in a previous chapter, the authorities of Birmingham for some time past had manifested their disapproval of the Bull Ring meetings, and the time at length arrived when they resolved to put those meetings down by force. To be sure, there were still existing some old-fashioned notions upon the constitutional right of Englishmen to meet for the discussion of their grievances, but, as before intimated, some of the Birmingham officials were regenade Chartists who set these old notions at nought. On the 8th of July the people had assembled as usual in the Bull Ring, and a working man had mounted the rostrum to read a newspaper. He was not, however, allowed long to proceed, before a body of the metropolitan police, who had just arrived by rail, entered the Bull Ring, headed by the mayor and another magistrate, and, without the slightest provocation, commenced an indiscriminate attack on the people. Not even the most defenceless women and children escaped the effects of their hired ferocity. The people were without arms of any description, and were, therefore, utterly unprepared for resistance. The consequence was, that panic-stricken, they for the moment fled in all directions; but the flight was only momentary, for they immediately rallied, and with fury depicted in their countenances, returned the attack of the police, who in their turn were compelled to fly,—several of them in the encounter being dangerously wounded, and carried off in a hopeless state. Two of the police would certainly have been sacrificed to popular vengeance, but for the arrival of Dr. Taylor, whose popularity enabled him to save them from the fury which was burning to be wreaked upon their heads.

After this brutal and unjustifiable onslaught upon the unarmed multitude, the mayor, protected by the military, proceeded to read the Riot Act, after which the police again attacked the people, and took several of them prisoners. The military then scoured the streets, and detachments were placed

at all the thoroughfares leading to the Bull Ring, so as effectually to block them up, and prevent any person passing.

The attack took place at nine o'clock; at half-past ten the
fighting ceased. But shortly after that time the people, who
had again gathered, indulged in loud shouts, and commenced
singing the Chartist anthem, " Fall, tyrants fall !" which was
followed by deafening cheers. Between eleven and twelve
o'clock, there arose a loud cry of "Holloway ! Holloway !"
and the people immediately marched for Holloway Head,
where they swore vengeance against the metropolitan police,
and then marched to St. Thomas's church, tearing down the
palisades and making them into arms. Seventy feet of this
railing, with all the masonry work, were torn down, and the
rails made into weapons about three feet in length. The large
and strong iron gates were wrested off, and the massive pillars
on which the gates swung were twisted from their positions,
giving evidence of the power of even an unarmed people, when
roused to fury by injustice. Armed with the above weapons,
they were again rushing to the scene of conflict, when they
were met by Drs. Taylor and M'Douall, who with the utmost
difficulty persuaded them to throw down their arms and
abandon their design. The reward which Dr. Taylor received
for saving the lives of two policemen, and inducing the people
to throw down their arms, was an arrest without a warrant,
at two o'clock in the morning, and made with all the brutality
common to Jacks-in-office. The magistrates sat as early as
six o'clock to examine the prisoners, and at an early hour, Dr.
Taylor, with ten others, was committed to Warwick gaol, the
magistrates requiring bail to the amount of £1000 for his
appearance.

The Convention met at the Golden Lion, at nine o'clock, and
of course the proceedings of the previous night formed the principal topic of discussion. Ultimately the following resolutions
were passed, and ordered to be placarded about the town :—

" 1st.—That this Convention is of opinion that a wanton,
flagrant, and unjust outrage has been made upon the people
of Birmingham, by a bloodthirsty and unconstitutional force
from London, acting under the authority of men, who when
out of office, sanctioned and took part in the meetings of the
people ; and now, when they share in the public plunder, seek
to keep the people in social and political degradation.

" 2nd.—That the people of Birmingham are the best judges
of their own right to meet in the Bull Ring or elsewhere; have
their own feelings to consult respecting outrage given, and
are the best judges of their own power and resources to obtain
justice.

" 3rd.—That the summary and despotic arrest of Dr. Taylor, our respected colleague, affords another convincing proof of all absence of justice in England, and clearly shows that there is no security for lives, liberty, or property, till the people have some control over the laws they are called upon to obey."

There was a large number of delegates present when these resolutions were passed, and every member, to his honour, desired to sign them ; and it was then Lovett, in the true spirit of chivalry, said that they could not spare victims, and a sacrifice of one being sufficient, he would alone sign them. He did so; and Collins undertook to get them published. The consequence was the immediate arrest of both these gentlemen. In the meantime, the people continued to meet at Holloway Head, but were dispersed by the military. Business was brought to a stand, and everything wore a gloomy and threatening aspect. Dr. Taylor was treated in prison with the utmost harshness. His hair was cropped, and he was subjected to all the indignities of the common felon.

In a short time after the resolutions of the Convention were posted on the walls of Birmingham, Lovett and Collins were brought up for examination, and these gentlemen conducted themselves with a deportment which conferred honour on the cause for which they had been arrested. When Lovett was asked by the Recorder whether the resolutions were published by his order, he unhesitatingly answered—yes! His other replies were equally candid, and they drew forth a well-merited compliment from the Recorder. One of Lovett's replies merits the eternal approbation of all lovers of liberty, and admirers of honesty and candour. " Were you aware," asked the Recorder," that certain members of the police force were wounded dangerously by weapons?" Lovett replied, "I heard that several of them were wounded, and at the same time thought that the people were justified in repelling such despotic and bloodthirsty power by any and every means at their disposal, because I believe that the institution of a police force is an infringement on the constitution and liberties possessed by our ancestors; for if the people submit to one injustice after another, which self-constituted authorities impose upon them, they may be eventually ground to the dust, without the means of any resistance." The Recorder tried very ingeniously to entrap Collins, by asking him if he was a member of the National Convention; but Collins replied that he knew of no such body, but there was the General Convention of the industrial classes. He was then asked whether he was a member of the General Convention. His reply was such as perhaps was little expected : " I am a member

of that, and was elected at the same time as Mr. Muntz."
Poor Muntz was sitting on the magisterial bench ! He put in
a paper as he was leaving, denying that he had ever accepted
the office of delegate, or acted as a member of the Convention.
But one thing is certain, that Mr. Muntz had taken an active
part in the movement—had never objected to his election, and
had allowed his name to be advertised as one of the trustees of
the national subscription, after that election had taken place.
Neither Lovett nor Collins could be induced to utter a syllable
in any way criminating a third person in the affair ; and their
conduct gained them the warm approbation of the Chartist
body, and the admiration of all.

The military and police still continued to parade the streets,
dispersing the people, and severely wounding numbers of persons with whom they came in contact. Martial law was proclaimed, and all public-houses ordered to be shut by eight
o'clock. Guest had printed the address of the Convention
recommending the ulterior measures to be adopted by the people, and was arrested when he presented himself at the public
office to offer bail for Dr. Taylor. Ultimately Messrs. O'Connor
and Smith became bail for the latter. There were about eighty
persons in all arrested for this riot, which was in reality a riot
of the authorities against the people. On the Tuesday, George
Julian Harney was brought into Birmingham under arrest,
having been taken on the previous night at Bedlington, a village in Northumberland. On his arriving at Carlisle, though
it was late at night, the news became known ; and a large
crowd assembled in front of the inn where he was in custody,
and demanded his release. Harney exhorted them not to
interfere, but to no purpose ; and a chaise had to be brought
to the back of the inn while the people were in front, and
Harney and the officer getting into it, were driven off.
The warrant on which he was arrested had been issued for
some time past. His offence was the delivery of a seditious
speech ; that speech being one of the mildest he ever delivered.

Debarred from meeting in the open air, the people applied
for the use of the Town Hall, but were refused ; and again
they met at Holloway Head. The military interfered, and the
people commenced pelting them with stones. They had orders
to load and make ready ; but a reinforcement arrived, and the
firing was prevented—many of the people being made prisoners.
The military continued to parade the streets, and to chase the
people. A large number were in St. Martin's Lane when they
were attacked by the police, who gave orders to the occupiers
of houses to close their doors in order to prevent the people
obtaining shelter. A large number were wounded severely by

their brutal pursuers. Things continued much in this state until Monday the 15th, when the pent-up feelings of the outraged people burst forth with terrific fury. About eight o'clock crowds of people began to assemble in the Bull Ring, and the police issued forth in order to disperse them. The sight of this force only tended the more to exasperate the public feeling, and at nine o'clock the cry arose of "Put out the gas!" The utmost confusion ensued. The police were powerless. Some of the shopkeepers had rendered themselves obnoxious to the people, who set the house of Messrs. Bourne, grocers, on fire. The buildings of Messrs. Leggett, wholesale and retail feather and bed tick dealers, were next in flames. Mr. Banks, druggist, Messrs. Dakin and Naden, grocers, Mr. Horton, silversmith, next had their houses fired. On Snow Hill fires also raged with fury. The desperation of the people knew scarcely any bounds. They entered the shops—completely gutted them of their contents—brought them into the Bull Ring, and committed them to the devouring flames, not permitting an engine to come near the spot. The soldiers took up their position in the Bull Ring; when immediately four other fires were discovered in different parts of the town.

Amid all these desperate proceedings the people exhibited a disinterestedness worthy of all imitation. Not even the most costly goods for a moment tempted their cupidity. They even trod under foot the splendid silver plate of Mr. Horton, proving that however great their provocation, plunder was not their object. They were at war with the ruling classes, but they scorned to avail themselves of the common privileges of warriors. That they had become desperate was not their fault; their vices belonged to their oppressors, their virtues were their own. Meetings continued to be held, to which the people flocked in crowds. The process of trade was stopped, and a large number of the gentry fled the town; even the valiant mayor was terrified into flight. Several persons were arrested for taking part in the firing and demolishing of the houses, and were committed for trial at the approaching assizes.

The conduct of the Birmingham officials excited the indignation of the Chartists throughout the country. As soon as the news reached Newcastle, a public meeting was convened for Sunday evening, in the lecture room, which was crowded to suffocation. James Ayr presided. Bronterre O'Brien who was in the town, was introduced to the assembly amid tremendous cheering. He read from the *Sun* newspaper an account of the proceedings, which produced a profound sensation. O'Brien said :—

" He foresaw, seven years ago, that the middle class would attempt to shed the blood of the people, rather than give them their rights. He had advised the working class to form themselves into agitation committees, knowing that the authorities would attempt to suspend trial by jury. He had advised the people to be armed to the teeth, to put down tyrants who relied on nothing but the physical force of hired homicides. If the Government met them with reason, they might settle the whole matter peaceably ; but when they dispersed the people for meeting peaceably, it was a mockery to ask the people to meet without they were prepared to defend themselves. When these minions attacked the people they created the riot ; and if there was either law or justice in England, these ruffians would be in gaol instead of the peaceable people. But there was no law in England, except for the seven hundred thousand living on rents, profits, and interests, who attempted to govern England by physical force. Talk not to him of the Queen, or of the ministers, or the House of Commons ; they were but the tools of the seven hundred thousand monopolists whom he denounced as conspirators against the people." (Here a middle class man complained of O'Brien's observations.) O'Brien said, " If the gentleman did not resist the demands of the people, then was he not comprised in the charge at all ; but if he were one of those who would keep to himself the rights which he denied to the people, then he called him a conspirator, because it was his proper name. He did not call any man of the middle class a conspirator, except he conspired to keep him from his just rights. A military force could not act in a borough without the aid of the borough magistrates. Had the Birmingham magistrates intimated to Lord John Russell that they did not require a military or police force? No ; for if they had done so, Lord John Russell dare not move one step towards suppressing public meetings in Birmingham. If the people's blood was shed in Newcastle, let them not rush upon the military. No ; let them go to the corporation who ordered them out. If the people's blood was shed in the peaceful discharge of their right of meeting, why, let the borough authorities be answerable in life and property. They should have no escape from despotism but by those means. These despots were not a few men on the banks of the Thames. No, their tyrants were to be found among all men who wrung a fortune from the sweat of the people ; and so long as the electors, who usurped the government, got the people to expend their force against the military and police, they would have no peace ; so let them hold those men accountable—he said it again—in life and property. Their plan was to gather up under the law a power greater than the law itself; and the moment the local authorities attempted to break the law, why let them never more meet till they met with arms in their hands to defend the Queen, to defend the constitution, but above all, to defend the rights of Englishmen, for whom the Queen and constitution exist."

O'Brien was greeted throughout a long and eloquent address with terrific bursts of cheering. Messrs. Mason, Thomason, Devyr, Cockburn, and others delivered spirited addresses. The latter said :—

"If the authorities resisted the people, and attempted to put down their constitutional meetings then were the people bound to resist those authorities by force. He never knew of any attempt made by the people to vindicate their rights, but they were met by brute force on the part of their oppressors. The present system was kept up by physical force. If it was not, why keep up a standing army, and an armed and unconstitutional police? If the people did not now exert themselves, and right suddenly, they would soon lose the last vestige of their rights. He recommended the people to arm, but he did not recommend bloodshed, for if the people were all armed, the Government would not dare to oppose them. The Whigs carried their Reform Bill by physical force. Had not the Aristocracy been afraid of their estates, they would never have granted the Reform Bill. He who wished for peace and detested bloodshed, must now or never prepare for war."

O'Brien appealed to all who were ready to strike should the Convention be arrested, to hold up their hands, when the whole meeting raised their hands and cheered enthusiastically. The following resolutions were unanimously carried :—

"1st.—That the Government and local authorities have committed high treason against the Queen and constitution, by attempting to disperse the people of Birmingham peacefully assembled for the discussion of their mighty grievances.

"2nd.—That in case the Government shall persist in dispersing the constitutional meetings of the people by physical force, we, the men of Newcastle, putting our trust in God, and resting upon our rights and the constitution, are determined to meet illegal force by constitutional resistance."

At Sunderland, a few hours' notice brought twenty thousand people from various parts of the county to the Town Moor, who expressed their indignant abhorrence of the proceedings of the Government and the Birmingham authorities. At Glasgow a similar spirit was manifested. Indeed from all parts resolutions poured into the offices of the *Northern Star* and other democratic papers. A resolution passed at Northampton will

s

give an idea of the feelings excited by the above events.

"That this meeting would caution the liberty-loving whig Government, that if they will persist in putting down the present peaceful and legal agitation of the people by brute force, that they (the Government) will be held responsible for the consequences, even if the suffering people, writhing under a sense of the many acts of injustice inflicted on them, should leave at midnight their miserable homes in a blaze, and the destructive element communicating with everything around, reduce to one common ruin and desolation, the mansions of the rich and the hovels of the poor."

When the chairman read this resolution, the effect was electrical.   For a moment the meeting seemed transfixed. The next moment every hand was raised, and then followed a loud burst of applause.   Such is a specimen of numbers of resolutions agreed to by the Democrats of Great Britain on the above exciting occasion.

While the greatest excitement reigned in the agitated districts, Messrs. Atwood and Fielden were not idle in the Legislature.   Atwood presented the Petition on the 14th of June.   It was signed—not by two or three millions, as was anticipated, but by one million two hundred and eighty thousand persons.   The House of Commons paid unusual deference to the public on the occasion, by throwing open its gallery for the admission of strangers ; and Atwood was allowed not only to state the objects of the Petition, but to speak at some length in their favour—a proceeding at variance with the standing rule of the House.   G. H. Smith objected to this course, but the objection was over-ruled by the Speaker.   Fielden was also allowed to address the House.   On the motion of Atwood, the Petition was ordered to be printed ; and he then gave notice that on an early day, he would move that the House resolve itself into committee for the purpose of considering the prayer of the Petition.   This having been done, the Petition was borne away by twelve men, to share the fate of all petitions for real reform.

On the 12th of July, Atwood accordingly made his motion in a very able speech.   He told the House that he had been personally connected with the getting up of the petition, giving, as his reason, his conviction of the last twenty years, that the people of England had not had common justice or common humanity extended to them.   He referred to petitions that had been presented in the years 1816, 1819, and 1825, when the people were in great distress from the operation of the government measures on the currency, showing how their complaints had been disregarded, while they (the members of

THOMAS ATWOOD

FROM A SCARCE ENGRAVING

Mr. Pitt, Sir Francis Burdett, and others in high station, and quoted from speeches of Lord John Russell and Earl Grey, in favour of their views.

O'Connell delivered a speech abusing the Chartists, and accusing them of high treason in talking of physical force ; although he had previously recommended the people to get a petition signed by five hundred thousand, who were in the petition to state themselves as being fighting men.   He admitted at the same time, that it was unfair to call for obedience from those who had no vote in the election of the Legislature.

Wallace was for household suffrage, vote by ballot, and payment of members.   He should support the motion.

General Johnson supported the motion, and charged the majority of the House with denying that the working class had any rights at all.   He was for universal suffrage, and vote by ballot.

Villiers thought that the petitioners had some ground for saying that that House should be differently constituted.   He did not see how the House could reasonably oppose the consideration of this gigantic Petition.

Oswald thought that if a committee were appointed, it could end in nothing but in its throwing out the first and leading principle of the Petition:—viz., universal suffrage.   He should hold himself exceedingly wrong to go into committee upon it.

Warburton, though not agreeing to the full extent with the petitioners, was for going into committee.   If he thought that a more extended representation would lead to a grappling with the National Debt, he would be the first to oppose it ; but he did not believe that such would be the case.

Wakley said the noble lord had referred to deposits in the savings' banks of Exeter.   It was impossible that these deposits could be made by the labouring people of that county out of six or seven shillings a week, which was the general amount of wages paid; and the deposits must be made by another class of people.   The agricultural population in the neighbourhood of the metropolis was in the greatest distress, and the labourers were lying in sheds, barns, and outhouses. (An hon. member—They are harvest men.)   He knew they were harvest men; but was that the way in which labourers ought to live, who were sweating and toiling under a burning sun all day to have no resting-place but a barn or a shed, and be clothed in rags ?   He wished the people to know that there was not the slightest chance of their being heard in that House. He would say to them, don't waste your energies by again presenting a petition to this House.   Don't waste your time by presenting petitions to persons who will never lend a willing ear to them. He would say to them, if he were speaking to them out of doors, form your associations, discuss your grievances, make known your wants, and make friends and not enemies of your neighbours. Try to win by constant discussions, and to advance in the good will of the middle class of society. Join with them in such a demand, as shall at last have an effect on this assembly. But as the House was at present constituted, they might as well petition the rock of Gibraltar, as address a petition to that House.

Messrs. Slaney, A. White, Fox Maule, T. Acland, and Sir J. Y. Buller, opposed the motion.

Schofield rose and addressed the House, but the calls for a division were so loud and frequent, that it was with great difficulty a few sentences were heard. He said that he was an advocate for keeping faith with the public creditor, and he was not for a division of property. He was in favour of a property tax, which would make taxation more equal on classes, rich and poor.

Atwood in reply, combatted Lord John Russell's argument on deposits in the savings' banks; stating that the whole amount deposited was £22,000,000, but of that sum there was but £2,000,000 in sums under £20. The remainder was the deposits of people in middling circumstances, and a large proportion of what might be called rich individuals—persons whose deposits amounted to £200, and many to more—and who thus received more for their money than they could by investing it in any other securities.

A division then took place, when out of the whole collective wisdom there appeared forty-eight, including tellers, in favour of the motion. Against it there appeared two hundred and thirty seven ; leaving a majority against taking into consideration the complaints of one million two hundred and eighty thousand of their countrymen, of no less than one hundred and eighty nine, exclusive of all the absent members, who almost without exception would, if present, have gone with the majority. Of those members who voted in favour of the motion, many who had been radical leaders, and who were qualified to speak, contented themselves with giving a silent vote. Among those were Sir W. Molesworth, D. W. Harvey, J. T. Leader, and W. Williams—thus proving how poor is the support the people have to expect from parliamentary Radicals. Lord John Russell's speech was a continued tissue of illogical absurdities, which would have disgraced a dunce at school ; and as to the amount of sympathy shown for the people, why he strained every nerve to disprove the existence of distress which was every day draining the hearts of hundreds of thousands. This was a greater insult than that of the wretched abortion of humanity, who, in answer to Wakley's statement about the distress of the agricultural labourers, exclaimed, " They are harvest men," as if harvest men were not entitled to the common necessaries of life, but were doomed to waste their lives in gathering riches for their lords and masters. Altogether there could not well have been exhibited a more utter regardlessness of the people's rights, or a more supreme indifference to their condition, than was shown on the above occasion by the House of Commons ; and that House only tended by its heartless conduct to confirm the opinion, already widely spread, that nothing short of a bloody revolution could ever enable the people to wrest their rights from their oppressors.

The Convention re-assembled at Johnson's Tavern, Bolt Court, Fleet-street, in accordance with the motion agreed to at Birmingham, on Wednesday July the 10th. Even if that day had not been fixed, their removal would have been a matter of necessity ; for so great was the terrorism exercised by the authorities, that they were left without a room in which to hold their sittings. At the first London sitting, Cardo moved the suspension of the standing orders, in order that the Convention might proceed with the discussion on the sacred month, which was seconded by Neesom, but strongly opposed by Dr. Fletcher, and negatived without a division. The Convention then adopted the following resolution, on the motions of Messrs. Carpenter and Cardo, and which was strongly supported by Messrs. Hetherington, Neesom, Woodhouse, and Burns. Resolved :—

" That this Convention has read with feelings of inexpressible indignation, the statements said to have been last night made in the House of Commons by the Secretary of State for the Home Department, relative to the necessity and propriety of employing the metropolitan police force in various parts of the country, for the suppression of public meetings of the people, peaceably conducted. And further, the approbatory remarks of the same minister, of the bloody-minded and atrocious assault made upon the people of Birmingham, by a portion of that unconstitutional and obnoxious force. And this Convention is of opinion, that wherever and whenever persons assembled for just and legal purposes, and conducting themselves without riot or tumult, are assailed by the police or others, they are justified upon every principle of law and self-preservation, in meeting force by force, even to the slaying of the persons guilty of such atrocious and ferocious assaults upon their rights and persons."

On the 13th of July, the motion of Atwood having been rejected, the Convention proceeded to the discussion of the sacred month. There was but a thin attendance, a large number of the members, for various reasons, being in the country. Lowery said it was useless to expect anything from the House of Commons. Belgium and America did not get liberty until they took it, nor would the people of this country. He had been in Scotland, Cumberland, and Westmoreland, and the people were of opinion that the best time for commencing the sacred month was when the corn was ripe, and the potatoes were on the ground. He agreed with that opinion, and he would move the following resolution :—

"The House of Commons having refused to go into committee on the prayer of the National Petition, it is vain to expect redress from that House. It is therefore the opinion of the National Convention, that the people should work no longer after the 12th of August next, unless the power of voting for members of parliament, to protect their labour, is guaranteed to them."

A member was about to address the assembly, when a message arrived from Messrs. Atwood and Fielden, requesting a deputation from the Convention. A deputation was appointed, who waited on the hon. members, and asked them what the Chartists were now to do? They recommended more petitions, as those who spoke in the debate against the motion, denied that the Petition was the petition of the people. Atwood thought they ought to get up petitions in all the parishes of Britain. They replied they would never petition again, as they found it was of no use. The deputation having reported, a letter was read from Dr. Taylor, stating that in the manufacturing districts, the organization for the sacred month was going on like a house on fire. Messrs. Deegan and Moir both recommended caution in fixing the day for the sacred month—the discussion on which was adjourned to Monday, and re-adjourned to Tuesday, when Lowery's motion was carried for the holiday to commence on the 12th of August.

As might have been anticipated, from the thinness of the numbers who adopted the above motion, the subject of the sacred month again came under discussion. O'Brien had been addressing numerous meetings in the country, and making strict enquiries of the leading men in the various districts, as to the preparedness of the people ; and the results led him to doubt the propriety of the motion which had been agreed to in the absence of many important members ; and in accordance with his views, he introduced a resolution to the

T

Convention on the 16th of July, adding reasons for its adoption. Resolved :—

" That while the Convention continues to be unanimously of opinion, that nothing short of a general strike, or suspension of labour throughout the country, will ever suffice to re-establish the rights and liberties of the industrial classes, we nevertheless cannot take upon ourselves the responsibility of dictating the time or circumstances of such strike, believing that we are incompetent to do so for the following reasons :—

" 1st—Because our numbers have been greatly reduced by the desertion, absence, and arbitrary arrests of a large portion of our members.

" 2nd—Because great diversity of opinion prevails amongst the remaining members as to the practicability of a general strike, in the present state of trade in the manufacturing districts.

" 3rd—Because a similar diversity of opinion seems to prevail out of doors amongst our constituents and the working class generally.

" 4th—Because, under these circumstances, it is more than doubtful whether an order from the Convention for a general holiday would be generally obeyed, or whether the strike would not be a failure.

"5th—Because, while we firmly believe that an universal strike would prove the salvation of the country, we are at the same time equally convinced that a partial strike would only entail the bitterest privations and sufferings on all parties who take part in it, and, in the present exasperated state of public feeling, not improbably lead to confusion and anarchy.

"6th—Because, although it is the duty of the Convention to participate in all the people's dangers, it is no part of our duty to create danger unnecessarily, either for ourselves or others. To create it for ourselves would be folly—to create it for others would be a crime.

"7th—Because we believe that the people themselves are the only fit judges of their right and readiness to strike work, as also of their own resources and capabilities of meeting the emergencies which such an event would entail. Under these circumstances, we decide that a committee of three be appointed to reconsider the vote of the 16th instant, and to substitute for it an address, which shall leave to the people themselves to decide whether they will or will not commence the sacred month on the 12th of August, at the same time explaining the reasons for adopting such a course, and pledging the Convention to co-operate with the people in whatever measures they may deem necessary to their safety and emancipation."

Pitkeithly seconded the motion.

O'Connor moved, and James Taylor seconded the following amendment :—

"That the Secretary be directed to summon forthwith, by letter and advertisement, every member of the Convention, for Wednesday, the 31st of July, for the purpose of taking into consideration the most effectual means for carrying out the ulterior measures for the accomplishment of universal suffrage, and to impress upon the minds of the delegates the absolute necessity of coming prepared with the views of their constituents."

A long discussion followed, during which many of the delegates did not appear to be animated by any very amiable feelings. O'Connor, in the course of his speech, argued both for and against the holiday, which drew forth from Dr. Fletcher an observation, that with regard to his speech he could make nothing of it. It was evident that O'Connor was opposed to the sacred month, while he feared to brave the disapprobation of its supporters. Ultimately O'Brien's resolution was carried by a majority of six; twelve voting for, six against, and seven remaining neutral. The committee on the subject was extended to five, consisting of Messrs. O'Connor, O'Brien, Fletcher, Lowery, and Neesom. That the Convention took the wisest course which it was in their power to take, we will make evident from the fact, that for O'Brien's motion there voted, Burns for Dundee, Carpenter for Bolton, Hetherington for London, Knox for Durham, O'Connor for Yorkshire, O'Brien for London, Manchester, Stockport, and other places; Pitkeithly for Yorkshire, Smart and Skevington for Leicester, Derby, and Loughboro', Taylor for Rochdale, Woodhouse for Nottingham, and Cleave for London. Against these were Lowery for Northumberland, Mealing for Bath, Marsden for Preston, Neesom for Bristol, Osborne for Brighton, and Wolstoneholme for Sheffield. It will be seen that the majority represented most of the populous districts. True, some of that majority voted for the holiday; but the very fact of their supporting O'Brien's motion, was proof that they had their doubts of its propriety. With regard to Bristol, there was a letter from Frost, who was on the spot, and who stated his conviction that the people would not strike. He also stated that the people of Wales were not prepared. A strike at Bath would have been ineffectual, as that city has no trade, and is dependent in a great measure on the Aristocracy and gentry, who could leave it at their pleasure; the same remark applies to Brighton. At Preston the Democrats, though warm in the cause, were comparatively few in number.

Peter Bussey, though the first to propose the strike, had become convinced of its impracticability. Craig, who signed the resolution for the holiday, declared that the Convention had committed suicide, and resigned his post. Duncan, the Dumfries delegate, was opposed to it. Dr. Fletcher, who voted for it, declared that the evidence in its favour was anything but satisfactory. Richardson had written a letter from Manchester, stating the unpreparedness of the people, which was corroborated by his colleague Dean. Under these circumstances, who but a man whom excitement had driven to the verge of madness, or a traitor in the interest of the enemy, would have continued in favour of the holiday? And yet, so reluctant are men to retract their errors, that a few clung to the project like men leading a forlorn hope, and tried to persuade themselves that they were the nation, or at least its representatives. Happy was it that they were frustrated in their efforts, or a portion of the country would have been deluged with its best blood, the blood of the most honest and enthusiastic devotees of justice and liberty ; and that, too, without a single advantage accruing to the cause.

The proceedings at Birmingham still continued to be productive of intense excitement, more especially in the North of England. After the meeting held at Newcastle in the Lecture Room, large gatherings of the people took place every day in the open air. On the Monday two bands arrived from Winlaton and Swalwell, followed by immense multitudes of people, who made their way to the Forth, which was filled with one vast crowd of human beings excited to the highest degree. The announcement of the arrest of their delegates, Taylor and Harney, only fanned the flame, and strong resolutions were passed on the subject. The chairman, Mr. Hepburn, requested them to abstain from cheering; but he was answered by tremendous shouts. Meetings of the same enthusiastic character continued to be held during the week, attended by thousands upon thousands of the toiling classes. On the following Sunday the rain poured down in torrents; but despite the weather, a band played through the streets to the tune of "Rule Britannia," and thousands collected in the Forth under the drenching rain. On Monday, Tuesday, and Wednesday, the meetings were continued, and were addressed by Messrs. Ayr, Charlton, Cockburn, Byrne, and others; some of whom read accounts from the papers as to the state of the country. On Monday, July the 22nd, news arrived of the arrest of Williams and Binns at Sunderland, on a charge of sedition ; and the consequence was another public meeting in the Forth on the following evening, equal to any that had previously taken place, when resolutions of sympathy with the persecuted, and pledging the meeting to the sacred month, were unanimously passed. But the authorities of Newcastle were in the meantime, in imitation of their Birmingham brethren, preparing to strike a blow at the right of public meeting. On the Assizes being held, the grand jury, without any previous notice, found true bills against Bronterre O'Brien, William Thomason, John Mason, James Ayr, and Thomas Devyr, for the speeches delivered by them in the Lecture Room on the 7th of July, and those gentlemen were speedily arrested. Proclamations were also issued against public meetings, which were met by the Democrats presenting a requisition to Mr. John Fife, the Mayor, requesting him to convene a public meeting to address the Queen against any increase of the standing army, and the establishment of the rural police, both of which measures were before the Legislature. At the last hour the Mayor declined calling the meeting, and the requisitionists called it themselves in the Forth. On Sunday the Chartists went in a body and filled St. Nicholas' church during divine service, to the great annoyance of the regular attendants. The meeting in the Forth passed off with the strictest order and decorum ; but just as the multitude was dispersing, the Mayor appeared at the head of the special constables, police, and military, and was loudly groaned at. This physical force party seized some of the banners, and maltreated several of the people in a shocking manner. The unarmed people acted with the utmost possible forbearance ; and though plenty of missiles were at hand, but few were made use of. This attack took place after nightfall, and it was not owing to the discretion of the authorities that Newcastle was not placed in a similiar state to Birmingham. The traitor Mayor received the doubtful honour of Knighthood for his share of the transaction. We say traitor, for this man had formerly been one of the loudest advocates of the right of public meeting ; but then it was to serve the purposes of the middle class. In justice to Fife, we must insert a specimen or two of his former eloquence. A great meeting was held in the Spital, Newcastle, on the 13th of May, 1832. Earl Grey had resigned office in consequence of the King refusing to create Peers for the purpose of carrying the Reform Bill, and the meeting was convened to express its opinion on the subject. Fife was one of the speakers, and he took occasion to allude to a speech of Fox on the Seditions' Bills of 1795. " During that discussion he (Fox) said, 'The Houses of Commons and Lords may pass these bills, they may even receive the royal sanction, and yet be so unconstitutional, so grevious to the sense of the nation, that obedience is no longer a moral duty, and insurrection itself justifiable.' On a future occasion, when he was called upon by Pitt to explain, he only repeated the words, and said, ' In these principles I will live and die.' " " Here," said Fife, " is an immense multitude ; and is there one man who will not join me in holding up his right hand, and repeat after me—In these principles I will live and die ?" At this appeal, the immense multitude upraised their hands, and repeated the vow ; and immediately after, the same multitude again upraised their hands, each of which grasped an oak sapling. The above scene continued for several minutes, and then Fife resumed, " I know that many of my fellow country-men are armed, that many others are arming, and every man in this country has as good a right to his arms as the Marquis of Londonderry ; and I hold that the most ignorant and simple-minded man in this assembly is as likely to make a proper use of them. I, however, call upon you to remember, that the recourse to violence is the last and worst resort. The House of Commons still stands between this country and a revolution. If it only prove that it is the representative of the nation, the people may obtain their rights without confusion and bloodshed. Let us, therefore, with one voice exclaim—Privilege of parliament, privilege of parliament! But, remember, until that cry is disregarded—until privilege of parliament ceases to exist, or is grossly violated ; then, and not till then, shall I for one exclaim, ' To your tents, oh Israel.' "

At a meeting on the Town Moor, on the 27th of May, 1833, Fife said:—

"Your crowd is weeded of all those timid, self-interested, half-whig men, who swelled our numbers on former occasions, though they were the mere tools of the whig Aristocracy. You are stronger without them; your masses to-day contain none but the best. Half a million of honest men were ready to sacrifice their lives for the achievement of the Reform Bill, and could the Tories have relied upon the slavery of the army, they would have deluged this unfortunate country with all the bloodshed and horrors of civil war, to preserve their own ascendancy. The army sympathized with their fellow country-men. Our brave soldiers would not turn their swords against their fathers and brothers at the bidding of a dishonest Aristocracy. The Aristocracy have broad lands, superb castles, monstrous privileges; can they not be content with these? Have they forgotten the fate of the French *noblesse?* Do they know that the destruction of the French *noblesse* might have been prevented by giving bare justice to the people? As they value their privileges, as they would retain their property, as they regard their very existence, I warn them to relax their grasp from the rights and the property of the people while it is yet time, and before that grasp is paralysed by the people's vengeance."

Such, in former days, was the Mr. Fife who caused his townsmen to be bludgeoned and sabred for meeting peaceably, to enter their indignant protest against a system of despotism, worse than any existing before the Reform Bill; the despotism of a spy police, in the hands of such petty usurpers as Fife, and his infamous, traitorous faction.

On the following day, John Bell, printer of the *Northern Liberator*, was arrested for printing an address to the middle class; and on Friday, eight persons were examined for the proceedings in the Forth, and committed for trial at the assizes. It was admitted, in evidence, that the Riot Act was not read previous to the attack on the people.

Other parts of the country were no more fortunate than Newcastle. At Stockport, James Mitchell, Charles Davies, John Wright, James Briton, Isaac Armitage, Cornelius Armitage, George Brushworth, Isaac Armitage, junior, David Roberts, aud Timothy Higgins, were arrested for possessing arms ; the police bursting into their houses at dead of night, and using the utmost violence ; breaking valuables, seizing papers, and committing many acts of the pettiest malignity, though not the slightest violence was offered to them.

At the Montgomeryshire assizes, forty persons were tried and found guilty of training, drilling, riot, &c., and were sentenced to various terms of transportation and imprisonment. At Llanidloes the Chartists were so strong during the excitement, that the magistrates committed the peace of the town to their keeping, imploring them to use their power to save life and property, which for a period of fifteen days they performed most faithfully. At the assizes a bench warrant was issued against Charles Jones, delegate to the Convention, and a reward offered for his apprehension ; but he was never taken, and died some time after of consumption, accelerated by the difficulty of his position.

At the Warwick assizes, the trial of Lovett and Collins was proceeded with. Lovett conducted his own defence, making an able exposure of the authorities, and manfully maintaining the right of public meeting, in support of which he quoted many authorites, and amongst others, Lord John Russell. As a matter of course, both the defendants were found guilty—it could hardly be otherwise, when two of their jury had previously declared that they should like to see all the Chartists hanged. These men were challenged by Lovett, but the objection was overruled. The jury did not deliberate more than two or three minutes, before they returned their verdict, and the defendants were each sentenced to twelve months' imprisonment. Jeremiah Howell, Francis Roberts, John Jones, and Thomas Aston, were sentenced to death, but the punishment was, after strong representations made to the government, commuted into one of transportation for life. Many other prisoners were visited with various terms of imprisonment.

At Monmouth, Vincent, Edwards, Dickinson, and Townshend were put upon their trial for sedition, and attending illegal meetings; witnesses swore that people attended the meetings with sticks, and that Vincent said, in the course of his speech, their cry should be, "To your tents, oh Israel! and then with one heart, one voice and one blow, perish the privileged orders, death to the Aristocracy, up with the people, and the government they have established." Roebuck defended the prisoners, but they were found guilty, and sentenced, Vincent to twelve, Edwards to nine, and Dickinson and Townshend to six months' imprisonment. Vincent applied for the use of books and writing materials, but was told that he could have none but religious books.

The arrests continued. Deegan was apprehended for having at a public meeting in Rochdale recommended the people to arm. William Benbow, John Livesey, and Timothy Booth were arrested, the first for attending an illegal meeting, the second for dealing in arms, and the third for having arms in his possession, and the whole of them were committed for trial. Dr. M'Douall and John Bradley were also committed for attending an unlawful meeting at Hyde.

At Devizes the grand jury returned true bills against Messrs. Roberts, Potts, and Carrier, who had been arrested for sedition and attending unlawful meetings; but no notice was even taken of an organized attack made on the Chartists at Devizes, by a mob of five hundred persons, under the patronage of the upper class, who assailed Vincent and others with stones, brickbats, and knives, and exposed their lives to imminent danger.

At Stockport, two other persons were arrested for sedition, by the names of Isaac Johnson, and the Rev. W. Essller; and at Manchester, Messrs. Richardson, Smith, Tillman, Finney, and Doyle, and Rev. W. V. Jackson, were arrested for various political offences. Feargus O'Connor was also brought before the court at Manchester, in consequence of five true bills that had been found against him at the Liverpool assizes, and he was fully committed for trial; but what seemed remarkable was, that while bail to the amount of £1,000 had been demanded of working men for their appearance, only £600 was demanded of O'Connor, a fact which drew from that gentleman some deprecatory observations. Bronterre O'Brien was not only visited with the persecution of the Newcastle authorities, but a second warrant of arrest was made out against him in Lancashire, and he was seized in London, and subjected to many hardships and indignities.

At Sheffield things began to look ominous. Large meetings assembled in the open air at night, at which not a word was spoken. Several persons were arrested in connection with these meetings, which were dispersed by the military. The above persons were but a few of those arrested; large numbers continued to be seized by the authorities in numerous districts throughout England. In modern times there was never previously so determined an attempt made by any government to crush a political party, as was made by the whig Government to put down the Chartists. When the working men found their right of public meeting infringed, they resorted to a novel method of displaying their numbers. Hundreds, sometimes thousands, of them assembled on Sundays, and crowded the churches, of which they generally sent previous notice to the clergy recommending them to preach from certain texts, such as, " The husbandman that laboureth shall be first partaker of the fruits;" " He who will not work, neither shall he eat;" and texts of a kindred character; but it was seldom that the clergy complied with their requests. They chose rather to preach upon passive obedience, and the folly of looking to the things of this life; a doctrine which only served to exasperate their hearers, who could not always be restrained from expressing their indignant feelings at the hypocrisy of the men who could preach this doctrine, while they were themselves in the enjoyment of every luxury. Sometimes the Chartists attended the churches in such numbers as to leave room for nobody else. They took possession of the pews of the gentry, who had to return home, or stand in the aisles all the time that the service was performed. The numerous arrests that took place led to the establishment of a defence fund, and collectors were appointed in the various towns to raise subscriptions. Sometimes these collections almost amounted to a levying of black mail, for the collectors carried with them two books, one of which was styled the " black book," in which were entered the names of those who refused to subscribe.

At Leeds, two persons named White and Wilson, were

arrested for using threats to the shopkeepers, on whom they waited to solicit subscriptions. George White was a working man, a native of the sister isle, and had long taken an active part in Radical movements. He was noted for his inflexible perseverance, and determination in everything which he undertook to perform. He was ever ready for whatever kind of work fell to his lot; whether it was to address a meeting, write a report, or collect a subscription, he was equally clever in each transaction. In battering the head of a policeman he was quite at home, and if circumstances had favoured, he would just as readily have headed an insurrection, quite regardless, we believe, of the danger to himself. George's chief talent as a speaker lay in his ready wit and poignant sarcasms, which were launched forth in language anything but classical, and by no means agreeable to the polite circles, though exceedingly well relished by men of a similar stamp to himself. George never did things by halves, but went the whole hog in everything which he undertook; and he never stooped to dissimulation. If he committed a wrong, he acknowledged the act, and defended it as frankly as though he had performed the most meritorious action. When accused by an opponent of having used unfair means to disparage him, he replied, "Well, did not I tell you that I meant to put you down? and I have done it." It is possible to justly charge George White with his almost utter want of courtesy; but his veriest enemy could never accuse him of anything approaching to cant, to which he always appeared an entire stranger.

The committee which had been appointed by the Convention to collect evidence regarding the practicability of the sacred month, proceeded with their labours, making every enquiry which could enable them to come to a right decision on the subject; and that enquiry led them to conclude, that the project, if sought to be carried out, would prove an utter failure. Although three of the members of the committee had voted for the holiday, this opinion was unanimous. Acting on their report, the General Council of the Convention passed the following resolution on the 6th of August. Moved by Bronterre O'Brien, and seconded by Feargus O'Connor :—

"That from the evidence which has reached this Council from various parts of the country, we are unanimously of opinion, that the people are not prepared to carry out the sacred month, on the 12th of August. The same evidence however, convinces us that the great body of the working people, including most of the trades, may be induced to leave work on the 12th instant, for two or three days, in order to devote the whole of that time to solemn processions, and solemn meetings;

for deliberating on the present awful state of the country, and devising the best means of averting the hideous despotism with which the industrious orders are menaced by the murderous majority of the upper and middle classes, who prey upon their labour. We, at the same time, beg to announce to the country, that it is the deliberate opinion of this Council, that unless the trades of Great Britain shall co-operate as united bodies with their more distressed brethren, in making a grand national moral demonstration on the 12th instant, it will be impossible to save the country from a revolution of blood, which after enormous sacrifices of life and property, will terminate in the utter subjection of the working people to the monied murderers of society. Under these circumstances, we implore all our brother Chartists to abandon the project of a sacred month as being for the present utterly impracticable, and to prepare themselves forthwith to carry into effect the aforesaid constitutional objects on the 12th instant. We also implore the united trades, if they would save the country from convulsion, and themselves and families from ruin, to render their distressed brethren all the aid in their power, on or before the 12th instant, towards realizing the great and beneficent object of the holiday."

The publishing of this resolution had the effect of putting a stop to the national holiday; and, in conformity with its advice, the people met in large numbers in the Chartist districts, and passed addresses to the Queen, praying her to dismiss her advisers, and call men to her councils who would redress the grievances of the people. The 12th of August did not, however, pass off without some little disturbances in a few places, at Bolton, Wigan, Chorley, Hendley, and some other towns; but considering the state of the country, the attempt of the Convention to prevent the shedding of human blood was highly successful. The Convention deputed Feargus O'Connor to attend a large delegate meeting in Glasgow, which took place on the 21st of August, there being fifty seven delegates in attendance. The delegates gave in reports on the state of the towns from whence they were deputed, from which reports it appeared that although in some places the Chartists were ready to adopt extreme measures, the majority were for moral agitation only, combined with some of the milder ulterior measures adopted by the Convention. Scarce any were favourable to a sacred month, and the majority deplored the want of better organization. O'Connor, and Mason from Newcastle, laid before them the state of feeling in England, and were received with great applause. It soon became evident, however, that if there were a number of enthusiastic

U 2

spirits, who were ready ro make any sacrifices for the cause, even to the carrying out of the sacred month, and the sacrifice of their lives, the great majority were not prepared to act even upon the other ulterior measures; a comparative few carried them out; but, generally speaking they were disregarded, and the Convention soon found itself in a position to dissolve. That body had become materially weakened in numbers through resignations and arrests. From the time of its first assembling to the close of its labours, no less than twenty-one resigned their seats, The names of these were J. P. Cobbett, Dr. Wade, R. K. Douglas, T. C. Salt, B. Hadley, J. Pierce, P. Matthews, H. Craig, W. N. Lankey, J. Wroe, J. Wood, J. Good, J. Harris, J. Whittle, B. A. Fight, R. J. Richardson, W. Rider, A. Halley, W. Gill, J. Finney, and J. Mills, while five or six others who were elected, never attended any of the meetings ; and although some of the vacancies were filled up, the resignations considerably detracted from the power of the Chartist body, by causing dissensions in the various localities where harmony and strength had previously existed. Under these circumstances, at a sitting of the Convention on September the 6th, O'Brien made a motion that the body should dissolve, which was seconded by Dr. Taylor ; eleven voted for, and eleven against the motion. Frost, the chairman, gave his casting vote for the dissolution. Those who voted for the resolution, were Messrs. Bussey, Skevington, Richards, Barry, Jones, Cardo, Pitkeithly, O'Brien, Harney, Hetherington, Frost, and Dr. Taylor. Against it were Messrs. Burns, Lowery, Neesom, Hartwell, O'Connor, Wolstoneholme, Carpenter, Jackson, Smart, James Taylor, and Deegan. Such was the end of the first Convention, which numbered amongst its members many men of superior talents, but who were so divided upon matters of policy, as to bring about results fatal to the glorious mission which they had undertaken. The great mistake of the Convention was in presuming to act before they were possessed of the requisite power to ensure success. A portion of the body were too timid and sluggish, another portion too hasty and precipitate, and those possessing the requisite energy to accelerate the cause, and preserve the even balance between the two extremes were but few, too few to turn the current of popular opinion in the right direction. A considerable number were ever vacil-lating between the fear of danger on the one hand, and the taunts of cowardice on the other. The paucity of signatures to the petition was a proof that much of the work of conver-sion was yet to be accomplished ; and if they had set them-selves steadily about that work, instead of seeking to force

DR. M'DOUALL
FROM A SCARCE ENGRAVING

ulterior measures on a people as yet unprepared for their adoption, they would have produced fifty times as much good, without a tithe of the mischief which resulted from their policy. Still that mischief might have been greater. The untiring perseverance of O'Brien, and a few others, saved the country from a horrible carnage, which must inevitably have followed any attempt to carry out the sacred month. If the Convention had its shortcomings, it had also its virtues. Many of its members showed an energy, an inflexibility of purpose, and a patriotism which could not fail to win for them a large amount of admiration and esteem, and their efforts will long be engraven on the memories of thousands of their countrymen.

Before the Convention had dissolved many of the trials of Chartist leaders had already taken place. Exclusive of the convictions at Warwick and Montgomery, several were arraigned at the Chester assizes. A short time previous to those events, the Rev. Joseph Rayner Stephens had become more moderate in his expressions, and in a sermon, the last he delivered before surrendering himself for trial, he shifted completely round ; and instead of teaching that doctrine of resistance which previously had formed the staple of all his exhortations, he told his hearers to be content with whatever might be their lot. There were some slight expressions of disapprobation at this wondrous change; but such homage as had been accorded to Stephens is not destroyed in a day, and generally, but little notice was taken of the matter. He was about to suffer for his past denunciation of oppression, and, that thought seemed uppermost in the minds of his audience. On the 15th of August, the reverend gentleman was tried at Chester, before Mr. Justice Pattison, and a special jury. He defended his own cause, unassisted by counsel, and in the course of his address, which occupied five hours in the delivery, he repudiated radical principles, which, he told the jury, he had done all in his own power to oppose amongst the people. He chiefly directed his observations to the question of the New Poor Law, which he quoted authorities to show was a law which ought not to be obeyed, because contrary to the word of God, and he carefully refrained from alluding to the evidence of his violent language. Despite his eloquence, however, the jury found him guilty, and he was sentenced to eighteen months' imprisonment. Very different however, was the treatment of Stephens, to that of many others; for he was allowed all the comforts which a man under imprisonment could enjoy.

At the same assizes, Dr. M'Douall, with Bradley of Hyde,

was put upon his trial for sedition, and attending an unlawful meeting, over which Bradley presided. M'Douall also defended himself, and delivered an address which lasted four hours, and which for force, eloquence, and boldness, was equal, if not superior, to any of the defences of the Chartist prisoners. His description of the altered condition of the working class was most pathetic, and he cleverly alluded to the former proceedings of his prosecutors, who had, when out of office, committed the very offences with which he was charged. The force of his eloquence, however, was turned against himself; for the Attorney General alluded to it as a proof of the danger in allowing men of such talent to be at large. Both the prisoners were found guilty, and were sentenced, Bradley to eight, and M'Douall to twelve months' imprisonment. In order to prejudice M'Douall's case the more, the grand jury brought into court, during the trial, a second true bill against him for conspiracy, which led him to ask, whether that was the sort of justice he was to expect?

Messrs. Thompson, gun makers of Birmingham, Mitchell and Davies, of Stockport, and Higgins, of Ashton, were indicted for sedition, attending illegal meetings, exciting to disturb the public peace, and unlawful possession of arms. The grand jury requested leave to alter the bill to a charge of high treason, but were overruled by the Judge. All the prisoners were found guilty, and each was sentenced to eighteen months' imprisonment. Twelve other prisoners traversed to the next assizes. At Liverpool the work of imprisonment was also briskly proceeded with. John Holmes was found guilty of walking at the head of a procession with a red cap on the top of a pole. Edward Riley was convicted of military training and riot near Manchester. T. Radcliffe was indicted for seditious conspiracy and riot at Wigan, and found guilty of the latter. J. Fairplay was tried for illegal training, and convicted; and between twenty and thirty others were tried for various offences of a similar nature, and found guilty. They were all sentenced to various periods of imprisonment. A large number of the accused traversed to the following assizes.

Notwithstanding the raging persecution of the Government, the Chartists continued to hold their meetings, though generally within doors. An attempt was made to introduce the question into the sister isle. There was a small band of Chartists at Dublin, at the head of whom was Patrick O'Higgins, a merchant. Lowery was invited to the fair city, and a meeting was got up for his reception. O'Connell sounded the note of alarm, and a *posse* of the coal-porters crowded to the meet-

ing, and made a dreadful uproar.   It was impossible for
Lowrey to make himself heard, even for a minute, and his
person was in danger of physical violence.   Availing himself,
however, of the known generosity of the Irish character, he
accosted the leader of the assault—an enormous sized man—
observing, " You see I am lame ; I place myself under your
protection."   Taking Lowrey by the arm, he exclaimed,
" Come on, my boy ; damn the man that shall touch you !"
and he led him safely out of the meeting.

   After the breaking up of the Convention, Dr. Taylor spent
a considerable time in the North, the authorities of Birmingham having abandoned the prosecution against him.   He addressed numerous meetings at Carlisle, Newcastle, and the
neighbourhood, and still spoke hopefully of the success of the
cause.   A curious incident occurred at one of the Newcastle
meetings.   The magistrates of Carlisle had issued a warrant
for his arrest, and the officers came to Newcastle to seek him.
Seeing him advertised to lecture, they purposed seizing him as
he entered the meeting.   The Doctor, however, had intimation
of their purpose, and did not make his appearance; but Byrne,
dressed in some of the Doctor's habiliments, marched up to
the lecture room, and the officers thinking their prey was at
hand, waited the favourable moment, and took him into
custody, and were a considerable time before they discovered
their mistake, which afforded food for merriment when related
to the meeting.   Julian Harney also repaired to the North,
after the dissolution of the Convention—for he was still at
liberty—being merely bound over to appear at Warwick when
called upon, which was tantamount to an abandonment of the
prosecution.   In the neighbourhood of Bradford, Peter Bussey
kept alive the democratic spirit, often addressing meetings in
that and the surrounding towns.   Feargus O'Connor was by
no means idle, visiting Sheffield, Nottingham, and numerous
other places, in all of which he was received with the
usual enthusiasm which attended his arduous labours.   In the
county of Durham, Williams and Binns, notwithstanding their
arrest, traversed the district, and kept alive the yet kindling
fire of agitation.   Indeed, all over the radical parts of the
country, the Democrats seemed resolved to continue their
career of agitation, and, if possible, to secure the triumph of
their cause.   Dr. Taylor was afterwards arrested, and bound
over for his appearance at the assizes ; and to show the lengths
to which the Government were resolved to go in crushing
every influential leader, it is only necessary to mention that,
they, through the local authorities, offered £100 to the editor
of the *Carlisle Patriot*, to induce him to appear as evidence

against the Doctor—an offer which, however, that gentleman magnanimously treated with the contempt which it deserved. Feargus O'Connor had not yet had enough of Conventions, and he proposed a scheme for the organization of another body, to consist of twenty-one members—thirteen for England and Wales, and eight for Scotland. The thirteen English delegates he offered to pay £2 per week each out of the proceeds of the *Northern Star*. His proposal met with little favour, it being regarded as a scheme for wresting the movement to his own purposes. It is needless to say, that such a body must necessarily have acted rather under his directions than under those of his constituents. It would indeed have made the Chartist movement not the movement of the body generally, but the movement of Feargus O'Connor, and there was yet enough of public virtue left to save them from such a degradation.

INTERIOR OF MONMOUTH COURT HOUSE
FAITHFULLY REPRESENTED
DURING THE TRIALS OF FROST, WILLIAMS, AND JONES, FOR HIGH TREASON
IN 1839-40

CHAPTER VIII.

THE WELSH INSURRECTION

It was not long after the occurrences noted in the previous chapter that an event happened which eclipsed all previous events in connection with the Chartist movement. It will be borne in mind that at the Liverpool dinner, Lord John Russell pointed out the dangers that always followed any attempts at suppressing public opinion. Those dangers had already been realized in the unfortunate occurrences at Birmingham and elsewhere, and they were now about to be realized on a more extensive scale. The important mining districts of Wales had sunk into a state of apparent apathy. Public meetings were abandoned, and the masses retired to nurture their burning resentment in secret. To add to their angry feelings, the authorities of Monmouth treated Vincent and the other Chartist prisoners with all the rigour dictated by the spirit of relentless persecution. They were subjected to the food, dress, and discipline of the most abandoned felons. Frost had, by memorials and other means, sought to obtain an alleviation of their miserable condition ; but all appeals to the clemency of their persecutors were in vain. The Welsh working class, possessed, as before observed, of warm and generous feelings, were highly indignant at this severe and uncalled for mode of treatment, and their resentment was speedily worked up to an uncontrollable pitch. The magistrates of Newport had received intelligence to the effect that an important movement was afoot. This they admitted ; perhaps they might with equal truth have admitted that they, through their agents, had taken a share in organising that movement for the pleasure of striking a blow at Chartism. Be this as it may, on the morning of the 4th of November, 1839, a large body of the working class from the hills of that district was observed to approach Newport. What the precise numbers were cannot correctly be stated, as the estimates were so various and conflicting   *The Times* stated them at eight thousand, the *Morning Chronicle* at one thousand, while an-

v

other account swelled the number to twenty thousand. A Chartist report estimated the gathering at ten thousand persons, which was probably correct. This large body of men had met on the previous night, despite the elements which were opposed to them, a heavy rain falling the whole of the night and drenching them to the skin. A considerable number had provided themselves with arms. A portion of them shouldered the musket, others were armed with pikes, a third detachment appeared with pitchforks, and a fourth with bludgeons, while a considerable number were destitute of any other arms than those supplied by nature. This mass of men marched through the dreary dark of a November night, halting in their course at various public-houses for the purpose of obtaining refreshment, and then remarching towards their destination, the town of Newport, which they reached about nine o'clock, accompanied by Frost their delegate to the late Convention. What their intended plan of operations was cannot with certainty be arrived at from the conflicting evidence given at the examinations, and on the trial; but one of their objects appeared to be the release of Vincent and his fellow-prisoners, whose harsh treatment in prison had so excited their indignation and abhorrence. A company of the 45th Regiment was stationed at the Westgate Hotel, and thither the multitude marched, loudly cheering as they proceeded through the streets. Arrived in front of the Hotel, an attack was immediately commenced; the magistrates, police, and specials were driven from the streets, and fled into the Hotel for refuge. The soldiers were stationed at the windows, through which a number of the people began to fire. It would appear, from some of the statements, that the attack was commenced by a man who was reported to be a deserter from the 45th Regiment, and who was shot dead in the encounter. The soldiers, as a matter of course, returned the fire. Holding such an advantageous position they were enabled to do so with effect, without themselves incurring any considerable danger; and the consequence was, that in about twenty minutes ten of the Chartists were killed upon the spot, and about fifty others wounded, some of them severely, and even dangerously. Having so far stood the fire of the soldiery from the windows, they then made an attempt to force their way into the Hotel; but this, which if attempted at first might have succeeded, they now found themselves unable to accomplish. The greater part of the people had taken their departure, and the remainder were defeated in their purpose by the various forces which were combined against them. One of those who fell in the attack upon the Westgate Hotel, was a youth whose enthusiasm and courage must command admiration even from the veriest opponent. He bore the name of Shell. That his whole soul was with the movement, and that he breathed the purest aspirations for liberty, will be found from the following letter to his parents:—

"Pontypool, Sunday Night, Nov. 4th, 1839.

"Dear Parents,—I hope this will find you well, as I am myself at this present. I shall this night be engaged in a glorious struggle for freedom, and should it please God to spare my life, I shall see you soon; but if not, grieve not for me, I shall have fallen in a noble cause. Farewell!

"Yours truly,

"GEORGE SHELL."

This youth had but just attained the age of eighteen, and while volumes are written in praise of the heroes of despotism, the sublime and courageous devotion of this young apostle of liberty, who feared not to die for the object of his worship, is surely worthy of a place in history.

The whole district in and about Newport was thrown into a state of the utmost excitement by these unfortunate proceedings. A reward of £100 was at once offered for the arrest of Frost, for whom a search was immediately made at his own house, but without effect. The authorities, however, seized all the papers which fell in their way. On the same night they proceeded to the house of Mr. Partridge, a printer of Newport, to search for papers; and on forcing open the door, the first object that met their gaze was Frost, whom, together with Partridge, and a third person of the name of Waters, they forthwith arrested. The first appeared calm and collected, and partook of some bread and cheese and beer, previous to departing with the officers. These arrests were followed by several others; among the rest were those of Henry, son of Frost, a youth of fourteen, who was alleged to have been with the party that made the attack, and Zephaniah Williams, and William Jones, who were charged with leading other divisions of the Chartists, and who were to have joined the main body at Newport, but from various circumstances were delayed in their march. It was immediately ordered that a Special Commission should be held for the purpose of bringing the numerous prisoners to trial; every method being taken in the meantime to prejudice the public mind, more especially against Frost and the various members of his family. Some of the reports went so far as to assert, that Mrs. Frost and her daughters were in company with the insurgents at Blackwood, disguised as peasants. Others affirmed that they waved their handkerchiefs from the windows, as the attack was made upon the Westgate Hotel, and to these reports, neither of which con-

tained a particle of truth, the infamous press gave currency ;
for what object is sufficiently obvious.   If these reports had
been as true as they were notoriously false, and the movement
had been successful, the very same papers would have trumpeted these noble women to the world as heroines, and have
demanded honours for their patriotism.   Such is the press'
justice.   The infamous *Times* entered on a career of defama-
tion with respect to the character of Frost as cruel as it
was unprincipled, and outrageous to the feelings of every lover
of justice and humanity.   " Our own correspondent " raked
up every little incident of his past life, and so coloured the
whole as to make it tell fearfully against him ; and the paper
devoted leader after leader to the subject, all of which went to
show that nothing short of the blood of its victim would slake its
inordinate thirst for vengeance.   *The Times* found John Frost
guilty long before his trial, and prepared the way for the verdict of a perjured jury.   The apostate O'Connell contributed his
share to the sum total of prejudice ; and though in the same
speech in which he denounced Frost, he declared that he
would take the field rather than Ireland should be ruled by the
Tories, he at the same time offered 500,000 of his moral force
army to put down the Chartists.   Such were the freaks of that
incomparable specimen of political hypocrisy.   There was but
one thing wanting to complete the array of prejudice against
the doomed victims of the law of treason ; this was supplied by
the meek and lowly preacher of the sermon before the judges,
previous to the opening of the Special Commission.   The
reverend gentleman tried his best to impress his hearers with
a conviction of the guilt of the parties about to be tried.
Every effort was made by the authorities to suppress the circulation of anything bearing the name of Chartist.   The
Western Vindicator, Vincent's paper, which circulated widely
amongst the Welsh people, was seized wherever it could be
found, and was obliged at last to finally disappear.   The great
offence which the *Vindicator* had committed, was that of urging the Chartists, by all and every means, to save Frost and
his fellow-prisoners from an ignominious death.   Vincent,
from his prison, had continued to send a letter for insertion ;
plainly intimating, that the only way to effect that object, was
to assure their prosecutors that in case they carried out the
last sentence of the law, from that hour their own doom would
be sealed.   The cause of the prisoners was warmly taken up
by the Chartists throughout the country ; defence committees
were established ; O'Connor, O'Brien, Harney, Taylor, and the
various other leaders, addressed meetings in their behalf ; funds
rolled in.   O'Connor gave one week's profits of the *Star* to the

all-engrossing object. It was resolved to employ the best counsel for the defence. A Convention met in London to aid the cause, and a determination was manifested to try every available means to secure a verdict which would set the captives once more at liberty.

As the time for the sitting of the Special Commission approached, the greatest anxiety and excitement pervaded the public mind. Parties of Lancers were out scouring the neighbourhood of Monmouth, in order to prevent any gatherings of the discontented people, and on the 6th of January, the day for opening the Commission, the military were drawn up and reviewed in the Square. All the streets in the vicinity of the court-house were guarded by soldiers, and the London and Monmouth police. The applications for admission to the court were so numerous as to be exceedingly annoying to the officials. At half-past nine o'clock the prison van conveyed the prisoners from the gaol to the place of trial. It was guarded by the 17th Lancers, and the military were so stationed in the streets as to bar all approach on the part of the people. The prisoners, thirteen in number, descended from the van. Frost was escorted to the court by the gaoler; the others walked in two parties of six each, handcuffed and chained together. The whole of them exhibited a firm and unshaken demeanour. The Chief Justice, Sir Nicholas Tyndal, Mr. Baron Parke, and Sir John Williams arrived at ten o'clock. Sir John Campbell, Attorney General, Sir Thomas Wilde, Solicitor General, Mr. Sergeant Talfourd, Mr. Sergeant Ludlow, Mr. Whiteside, and Mr. Talbot, were counsel for the Crown, and Sir Frederick Pollock, Mr. Fitzroy Kelly, and Mr. Thomas, appeared for the prisoners. Feargus O'Connor sat next to the solicitors for the prisoners. The names of the prisoners called over were John Frost, Charles Waters, John Lovell, Richard Benfield, John Reece, George Turner, Zephaniah Williams, Edmund Edmonds, Jacob Morgan, Solomon Briton, William Jones, James Aust, and David Jones. The whole of the prisoners pleaded not guilty, and resolved to separate in their challenges. The names of a large number of jurors were called over, and challenged by the prisoners' counsel. On the name of one gentleman being called, he was challenged by the Atorney General on the part of the Crown, to which Sir Frederick Pollock objected, and urged that if the Crown was allowed peremptorily to challenge every juryman, a jury might be packed so as to deprive the prisoners of any chance of a fair trial; but the judges overruled the objection. Ultimately, the following gentlemen were sworn in as jurymen : John Daniel, Thomas

Davies, Richard Lewis, Edward· Brittle, James Hollings, Thomas Jones, Edward Reece, Edmund Smith, Christopher John, William Williams, John Richards, and John Capel Smith. On the following day the Attorney General was about to open the case against Frost when he was stopped by Sir Frederick Pollock, who said it would be useless for the learned gentleman to proceed with a case which could not be borne out by proofs. He then urged that the trial could not proceed, as the forms of law necessary in such cases had not been complied with. The law required that a copy of the indictment, a list of the jurors, and a list of the witnesses, should be at one and the same time furnished to the prisoner, ten days before the trial. The latter list had not been supplied at the same time as the other documents, a fact which the learned counsel argued was fatal to the proceedings. The objection was for the moment overruled ; but on the first witness being called, Sir Frederick renewed the objection, and it was ultimately decided that the trial should proceed, and the point left for the decision of the judges. On the following day a large number of witnesses were called. On Samuel Simmonds, the first witness, being put into the box, Sir Frederick Pollock objected to the evidence, inasmuch as·the residence of the witness had not been correctly described ; but this objection was likewise overruled. There were not fewer than thirty-seven witnesses called, and considering who those witnesses were, it is impossible to escape the conclusion that there must have been most extraordinary exertions made by the Government either to assist in organising this armed demonstration, or in using its influence afterwards to induce persons engaged in it to appear as accusers against their associates, for not fewer than twenty-five of the witnesses gave what is termed " Queen's evidence ;" in other words, they had more or less taken part in the demonstration. That the authorities adopted some underhand means of aiding the so-called insurrection was at the time very seriously believed. There was one man, who was described in the evidence as wearing a glazed hat, and who was stated to be one of the first in urging on the demonstration, but who was never seen afterwards. The prisoners' counsel subjected some of the witnesses to a searching cross-examination. When the case for the prosecution had closed, Sir Frederick Pollock addressed the jury on behalf of Frost, in a speech which occupied six hours in the delivery. He alluded in very pointed terms to the large demonstrations made by the Whigs in the reform agitation, comparing those demonstrations to that joined in by Frost. In reply to one witness, who stated that the prisoner's design was to take Newport, blow up the bridge, and prevent the Welsh mail from proceeding to Birmingham, Sir Frederick showed that the Newport mail only went as far as the Short Ferry, that another coach crossed the Ferry to Bristol, and that a third proceeded from Bristol to Birmingham; thus showing the absurdity of supposing that the Newport mail could act as a signal to the people of Birmingham. He then showed that the object of the demonstration was to procure the liberation of Henry Vincent, which line of argument he supported by numerous references to movements that had been set on foot for that object. Sir Frederick concluded his address in these words :—

" However differing in opinion from those who are called Chartists, I must do them the justice to say, that Chartism so far is not treason, nor the assertion of public conviction of it, rebellion. And I must go farther ; fatal as I think it will be to the happiness, prosperity, and well-being of this country, when these principles should be established, yet I must say, if it should be the confirmed opinion at any time of the large mass of intelligence and numbers—if the strength and sinews of the community, and if the intelligence which controls that strength, should finally determine to adopt the Chartists' code, doubtless adopted it will be, as the Reform Bill was, and mere wealth will struggle against it, in my opinion, in vain."

At the conclusion of this address, Kelly examined witnesses for the defence, and produced testimony counter to that which had been given on behalf of the Crown. One of the witnesses had stated in his examination, that some of the armed people accosted the officers at the Westgate Hotel, exclaiming, "Surrender yourselves our prisoners;" the counter evidence showed that the demand was, "Surrender our prisoners;" referring to some persons who were confined in the Hotel. The constable of Newport was one who gave this counter testimony. Several witnesses deposed to the excellent character for humanity which had been invariably borne by Frost. On the following day Fitzroy Kelly addressed the jury on behalf of Frost, in an eloquent speech of five hours and a half duration. Frost was asked whether he wished to add anything to what had been advanced by his counsel ; but he expressed himself so well satisfied with their exertions, that he declined making any observations. The Solicitor General addressed the court in reply, bringing prominently before the jury every tittle of evidence that could bear against the prisoner. The evidence of one Harris he never even alluded to, because it was of a contradictory character. Throughout his address, which occupied several hours during two days, there appeared a most anxious resolve to secure a conviction at any price. It is seldom, since the days of the notorious Jeffries, that a speech so breathing the spirit of vengeance has been delivered in a court of law.   After the Chief Justice had summed up the evidence, the jury retired, and in the short space of half an hour, returned into court with a verdict of guilty, accompanied by a recommendation to mercy.   The verdict caused great disappointment to the public generally, for it had been generally hoped and anticipated, that Frost would be acquitted of the capital charge.   It certainly is abhorrent to our feelings to reflect that twelve men, holding the life of a fellow-man in the balance, should have devoted so short a period as half an hour to a consideration of such weighty import, but as certainly it is not very surprising when we consider the undue exertions of a portion of the press, and other parties, to decide their minds beforehand against the accused.

After the trial of Frost had concluded, that of Zephaniah Williams was proceeded with, and many of the witnesses in the former case appeared against him.   Joseph Box Stockdale, deposed that he arrested the prisoner at Cardiff, on board the "Vintage," which was bound for Oporto.   Thomas addressed the jury for seven hours, entering into a clever critical analysis of the evidence, and declaring that there was not a single point of the People's Charter with which he did not agree.   He then brought forward witnesses in defence.   Thomas Lewis stated that the prisoner repeatedly admonished the people to keep the peace.   Daniel Lewis, a shopkeeper, swore to several acts of embezzlement of which Thomas Saunders (one of the witnesses for the crown) had committed while in his employ, and he swore that he would not believe him on his oath.   Richard F. Marsden, linen draper, had also been an employer of Saunders, he could not say whether he would believe him on his oath, and proved that he had stated a falsehood in giving his evidence.

On Monday, the 20th, Williams was again placed at the bar, and intimated his desire of addressing a few words to the court.   He stated that he was entirely innocent of the charge; that he had not the slightest intention of levying war against the Queen; and that most of what the witnesses had stated was false—so help him God!   Williams seemed deeply affected during this declaration.   The Attorney General having replied, Thomas rose, and again protested against any part of the evidence going to the jury, in consequence of the forms of law not having been complied with; but the question as in the case of Frost, was left for further consideration, and the learned Baron Parke proceeded to sum up the evidence; after which the jury retired, and in twenty-five minutes returned with a verdict of guilty ; and, as in the previous case, recommended the prisoner to mercy. William Jones was then placed at the bar, and shortly afterwards the court adjourned till the following day. The evidence against Jones was of course similar to that which had been given against Frost and Williams, and the verdict, and recommendation to mercy, were precisely the same as in those cases.

On Thursday, January 13th, 1840, Frost, Williams, and Jones were brought up to receive sentence. Frost exhibited the same calmness of demeanour that he had manifested throughout the trial. Williams appeared low and desponding, and Jones's manner was calm and dignified. The prisoners were then asked if they had anything to say why judgment should not be pronounced against them according to law. Mr. Geach applied for arrest of judgment on the ground that one of the jurors summoned was wrongly named. The objection was overruled, and the learned judges then put on the black caps, and proclamation was made for silence; when the Chief-Justice addressed the prisoners, and spoke of the awful crime of which they had been found guilty, the prevention of the consequences of which crime, he ascribed to the interposition of Divine Providence. He exhorted them to prepare for the great change which awaited them, and then proceeded to pass upon them the old and barbarous sentence, that they be taken to the place from whence they came, and from thence to the place of execution, there to be hanged by the neck until they were dead—that afterwards their heads should be severed from their bodies, their bodies quartered, and disposed of as Her Majesty should think fit ; and he concluded with the usual hope that the Lord would have mercy upon their souls. During the latter part of the sentence Frost raised his eyes, but neither Williams nor Jones manifested any signs of emotion ; and then all three were removed from the dock. Charles Waters, John Lovell, Richard Benfield, John Rees, and Jacob Morgan, pleaded guilty, and sentence of death was passed accordingly, with an intimation, however, that their punishment would be commuted to transportation for life. Fourteen other prisoners were placed at the bar ; some pleaded guilty, and were sentenced to various terms of imprisonment, while others were bound for their future good behaviour. A large number traversed to the assizes, and the Commission then terminated. Intense excitement reigned among the Chartists at the news of Frost's condemnation, and public meetings were summoned in the various towns of England and Scotland without delay, at which addresses to Her Majesty were adopted, praying her merciful consideration for the prisoners.

W

On Saturday, February the 1st, the objection raised by Sir F. Pollock on behalf of the prisoners, came before the fifteen judges in the Court of Exchequer. Sir Frederick Pollock, Mr. Fitzroy Kelly, and Sir William Follet appeared for the prisoners, and the Attorney General and Solicitor General on behalf of the Crown. The case was argued on both sides at considerable length, and ultimately their lordships decided by a majority, that the objection was valid. They, however, decided that the said objection, though valid, was not taken at the proper time; under these circumstances the Government deemed it the wisest course to effect a compromise, and it speedily became known that the extreme sentence of the law would not be carried into execution, but that the prisoners would be transported for life. Public opinion appeared to be decidedly opposed to the carrying out of the capital sentence, and the meetings to prevent it became more numerous than ever. Twenty-six gentlemen of wealth and influence, many of them members of parliament, addressed Lord Normanby on the subject, and doubtless this strong expression of opinion had its weight with the Government.

On Monday, February the 3rd, the prisoners, under escort of the military, were removed in the prison van from Monmouth, under an order from the Secretary of State, and conveyed to Chepstow, where a vessel was in waiting to receive and convey them to Bristol, from which place another vessel was despatched with them to the hulks at Portsmouth. On the day that the prisoners were removed from Monmouth, a Chartist meeting of thirty-three delegates was held at Manchester, when it was agreed to recommend the country to use every effort to save them from transportation. The family of Frost addressed a most feeling memorial to Her Majesty on their behalf; but Lord Normanby replied that he could not, consistently with his public duty, advise Her Majesty to accede to their prayer.

On Tuesday, March the 10th, Leader brought forward a motion in the House of Commons for an address to Her Majesty, urging her to grant Frost, Williams, and Jones, a free pardon; but his motion was supported only by seven members, including tellers. All efforts to save these victims of the law from transportation proved ineffectual; in a few weeks from the time of their conviction, they bade farewell to their native land. Mrs. Frost had a strong desire to accompany her husband, together with her family; but to this course Frost strongly objected. The following letter, the last he wrote previous to his exile, will show the state of his feelings on the subject, as well as the strong affection he bore towards those who were bound to him by the ties of kindred :—

"February 28th, 1840.

"My Dearest Mary,—While sailing down the Channel on Wednesday evening, our main and mizzen topmasts were carried away, and we were obliged to put in to refit. I thought I would embrace the opportunity of dropping you a few lines. I am quite uncertain as to our sentence; I have nothing but reports to guide me; you probably may be better informed. I have just seen a gentleman, high in authority, and his opinion is, that it would be most imprudent that you should remove to follow my fortune; besides, my love, life is uncertain. Suppose that anything should happen to me, what would become of my family in a foreign country, without a friend? In your own native land, no matter how the conduct of your husband may be censured (and my conduct is now public property,) you will be safe from the finger of scorn. Englishmen are too brave and too generous to allow either you, my now, alas! five orphan daughters, or the two boys to be insulted. I would not even charge my personal enemies, who now rejoice at the melancholy position in which their victim is placed, with being capable of such baseness. In your own native land, I repeat it with confidence, a confidence that wonderfully soothes my sufferings, you will experience that protection, that sympathy you could not expect at the hands of strangers. Follow, then, the advice that I give you; commence business, and trust to Providence for the result. A ship will sail in about three weeks; write by it, and give me every intelligence you possess. We are likely to sail this evening. Now then, my love, you have occasion for the exercise of your religion, your fortitude, and your resignation. Above all, place your confidence in that Being, without whose permission "not even a sparrow falls to the ground," Who is so jealously fond of us erring mortals, that He counts "the very hairs of our heads." Remember what you owe to our dear children, and oh! remember what a charge you have in so many young, unprotected, and delicate females. Be assured it is to them you must show your affection for your husband. To follow me would add to my present troubles. Once more, then, my dear Mary, exercise your judgment, and do not suffer your feelings to lead you from your home, or the sight of your countrymen. I trust your home will yet be a comfortable one. You will employ your daughters and yourself, and possibly you may yet see your husband in that son whom he so dearly prized. Surely, although the Government has been opposed to my politics, they will not persevere in inflicting

W 2

punishment when no legal conviction took place. The laws form the only protection Englishmen can boast of; and in seeking to be restored to my native land I only seek the protection and the exercise of those laws. Once more a belief that you and my family are as comfortable as you can be in my absence, would greatly lessen my affliction. Alas! my children—yea, my unhappy, my unprotected children—those pledges of our mutual love and affection haunt me day and night. My first prayer, my last prayer is for them, and that heaven may protect them. Branded as I am with the infamy of treason—a crime I never contemplated—I beg of you to give them the blessing of their wretched father, and to assure them, that though an exile, my hands are raised each morning and night to heaven for them. May the Comforter of the afflicted, and the Father of the fatherless, be your and my dear children's support and guide in all things! God bless you! my love.

Ever yours,

" JOHN FROST."

We must for the present take our leave of Frost and the Welsh Insurrection; but we shall yet have to notice in connection with it some important matters.

While the Government were using vigorous measures for putting down Chartism in Wales, they were no less active in other quarters, and that, too, in such a way as drew down upon them the charge, apparently but too true, of using the most unworthy instruments for accomplishing their end. On Thursday, January the 16th, 1840, a meeting was held in the Trades' Hall, Abbey-street, Bethnal Green, for the purpose of making known the state of misery and destitution of the industrious classes, over which meeting C. H. Neesom presided. Spurr had but just proceeded to address the parties assembled when a body of police rushed into the room, and seized several persons with arms in their possession. There was a rush made by the people to get out of the room, in which the majority succeeded. The chairman called upon the remainder to be firm, and Spurr continued his address; but a Mr. Moor demanded the chairman's name, which was given, and Spurr, on being advised to leave off speaking, complied with the advice. The police having fastened the doors, arrested the persons who remained, and on the following day they were brought up for examination. Messrs. Byrne, Clark, Reynard, Hobb, and Wilkins, were charged with having arms in their possession; and Messrs. Joseph Williams, David Williams, Neesom, Spurr, Cherry, Livings, and Evans, were charged with using inciting language at an illegal meeting, and were committed for trial at the Central Criminal Court. Neesom, Joseph Williams, Reynard, Hobb, and Spurr appeared at the sessions, but were allowed to traverse to the following session, Neesom being bound to the amount of £1000. The above case had every appearance of being got up by the police, for they knew exactly the persons on whom to lay their hands, while others who were armed were allowed to escape; they probably being the parties who were made instruments for the purpose of getting their fellow men within the meshes of the law.

About the same time a large number of the Chartists of Sheffield were arrested for conspiracy and administering illegal oaths. The principal witnesses against them were persons who professed to have been engaged with them in the conspiracy. One Thompson deposed that a large number of persons were formed into classes, and that they had provided themselves with arms, and fixed upon a plan for taking some, and firing other, parts of the town. That they had agreed to strike down every policeman and watchman that they might meet, and catch the soldiers before they could fire upon them. The barracks were to be fired, and the insurgents were to possess themselves of the Town Hall and Tontine, which they were to defend with barricades. After the evidence had been given, Samuel Holberry, William Booker, Thomas Booker, John Clayton, Samuel Bentley, John Marshall, Thomas Penthorpe, Joseph Bennison, and William Wells, were fully committed for trial. Mrs. Holberry, a very interesting woman, was also arrested ; but the evidence against her not being sufficient, she was discharged.

Speedily following the above, another event occurred at Bradford, of which the authorities knew all beforehand. It appeared that a number of Chartists met in the night ; there might be from 50 to 100. The police were on the watch, and seeing some men pass, called out to their fellow officers to assist them. These, however, replied that they were themselves prisoners in the hands of the Chartists ; and on examination, such turned out to be the fact. In a short time, however, the tables were turned ; and the Chartists were compelled by superior numbers to relinquish their hold, and were themselves taken into custody. Eight of these were committed to York for trial. Following this affair, letters appeared in the *Northern Star* from Harney and Ryder, denouncing a Mr. Peddie, who, they asserted, was at the bottom of a plan for entrapping the Chartists, as a government spy. Harney retracted his charge on the following week, but it was too late. Peddie was seized by the authorities, and committed for trial ;

and he has ever since thanked Harney and Ryder for his arrest. Certainly, the former should have paused before preferring such a charge against any other man ; for he had but too often been himself suspected, and this should have led him to be wary in the case of another, who might be as innocent as he doubtless knew himself to be. The fact is, that Peddie was not unknown to the Chartist body ; he had frequently addressed public meetings, especially in Newcastle, and his speeches had often appeared in the public press.

On the 29th of February, the trial of O'Brien and the Newcastle Chartists was proceeded with, before Mr. Justice Coleridge. The only witness for the prosecution was Mr. Henderson, the reporter for the *Tyne Mercury*, who had attended the meeting in the Lecture Room, and who professed to have taken notes of the speeches. From these notes he gave his evidence ; after which O'Brien, who conducted his defence in person, subjected him to a searching cross-examination, when, in answer to almost every question, he completely invalidated his own testimony, and proved a case for the defendants as strong as case could be. The examination being concluded, Cobbett addressed the jury for Thomason. He was succeeded by O'Brien, whose address was able and logical, and well calculated to convince. He exposed the conduct of the Birmingham authorities in the affair of the Bull Ring, which he contended was a justification of the course he had pursued. Messrs. Ayr and Mason followed O'Brien, after which the jury retired, and shortly returned with a verdict of not guilty. Some of the prisoners were charged upon other indictments ; but their trials were postponed to the next assizes, and they were discharged upon their own recognizances. John Bell was found guilty of a seditious libel, and sentenced to six months' imprisonment ; he being the only one convicted of a political offence during the assizes. Even the prisoners taken at the Forth, for the riot got up by the knightly Fife, were liberated on their own recognizances. When the verdict of acquittal was given, in the cases of O'Brien and others, a tremendous cheer burst forth in the crowded court, which was taken up and echoed by anxious thousands who were outside awaiting the result of the trial. In the evening a public meeting was held, which was addressed by O'Brien. The Lecture Room was crowded to suffocation ; and the gifted speaker was received with all the enthusiasm which his public services entitled him to expect. Messrs. Harney and Lowery also addressed the meeting, the former proposing three cheers for O'Brien, which was responded to right heartily. At the Durham assizes, Messrs. Williams and Binns were put upon their trial for sedition, and the case was opened ; but the judge having to leave for York, the trial was postponed, as was also that of Messrs. Bryne and Owen, who were indicted for a similar offence. On Monday, March the 16th, the Yorkshire assizes commenced, before Mr. Justice Erskine and Mr. Justice Coleridge when the Sheffield Chartists were brought to trial. The court presented from the outset a very animated appearance; the gentlemen of the legal profession attending in large numbers both for and against the prisoners. Holberry, the two Bookers, Duffy, and Wells were first indicted for conspiracy and riot. By way of supporting the evidence against the prisoners, a large basket full of hand-grenades, and other combustible materials, was placed upon the table, and a great number of pikes and daggers were also produced. The evidence went to prove that these were found in possession of the prisoners at the time of their arrest. The charges appeared to weigh most heavily against Holberry, who did not, when arrested, deny, but on the contrary, admitted, that his object was to upset the Government, and he professed his willingness to die for the Charter. The principal witnesses for the prosecution were Foxhall and Thompson, who were admitted as Queen's evidence, and who had taken an active part in the proceedings of the accused. The Attorney General prosecuted, and Sir Gregory Lewin, Mr. Watson, and Mr. Murphy defended the prisoners, and dwelt in strong terms on the evidence of the witnesses; but after Justice Erskine had summed up, the jury found all the prisoners guilty. William Wells, John Clayton, John Marshall, Thomas Penthorpe, Joseph Bennison, and Charles Fox were charged with similar offences, and pleaded guilty. Robert Cox, George Gullimore, James Bartholomew, Joseph Lingard, Thomas Powls, and Joshua Clayford, who had been out on bail, were also indicted for riot and conspiracy. Mr. Baines and Mr. Wortley prosecuted; Mr. Murphy and Mr. Wilkins defended the prisoners in able addresses, and succeeded in procuring a verdict of acquittal. John Marsden was indicted for riot, and attempting to liberate from prison Peter Foden, one of the arrested Chartists, to which charge he pleaded guilty. William Martin was indicted for sedition. Messrs. Baines and Wortley conducted the prosecution. The prisoner was most eloquently defended by Mr. Watson, but the result was a verdict of guilty.

On the following day Feargus O'Connor was put upon his trial for a seditious libel, when the court was literally beseiged by applicants for admission. The number of barristers was larger than ever, and the magistrates were present in considerable numbers. Mr. Justice Coleridge presided. O'Connor was allowed a seat at the counsellors' table. The case was tried by a special jury. The indictment charged O'Connor with seditious libel. The offence was that of publishing certain speeches in the *Northern Star*. The first speech so published was one of his own, delivered at Rochdale, on behalf of the defence fund. The second was delivered by William Dean Taylor, at Manchester ; and the third was reported to have been delivered by O'Brien, at Stockport. He was also charged with publishing a report of the proceedings at the Newcastle meeting, for addressing which O'Brien and others had been tried and acquitted, after that gentleman's able and eloquent defence. The Attorney General addressed the court at great length, in the course of which he read the speeches referred to. The publication having been proved, O'Connor addressed the jury. He alluded to the torch-light meetings, and censured the Government for suppressing them, when the Attorney General had himself, in bygone days, threatened to prosecute the magistrates of Dudley for putting down a similar meeting. He dwelt on the sacrifices he had made for the people, declaring that he had spent eight or nine thousand pounds on the Chartist movement. He then read extracts from about fifty speeches which he had delivered, and declared that so far from advocating physical force, he had always reprobated it, though at the expense sometimes of a fleeting popularity. He denounced at some length, Fife, the late mayor of Newcastle, Muntz, and Daniel O'Connell ; and declared that he would always stand by his principles. O'Connor's address occupied four hours and a quarter in the delivery. The judge summed up most impartially ; but the jury, after retiring for ten minutes, returned a verdict of guilty. At O'Connor's request, judgment was postponed.

On Wednesday, Robert Peddie, William Brooke, Thomas Drake, James Holdsworth, and Paul Holdsworth, were indicted for riot and conspiracy at Bradford. The Attorney General, Mr. Wightman, and Sergeant Atcherley, were for the prosecution. Mr. Watson, Mr. J. Wortley, and Mr. Wilkins appeared for the prisoners. At the conclusion of the evidence the jury found them all guilty, with the exception of James Holdsworth. It appeared upon the trial, that so far from Peddie having been a government spy, he had been the victim of one of that detested class. The name of this wretch was Harrison, and we have the strongest reasons for asserting that he was the main concocter of the conspiracy. At the very time that he was ensnaring his dupes, he was in communication with the authorities, giving them every information necessary for the success of his vile schemes. On being cross-examined this sublime rascal refused to swear that he had not received £100 for his share in the transactions. He likewise refused to swear that he had not been the means of bringing at least twelve men to the gallows. We have good grounds for believing that although Peddie had some knowledge of what was going forward, he had no share in the business, further than frustrating to some extent the wicked designs of the entrapper. In justice to him it should be stated that magnificent offers were made to him on condition that he would betray others to the vengeance of the law; which, to his honour, he indignantly spurned. As a test of the value of the evidence given by Harrison, it will only be necessary further to state, that he afterwards appeared as informer against two poor boys for stealing a horse. Justice, however, in this case pursued the guilty. Suspicion being excited, he was himself tried for the offence which he sought to fasten upon his victims, found guilty, and met his deserts by being transported for the term of his natural life.

On the 21st of March the Sheffield and Bradford prisoners were brought up to receive sentence. Holberry was sentenced to four years' imprisonment, and bound over in fifty pounds, and two sureties of ten pounds each, to keep the peace after the term of his imprisonment should expire. Thomas Booker was sentenced to three years' imprisonment, and bound to keep the peace in thirty pounds, and two sureties of ten pounds each. William Booker, his son, was imprisoned for two years, and bound over to keep the peace in the sum of twenty pounds. James Duffy was sentenced to three years' imprisonment, and bound over in the sum of twenty pounds, and two sureties of ten pounds each. William Wells received a sentence of one year's imprisonment, and was bound over in the sum of twenty pounds. Marshall, Penthorpe, and Bennison, were each sentenced to two years' imprisonment, and bound over in the sum of twenty pounds; and William Martin was sentenced to twelve months' imprisonment. Of the Bradford Chartists, Robert Peddie was sentenced to three years' imprisonment, and bound to keep the peace in the sum of thirty pounds, and two sureties of ten pounds each. William Brooke, three years' imprisonment, and bound in the sum of thirty pounds. Thomas Drake, imprisoned for eighteen months, and bound in the sum of thirty pounds; and Paul Holdsworth, three years' imprisonment, and bound over in the same amount. John Walker, Joseph Naylor, John Rhyding, and John Rishworth, were convicted of riot at Bradford, and each sentenced to two years' imprisonment, and bound over in the

x

sum of thirty pounds.   Messrs. Hutton and Smithies, for a similar offence, were each sentenced to eighteen months' imprisonment, and bound in the sum of thirty pounds.   Peter Hoey, John Crabtree, and William Ashton were convicted of unlawfully assembling at Barnsley, and each imprisoned for two years, and bound over in the sum of fifty pounds.   These severe, we might say unmerciful sentences, finished the Chartist business at the York assizes.

At the Monmouth assizes Vincent and Edwards were a second time put upon their trial for having conspired, together with John Frost, to subvert the constituted authorities, and alter by force the constitution of the country.   In another count they were charged with seditious language.   Sergeant Talfourd again conducted the case for the prosecution.   Mr. Carrington appeared for Edwards, and Vincent conducted his own defence, addressing the jury at considerable length. They were both found guilty, but recommended to mercy, and Baron Gurney sentenced Vincent to twelve, and Edwards to fourteen months' imprisonment.   Let us state, that on the cases of these defendants being afterwards brought before the House of Commons, Sergeant Talfourd declared that after hearing Vincent's defence, he regretted having undertaken the case for the prosecution ; and he condemned the unjust and severe treatment inflicted upon the Chartist prisoners generally.

At the Liverpool assizes the Rev. W. V. Jackson, William Butterworth, R. J. Richardson, and James Bronterre O'Brien, were tried for maliciously conspiring and inciting the people of this country to make riots, to arm with weapons of offence, and with divers other acts for the promotion of rebellion.   O'Brien, as on his trial at Newcastle, defended himself; the trial lasted the whole day, but O'Brien was not as successful as in the former case, and the jury found all the defendants guilty.   O'Brien had depended on a number of witnesses coming forward in his defence, but for some reason or other they were not forthcoming.   He afterwards charged O'Connor with having in this matter dealt with him unfairly, and with saying to him, loud enough for the jury to hear, "O'Brien, you must not call witnesses."   George Henry Smith, Christopher Doyle, and John Kaye, were tried for seditious proceedings at Manchester, and found guilty. Messrs. Barker and Davidson were also convicted of conspiracy and riot at Manchester, and James Luck pleaded guilty of a similar offence. On Messrs Richardson, Jackson, Butterworth, and O'Brien being brought up to receive sentence, Richardson begged that his Lordship would inflict a fine on him instead of imprisonment, and produced affidavits to show that imprisonment would have a serious effect upon his health. His Lordship however declined, and sentenced him and Butterworth each to nine months' imprisonment, and afterwards to be bound in the sum of one hundred pound, and two sureties of fifty pounds to keep the peace for three years. In the case of Jackson, his Lordship regretted a minister of religion making use of such language as that of which he stood convicted; and considering his position, abilities, and means to do mischief, said he must sentence him to eighteen months' imprisonment, and bind him over in the sum of five hundred pounds, and two sureties of one hundred and fifty pounds each, to keep the peace for three years. O'Brien wished to move an arrest of judgment, and stated that he had been deceived in the course which the trial had taken, as there were certain witnesses, whom he had expected would have been called for Jackson and Butterworth and who would have contradicted the testimony of the reporter. His Lordship replied, that these considerations were now too late. O'Brien then desired that instead of imprisoning him, his Lordship would banish him for life, he having no wish to stay in this country, and having no hope of it in its present state. His Lordship said he could do nothing else than pass sentence of imprisonment, and he accordingly sentenced O'Brien to eighteen months' imprisonment, and to be bound to keep the peace, himself in three hundred pounds, and two sureties of one hundred and fifty pounds. Jackson received sentence, on a second conviction, of six months' imprisonment, and was bound over to keep the peace, himself in five hundred pounds, and two sureties in one hundred pounds each. John Kaye was sentenced to six months' imprisonment, and bound over to keep the peace, himself in two hundred pounds, and two sureties of fifty pounds. Christopher Doyle was imprisoned for nine months, and bound, himself in three hundred pounds, and two sureties in one hundred pounds each. William Barker received eighteen months' imprisonment with hard labour. Frederick Davidson six months with hard labour. Samuel Scott eight months' imprisonment, and bound, himself in one hundred pounds, and two sureties of fifty pounds each. Charles Morris twelve months' imprisonment, and bound in one hundred pounds, with two sureties of twenty pounds each. Daniel Ball eighteen months' hard labour, and a similar bond. Peter Murdin six months' hard labour, and Willoughby three months with hard labour.

At the Chester assizes, William Benbow, who had traversed from the last assizes, was called up and pleaded not guilty. This sturdy veteran in the cause of radical reform addressed

the jury for ten and a half hours ; at the conclusion of which
he was found guilty, and sentenced to sixteen months' imprisonment, having been confined before trial for a period of eight
months.   Isaac Johnson was then arraigned on a charge of
uttering seditious language at Stockport.   He addressed the
jury in a bold and eloquent speech, which occupied several
hours.   He was found guilty, and sentenced to twelve months'
imprisonment, and to find security for keeping the peace for
two years, himself in two hundred pounds, and two sureties in
one hundred pounds each.   Messrs. Stubbs, Barnet, Savage,
Lowe, Weaver, and Jackson, were charged with conspiracy
and riot at Macclesfield.   With the exception of Weaver they
all pleaded guilty, and were discharged, on entering into a bond
of one hundred pounds each, to appear when called upon to
receive judgment.   James Duke, of Ashton, and John Livesey,
of Manchester, were arraigned on a charge of conspiracy,
and found guilty.   They were each sentenced to twelve
months' imprisonment, and to find security in one hundred and
fifty pounds to keep the peace for three years, and to be further
imprisoned until such security was given.   On Monday, May
11th, 1840, after repeated adjournments on the ground of ill
health, O'Connor was brought up before the Court of Queen's
Bench to receive sentence.   He put in a long affidavit to the
effect that he had always advised the use of moral force.   The
judge, before passing sentence, observed that according to
O'Connor's own showing, his moral force was little short of
physical force.   He was then sentenced to eighteen months'
imprisonment in York Castle.
    At Devizes, William P. Roberts, William Potts, and William
Carrier, were indicted on a charge of sedition, and were all
found guilty.   Roberts and Potts were each sentenced to two
years' imprisonment.   Carrier, being a working man, was
sentenced to the same term of imprisonment with the
additional punishment of hard labour.   In a few weeks, however, Roberts was released on the ground of ill health.   At
Taunton, Messrs. Young, Bolwell, and Bartlett were charged
with sedition, found guilty, and sentenced, Young to three
months, Bolwell to six months, and Bartlett to nine months'
imprisonment.   In July Marsden was arrested on a bench
warrant, and brought to Newcastle.   He looked the very
personification of misery ; so much so, that when the reporter
who appeared as a witness against him was confronted with
him, he could scarcely identify him.   When the assizes came
on, Marsden, together with Messrs. Hume, Devyr, and
Thomason, was placed in the dock; but the prosecuting counsel
informed the court that he had no evidence to offer, and all

the prisoners were thereupon discharged. John Mason was again indicted on a charge of sedition ; but after he had addressed the jury, they returned a verdict of acquittal. At the Durham assizes the long-delayed trial of Williams and Binns was brought to an issue. These gentlemen very ably and eloquently pleaded their own cause. The principal witness who testified against them was H. F. Hetherington, the reporter for the *Sunderland Herald.* The jury found them guilty, but recommended them to mercy on account of their youth. Williams, speaking in mitigation of punishment, said that he claimed no consideration on the ground recommended by the jury, as all that he had done was the result of calm deliberation. He only claimed consideration for the utility of his public conduct. They were each sentenced to six months' imprisonment. Messrs. Byrne and Owen were also tried and found guilty, and were each imprisoned for three calendar months. White and Wilson were indicted for attempting to extort money by means of threats and intimidation. White was awarded six, and Wilson four months' imprisonment. Although the Government had so vigorously prosecuted the Chartists, and condemned most of their leaders to imprisonment and transportation, the spirit of reform did not entirely die out. In Scotland, particularly, the agitation was carried on with a great degree of vigour. Besides Moir and others of Glasgow, and a host of local leaders in the various towns, Messrs. Lowery and Duncan made an extensive tour through that part of the kingdom, addressing public meetings ; and Julian Harney, like the apostles of old, went from town to town on foot, and even penetrated into the Highlands, to proclaim the doctrines of the Charter. In England, too, numerous meetings were still held, although chiefly sustained by the local talent of the respective localities. Poor Dr. Taylor, utterly disappointed in the results of the Chartist movement, and broken in health by incessant agitating, retired to the house of his brother-in-law, an Irish clergyman, where he rapidly sank, and in a short time breathed his last. His death caused profound regret amongst all who had known him in the course of the movement. Even his political opponents could not refrain from breathing a sigh at the loss of one who, with all his trifling faults, and his somewhat reckless bearing, had a noble heart that ever beat warmly for humanity, and in favour of the oppressed against the oppressor. The *Ayr Advertiser* contained a feeling notice of his decease, which reflected credit on its author, and showed how highly the subject of it was esteemed even by his political foes.

The Whig Government having got the Chartist prisoners in their power, in many instances inflicted punishments on them harsher than persons convicted of similar offences had ever been subjected to by the Tories. O'Connor was at first treated in every respect like a common felon ; and it was only the outcry made by his friends, and the strong representations of some members of parliament, and of even a part of the press, that secured him better treatment. O'Brien had inflicted on him the greatest punishment which a man of his vast intellect and great acquirements can suffer, by being deprived of the use of books, except such as were approved of by the authorities, which of course were of a very exclusive kind. Vincent was for the greater part of his time subject to felons' fare, to wear the prison dress, and to work as a tailor, a trade to which he had never been accustomed. Lovett and Collins were supplied with filthy and loathsome food, which at length they were compelled positively to refuse. Carrier and Potts were subjected to treatment which ruined their health. Peddie was put to hard labour, which caused him frequent vomiting, and materially preyed upon his constitution; and very similar was the treatment of most of the Chartist prisoners in the several gaols throughout the country. After the onslaught made by the Government upon the Chartists, a portion of the Chartist press went out of existence. The *Operative* died through want of means on the part of the proprietor to carry it on, together with the secret workings of some of the leaders to prevent its circulation. The *True Scotsman*, the *Charter*, the *London Despatch*, and the *Champion* followed,—the latter being incorporated with the *Northern Liberator*,—and the *Birmingham Journal* returned to Whiggery. Messrs. O'Brien and Carpenter, however, in the winter of 1839-40, started the *Southern Star;* but the imprisonment of the former prevented his long attending to his editorial duties, and it followed in the wake of the *Operative.* The Glasgow Democrats established a paper under the title of the *Scottish Patriot*, and some small periodicals were established. In the West, R. K. Philip edited the *Regenerator.* In Manchester, one of the same name was brought out by R. G. Richardson. The *English Chartist Circular* was established by Cleave; and in Glasgow, the *Scottish Chartist Circular,* a very able little paper, was launched on the waves of public opinion. Thus there seemed a determination by some means to supply the loss of the newspapers ; and these periodicals—especially the *Circulars* —had considerable influence with the Chartist body.

CHAPTER IX.

The last of the Chartist prisoners had not been put upon his trial before an effort was made to remodel the organization of the Chartist body. As our readers have already seen, the first associations formed for the Charter were local, though all converged towards the national object. Many of these bodies had become disorganized ; and on Monday, the 20th of July, 1840, a meeting of delegates assembled at Manchester to take the subject into consideration, and to devise a plan for placing the body on a better footing. John Arran and Joseph Hatfield sat for the West Riding of Yorkshire ; James Leach and James Taylor for South Lancashire ; J. Deegan for Staleybridge and Liverpool ; David John for Merthyr Tydvil and Monmouth ; J. B. Hanson for Carlisle ; W. Tillman for Manchester ; George Halton for Preston ; Samuel Lees for Stockport ; Richard Littler for Salford ; Mr. Andrew for Glossop ; Mr. Lowe for Bolton ; Samuel Royse for Hyde ; William Morgan for Bristol, Bath, and Cheltenham ; James Cooke for Leigh ; George Black for Nottingham ; James Williams for Sunderland ; Thomas Raynor Smart for Leicester and Northampton ; James Taylor for Loughborough ; Richard Spurr for London ; and Richard Hartley for Colne—making in all twenty-three delegates. After coming to various resolutions with respect to the wives and families of the incarcerated Chartists, the delegates proceeded to discuss various plans of organization ; and after several days' sitting, it was ultimately resolved to merge all the local bodies into one association, to which they gave the name of the " National Charter Association of Great Britain." The basis of the Association was of course the People's Charter ; and it was agreed that none but peaceful and constitutional means should be employed for gaining that object. All persons might be admitted as members on declaring that they agreed with the principles of the Association, and taking out a card of membership, to be renewed quarterly, for which they should be charged twopence. Where practicable, the members were to be divided into classes of ten, and a leader appointed to each class by the Executive. The latter was to be composed of seven persons, including a secretary and treasurer, who were to appoint a Council, with a sub-secretary and sub-treasurer to be nominated by the members in each locality. The Executive, as well as the General Council, were to be elected annually —the former by a majority of the members throughout the country. The salary of the general secretary was fixed at the rate of two pounds per week, and the other members of the Executive were each to receive a weekly salary of thirty shillings during their sittings. One half of the monies collected throughout the country were to be at the disposal of the Executive, who, when practicable, were to act as missionaries, and appoint other missionaries to agitate the various districts in favour of the Charter. It was agreed that at the next general election, the Chartists should, wherever practicable, adopt O'Brien's plan of putting forward Chartist candidates to advocate their principles, and that the Chartist body should attend all public meetings of a political character in order to make known their views, and, if necessary, move amendments to the objects of those meetings. After the plan of organization had been adopted, the delegates issued an address to the country, and nominated twelve persons out of whom were to be chosen the provisional Executive, which was accordingly appointed, and of which James Leach was the first president, and William Tillman the secretary. The above plan of organization was adopted by the Chartist body generally, and in many towns considerable numbers joined the Association. Still those numbers were anything but equal to the masses who had been enrolled under the local associations. But events were now about to occur, which were calculated to re-kindle the old fire of the Chartist movement. The time of imprisonment of some of the leaders had expired, and their release was looked forward to with much interest and expectancy.

On July the 24th, 1840, the doors of Warwick gaol were opened, and forth from their living tomb issued William Lovett and John Collins. The former had evidently suffered much from his confinement; he was considerably emaciated, and had some difficulty in walking unsupported. Collins appeared to have better resisted his treatment under prison discipline. The liberated victims, accompanied by a deputation, made their way to the house of Mr. French, where a breakfast had been provided. Thompson on behalf of the Birmingham Chartists, gave an invitation to Messrs. Lovett and Collins to a public entertainment in that town.

Collins accepted but Lovett, both on the grounds of ill health
and prior engagements, declined with thanks the invitation.
On the following day the Chartists of Warwick gave an
entertainment in honour of the above gentlemen, which was
attended by Collins. Cardo presided, and several speeches
were made by Collins, Donaldson, and others. Songs were
sung, and all passed off with great harmony and spirit.

The Birmingham demonstration came off on Monday
July the 27th, 1840, and was everything that might
have been anticipated both in numbers and enthusiasm.
A procession started at ten o'clock from the Cross
Guns, Lancaster street, in the following order: 1st.—two
marshals on horseback ; 2nd.—members of committee two
abreast ; 3rd.—body of collectors and subscribers four abreast ;
4th.—a large and appropriate banner; 5th.—union band in their
uniform; 6th.—carriage drawn by four greys, containing Collins
and family; 7th.—carriages with deputations from several parts
of England and Scotland ; 8th.—carriages containing the
committee of the Female Political Union ; 9th.—trades four
abreast ; 10th.—a large banner ; 11th.—a brass band ; 12th.—
trades four abreast ; 13th.—friends from the surrounding districts four abreast ; 14th.—two marshals on horseback to bring
up the general procession. In this order the procession made
its way up Lancaster-street, Stafford-street, Dale-end, High-
street, Deritend, Bordesley, Camp Hill, and along the
Warwick road as far as the Mermaid, and returned by the same
route to Ashton-street, and then proceeded to Gosta Green ;
the order of the procession being kept by the police, who were
placed at the disposal of the committee. Such was the
demand for vehicles on the part of the committee that scarce
one could be hired for any other purpose. The sun shone
brilliantly just as the procession was about to form. The
sight of the dense masses of people was extremely grand and
exciting. The procession reached a full mile in length, and
on its return it was extended to double that distance ; the
streets being literally crowded by a dense mass of human
beings. The lamp-posts, windows, and roofs of houses,
shewed interested faces viewing the scene, and the vast multitude rent the air with their cheers, and numbers of ladies
waved their handkerchiefs in token of welcome. The gigantic
crowd having reached Gosta Green, silence was proclaimed,
and Collins addressed them as " Friends, fellow-townsmen,
and brother slaves." He reviewed the past, spoke hopefully
of the future, and promised them his continued co-operation
in furtherance of their rights. In the evening a banquet was
given in honour of Collins, at which upwards of eight hundred

persons sat down. Mr. Farebrother Page, town councillor, occupied the chair, and proposed the usual radical toasts and sentiments. Messrs. Cardo, Warden, Thomason, Thompson, Charlton, Greaves, and Watson responded ; and Collins, on his health being drank with three times three, acknowledged the compliment with an animated address. On the following morning there was a meeting of the delegates, who had been deputed to attend the demonstration. Messrs. Holman and Jackson attended from Totness, Leach from Manchester, Spurr from London, Messrs. Carter and Greaves from Oldham and Saddleworth, Chappel from Stockport, Thomason from Newcastle-upon-Tyne, Chance from Stourbridge, Chadwick from the Potteries, Griffin from West Bromwich, Cook from Dudley, Lewis from Bristol, Morgan from Bath, Millson from Cheltenham, Sankey from Edinburgh, and O'Neil from Lanarkshire. On the motion of the London and Lanarkshire delegates, the following resolution was unanimously adopted :—

"That we, the delegates from various parts of England and Scotland, for the purpose of congratulating our friends, John Collins and William Lovett, on their liberation from prison, after considering the plan of organization adopted at the Manchester delegate meeting, which was assembled for that purpose, express our approval of the same and our determination to give it our most cordial support in our various localities."

Another out-door meeting was held in the evening, on a piece of ground purchased for a new People's Hall, which was addressed by Messrs. Chadwick, Chappel, Spurr, O'Neil, Empson, Smallwood, and Mumford; and an address previously adopted by the delegates was read to the meeting and carried unanimously, as were also various resolutions; and thus ended the great Birmingham demonstration of the Chartists in honour of two of the foremost sufferers in their cause.

The Chartists of London, though in a more humble manner, testified their appreciation of the services of Lovett and Collins, by honouring them with a public dinner at White Conduit House, on Monday, August 3rd. The Chair was taken by Mr. Wakley, M. P., who was supported on his right by Lovett, and on his left by Collins. Mr. Duncombe, M.P., was also present. Wakley denounced strongly the treatment to which those gentlemen had been subjected. Lovett, on his health being proposed, made an able speech. The first paragraph will show whether his imprisonment had effected the object desired by his persecutors.

"Those who had not experienced the monotony and misery

of a prison, could scarcely estimate how wholesome and refreshing were the grateful blessings of freedom. Notwithstanding these feelings, he would say, welcome once more the starving imprisonment of Warwick gaol—welcome again all the misery he had suffered, rather than the right of public meetings should be questioned, and peaceful bodies of people dispersed by blue-coated bludgeon men, and not a voice be found to denounce the oppressor, and publish his infamy to the world."

Collins spoke in a humorous strain, to the great delight of the meeting. Cleave introduced Messrs. Morling and Londsell, from Brighton, who presented an address from the Chartists of that fashionable town to Lovett and Collins ; after which Duncombe addressed the assembly, entering into the facts of the Government persecution, which he cordially denounced. Mr. J. Watson and Dr. Epps, with several others, responded to various toasts and sentiments, after which the meeting separated, highly delighted with the evening's entertainment.

The liberation of Dr. M'Douall from Chester Castle, gave rise to other demonstrations of a similar kind to the above. On Saturday, August the 22nd, M'Douall and Collins entered Manchester, when a procession paraded the streets ; and on the following Monday about five hundred persons entertained them with a dinner in Carpenter's Hall, which was tastefully decorated with flags, portraits of eminent patriots, and various other Chartist emblems. After dinner the meeting was entertained with the usual toasts and speeches, and a great number of gentlemen took part in the proceedings. The Rev. James Scholefield was called to the chair. M'Douall on being introduced, met with a most cordial reception. Alluding to his imprisonment, he said :—

" He had gone through the dungeon, and an ill effect it had produced upon his constitution ; but he had forgot the persecution, and now began to remember his persecutors. He would now begin to pay his debts to them ; that debt was a long one, and from the moment he left the dungeon gates, he swore in his heart that he would have revenge. He would not have that revenge, however, which they might understand from the general acceptation of the term. The revenge that he would seek was—The Charter. His course would be to contend peacefully, if they must, for the Charter, for which all of them he trusted were ready to suffer, and if necessary to die."

M'Douall spoke throughout with remarkable energy and effect, and was warmly applauded. Tillman followed, and then came Collins, who spoke of the illness of his friend Lovett, and justified the course which had led to their joint imprisonment.   Messrs. Littler, Deegan, and others afterwards addressed the meeting, which was most enthusiastic throughout.   M'Douall subsequently visited all the principal towns in the North of England.   In some of them he was met by large processions ; and in all he was received with every demonstration of welcome.

The expiration of the sentence on White, added another to the list of liberated Chartists, and he, in company with Collins and M'Douall, was invited to visit numerous places in Scotland.   At Glasgow an imposing demonstration of the people took place.   Tens of thousands of the industrial classes turned out, and formed into a vast procession, to do honour to their liberated champions, whom they no sooner recognised than they greeted with the loudest acclamations. The assembled mass was drawn up on Glasgow Green, over whom J. Moir presided.   Messrs. Collins, White, and M'Douall, severally addressed the meeting.   It was computed that not fewer than two hundred thousand people attended this demonstration, which was followed in the evening by a soiree, when the liberated advocates of the Charter were presented with testimonials of the esteem of the Radicals of Glasgow, and in recognition of their exertions and sufferings in the cause.   After the Glasgow demonstration, however, M'Douall parted company with his colleagues, they preceding him, and attending open-air meetings, and he following, and delivering instructive in-door lectures, which were always numerously attended.   In this way they made a regular tour of Scotland, and quite revived the agitation wherever they appeared.   Messrs. Byrne and Owen were shortly afterwards released from Durham gaol, and attended several meetings in the neighbourhood.   At Newcastle the Democrats got up a demonstration in honour of the above persons and White, who had returned from Scotland. Collins was unable from the state of his health to attend.   A procession with bands and banners met White at the Railway station.   He was escorted to the Spital, where he addressed the crowd at considerable length in his usual caustic style. Deegan and others also delivered their sentiments.   After the meeting about a hundred and twenty persons sat down to dinner at Macdonald's hotel, when that tried and sterling friend to the cause, Thomas Doubleday, was called to the chair, and Messrs. White, Byrne, and Deegan, entertained the company with speeches.   In the evening a soiree was held in the Music Hall, which was filled by the Democrats of both sexes. The women Chartists presented an address to the liberated victims; after which a silver chain was placed round the neck of Byrne by Mrs. Holmes, and a similar tribute of respect paid to White, which those gentlemen gracefully acknowledged. A variety of sentiments were given and responded to during the evening, and the meeting broke up with cheers for the *Northern Liberator*, *Northern Star*, the ladies, and the chairman.

While the liberated Chartists were re-awakening the people to the importance of the Charter, another movement of no mean significance was taking some hold of the public mind. We should not allude to it in this history but for its effect upon the Chartist agitation. The movement alluded to was concerned with the foreign policy of Lord Palmerston. Newcastle-upon-Tyne was the head-quarters of this movement. The prime mover in the affair was David Urquhart, a gentleman who had made our foreign affairs his particular study. He was seconded in his efforts by Charles Atwood, brother of the late popular member for Birmingham. William Cargill also took a leading part in the movement. These gentlemen all charged Lord Palmerston with playing the interests of the British nation into the hands of Russia ; and they even went so far as to charge him with having been corrupted by Russian gold to embroil this country in a war with France. The *Northern Liberator* was the organ of the anti-Palmerston party in the North, and Doubleday, both by speech and pen, enforced their sentiments and opinions. The Chartist body was the only party of politicians likely to favour their views, and an attempt to enlist their favour was to some extent successful. Public meetings were held in Newcastle, at which Messrs. Urquhart, Charles Atwood, Doubleday, and Cargill, were the principal speakers, and many of the Chartist leaders joined them. Messrs. Ayr, Mason, and Lowery, were the principal of these, and the agitation of the question in this town was carried on with vigour. Cardo, Richards, and Warren, all members of the late Convention, were engaged as missionaries, and meetings were addressed in Birmingham, Northampton, Carlisle, and many other places ; but with the exception of Newcastle, the movement was not long successful. This did not arise from any confidence that the Chartists reposed in the British minister; but from the fact that they looked upon it as a scheme to divert them from their own favourite measure, and of this they were assured by O'Connor in the *Northern Star*, who discountenanced it in every possible way, and in a short time, Newcastle almost alone paid any particular attention to the subject. In this matter the Chartist body, through the influence

of O'Connor, evinced a narrow spirit. Undoubtedly it was
their duty to keep the question of the Charter first and foremost,
but it was their interest to gain every sort of information,
which would show the worthlessness of their rulers, and so have
made out a stronger case for the establishment of their
principles.

In the winter of 1841, an attempt was made by the whig-
radical section of reformers, to inaugurate a new movement
for amending the representation of the people, which led to
the project of holding a great public meeting in a new mill
built by Messrs. Marshall of Leeds, in that important town.
The names of O'Connell, Roebuck, Colonel Thompson,
Sherman Crawford, and Joseph Hume, were paraded to give
importance to the movement. If there had existed no other
reason the very name of the first of these men would have
been sufficient to ensure its condemnation. The virulent
opposition he had given to the Chartists, and the bitter and
unsparing language of denunciation which he had dealt out
regarding them, coupled with the fact that he had caused to be
broken up by physical force a meeting called in Dublin to
listen to one of their advocates, aroused the ire of that body ;
and in an address, extensively posted throughout the West
Riding, every Chartist was urged to attend, and give him such
a welcome as it was declared he so richly deserved. The
meeting was fixed to take place on Thursday, the 21st of
January, and the Chartists resolved on meeting this movement
by a counter demonstration, to aid which delegates arrived from
various parts of England and Scotland. A soiree to welcome
these delegates was held on Wednesday, the day previous to
the meeting, in the Music Hall, over which the Rev. William
Hill, editor of the *Northern Star*, presided. On the following
day, notwithstanding the severity of the weather, a procession
was formed, which, after traversing various streets, proceeded
to Holbeck Moor, bearing numerous banners, with the usual
mottos and devices. Mr. Joshua Hobson presided over the
meeting, and read a list of the delegates, from which it
appeared, that Moir was in attendance from Glasgow,
Collins and O'Neil from Birmingham, John Mason from the
Midlands, James Leach from Manchester, William Tillman
from Manchester and London, C. Doyle from Manchester and
the Metropolitan districts, J. Deegan from the county of
Durham, W. G. Burns, Samuel Healey, John Peck, and
William Worsdale from Hull, Lawrance Pitkiethly and
Edward Clayton from Huddersfield, John Wright from
Stockport, George Halton from Preston, Job Midgley from
Hebden Bridge, James Vickerman from Halifax, John Greaves

from Oldham, William Beesley from Burnley, Robert Lowery from Newcastle, Thomas Baldwin from Colne, Thomas Knowles from Keighley, John Sawdon from Great Horton, and J. R. Bairstow from Liverpool. Resolutions were unanimously carried in favour of keeping to the agitation for the Charter, and of distrusting the initiators of the new movement, more especially for having invited O'Connell to the meeting, who, it was contended, was the most profligate politician of the age. Resolutions of confidence in Feargus O'Connor, and for the dismissal of the ministry, were also agreed to, and an address to the Queen for the latter object was passed unanimously. The meeting having dispersed, the delegates proceeded to Marshall's Mill, followed by numbers of people, who speedily filled that part in which the middle class meeting was held, and which was calculated to hold seven thousand people. At the back of the president's chair were painted various devices; such as, "Justice to one and to all;" "No property qualification for members;" "Household suffrage;" "Vote by ballot, and triennial parliaments;" "Re-distribution of representation;" &c. James Garth Marshall occupied the chair; but the Chartists were prevented from giving their peculiar kind of welcome to O'Connell, for the great agitator had very valorously, that is to say, discreetly kept away. Joseph Hume moved the first resolution in a speech of an hour's duration; but his reception at times was anything but gratifying. This, at the least, was very undeserved and unjust; for whatever the political principles of Hume might have been, he had always laboured to secure a hearing for the working class both in and out of parliament. The resolution was so general in terms that the Chartists were enabled consistently to give it their support. It ran as follows:—

"That the great experiment made by means of the Reform Bill to improve the condition of the country, hath failed to attain the end desired by the people, and a further reform having therefore become necessary, it is the opinion of this meeting, that the united efforts of all reformers ought to be directed to obtain such a further enlargement of the franchise as should make the interests of the representatives identical with those of the whole country, and by this means secure a just government for all classes of the people."

Moir, of Glasgow, seconded the resolution, and was followed by Collins, who, like his predecessor, argued in favour of universal suffrage. Roebuck next spoke, and in the course of his remarks denounced the severity of the Government towards the persecuted Chartists. He was followed by O'Neil, who declared that the Chartists would never relinquish the high ground they had occupied.   Sherman Crawford next spoke, exposing the system of class-representation, and advocating such a household suffrage as would include lodgers; but, like Hume, he was met with frequent disturbance.   Lowery followed, and made some hard hits at Daniel O'Connell.   W. Williams, M.P. for Coventry, succeeded Lowery, and spoke in favour of household suffrage, though declaring himself for universal suffrage.   Mason next addressed the meeting in an energetic speech; and then came Colonel Thompson, who declared himself a "despised Chartist."   Deegan was the last speaker, and when he had concluded, the resolution was put and carried amid the most rapturous cheering.   A vote of thanks being given to the chairman, the meeting concluded with three cheers for Feargus O'Connor, three for Frost, Williams, and Jones, and three terrific groans for Daniel O'Connell.   The object, then, for which the meeting was called completely failed. It was to all intents and purposes a Chartist meeting; and it appeared evident enough that all attempts to secure a union between the middle and working classes for anything short of the Charter would, at least for the present, prove abortive.

The summer of 1841 brought with it a general election. The Chartists had vowed vengeance on the Whigs, and as their termination of office drew near, they prepared to put their threats into execution.   The Melbourne ministry having perceived its sinking popularity, resolved to take a bold course in order to redeem its public credit, and three important measures were the fruit of that resolve.   They proposed to abolish the existing corn-laws and substitute a fixed duty of eight shillings per quarter ; to equalize the duties on free and slave-grown sugar, and to reduce those on foreign timber. They hoped by the proposal of these measures to win back that public confidence which a long course of perfidious legis- lation had caused them to lose ; but with whatever favour these measures might formerly have been received, the Government got but little credit for its good intentions.   A strong current of public feeling had set against everything relating to Whigs and whiggery, and when they came to propose their measures, they were defeated in the Commons, and there was no alternative but a dissolution of parliament.   The question came, what policy should the Chartists pursue ? Some were for voting for what were called the most liberal members, while others were for ousting and defeating the Whigs even by the substitution of Tories.   A controversy took place between O'Connor and O'Brien, both of whom were still confined in prison.   The former advocated the pro-tory policy, the latter opposed it, maintaining that the Chartist who would vote for a Tory, except on condition of the Tories assisting them to return a man of their own, was to all intents and purposes a tool of that party. O'Brien, however, held the same doctrine with regard to the Whigs, and set forth that the true policy of the Chartists was to vote for neither party except for mutual advantage. Undoubtedly O'Brien had the best of the dispute, but the feeling against the Whigs was so strong, that the sentiments of O'Connor were received with far greater favour than those of O'Brien, and his policy was declared to be that of the party generally. A more fatal policy could not possibly have been adopted; but for it the Whigs might have sunk into everlasting contempt, but this step armed them with a powerful weapon wherewith to fight the Chartists, and the term "Tory Chartist" was adopted in order to load the Chartists with opprobrium, and too well it had its effect. We even go farther than O'Brien in this matter; *we would never coalesce with either party on any terms whatever.* To do so is almost the height of inconsistency. What, to say the least, can be more ridiculous than supporting a friend with one vote, while you support, it may be, a most deadly enemy with the other. Such a policy as this never yet accomplished the slightest permanent good. It may be that a victory is for the moment gained, but it is a victory worse than defeat. Can any good ever come by linking together truth and error, virtue and vice? If there are but three men of right principles, let them stand or fall by those principles; it at least secures them the respect even of their foes. A far better resolution than that of supporting the Tories was also adopted at the election; it was that of bringing forward candidates on the hustings to explain and defend the principles of Chartism. A number were taken to the poll, but some of these were of the mere Roebuck-class of politicians. All who held the principles of the Charter were recommended, through the medium of the *Northern Star,* in a long letter from Feargus O'Connor. Roebuck stood for Bath, and was returned; Colonel Thompson for Hull, but he was unsuccessful; Oakely and Duncombe were returned for Finsbury, Fielden and Johnson for Oldham. Vincent contested Banbury and secured fifty one votes; the highest number polled by any candidate being one hundred and twenty-four. M'Douall was brought forward for Northampton, where an open coalition took place between the Chartists and the Tories; the battle was fought desperately between Whigs and Tories, but the former triumphed, and M'Douall polled but one hundred and seventy votes, out of a constituency of about two thousand. At Newcastle-on-Tyne Bronterre O'Brien was proposed as the

z

Chartist candidate, though still in prison, and the result was a tremendous show of hands in his favour, far outnumbering those held up for both the successful candidates; that is to say, those who were successful in securing the suffrages of a majority of the electors on a poll. The friends of O'Brien withdrew their candidate after securing a hustings victory. Harney and Pitkeithly contested at the hustings with Lords Morpeth and Milton, the West Riding of Yorkshire, where they carried public opinion in favour of the Charter. At the aristocratic borough of Marylebone W. V. Sankey was the Chartist candidate, and he had the courage to go to the poll against all odds, which were fearful, for he only succeeded in polling seventy votes. Even at Brighton the Chartists were not without their candidate in the person of Charles Brooker, a gentleman of the county, who, however, only commanded eighteen votes out of that large constituency. The Chartists of Carlisle proposed as their candidate Mr. Hanson, a journeyman weaver, who carried the show of hands against his aristocratic competitors. In numerous other places, both in England and Scotland, Chartist candidates were proposed, and in almost every case the vast majority at the hustings appeared in their favour. This was the case even where they went to the poll, and were left in a minority by the electors; thus proving the little sympathy between the electoral and non-electoral classes. There was one exception, and that was the borough of Leeds, where the middle class feeling was strong even among the unrepresented. Messrs. Leach and Williams were the Chartist candidates, but the show of hands was against them; and when their friends announced that result, they as the advocates of universal suffrage, bowed to the public decision, and retired from the contest. Had it not been for the pro-tory policy recommended by O'Connor, the election of 1841 might have conferred immense benefit on the cause. Had the Chartists never taken a single candidate to the poll, but left the Whigs and Tories to fight their own battles, standing aloof from both, and contenting themselves for the time being with carrying their men by show of hands, they would have necessarily increased their influence, and have laid the foundation for future triumph. But the policy pursued brought endless division into the ranks, worse even than was introduced by the discussion of moral and physical force; for although the policy of O'Connor met with the approbation of the majority, there was a considerable minority, consisting generally of the more influential members, who were opposed to it, and who ran into the opposite extreme of throwing themselves into the arms of the Whigs, in sheer disgust at the opposite policy. Thus the ranks were completely divided, and the elections, which if wisely taken advantage of would have materially aided the cause, only retarded the glorious object which the Chartists had in view. The Tories secured by the election a majority of nearly a hundred members over their Whig opponents; but with the exception of men who, like Roe-buck, had previously occupied seats in the House of Commons, not a single Chartist candidate was returned. Even where the Tories professed to coalesce with the Chartists for mutual advantage, they, with some few exceptions, withheld their votes from the Chartist candidates. This might have been expected. The distance between Whigs and Tories is but slight; but between Tories and Chartists, there is in principle an almost immeasureable distance. Whigs and Tories, from the social position of the classes they represent, are alike the upholders of monopoly ; is it likely then, that either the one party or the other will cordially unite with the advocates of Democracy, who are necessarily opposed to all monopoly? It was the want of viewing the question in this light that brought about all the disgrace of 1841, and which resulted, as before observed, in disunion in the ranks, and the most disastrous consequences to the Chartist movement.

The National Charter Association had not long been estab-lished before another quarrel broke out; and, as usual, upon a question of policy. Messrs. Lovett and Collins had written, while in prison, a work under the title of "Chartism," which contained a plan for the organization of the Chartists through-out the kingdom. This plan embraced the appointment of missionaries, the printing and circulating of tracts, the establishment of circulating libraries, the erection of public halls and schools for the education of the people in physical, mental, moral, and political science, and the establishment of normal schools for the training of teachers of both sexes. It was shown that if every person who signed the National Petition would subscribe less than one penny per week, there might be established every year eighty district halls, or normal, or industrial schools, at £3000 each, £240,000 ; seven hundred and ten circulating libraries at £20 each, £14,200; that four missionaries might be employed at £200 per annum each, travelling expenses included, £800 ; 20,000 tracts, at fifteen shillings per thousand, might be circulated every week, £780 ; for printing, postage, salaries, &c., £700 : thus expending every year, for the purpose of promoting the enlightenment and organization of the people, £256,200. No sooner, how-ever, did the above plan appear, than it met with a howl of denunciation. Feargus O'Connor and the *Northern Star* sounded the note of alarm, and denounced it as a middle-class scheme for destroying the Chartist movement, and the " new move " was pretty freely denounced in the great majority of Chartist localities. The *Northern Star* contained from time to time letters and articles setting forth that the plan adopted at Manchester was the only one worthy the adoption of the people, and denouncing all as traitors who favoured the plan of Lovett and Collins. Another cause of dissension soon appeared. Vincent had from his prison at Oakham addressed a letter to the Chartists, recommending them all to become teetotallers ; and on his release in March, 1841, he made an extensive tour through the principal towns, at the invitation of the friends, and at the close of the meetings recommended the formation of Temperance Chartist Associations, and administered the pledge to considerable numbers of the body. The denunciation of this plan did not, however, meet with the success of that which was hurled at the plan of Lovett and Collins. Mr. Hill, the editor of the *Northern Star*, appended his name to Vincent's address, and the same step was followed by a considerable number of the local leaders ; but it met with no favour from O'Connor, who denounced any plan other than the one adopted at Manchester.

A third party soon appeared which met with an equal amount of disapprobation from that leader. The Chartists of Scotland had in numerous places established Christian Chartist Churches, in which every Sabbath were preached political sermons, and these were to some extent established in England. At Birmingham, Arthur O'Neil was the pastor of a church of that description. In the *Northern Star*, O'Connor wrote a letter on " Knowledge Chartism, Teetotal Chartism, and Christian Chartism," in which he emphatically denounced all three as organized systems ; but against the first his letter was more especially directed. This, of course, led to no very good feeling between O'Connor and the parties in question, who looked upon his conduct as nothing less than an effort to establish a dictatorship, by throwing the mantle of his favour round one body alone, which he sought to mould to his own particular purposes. In this conclusion they were perfectly right. It was a piece of the veriest arrogance for any man to assume that all men holding similar principles were bound to pursue a certain line of policy, and that any man diverging from that line was an enemy to the cause. With regard to the plan of Lovett and his friends, there was in it all the elements of the people's regeneration, supposing it to be fully, faithfully and honestly carried out, which it might have been if set about in a proper manner. Happy would it have been if that plan had met with general adoption, always taking care that it was never perverted to mere middle class purposes. We might then in a few years have seen a popular power built up, of sufficient strength to have withstood all the blasts of the enemies of Democracy. But this was the very last thing that O'Connor desired. He never sought to raise the Chartist body by enlightening its members. He had no wish for that body to be anything more than a mob, which should conclude every meeting with three cheers for Feargus O'Connor and the *Northern Star*. The building of halls and schools, and the establishment of circulating libraries, would not only have led to the better instruction of the people, but it would have given them a material interest, not only in joining, but in sustaining the movement, which would then have been something better than a record of absurdities, disasters, and defeats.

The latter end of the summer of 1841 brought with it the release of O'Connor and O'Brien, and this for the time gave a great impetus to the Chartist movement, which had now a regular Executive Committee in the persons of M'Douall, Leach, Philp, Campbell, and Morgan Williams. O'Connor had announced through the *Northern Star* that when he should be released from prison, he would appear in a suit of fustian, to show how completely he identified himself with the working class. A suit of that material was accordingly made and presented to him. On the day of his release, a large number of delegates from various quarters met in York to congratulate him on behalf of their constituencies; these delegates amounted in number to fifty-six. A triumphal car was manufactured for the occasion, in which O'Connor was placed, clad in his fustian suit, and followed by thousands, who walked in procession through the streets of York, cheering at intervals the liberated " Lion of Freedom." The delegates before separating issued an address to the country, calling on the people to organize for the purpose of accelerating the movement. At Lancaster, on O'Brien's liberation, he was treated to an entertainment by the Democrats of that town, whom he addressed in his usual instructive and eloquent manner, and by whom he was greeted with the warmest enthusiasm. O'Connor and O'Brien were shortly afterwards invited to Manchester, where they were met by a vast procession of people, who greeted them with all the honours usual on such occasions.

O'Connor continued to attend demonstrations throughout the country ; and after a tour in Scotland, notwithstanding he had previously asserted the impossibility of a union between the middle and working classes, he announced that he would unite them in the short period of three months. O'Brien, on the other hand, stated his determination to attend no more processions or demonstrations of that kind, as he considered such demonstrations to be, for the present, productive of no good ; but he traversed the country at the invitation of the various bodies, and delivered those eloquent, brilliant, and instructive lectures for which his fame was so widely spread. O'Connor did not enjoy his tour through Scotland uninterrupted, for the Rev. P. Brewster followed him through a portion of his travels, and opposed him on the question of physical force, not without considerable effect.

In the spring of 1842, a fresh source of disunion arose in the Chartist ranks. Joseph Sturge, who had abandoned the Anti-Corn-Law movement on account of the want of principle evinced by its leaders, began to move on the question of the suffrage. He put forth a declaration, affirming the right of every man to the franchise. This declaration he called upon the friends of parliamentary reform to sign, and those who signed he invited to meet him in conference at Birmingham, to devise the best means of forwarding their object. A number of the Chartists, particularly in the West of England, looked with some degree of favour on this movement. Vincent and Philp were then residing at Bath, conducting the *National Vindicator*, a twopenny unstamped Chartist publication. Philp, as was observed previously, was a member of the Chartist Executive. These gentlemen signed the declaration of Sturge, and thus qualified themselves for the Conference to which they were elected. The Chartists of Wootten-under-Edge appointed Bronterre O'Brien to attend the Conference. Mr. McCartney was sent from Liverpool. Mr. Dewhurst and four others represented the Chartists of Bradford. John Humphries Parry was deputed from London, as well as several other delegates from various localities ; the greater number being middle class men who had never mixed in the Chartist movement. The organ of this new movement was the *Nonconformist* newspaper, which was edited by Mr. Miall, a dissenting minister, in which had appeared a series of able and eloquent articles setting forth the right of the working class to the suffrage. But however favourable were a portion of the Chartists to the efforts of Sturge, O'Connor and his party denounced those efforts, and when the Conference assembled, O'Connor repaired to Birmingham to watch the proceedings. The question of representation was brought before the body; and after a discussion of two days, during which time O'Brien and the other Chartist delegates used all their efforts in favour of their cherished principles, the Conference unanimously affirmed the six points of the People's Charter; and, on the motion of Messrs. Lovett and O'Brien, it was resolved to call a Conference of a more national character, the members of which should be elected by public meetings, and whose object should be to fix on the details of a measure of which those points should be the basis.   In the following number of the *Northern Star* appeared a leading article denouncing the Conference, and especially singling out O'Brien for animadversion.   He was pointed to as betraying the Chartist body to the middle class, and endeavouring to sink the National Charter Association in the new one of Sturge.   Philp was also held up by O'Connor to the execration of the Chartist public for having signed the declaration, which it was alleged was inconsistent with his duty as a member of the Executive.   The renowned agitator took a characteristic method of telling his admirers to oust that gentleman from his post.   He addressed a letter through the *Northern Star* to Leach, M'Douall, and Campbell, full of his usual flattery on such occasions, and declaring that when the election for the Executive should take place, his vote should be given in their favour.   The letter having the desired effect, Philp was ousted, and his place supplied by Jonathan Bairstow, a young man of good oratorical ability, who had been long engaged as lecturer in the West Riding of Yorkshire, and other districts.

O'Brien resolved his assailants should not put him down without a struggle, and accordingly addressed a letter to the editor of the *Northern Star,* complaining of his injustice, and challenging both him and O'Connor to meet him before the public of Birmingham, where the proceedings in question had taken place, and he would engage to prove that the charges made against him were entirely at variance with fact; but the only answer to this challenge was another tissue of misrepresentations.   O'Brien wrote a second letter to the editor, which that functionary, however, refused to insert, on the ground that it contained nothing but "blackguardism and Billingsgate, and the ravings of an angry man."   Nothing was farther from the truth than this statement.   It is true that O'Brien repelled the charges made against him with a manly indignation; but the terms of his letter were such as would have been far from disgracing any public journal.   Denied all justice in the *Northern Star,* which gave no fair report of the proceedings of the Conference, but contented itself with giving garbled extracts from other papers, O'Brien published his vindication in a small pamphlet, in which he clearly showed the injustice that had been done him.   The editor of the *Star* had charged him with opposing a resolution of thanks, moved by one of the Bradford delegates, to the working class for their past exertions in the cause ; the fact being that he supported that motion, until Mr. Parry, seeing that the general impression was that the motion was made from factious motives, moved as an amendment a vote of thanks, not only to the working class, but to all others who had advocated the cause ; when O'Brien seeing no chance of carrying the original motion, supported the amendment, which indeed embodied all contained in the original motion, besides being free from its exclusive character. O'Brien, in answer to the charge that he had sought to play the Chartist movement into the hands of Sturge and his party, explained clearly the position he had taken, which was that of recommending the working class to rely mainly on their own strength ; but at the same time not to stand in the way of any portion of the middle class who chose to advocate the principles of the Charter in a different manner.   In short, O'Brien showed that his aim was not the predominance of a faction, but the assertion of just principles, from whatever quarter the advocacy might come.   The conduct of O'Connor appeared all the more strange, as he had at a public meeting at Birmingham, after the Conference had broken up, actually supported a resolution strongly approving the proceedings of the Conference, and congratulating the country on the tone manifested by its members ; but then he took all the credit to himself for the good which had been accomplished.   It was evidently his intention to disparage O'Brien ; for although he had paid a reporter in Birmingham, no fair report was inserted of the proceedings, as that course would have frustrated the desired effect.   These one sided proceedings drew forth resolutions from the vast majority of the localities, denunciatory of O'Brien and the Conference.   Every paid servant of O'Connor's (and they were numerous) felt himself bound to follow in the wake of his master.   Still the most intelligent of the Chartist body were on the side of justice, and some resolutions in accordance with their sentiments were sent to the *Northern Star*, but they were either burked altogether, or kept back until such time as the poison had taken root.   O'Brien had but slender means of doing himself justice ; for he was without an organ, and the *Northern Star* reigned omnipotent over all.   Despite, however, all influences, O'Brien was invited to several places to lecture ; but an organized system was put in force to upset his meetings, and destroy his influence. Leicester was one of the towns where the O'Connor influence was widely felt.   In the spring of 1842, the working class of that town were in deep distress.   Thousands were out of any

THOMAS COOPER

FROM A WOODCUT

employ, save what the parish afforded; and for the work so performed, each man received the starvation pittance of twopence halfpenny per day. A multitude of men, wrought almost to madness by such severe privation, were easily excited against the rich, particularly when led by a man capable of the most vehement passions, and who could communicate his own burning nature to his adherents; such a man was found in the person of Thomas Cooper.

The subject of this brief notice was born in the town of Leicester; but his father dying while he was yet in his infancy, his mother removed with him to Gainsborough, in Lincolnshire, where she struggled amid much privation to obtain a livelihood for herself and child. This was often a very difficult matter, for frequently the mother was compelled to fast in order that her child might live, and her maternal fondness was such, that she subsequently deprived herself of many a meal in order to gratify his growing thirst for reading. It is no disgrace to Cooper, that in his earlier days he was in such a state of poverty as to be compelled often to be shoeless and stockingless. At that time he suffered from delicate health, in which indeed there is nothing surprising. At fifteen years of age he was put to the humble occupation of a shoemaker, and he continued to apply himself to his craft until he reached the age of twenty-three. But while Cooper was undergoing this mechanical drudgery, he was not idle in storing his mind with other branches of knowledge. He set himself to the task of learning languages, and mathematics. He acquired considerable proficiency in Latin, Greek, Hebrew, and French, and also in Geometry and Algebra. He also, in after life, obtained some knowledge of Italian, German, and other languages. During the period that he was thus struggling to make himself master of various branches of learning, he was earning but ten shillings per week at his trade of a shoemaker; and his mother's health being at the time but weak, his efforts to sustain her and himself were often severe. Some of Cooper's habits were similar to those of Cobbett, whom in the practise of early rising he even excelled, rising in summer as early as three o'clock, and walking until six, during which time he also applied himself busily to reading. At twenty-three, Cooper was persuaded by a friend, after a severe illness, to leave his trade, and follow the profession of schoolmaster. He accordingly opened a school at Gainsborough, which was highly prosperous. At about thirty he removed to the famous city of Lincoln, where he still carried on the same profession. While at Lincoln, Cooper became reporter for the *Stamford Mercury*, a journal which, until within a very recent period,

2 A

stood in point of circulation at the head of the provincial press. At first his salary as reporter was but twenty pounds per annum ; but it gradually advanced until it reached the sum of one hundred pounds, and he afterwards removed to Stamford, where he assisted in the editorship of the paper at a salary of three hundred pounds per annum. In this situation he did not long remain, but removed to London, and for some time had to struggle against difficulties ; being often compelled to sell some of his books, and at last to pawn clothes, in order to live. Occasionally, he received some trifling employment on some of the magazines; and at last he became editor of the *Greenwich Gazette*, which, however, enjoyed but a short existence. Just previous to leaving the situation of editor to the above journal, Cooper was offered a situation as reporter to the *Leicestershire Mercury*, a paper published in his native town. That situation he accepted; and he had not been many months employed before he had to attend a meeting to report a Chartist lecture by John Mason, of Newcastle. The result was that he became a Chartist, and afterwards opened a coffee-house, and a shop for the sale of Chartist publications. As before observed, the spring of 1842 was marked by great distress in the town of Leicester. Cooper warmly denounced the wrongs to which the working class were subjected. Possessed of a dashing style of oratory, restless energy, and indomitable will, he placed himself at their head. To the Chartist locality he gave the name of "The Shaksperian Brigade of Leicester Chartists," and the addresses of that body were signed by his hand under the title of "General." Excited by his harangues to the highest degree, the unemployed working class followed him by thousands through the streets, cheering in spite of their distress, and halting at the doors of the shopkeepers to receive their charitable contributions. When Cooper was unable to head these processions another man took his place, dressed in a military suit; but Cooper was the man to whose voice the people always listened, and whose dictates they always obeyed. It was astonishing to witness the good humour with which these half-starved multitudes went through their daily task of marching through the streets; but for their rags, and their haggard faces, one might have thought that the town was undergoing a general festivity. Now of all the worshippers of that day who bent the knee to Feargus O'Connor, first and foremost stood Thomas Cooper; and he was proud to declare himself a worshipper of his idol, as he did in a speech at Manchester. Whatever Feargus O'Connor said, Cooper endorsed. Whatever any other man said in opposition to Feargus, he was as sure to denounce.

In short, he was O'Connor-mad, and his acts corresponded with the state of his mind. On the release of his great idol Cooper composed a song, to which he gave the title of "The Lion of Freedom;" and at whatever meeting he appeared, the singing of this song was invariably the commencement of the proceedings. He always led the air himself—for music was one of his accomplishments—and his "Brave Shaksperians" lustily joined with him. Over this starving multitude he exercised the power of a king; he had but to command, and they were sure to obey. It was into this nest of hornets that Bronterre O'Brien fell, just after the proceedings of the Birmingham Conference.*

There was another party of Chartists in Leicester, distinct from the Cooper-O'Connorites, amongst whom was John Markham. Possessed of too much intelligence to bow to the dictatorship of the "Shaksperian General," they split from the main body. It was this party that invited O'Brien to lecture, and they engaged one of the largest and most splendid halls in Leicester. A charge of twopence was made for admission, to defray expenses; but the physical force "Shaksperians" burst into the hall without payment, and formed the majority of the meeting, while their "General" was on the platform to take advantage of his position. He had well trained and drilled his soldiers, and had made them understand the duty of passive obedience to his decrees. He had taught them that the rich were their enemies,—which was true enough—that Joseph Sturge was a rich corn-dealer, and that, consequently, he could not be honest; and that Bronterre O'Brien was the tool of Sturge, and the enemy of their great chief, Feargus O'Connor. He forgot to remind them that though the rich are generally the enemies of the poor, that all ages have furnished some men from their ranks who have had the justice and humanity to plead the cause of the people. The proceedings commenced by W. D. Taylor being moved to the chair, upon which Beedham, one of the "General's" subaltern officers, moved his master to that post. There was a dispute as to which had the majority; but O'Brien rose and declared that Cooper was elected, and he took the chair accordingly, and commenced the proceedings by giving out the "Lion of Freedom," which was roared, rather than sung, by the company. Cooper then sarcastically apologised for the unseemly behaviour of his poor fanatic followers, by stating that it was owing to their great anxiety to hear the "schoolmaster," and that they were too poor to pay for admission. He then introduced O'Brien, who gave one of

* See Cooper's letter in the appendix.

the most brilliant, as well as instructive lectures, ever delivered from a public platform.   From the more intelligent
portion of the audience he elicited the loudest applause.   He
entered into a lucid statement of the part he had taken in the
Conference, and declared that for himself he was still for the
Charter, details, name, and all.   Though this declaration was
received with tremendous cheering by a large portion of the
meeting, and although it was the standing declaration of the
O'Connorites, yet, the "General" not applauding, the "soldiers"
remained silent.   O'Brien, in the course of his observations,
referred to the Sturge-movement, and defended the right of
all men fighting for Democracy to join or form any association they might please, and that no man had a right to dictate
to any other man that he should join the National Charter
Association.   This sentiment was loudly cheered by O'Brien's
friends; but the "Shaksperians" remained silent, until Cooper,
thinking no doubt the lecture was beginning to carry conviction farther than was agreeable to the tenets of O'Connorism,
started up and exclaimed, "No, no! Chartists, Chartists!"
He then waved his cap and gave a counter cheer, which the
"soldiers" imitated as implicitly as a child would a parent.
Gazing on the faces of that distressed and trampled crowd of
men, it was easy to see the elements of which O'Connorism
was composed, viz., ignorance and fanaticism.   At O'Brien's
stern appeals to principle, his masterly arguments, and brilliant sallies, there was the ever listless look, the same vacant
stare.   It was only at the dictation of the chairman that they
displayed any signs of life, and then it was the life of passion,
and not of reason.   O'Brien spoke for about two hours, and
was then compelled through illness to conclude, being seized
with a fit of vomiting which rendered it impossible for him
to proceed.   This circumstance for the moment disarmed even
the rancorous devotees of O'Connorism, and Cooper announced that he should not on that evening put any questions
to Mr. O'Brien.   On the following night, however, before
O'Brien commenced his lecture, Cooper put a string of questions, such as, "Was Mr. O'Brien a member of the National
Charter Association ?" and others of a similar character.
O'Brien's answers to these questions were not equivocal.   He replied that he was not a member of the National
Charter Association; and that he preferred standing on his individual responsibility, and would not therefore at present belong
to any Association whatever.   Cooper then proposed a vote of
want of confidence in O'Brien, which his "Shaksperians" carried
against the rational portion of the meeting.   O'Brien attempted to speak, but in vain ; for an incessant clamour was

kept up by the "General" and his "troops," which baffled all attempts to gain a hearing, and the meeting broke up in the utmost confusion.

About the same time Vincent also was invited to lecture in Leicester. Cooper and the "Shaksperians" again were in attendance, and all attempts that Vincent made to gain a hearing were utterly fruitless. Cooper, standing on the platform, exclaimed aloud to Vincent's friends, " If Sturge or Spencer visit Leicester, the people will hear them ; but they will not hear that little renegade ;" and Vincent was compelled to retire from the meeting unheard.

Another freak played by Cooper was still more fantastic. William Dean Taylor was going to deliver a lecture. He had offended Cooper, and he, together with his party, attended. Of course the "Shaksperians" voted their leader to the chair. The platform consisted of a series of steps. Taylor had just elevated himself sufficiently high to speak, when the chairman demanded that he should stand on one of the steps below. Taylor refused to obey. " Chartists," exclaimed Cooper, " Mr. Taylor won't obey your chairman ;" and because the lecturer would not submit to this insolent demand, his voice was drowned for the evening in the clamour of Cooper's fanatical followers. Such were the freaks in 1842 of one of the greatest geniuses that ever sprang from the ranks of the working class ; and like most persons in a similar state of mind, Cooper had the presumption to declare that O'Brien was mad. Philp, however, had the coolness and self-possession to take an effectual stand against the deputy-dictatorship of Cooper. He paid a visit to Leicester with a view of giving a lecture, and waited on Cooper to arrange for the same. He was met, however, in the spirit of rebuke ; and told that before he could lecture in Leicester, he must go down on his " marrow bones," and beg pardon for the past. Philp replied in a calm and dignified tone ; and leaving Cooper, waited on the other body of Chartists, who arranged for him to lecture in their room. When Cooper heard of this he almost went down on his " marrow bones " to beg that Philp would renounce his intention ; but the cool, calm, and unassuming " boy," as Cooper called him, was not to be turned aside from his purpose. The same folly which reigned at Leicester pervaded more or less the Chartist body generally. Reason was trampled under foot ; passion, led by the spirit of demagogueism, was rampant; and no man stood the slightest chance who had courage enough to diverge from the path marked out by O'Connor and the *Northern Star.* In the then state of the public mind, what could be more unjust or irrational than to demand that all Democrats should join one particular association, while such a diversity of opinion prevailed amongst the leaders? This was the rankest arrogance. It is time enough to demand unity when you have sufficiently spread instruction to make it possible; but the mere demagogue is ever seeking to reach the end without compassing the means. Until the spread of knowledge is at least general amongst the people, it is vain to expect that they will ever enter into any organization sufficient for the accomplishment of their rights. In the spreading of that knowledge, it matters not whether there are one or a hundred associations, so that all have the one great object in view. The mischief which has been attributed to a diversity of opinion and action on points of policy, did not arise from that source; but from the fact that one section of the Chartist body could not tolerate a different policy to its own. Hence the strife and bickering—hence the dwindling down of the Chartist party from powerful bodies to comparatively insignificant sections.

Soon after these occurrences O'Brien became proprietor and editor of a journal which enjoyed the title of the *British Statesman*, and in that journal he vindicated most powerfully the right of every Democrat to perfect independence of action, so long as he remained steadfast to principle. It was impossible, however, for O'Brien, against all the power of O'Connor's established agents, and almost without capital, successfully to keep the field against his antagonist; and it was not long before the *Statesman* was beaten down. The Lovett party had its organ in the *National Association Gazette;* and Vincent and Philp continued to put forth their views in the *National Vindicator*; but neither of these papers enjoyed a very lengthy existence. To show the extreme inconsistency of O'Connor's policy at this period, we must not omit to mention one little circumstance that occurred at Bath. There was an attempt made to form a union in that city between the Corn Law Repealers and the Chartists, the basis of which was to be the repeal of the Corn Laws, and a full, fair, and free representation of the people. Vincent was the representative of the Chartists on the occasion of a public meeting to promote that object. We previously observed that Vincent generally excelled more in attitude, voice, gesture, and enthusiasm, than in matter; but that occasionally he made use of grand and beautiful language. The following is a specimen; it is decidedly one of the best selections that could be made :—

"The world is up against aristocratic institutions. True, the battle is fought on various fields. One day it is seen in the struggle of Dissenters against the domination of a law-made

Church. Another day it is heard in virtuous efforts to free the black slave. Another time it speaks in the exertions of our oppressed Catholic brethren. One moment in the cry against the Corn Laws; and at another moment in the erection of a school. These are but indications of a great and noble spirit. Higher principles are the springs of action; the belief in the brotherhood of humanity—a desire to realize Christian institutions. It is a mental and moral rebellion against the prejudices of ages. And gentlemen, why should you fear this indication of a new power? For myself, I rejoice at it. I see with Channing, that this is an age pregnant with events. I behold this rise of mind, and the tremulous pulsations of the democratic heart, with the greatest joy. Hail it! gentlemen, I beseech you. Do not despise it; encourage it—help it on. Look on this multitude; God is their and your common Parent. He made them, as He made you, in His own image. Sin and aristocratic institutions have marred that image; and just in proportion as the religious, intellectual, moral, political, and social elevation of the masses are secured, so in proportion will the image be restored to its original beauty. Do not wonder why the multitude reason on abstract rights instead of clamouring for bread; there's a nobility in it beyond all praise. To my mind, it is one of the sublimest spectacles to see a ragged and hungry people pondering over nice abstractions, and saying True, we want bread; but we demand rights long withheld. This is true magnanimity. It shows that a spark from the Deity has entered their souls. It is a proclamation of the Christian truth, "Man shall not live by bread alone, but by every word that proceedeth out of the mouth of God."

O'Connor visited Bath on the same day on which the above meeting was held; and though a portion of Vincent's speech was a thorough pandering to the middle class, O'Connor at a public meeting held in the evening, at which Vincent was present, exclaimed on alluding to it, "I knew that Henry Vincent, the Benjamin Franklin of Chartism, with his army of Bath Chartists, would achieve a glorious victory over our foes." It must be borne in mind that the so-called victory was a union between the Chartists and the Corn Law Repealers; that the Chartists, and particularly O'Connor, held that the Charter was necessary to render the repeal of the Corn Laws beneficial to the working class; and that the Charter, if carried, would have enabled the people to repeal the Corn Laws. Taken, then, from the above point of view, it was absurd to talk of a union for the two objects. O'Connor knew that the middle-class Corn-Law Repealers only meant to use the power of the Chartists for their own special object, and yet he called the policy of joining with the middle class for that object, "a glorious victory over our foes !"

When, however, the Chartist Executive, nearly at the same time, put forth an address in which was laid down a union between the Chartists and the Corn Law Repealers, on a better basis than that laid down by Vincent, O'Connor threatened to denounce their plan to the Chartist body, and his editor did denounce it in the *Star*. In the same spring in which these things took place, Joseph Sturge contested the representation of Nottingham with John Walter of the *Times*. At the previous election O'Connor had supported Walter. He now came forward and supported Sturge against that gentleman, although he had held him up as "a cunning tool of the Anti-Corn Law League," and he engaged a whole batch of Chartist lecturers in Sturge's interest, who for several days kept the town in a state of perpetual excitement. Sturge was not returned; but he polled more than eighteen hundred votes, which was within about eighty of his antagonist. O'Connor afterwards sent in to Sturge a bill for the payment of his lecturers, who consented to be paid by the very man whom most of them had been holding up as the enemy of their cause. Such were a few of the Chartist inconsistencies of that period; inconsistencies which could not fail to damage the movement, whatever temporary purpose they might serve.

Meanwhile the Executive were directing the attention of the country to the subject of another petition for the Charter, and they submitted a draft of the same for adoption. This second Petition did not, however, stop at the Charter; but, as well as stating a host of grievances, prayed for a repeal of the legislative union between Great Britain and Ireland. Here again was a bone of contention. A portion of the Scottish Chartists were opposed to the introduction of any other subject into the Petition than the Charter, and a controversy on the subject took place between Dr. M'Douall and John Duncan, one of the best and ablest of the Scottish Chartists. The majority, however, went with the Executive, and the signing of the Petition proceeded very briskly. A Convention was appointed to sit in London for three weeks, for the purpose of superintending its presentation. It consisted of twenty-five members, whose names were as follow:—Abraham Duncan, E. Stallwood, James Leach, J. R. H. Bairstow, C. Doyle, W. P. Roberts, George White, Feargus O'Connor, N. Powell, R. Lowery, James Moir, S. Bartlett, William Beesley, J. M'Pherson, G. Harrison, P. M. M'Douall, Morgan Williams, R. K. Philp, Ruffy Ridley, W. Woodward, J. Mason, William Thomason,

Lawrence Pitkeithly, J. Campbell, and J. Bronterre O'Brien. It will be seen that only six out of the twenty-five were members of the first Convention.   This body met in London on the 12th of April, 1842, and received the signatures to the National Petition, which in the aggregate were stated to amount to thirty-three thousand.   The Petition was presented to the House of Commons by Mr. Duncombe on the 2nd of May, on which occasion there was a large procession, which left the Convention Room and proceeded through several of the principal thoroughfares to the House of Commons.   The authorities had strictly ordered that no vehicles should pass along the thoroughfares, so as in any way to interfere with the procession, which order was rigidly enforced.   The concourse of people assembled on the occasion was immense ; many strangers being present from the country to witness the proceedings.   Duncombe presented the Petition, which was wheeled into the House, and stated the purport of its prayer ; he then gave notice of a motion that the petitioners be heard at the bar of the House, through their counsel or agents, in support of the allegations which the Petition con- tained.   When Duncombe brought forward his motion there was the usual quantity of speaking.   Macaulay was the great opponent of the motion.   He stated that he had no objection to any one point of the Charter but universal suffrage, which he described as amounting to nothing short of the confiscation of the property of the rich.   He uttered during his speech the most unfounded and abominable calumnies against the working class.   Duncombe's speech was noble and manly, and elicited the warm esteem of men of all parties ; but no amount of good speaking was sufficient to draw forth a response from the House of Commons, and only fifty-one members, including tellers, were found to vote in favour of his motion.   That House was too cowardly, or too callously indifferent to the condition of the people, to consent to meet the veritable representatives of the suffering poor face to face, and listen to an exposure of their wrongs from those who were best qualified to make it.   Duncombe declared that so much was he disgusted with the conduct of the House of Commons, that if the people ever got up another petition of the kind, he would not be a party to their degradation by presenting it.

While the Convention was sitting the differences of the Chartist body came under discussion.   The O'Connor policy was warmly denounced by Roberts, Philp, and O'Brien. O'Connor professed that he had never felt anything but affec- tion and love for O'Brien; to which the latter replied that he could not reciprocate the compliment : he had no love but for the other sex. The discussion ended by the passing of two resolutions against public denunciation, and private slander of public men by each other; which resolutions were respectively moved and seconded by O'Brien and O'Connor. O'Connor offered his hand to O'Brien, which the latter accepted on public grounds; but he declared that his opinion of O'Connor and his policy remained the same.

After the Convention had dispersed Chartist lecturers continued to agitate the various districts. A number of new men had since 1839 taken the field, or from an inferior had risen to a prominent position. Among these were Bairstow, William Jones of Liverpool, John Mason of Newcastle, W. D. Taylor, James Leach, and John Campbell. Of all these men, Bairstow was perhaps the man who possessed the greatest amount of power over a public meeting. His speeches were mostly declamatory, and his descriptions extravagant. He was not more than twenty-three years of age. His person was tall and well formed; his voice strong, clear, and musical; and his attitude commanding. He frequently indulged in figures of speech which set some of his audience gaping with wonder as to what could be his meaning. This was particularly the case when lecturing to the colliers, and similar bodies of men. The following extract will give an idea of Bairstow's usual style. It was delivered at a meeting at York in 1839, the speaker being then but twenty years of age:—

"Is this a state of things to be final? With an immense standing army, and an intended rural police—the curse of the country—whose annual expense amounts to four millions of money, for the purpose and with the intent to awe a free people into slavery—to buttress the citadel of aristocratic domination—to scour the country through every nook and cranny of its extent—to swamp the physical energy of the people, and render powerless their attempts at resistance—to keep in authority, maugre all the opposition, (and in defiance of the people's consent) a despicable, destructive, and damnable faction, sitting in silken repose on the couch of putrid insolence, or actively employed only in abstracting from the people the fragments of their liberties yet remaining; who draw as by magic all the wealth of the nation into their pockets, to uphold by physical force a system which has consigned its myriads of millions to a premature grave—has wrung thousands of bleeding widows' hearts with piercing anguish—has raised the orphan's voice to Heaven, crying for vengeance on its merciless murderers—has erased the last traces of God's image on man's physical form—has blasted beauty in its germ—struck the working population with disease, decrepitude, and untimely

death—has withered to ashes the energy of the labourer's arm
—has unstrung the very nerves of industry—has swept as with
a whirlwind's wing, the garland of Britain's proudest boast,
the honourable industrious labourer, to misery and starvation.
And not content with all this, when alive pursues him to the
bed of death in a bloody bastile, rent asunder from every one
he holds dear on earth; and even rushes beyond the precincts
of this mortal stage, consigns his last remains to the dissector's
knife, and erects itself on his tomb, opening its earthquake's
mouth, shouting give, give, give."

Mason was a very rousing and rapid speaker. His declamation was powerful, and his speeches were generally interspersed
with useful facts and solid arguments: he inclined to the O'Brien
school of politics. William Dean Taylor was one of those
men who are extremely dexterous at making something out
of nothing. Taking a single sentence for his text, he would
spin a speech two or three hours in length; and when he had
finished, one was convinced that the speech contained nothing
but "words, words, words;" and those words were delivered
in an unpleasant, and ridiculously ostentatious style. James
Leach was a man who never attempted to play the orator. In
addressing a public meeting he was just as free and easy as
in a private conversation; but for fact and argument there
were but few of the speakers at that period who excelled him.
John Campbell was more forcible than Leach; but being chiefly
confined to his business as secretary, it was not often that he
came before the public as a speaker. He was principally
famed for a pamphlet which he published under the head of
"An Examination into the Corn and Provision Laws," which
was directed against the Anti-Corn Law League, and
which at the time produced considerable effect. William
Jones was decidedly the best of the new orators who at that time
figured before the public. His style was easy and flowing,
and his diction pleasing and forcible, but void of that extravagance which characterised Bairstow. We give the following
as a fair sample of his style; it was delivered at the Queen's
Theatre, Liverpool, on the occasion of O'Brien's liberation
from Lancaster gaol. The orator had scarcely attained his
majority:—

"But it must not be supposed that though there are immoral
wretches amongst the working class, that vice has tainted
with its polluting touch the character of working men as a
body. The bulk of the people are moral and virtuous, and
there have been amongst working men instances of moral
forbearance and self-denial, which would lose nothing by a
comparison with the vaunted virtue of Rome's proud heroes.

When a working man, with his wife and family depending on his exertions for support, is thrown out of employment, and reduced to a state of destitution and indescribable misery, is depending for a temporary existence upon the charity of some kind friends almost as poor as himself, or upon the paltry pittance which a parish workhouse doles out for his support; when he reads in the pale and pinched features of his infant children, the havoc which hunger is making on their tender constitutions—when he sees the big tear of sorrow stealing silently down the cheeks of his beloved wife, whose countenance is deeply marked by the rude ravages of grief and want—when he hears the half-stifled sigh which rises from a broken heart, and tells of the mournful ruin that exists within ; and when he looks around upon society, and sees the glittering grandeur, and magnificent splendour so ostentatiously displayed by the rich —when he sees in the little gem that decorates the bracelet of some fine lady, or sparkles in the finger ring of some proud possessor of wealth, not only the means of relieving his present distress, but securing future enjoyment ; can we, my friends, can we sufficiently admire the heroic virtue of the man who could resist the strong temptation to become dishonest ? Must we not feel the glow of virtuous indignation burning in our breasts when we hear this man, who would prefer a life of want and suffering, to the enjoyments and plenty which might be purchased by an act of dishonesty, told that he has no respect for the laws of society, no regard for the property of his neighbours, that he is an ignorant and immoral wretch, who is unfit to exercise the rights of man ?   But should morality become the only qualification for an elector or law-maker, how many a proud and pampered Aristocrat would be compelled to surrender the reins of power, to give up the sweet enjoyments of place and pay, and hide his polluted character in the shaded obscurity of private life?   How many a petty shopocrat, who can rise with trembling hand, and eye-balls wild and red from the last night's debauch, and proceed to his daily employ-ment of dealing fraud and falsehood across his counter to improve his fortune ; who, when he hears the people demand-ing the restoration of their rights, can in the pride of his little greatness curl up into an expression of scorn and con-tempt the lip which is still quivering and blue from the effects of dissipation, and tell the working men that they are too immoral to be entrusted with the franchise,—how many such men as these would be deprived of those privileges which they refuse to the people upon the ground of their immorality ?"

R. K. Philp was another of the speakers who had come prominently forward since 1839.   He also was a young man

not more than twenty-five. His speeches were almost free
from declamation ; but many of them, though delivered with
but little force, were eloquent and instructive, and read better
in print than those of many a fiery orator.

The National Charter Association was never in so flourishing
a condition as in 1842. There were upwards of four hundred
localities in connection with that body, and forty thousand
names were on the books. County and district organizations
existed far and wide, and lecturers were engaged for several
months together to agitate the country. The county of
Northampton, which even in 1839 did not contain more than
two or three Chartist societies, now numbered nearly a
dozen. This organization was kept intact through the exertions of John McFarlan, a native of Scotland, who was county
secretary, and to whom the writer of this history stands
indebted for his first introduction to a public meeting. In a
similar state to Northampton, were Leicester, Nottingham,
Derby, Lancashire, Yorkshire, and many other counties; but
elements were in progress to break up this organization. A
secret blow was being aimed at the Executive by the O'Connor
party. Cooper of Leicester was the first to move in the affair
publicly. He got up a series of resolutions, all of them
amounting to nothing, finding fault with the Executive, who
were charged with neglect of duty. He addressed a letter to
a friend of the name of Mead, who was lecturing in the neighbourhood of Nottingham, in which was the following :—"You
see we have spoken out about the humbug Executive. George
and Julian, with the editor at Leeds, and our Generalissimo,
all go with me. Get your Notts chaps to approve our resolutions. Johnny Campbell is O'Brienizing : he must be
stopped."

Another event occurred on the 21st of June which produced
no little amount of sensation in the Chartist ranks—it was the
death of Samuel Holberry, one of the Sheffield prisoners. He
had for some time past suffered greatly from his confinement.
He was at first confined in Northallerton gaol, where the
treatment was very severe; but the death of Clayton, another
of the Chartist prisoners, caused applications to be made for
Holberry's removal. He was consequently removed to York
Castle; but he continued to suffer, and was constantly under
medical treatment. At last, on the representation of the
surgeon, the Home Secretary agreed to his release, on condition of his entering into security to keep the peace for five
years, in two hundred pounds, and finding two sureties in one
hundred pounds each; but while the matter was under
negotiation, poor Holberry died. In Sheffield the Chartists

were all astir.   It was resolved to honour his remains with a public funeral.   The body of Holberry was conveyed to the grave on Monday, the 27th of June.   Bands and banners were again brought into use.   A procession started from Sheffield to Attercliffe, where the remains of Holberry lay.   On the name-plate of his coffin was the following inscription,— "Samuel Holberry, died a martyr to the cause of Democracy, June 21, 1842, aged 27."   On one of the banners was the scriptural quotation, "Vengeance is mine, I will repay, saith the Lord."   A second bore the inscription, "Clayton and Holberry, the martyrs to the People's Charter;" and on the reverse side, "Thou shalt do no murder."   A third contained also the names of the martyrs; and on the reverse side, "The Lord hateth the hands that shed innocent blood."   An immense concourse of people followed the corpse, which was conveyed in a hearse to the cemetery; and as the mournful procession moved on, accompanied by some thousands of persons on either side, the sight was very imposing.   On reaching the town the numbers were immensely increased. Windows, roofs of houses, and other available spots, were crowded by spectators of the solemn scene.   The procession proceeded through what is called the Wicker, up Waingate, the Haymarket, High-street, Far Gate, Barker Pool, down Coal-pit lane, to Sheffield Moor, by which time a vast multitude of people were to be seen taking part in the proceedings. The *Sheffield Iris* estimated the number at twenty thousand, while the reporter for the *Northern Star* set it down at fifty thousand.   The correct number perhaps lay between these estimates.   Many of the shopkeepers paid the deceased the respect of closing their shops as the procession moved by. From Sheffield Moor the procession moved along the new road to the cemetery, in the grounds of which hundreds of persons were already assembled, who had obtained admission by a private road.   As soon as the gates were opened, there was a tremendous rush into the cemetery ; it was, however, but momentary, and was of course caused by an anxious desire to get near the grave.   The band remained at the gates, while the hearse, coaches, and people proceeded up the path to the chapel, where the burial service was read by the Rev. Mr. Landells, independent minister.   The coffin was then taken and lowered into the grave, and Mr. Landells, having offered up a prayer, retired.   Mr. S. Parkes then gave out the following hymn, composed by J. H. Bramwich, of Leicester, one of the Chartist poets of that day :—

"Great God ! is this the patriot's doom !
Shall they who dare defend the slave

Be hurled within a prison's gloom,
To fit them for an early grave?

Shall victim after victim fall
A prey to cruel class-made laws?
Forbid it, Lord! on Thee we call,
Protect us, and defend our cause!

In vain we prayed the powers that be,
To burst the drooping captive's chain;
But mercy, Lord, belongs to Thee,
For Thou hast freed him from all pain.

Is this the price of liberty!
Must martyrs fall to gain the prize?
Then be it so; we will be free,
Or all become a sacrifice.

Tho' freedom mourns her murder'd son,
And weeping friends surround his bier;
Tho' tears like mountain torrents run,
Our cause is watered by each tear.

Oh! may his fate cement the bond
That binds us to our glorious cause!
Raise, raise the cry, let all respond,
Justice, and pure and equal laws."

As soon as the singing of the hymn was concluded G. J. Harney, standing on the edge of the grave, addressed the vast concourse of people. We give the following extract from his speech, as reported by himself at the time. It will be seen that the language used by Harney was eloquent, however imperfect his delivery as an orator:—

"Our task is not to weep; we must leave tears to women. Our task is to act; to labour with heart and soul for the destruction of the horrible system under which Holberry has perished. His sufferings are over: he is where the 'wicked cease from troubling, and the weary are at rest.' He sleeps well; he is numbered with the patriots who have died martyrs to the cause of liberty before him. His is the bloodless laurel, awarded him by a grateful and admiring people. How different to the wreath which encircles the brow of the princely murderer, and the conquering destroyer! Compared with the honest, virtuous fame of this son of toil, how poor, how contemptible appear the so-called glories that emblazon the name of an Alexander or a Napoleon! Desolated empires, or slaughtered myriads, have saved their names from oblivion, but will not, in a future and a better age, save them from execration; whilst with the Tells and Tylers of the earth, the name of Holberry will be associated, venerated, and adored. Be ours the task to accomplish by one glorious effort the freedom of our country, and thereby prevent for the future the sacrifice of the sons of freedom.   Tyrants have in all ages, and in all countries, striven by persecution to crush liberty, and by torture, chains, and death, to prevent the assertion of the ' Rights of Man.'   It would appear that our haughty rulers are bent upon following the same, and seeking, by the same means, to arrest the progress of Democracy.   We bid them defiance !   We tell these puny Canutes, that despite their bidding, the ocean of intellect will move on.   Here, by the graveside of the patriot ; here, under the bright blue canopy of the skies, let us enter into a solemn league and covenant. Let the honest and true embrace in fraternity, and swear with me,—swear by the imperishable truth of our principles, by the dead relics of our murdered brother,—swear while the spirit of Holberry hovers over us, and smiles approval of the vow,— swear to unite in one countless moral phalanx, to put forth the giant strength which union will call into being, and aid, assist, and fraternize with each other to burst the bonds which bind us.   Swear as I now swear, that neither persecution, nor scorn, nor calumny ; neither bolts nor bars, nor chains, nor racks, nor gibbets ; neither the tortures of a prison death-bed, nor the terrors of the scaffold, shall sever us from our principles, affright us from our duty, or cause us to leave the onward path of freedom ; but that come weal, come woe, we swear, with hearts uplifted to the Throne of Eternal Justice, to have retribution for the death of Holberry ; swear to have our Charter law, and to annihilate for ever the blood-stained despotism which has slain its thousands of martyrs, and tens of thousands of patriots, and immolated at its shrine the lovers of liberty and truth."

Parkes then addressed the assemblage in a forcible speech ; after which the parties left the grave, and the people once more formed into procession and walked back to Sheffield. The mourners returned home, but the mass of spectators made for Paradise-square, and immediately broke up, after having been engaged for seven hours in the above proceedings.

At this time the battle between the Chartists and the Anti-Corn Law League was fought severely.   Campbell's pamphlet served as a text-book for the local leaders of the Chartist body, and they, as well as the itinerant lecturers, met the League on every platform, and contested their right to popular sup-port, sometimes in the fiercest manner.   There was—whatever may be thought of the policy—something heroic in the attitude assumed by working men on this question.   It was a battle of the employer and the employed.   Masters were astonished at what they deemed the audacity of their workmen, who made no scruple of standing beside them on the platform, and contesting with them face to face their most cherished doctrines.   Terrible was the persecution they suffered for taking this liberty.   Loss of employment usually followed, but it was in vain that their employers endeavoured to starve them into submission: they braved every such effort, with more determination than ever.   But now a blow was about to be struck which produced an effect upon the progress of Chartism from which it took years to recover.

The distress in the factory districts in 1842 was of such a nature, and was so wide spread, that it produced the utmost discontent amongst the operative classes.   There had been made reduction after reduction in their wages, until thousands were reduced to the merest pittance.   Towards the latter end of July meetings were held at Ashton, Staleybridge, and Hyde, at which the speakers recommended abstinence from work until such time as something like justice was rendered by the masters to the men.   On the 5th of August the men of Ashton struck work accordingly; and on the 7th of August two meetings were held at Mottram Moor, at the latter of which it was resolved never to resume work until the Charter should become the law of the land.   On the 8th of August another meeting was held at Haigh, near Staleybridge, which was attended by two or three thousand persons.   Placards were exhibited at the meetings, on one of which was printed, " The men of Staleybridge will follow wherever danger points the way."   After the speakers had addressed the meeting, the people proceeded to several factories in the neighbourhood—Harrison and Lee's being amongst the number—and turned out all the hands in accordance with a resolution come to at the meeting on Mottram Moor.   On the following day several thousands of persons formed into procession and marched upon Manchester, armed with bludgeons and carrying banners.   At the entrance to the town they were stopped by the military, and some conversation took place between the leaders and a magistrate, who was in company with the military force.   The leaders assured the magistrate that their motto was peace, law, and order, and they pledged themselves not to be guilty of disorder of any kind whatever.   The magistrate ordered the military away and accompanied the people on their march into the town.   When they had gone some distance the men separated themselves into various bodies, and proceeded from mill to mill, and from workshop to workshop, turning out all the hands, and suspending labour of nearly every kind.   From some of the shopkeepers they demanded bread and money, which were given ; the shops were shut, and for three days Manchester presented such a scene as perhaps had never been known in its history.

On the 12th of August a meeting of delegates from the factory districts was held in Manchester, at which three hundred and fifty-eight delegates were present. The question as to whether the people should continue the strike for a mere advance of wages, or whether they should stand out for the Charter, came under discussion, when three hundred and twenty delegates voted in favour of the latter. Another meeting of the same body was held on the 15th, at which an address was voted calling for the co-operation of the working class throughout the country for that object. On the 16th they again met, but the police appeared and allowed them ten minutes to disperse, which they accordingly did. On the same day another meeting of delegates took place. The original cause of the meeting was the unveiling of a monument to the memory of Henry Hunt; and it had been determined that a procession should be formed on that occasion. In consequence, however, of the excited state of the district, the procession was abandoned; and when the delegates met, it was to turn their attention to the all-absorbing subject of the strike. Ultimately, a resolution was adopted sympathising with the men on strike, and approving of the extension and continuance of the movement until the Charter should become a legislative enactment, and also pledging the Conference to assist the people in carrying out the same. This motion did not pass unanimously. The Rev. William Hill, editor of the *Star*, was present, and moved an amendment to the effect that the information laid before the Conference did not warrant the delegates in recommending any national strike or holiday, or in mixing up the name of the Charter with the strike movement, which it was believed was originated by the Anti-Corn Law League. Julian Harney supported Hill in his opposition to the resolution. The amendment, however, only secured six votes, and it was agreed that the minority should be bound by the majority. The Conference then issued an address to the country in accordance with the resolution agreed to; and in the address they spoke of the Executive Committee of the National Charter Association as a body having the confidence of all. That Executive also issued an address containing very forcible language, from which we select the following passages :—

"Englishmen, the blood of your brethren reddens the streets of Preston and Blackburn, and the murderers thirst for more. Be firm—be courageous— be men. Peace, law, and order, have prevailed on our side; let them be revered until your brethren in Scotland, Wales, and Ireland, are informed of your resolution; and when a universal holiday prevails—which will be the case in eight days—then of what use will bayonets be against public opinion? What tyrant can then live above the terrible tide of thought and energy which is now flowing fast under the guidance of man's intellect— which is now destined by the Creator to elevate His people above the reach of want, the rancour of despotism, and the penalties of bondage? The trades—a noble, patriotic band —have taken the lead in declaring for the Charter. Follow their example. Lend no whip to rulers wherewith to scourge you. Intelligence has reached us of the wide spreading of the strike, and now within fifty miles of Manchester every engine is at rest, and all is still, save the miller's useful wheels, and friendly sickle in the fields.

" Countrymen and brothers,—Centuries may roll on, as they have fleeted past, before such universal action may again be displayed. We have made the cast for liberty, and we must stand like men the hazard of the die. Let none despond; let all be cool and watchful, and, like the bridesmaids in the parable, keep your lamps burning; and let your continued resolution be like a beacon, to guide those who are now hastening far and wide to follow your memorable example. Brethren, we rely on your firmness. Cowardice, treachery, womanly fear, would cast our cause back for half a century. Let no man, woman, or child, break down the solemn pledge ; and if they do, may the curse of the poor and starving pursue them. They deserve slavery who madly court it. Our machinery is all arranged, and your cause will in three days be impelled onward by all the intellect we can summon to its aid. There- fore whilst you are peaceful, be firm ; whilst you are orderly, make all be so likewise ; and whilst you look to the law, remember that you had no voice in making it, and are there- fore slaves to the will, the law, and the price of your masters. All officers of the Association are called upon to aid and assist in the peaceful extension of the movement, and to forward all monies for the use of the delegates who may be expressed over the country. Strengthen our hands at this crisis; support your leaders; rally round our sacred cause; and leave the decision to the God of justice and of battle."

On the 15th there was a large meeting at Stockport, con- sisting of about five thousand persons, at which Richard Pilling, John Wright, and several others spoke. The mixing up of the political question with the strike caused a discussion in the meeting. Some of the speakers talked about going to London, but others opposed anything of the kind, and the proposers were charged with being tools of the Anti-Corn Law League. Some of the speakers recommended the people to return to their work. A meeting was held on the 13th at Roston. A person named Radcliffe spoke in opposition to any struggle for the Charter; he was for standing to the wage question; but he was most unmercifully hissed, and the general feeling appeared to be in favour of turning attention to the broader question of the Charter. This meeting was followed by another at the same place on the 15th, and again Radcliffe contended against struggling for the Charter, which, he said, they would never gain; but, despite his opposition, it was determined to make that document the basis of the strike. On the 17th a third meeting was held; Frederick Taylor was the orator of the day, and a Mr. Hoyle also addressed the meeting. Taylor reported that he had attended the delegate meeting at Manchester, and that they had determined to go for the Charter, and nothing less. Loud cheers greeted this announcement. At Bacup, on the 12th of August, the town was in a state of considerable excitement. A procession of people, amounting in number to two thousand, entered the town by the Rochdale road, armed with sticks, and immediately visited the several mills, demanding that the hands should turn out. In half an hour after they had entered the town every mill to the number of twenty was at rest; and the invading parties then went round in detachments to the various shops. Many of the doors were locked; but by persuasion and threats they got them opened, and demanded provisions, which the shopkeepers seemed afraid to refuse, and which they accordingly distributed. At Staleybridge, a crowd of from three to four thousand people paraded the streets, and went from mill to mill, crying, "Turn them out, turn them out;" an order which was speedily obeyed. From Staleybridge they proceeded to Dukinfield, stopping every mill which lay in their way, both leading to and in the town. They then went to Ashton, and proceeded in a similar line of conduct, running about from mill to mill and brandishing their sticks. The crowd was joined at Ashton by people from other places, and the aggregate body held a public open-air meeting, which was addressed by Messrs. Crossley, Pilling, and Aitkin, the latter of whom reproached them for their violent conduct. The Staleybridge people left Ashton immediately after the meeting, and proceeded to Denton and Hyde, where they also demanded of the workpeople a suspension of labour, until such time as they obtained a fair day's wage for a fair day's work, and the Charter became the law of the land. The people obeyed, and they were then ordered to fall into the ranks, which also they complied with ; going with their companions from place to place, and turning out all the hands. At Kingston they demanded of Mr. Ashton that he should stop his factory from working, an injunction he did not dare, or had not the inclination to resist. Many of the youths proceeded to acts of mischief which their elders had some difficulty in repressing. On the 11th the Staleybridge men proceeded to Saddleworth, to the number of eight hundred, stopping all the works on their line of march, and causing amongst the middle class the utmost consternation. On the 12th of August a meeting was held at Preston, in the Orchard ; which was addressed by Messrs. Aitkin and Challenger. On the following morning, as early as five o'clock, a crowd had assembled at the same place, from whence they moved off in order to stop a factory that was still working. From this factory they proceeded to others ; but while the people were busy, the authorities were by no means idle. The magistrates met and ordered out the police, as well as thirty of the 72nd Highlanders who were quartered in the town. The magistrates accompanied the soldiers down Fishergate, where they met an immense number of persons whom they prevented from passing up the street. Proceeding down Fishergate and Lunc-street the soldiers were pelted by the people with showers of stones, upon which they faced about with the view of effecting a dispersion, which they made great efforts to accomplish. The chief of the county constabulary told them that the Riot Act would be read ; but a stone was immediately thrown, which knocked the Riot Act out of the Mayor's hand. Showers of stones flew from all sides at the military. The Mayor, however, succeeded at last in reading the Riot Act, the stones meanwhile flying about him. The chief constable then informed the people that the Riot Act had been read. Women filled their aprons with stones, and brought them to the men; who from other streets threw them over the houses, causing very great annoyance, and harassing the military. It was in vain that the soldiers attempted to disperse them. All attempts to do so by a mere display of force were ineffectual, and the Mayor at last gave the order to fire. At the first discharge many of the people fell to the ground; the rest did not run away, but stood for two or three minutes in a state of consternation, as though they had not power to stir from the spot. Four were shot dead, and many others were wounded. The remainder speedily dispersed, and the military returned to their quarters. On the following day the mills resumed work. On the 16th of August a large body of men entered Stockport in order to aid in extending the strike, and proceeded to the mill of Mr. Bradshaw. Most of them were armed with sticks, which however, as in most of these popular gatherings, were carried rather from motives of personal convenience, than as weapons of offence. They encountered Bradshaw at the lodge door, and demanded admission for the purpose of turning out the hands. He refused their request, and gave as a reason that the men were gone to dinner. They told him that they would go and search, and made a push to get in; but were told by the owner that they had nothing to do with him or his men, and he locked the door in their faces. Not satisfied with this sort of reception they commenced breaking the lodge windows, and tried to force open the gates, which at last they succeeded in doing, and entered the yard. On this occasion, fired perhaps by the resistance they had met with, they laid their sticks about the person of Bradshaw, which caused him to be confined to his bed for several days. In the neighbourhood of Glossop the same sort of excitement existed. A body of persons proceeded to Chisworth, near that town, and made for the mill of Mr. Cooper, telling him that if he did not turn out his hands they would put out the fires of his mill. The whole of them, amounting to from one to two hundred, were armed with sticks. Cooper at once acceded to their demand; the hands left the mill, together with the crowd. The former wanted to return, but their employer was afraid to recommence running his mill. His men waited on him every day from the 11th (the day when they were turned out) until the 24th, each time requesting to be allowed to restart work, which they did at the latter date. They were, however, no sooner at work than a body of men went to the mill, and demanded that they should again leave their employment. This second body consisted of not less than from three to four hundred persons, who went into the yard and deputed two of their number to search the premises; the men, however, fled for fear of consequences, and some of the trespassers were arrested and examined before the magistrates, who were sitting at the barracks. The Messrs. Cooper appeared against them, and on leaving the magistrates' room, were assailed with stones, and compelled to run to save themselves from further assaults. The crowd also went to the mill of Mr. Rhodes, at Brookfield, and having presented themselves at the gates, demanded that the hands should cease work. They rushed into the yard, but the owner told them that there was no need for using violence, as they would stop without it. They ran into the mill, however, and turned the hands out by force, telling them that if they went to work again they would disable them from working altogether. These workmen returned to work on the 26th of August ; and a body of men speedily surrounded the mill, and attempted to force an entrance. Baffled in the first attempt, they made a second, breaking the windows, together with the frames, and ultimately the military had to be called out to guard the place. At Patricroft, in the neighbourhood of Eccles, a number of men, amounting to about three hundred, were going about on the morning of the 11th in bodies of ten and twelve. They gathered into a mass, and held a meeting, which was addressed by a person named Morrison. It was proposed that a deputation should visit the various works and request the hands to turn out ; but an amendment was carried that the meeting should proceed in a body for that purpose. They accordingly proceeded to the works of Mr. Nasmyth, but found that the men had gone to breakfast ; when they returned, a meeting took place between the two bodies. Those on strike requested the others to turn out. Morrison told them that, although they might think they were well off, the distress would ultimately reach them, and that if they did not turn out quietly, they would bring such a force as would compel them. "We are come," said one, "We are come, like a clock, to give you warning before we strike; and you may now consider that you have warning." They were told by the foreman of the works that the men should cease working. On the same day a meeting, held at Eccles, was addressed by Mr. McCartney of Liverpool, who strongly advocated the strike, and gave great hopes of its speedy success. The Lancashire men did not confine themselves to perambulations through their own county, but some of them made a tour into Yorkshire, in order to extend the strike. Large bodies, amounting to many thousands, went from Burnley and Bacup, on to Todmorden, and down the beautiful valley leading from there to Halifax, turning out the hands engaged at the mills between those towns. At Todmorden public meetings were held in order to keep up the agitation. On the 18th two meetings were held and were addressed by Mr. Brook, a schoolmaster, an old and consistent Democrat, who advised the men to stand firm until the attainment of the Charter. On the 15th of August a body of men assembled at the town of Blackburn, and proceeded about eleven o'clock in the day to the mill of Messrs. Rodgett and Brierley, where some of them commenced scaling the gates, and others knocking against them with their clubs.

The police were drawn up, and the military were present, ready to assist if necessary. A large number of the besiegers were taken into custody. Two hours afterwards another body numbering about two thousand came along the Burnley road, and approached the magistrates and military, who were still under arms. One of the party addressed the magistrates with, "Well chaps, how is it to be? Are we to go quietly or not; because if not, we will do so by force?" Some of the others spoke up and said, "Hush, hush, that is not what we want; we want to go quietly into the town to turn out the hands, until we get a fair day's wage for a fair day's work." The magistrates endeavoured to persuade them to leave the town, and told them that if they proceeded, all their efforts would be resisted. They refused, however, to go, and the police took about forty of them into custody. The rest made their escape across the fields and in various directions, and the police and military afterwards escorted their prisoners to the town. Another great crowd had gathered at the gates of a mill belonging to Mr. Eccles; but they moved away when the police and magistrates approched. On the following day a party of men went to the mill of Mr. Hopwood, and broke the windows of the lodge and counting-house, but speedily the military took sixty persons into custody, and dispersed the remainder. On the 18th some hundreds of men paraded the streets of Ashton, armed with sticks and other weapons. They stopped the brick-layers who were working in the streets, brandishing their sticks, and using threatening language; the Riot Act was thereupon read, but the men were nevertheless obliged to cease labour. They went to the mill of Mr. Hume, and requested the over-looker to stop the works, which he refused to do. They then went away, but returned shortly after with an increased force, and the hands turned out at their approach. They tried to exact from the employer a promise that the men should not resume work. Failing in this, they put out the fires, and drew the plugs from the boilers, so as effectually to stop the works. The military then came up and the crowd was dispersed. At Skipton, in Yorkshire, some two or three thousand men from Colne went to the mills belonging to Mr. Duhert, and Mr. Sedgewick, and asked them to suspend their works. They refused for about an hour, when the people were dispersed by the special constables; but speedily a reinforcement arrived, and although the Riot Act was read, they drew the plugs out of the boilers, and stopped the works. At Burnley all the mill hands were turned out on the 13th, and all the places around were in a very excited state. On the 15th, an attempt was made to stop the Habergham Eaves coal-pit, when the parties were dispersed by dragoons, headed by a magistrate.   The shop-keepers of Burnley were so influenced by the prevailing excitement, that they called a public meeting to petition for the People's Charter.   For fifty miles round Manchester the same excitement prevailed.   Bodies of men went from mill to mill, turning out the hands; breaking the windows and gates of the factories in cases of resistance; begging or demanding money or food of the trading classes, and otherwise exercising authority.   Committees sat in some places, and gave leave to the employers, in particular cases, to get their work finished to prevent it spoiling.

CHAPTER X.

While this excitement existed in Lancashire and Yorkshire the working class were no less excited in some other districts. In Staffordshire, particularly, things were carried to a very high pitch. Thomas Cooper, the "Shaksperian General" was lecturing amongst the colliers and other bodies of men in that district, on his way to the Manchester Conference. We have before alluded to the exciting nature of this gentleman's harangues; he worked the masses up to a perfect fury against the richer class. Thousands attended his meetings. He addressed the colliers at Wednesbury, Bilston, and Wolverhampton. At the first of these places thirty thousand persons were present; and resolutions to stand out for the Charter and to keep the peace were agreed to. From these places he proceeded to the Potteries, and on Sunday the 14th of August, 1842, addressed three meetings at Longton, Fenton and Hanley. He was requested to address another meeting at the latter place on the following morning, consisting of the colliers on strike; and on the same evening he addressed another meeting in the large room of the George and Dragon. Among other places he also visited Stafford—a town by no means celebrated for Democracy, and where there was great likelihood that he would be arrested. Cooper, however, was too cunning to be caught at Stafford. Seeing the police ready to pounce upon him if he but gave them the opportunity, he left off speaking seriously, and commenced to speak ironically. The following will give an idea of his method of baffling the authorities. It is an extract from a letter addressed to " My dear comrades," the "Shaksperian brigade of Leicester Chartists," and signed, "Your faithful General, Thomas Cooper."

"Great fears were entertained that I would be apprehended if I dared to stand up in the Market place that night. However, when seven o'clock had struck, there I was, mounted on a famous long bench procured by the friends. The Superintendent of police then took his station close at my right elbow.

The tory gentry and ladies threw up their windows to listen
and hear the rebel Chartist commit himself, and to see him
pounced upon and borne away in the dirty claws of the raw
lobsters. But no! I showed how excellent it was to have
a "sweet little silver-voiced lady," and pay one million and a
quarter yearly to support her and her establishment. I
demonstrated that loyal Chartists knew the land would be
ruined if the civil list were not kept up; and that working men
would all weep their eyes sore if Adelaide were to be bereft
of her £100,000 a year. I denounced any ragged shoemaker
(Stafford, like Northampton, you know, my brave Shaksperians,
is a famous shoemaking town) as a stupid fellow, if he dared
to talk about his aged grandmother being in a bastile, and
vegetating on skilly, while the Dowager had three palaces to
live in. The satire completely blunted the talons of the Blue
Bottle. His hard face relaxed; his teeth separated; and at
length he grinned outright, while the host of shopmates burst
into laughter."

The whole of Staffordshire was in a very excited state; in
the Potteries especially so. On the night following the meeting on Crown Bank, Hanley, the colliers began rioting, which
presently increased to a fearful height. At Longton a body
of men attacked the house of the Rev. Dr. Vale. They broke
into the cellar, where they found wine; many of them drank
until they reached a state of intoxication, and in that state
they set fire to the house, and other dwellings were also
speedily in a conflagration. The utmost terror prevailed
amongst the richer class. Immense masses of men went
about the streets; and throughout Longton, Fenton, Hanley,
Burslem, and the neighbourhood, there was one vast scene of
excitement, and the authorities quickly proceeded to arrest
certain parties who were supposed to be connected with these
movements. In the town of Stafford business was as completely at a standstill as though the men had struck work;
such was the effect which the strike in other places produced
upon it. At the time that Cooper paid his visit there were no
less than one hundred and fifty colliers in gaol for offences connected with the movement. J. Mason and several others
were also incarcerated for attending what the stupid magistrates designated an illegal meeting, though held some time
before the excitement connected with the strike commenced.
Cooper was so convinced of the certainty of an arrest if he
remained in the Potteries, that he set out on foot in company
with two youths at half-past twelve on the night of the riot,
in order to attend the Manchester Conference the following
day. He had not, however, got further than Burslem, when

he was arrested and taken before a magistrate, who, though in bed at the time, examined him; but after a little delay he was set at liberty, and resumed his journey, which he completed as he had designed. With the exception of Lancashire, Yorkshire, Staffordshire, and a few other places, there was not, however, any strike on the part of the working class; though the excitement in all the manufacturing districts ran very high— so high that the Government issued a proclamation denouncing the agitation, and cautioning all persons against taking any part in the riotous scenes that were being enacted; enacted, however, without any serious damage to property, except such as resulted from the stoppage of the works, and in many cases, as we have already stated, the strikers guarded even against this.

No sooner did the Executive issue their address, than the authorities proceeded to arrest the leaders of the Chartist body. O'Connor, Leach, Campbell, Bairstow, and a large number of others were seized, and committed for trial; but bail was taken for their appearance. The Government seemed very desirous to lay hands on M'Douall, as it well understood that he was the author of the Executive's address. A reward of fifty pounds was offered for his apprehension, and his portrait was exhibited in various public places throughout the country, together with a printed description of his person; and in some respects, a very erroneous description it was. The Doctor had many hair's breadth escapes from being pounced upon by the police. Alighting at the Leeds station, he saw a policeman looking at him very earnestly; he walked boldly up to the man, and asked to be shown to an hotel, in which request the policeman obliged him. He invited his conductor into the house, called for brandy; but speedily contrived to give his official companion the slip. He stayed in Leeds, however, for a short time, but was so disguised that he completely eluded the vigilance of his pursuers. On another occasion he was going into Manchester, and called at a house on the way, where he saw the *Northern Star* portrait of himself hanging against the wall; he was dressed in a short dirty working jacket, and a cap, and his graceful locks were turned up out of sight. He asked his hostess how she dare have the portrait of such a man in her house. Her reply was encouraging. Pulling off his cap, his hair fell down, and the woman recognised him at once. In order with greater security to continue his journey, he prevailed on the woman, who was in her working dress, to accompany him; he could not, however, on this occasion escape the eye of one of the police whom they met on the road. The woman looking back after passing him the policeman beckoned her to him, and advised her to get her companion out of the way as soon as she could, for the next policeman they met might not be so friendly.   After much dodging the Doctor escaped to Brighton and went with a friend to the races at that town.   Strange to say, they dropped by accident into the company of the Chief Constable, who told his friend that he had M'Douall's description and portrait with him, and that he was on the look out for him at that very moment.   The Doctor, however, by skilful manage-ment got over to France, where he remained in exile for a period of two years; it was by the advice of his political associates that he pursued this course.   While, however, he was placed in this critical position, the editor of the *Northern Star* indulged in the most ungenerous attacks on his character.   Money was wanted in order to assist him to live.   The editor, in reference to this matter, went so far as to say that any man with a spark of manly feeling, rather than thus hang on the skirts of the people, would hang himself on a tree.   O'Connor was in Manchester on the day that this attack appeared, and in an interview with Leach he sounded him as to the feeling of the Chartists with regard to his editor's attack.   He learnt that the feeling was in favour of M'Douall, and when addressing a public meeting in the evening, he strongly denounced the attack that had been made upon him.   The Executive had laid themselves open to an attack on money matters, having appropriated to their purposes about eight pounds more than was their due according to rule.   The editor did not lose this opportunity, but pointed out every trifling discrepancy.   He was opposed in this by O'Connor, and ultimately left the editor-ship of the *Star*, which made room for the admission of Julian Harney to the office of sub-editor, and ultimately principal editor of that paper.

In addition to Cooper being arrested for his participation in the Manchester Conference, he was arrested by the autho-rities of Stafford on a charge of arson, during the riots in the Potteries.   It was not pretended that he took any active part in the deeds of that night, but that his speeches were the cause of the mischief.   Cooper conducted his own defence, and made a most powerful appeal to the jury, who returned a verdict of not guilty.   William Ellis, another person tried on a similar charge, was not so fortunate as Cooper; he was found guilty and transported for twenty years, although he proved an *alibi*.   Ellis, however, was obnoxious to certain parties, and the jury had no scruple in finding a verdict against him.   In many other places the Chartist leaders were arrested on charges of sedition.   William Jones was seized at Leicester for making a seditious speech; and at Derby John West, another of the lecturers, met with a similar fate. Joseph Linney, of Bilston, was also arrested, as were George White and Arthur O'Neill, at Birmingham. West was afterwards tried before Baron Alderson, and pleaded his own cause; he was very politic in his defence, and the case being a very flimsy one, and the judge giving him very prudent advice, which he accepted, the jury returned a verdict of acquittal. Linney, when put upon his trial, was found guilty, and sentenced to two years' imprisonment. Arthur O'Neill, though a member of the Peace Society, was not deemed unworthy of a similar verdict, and he was sentenced to twelve months' imprisonment in Stafford gaol. George White was also brought to trial. When arrested he was very rough with the policeman; but of course he was ultimately overpowered. On White being put upon his examination he treated the magistrates to a very characteristic specimen of his audacity. He cross-examined the witnesses at great length, and sitting down in the midst of his examination, demanded a sandwich and a glass of wine. He was told that he could not be allowed such indulgences; but he rejoined, that he could not go on with the cross-examination of the witnesses unless his demand was complied with. Again he was assured that he could not be indulged, that it was contrary to the rules of the court. He replied, that he knew nothing about the rules of the court, but he knew that unless he was provided with the refreshments asked for, he could not go on. It was in vain that the magistrates reasoned; George was inflexible, and at last they yielded him the palm of victory. On his trial White was found guilty, and was afterwards sentenced to eight months' imprisonment in the Queen's Bench, where he frequently held a levee, at which attended the principal Democrats of the metropolis. Jones was brought to trial at the assizes before Baron Gurney; like many others he conducted his defence in person. The sedition with which he was charged, was such as no unprejudiced jury would have construed into guilt; but he committed the additional offence of delivering one of the most brilliant defences ever addressed to a jury; it lasted for four hours, and its eloquent diction even extorted the praise of the *Daily Times*. The conduct of Baron Gurney on this occasion must not pass without comment; it reminds us of the indecent interruptions indulged in by the bloody Jeffries when a victim was in his power. Jones cross-examined a witness, and among other questions, asked, "Did you think you were morally justified—" Baron Gurney, "Stop, stop; what have we to do with that?" Jones, "My Lord, I think—" Baron Gurney,

"You may think what you please, but we'll have no such nonsense as that about morally justified here." After the Judge had indulged in his triumph on this miserable technicality, Jones questioned the witness again, who replied, that injury was done to the London police before Jones arrived, but not after. Baron Gurney to Jones, "Why they took you up, you see; that's the way they quieted you. If you turn a dog down the street, and cry out 'mad dog,' there's no need to tell the people to knock him on the head; there's no occasion for it, it is not necessary, they will do it without." Jones, "I am quite aware of that, my lord; I, and those like me, have painfully learned that by experience." Jones had two friends in Court assisting him in arranging his defence. Baron Gurney said he should order them away if they kept prompting. Jones complained with great warmth of his interference. "My lord," said he, "may I beg that I may not be further interrupted, but permitted to conduct my defence according to the best of my ability, in the mode in which I have designed it." Baron Gurney, "That will depend upon whether you confine yourself within proper limits, and to the subject of the charge which you have to answer." Jones said, "He felt it useless to address them further." The above were not the only interruptions he received from his brutal persecutor. Among other things, he said that "He had always advocated peace and order, but it was true he had denounced the Government as tyrannical." Baron Gurney, with great vehemence, "Then you have done exceedingly wrong; we know nothing of you sir." Jones, "That was my conviction, my lord." Baron Gurney, "You may hold your convictions as you please sir, but you have no right to hold out to the people that the Government is tyrannical, that's a crime. You need not give yourself a bad character—we know nothing of you sir, but what you said and did on the occasion that we are enquiring into. Confine yourself to the present charge against you." On these indecent proceedings the *Morning Chronicle* asked, "Which is the judge, and which the criminal?" And it remarked, "Had Jones been the most unprincipled agitator, or even the most daring traitor that ever infested society, the treatment which he is reported to have received from Baron Gurney, would not the less violently have shocked every received notion of judicial decorum." A servile jury bowed to the ill-tempered caprice of the tyrannical judge, and delivered in a verdict of guilty; and Jones was sentenced to six months' imprisonment, for having actually assisted in restoring the peace of Leicester.

At the Lancaster assizes, March, 1843, Feargus O'Connor

and fifty-eight others were put upon their trial. They were all indicted in what was called a "Monster Indictment," containing nine counts, many of them of course resembling each other. The gist of them was that the said fifty-nine "did unlawfully aid, abet, assist, comfort, support, and encourage certain evil-disposed persons to continue and persist in unlawful assemblings, threats, intimidation, and violence; and in impeding and stopping of the labour employed in certain trades, manufactories, and businesses with intent thereby to cause terror and alarm in the minds of the peaceable subjects of this realm, and by the means of such terror and alarm, violently and unlawfully to cause and procure certain great changes to be made in the constitution of this realm, as by law established." This was the fourth count. The fifth charged them with "unlawfully endeavouring to excite Her Majesty's liege subjects to disaffection and hatred of the laws, and unlawfully did endeavour to persuade and encourage the said liege subjects to unite, confederate, and agree to leave their several and respective employments, and to produce a cessation of labour throughout a large portion of this realm, with intent, and in order by so doing, to bring about and produce a change in the laws and constitution of this realm." Mr. Baron Rolfe presided at this trial, which commenced on Wednesday, March the 21st. The counsel for the crown were the Attorney General, Sir F. Pollock, the Hon. J. S. Wortley, Sir Gregory Lewin, Mr. Hildyard, and Mr. Pollock. For the defendants there appeared Mr. Dundas, Mr. Atherton, Mr. Baines, Mr. Cobbett, Mr. Sergeant Murphy, and Mr. McOubrey. A large portion of the defendants, however, pleaded their own cause. There were no less than seventy two witnesses produced on the trial, the greater part for the prosecution. Sir James Graham was subpœnaed at the instance of O'Connor, and waited in court for several days, when, owing to another witness having come forward, O'Connor announced that he should not require to examine the Home Secretary, who, bowing to the court, took his departure for London. The trial lasted eight days, and considering the number of witnesses and defendants, it was a matter of surprise to many that it was over so soon. Sir F. Pollock, in opening the case, delivered a very temperate address, which contrasted strongly with some of the speeches made by the prosecuting counsel under the late whig Government. He did not appear to wish to take the slightest advantage of the defendants, maintaining throughout the most gentlemanly bearing towards every one engaged in the case. The examination of the witnesses for the prosecution alone lasted nearly five days. The two principal witnesses for the prosecution were persons named Cartledge and Griffin, men who had taken an active part in the movement. The former had been a defendant, but having been induced to turn Queen's evidence he stood in the witness box instead of the dock. These men laid before the jury an account of the proceedings which they alleged took place at the Conference; Cartledge having been one of the delegates, and Griffin present as a reporter for the *Evening Star*. Cartledge was the first of the two to be examined, and he deposed as to the meeting of delegates, and the part taken by them at such meeting. He was subjected to a long, tedious, and searching cross-examination, especially by O'Connor, who thus proceeded: Now, Cartledge, I want to have a word with you. When did you come to Lancaster? On Tuesday. Who did you come with? With Mr. Irwin and Mr. Griffin. How did you come? By the railway. By the third class? No. By the second class? No. By the first class? Yes. Is that your working jacket that you have on? It is. Have you not got better clothes than these? No, I have not. Will you swear that? I will. Have you not got a fancy waistcoat? I believe I have got a better waistcoat than this. What did you give for it? Three shillings. Did you give one pound fifteen shillings for anything lately? No. Where did you buy the waistcoat? I don't know; in a shop in Manchester. You don't know where; are you sure of that? In Manchester. In whose shop? I don't know. Will you swear that? Yes. Did you pay for it? I don't know. But you are not sure? No. Either me or my wife paid for it. Is it paid for? Yes. Do you know Mrs. Knowles? I do. Did you order a coat and waistcoat of her? Yes. When? A few weeks since. When did you get the coat? About a fortnight ago. Did you pay for it? I did not, and consequently it is not mine. Did you give any notice of your intention to leave your lodgings, or did you leave them in a hurry? I left them in a hurry. When I got the coat and waistcoat, I got them for the express purpose of pledging them, to bring me here. You picked up your traps after you got these things from Mrs. Knowles? Yes, for the express purpose of bringing me here. Did you pay for your seat in the railway carriage? Yes. Did you pledge the coat and waistcoat? I believe my wife has. What was got for them on pawn? I don't know. You never heard? No. Upon your oath? I don't know. How soon after you got the things from Mrs Knowles did you leave your lodgings? I don't know, I left my wife there. Were you what is called purveyor and secretary to a District Co-operative Store. Yes. For what district? Manchester. That is a large district; in what district of Manchester? Ancoats. Did you fill any post of distinction in the Brown Street district? I did. Were you purveyor and furnisher of the goods to the Association? Yes. And secretary? No. Did you settle accounts? So far as I was concerned I did. Was there a balance in your favour? No. Was it all the other way? I don't understand the nature of the question. Was the balance against you? No, not when explained. Do they charge you with owing the money? I believe not. Then what wants explaining? I had the selling of the *Northern Star*, the profits of which were to go to the Association; they did so, but certain parties ran into debt. A fresh committee came into office, and now they say I must be responsible for the debts of other parties, and they lodge that to my account. How much do you owe? I don't owe anything. With respect to the Co-operative Stores, do you owe anything there? I don't know how the matter stands. Do you owe money? No. Then do they owe you money? No. Then you don't know how it stands? No. You say that the Chartists behaved badly to your wife when she was at Chester? Yes. Did she go to Chester? Yes. Who sent her there? The Chartists. Did they give her money? Yes. Then it was at Chester that you first conceived the notion of coming here to give evidence? It was. And it was in consequence of the bad treatment of the Chartists to your wife that you came here? It was. Did you consider it bad treatment to have your wife sent to you? I did. You considered yourself badly treated by having your wife sent to you! Now, Sir, I think you stated in answer to the Attorney General, that on the 14th of August you were a Chartist? Yes. How soon after did you read your recantation? I have not read it yet. Are you still a Chartist? I still approve of the principles of the Charter. Are you still a Chartist? Yes. Are you for annual parliaments? Yes. Are you for universal suffrage? I am. Are you for vote by ballot? I am. Are you for equal electoral districts? I am. Are you for no property qualification for members of parliament? I am. And are you for payment of members for their services? I am. Then you are a good Chartist. In another part of the examination O'Connor asked, Where have you been for the last three weeks, Cartledge? In Manchester. For the whole time? A fortnight ago I was at Lymm in Cheshire. How long were you there? I went one day, and came back the next. And during the last three weeks you have never seen Griffin? Not before last Sunday night. When did you come here, and where did you come from? From Lymm, a fortnight ago. I thought you were at Lymm one day, and came back the next? I have been at Lymm twice. Ah, Sir, you are a limb! In this way did O'Connor keep the court in continual good humour during the cross-examination, and he obtained from Cartledge many admissions favourable to the defendants.

On the cross-examination of Griffin, O'Connor also elicited some important replies. Did you write to me for money to take you to America out of Irwin's way? No. You will swear positively that you never wrote for money to take you out of the country, because Irwin was tampering with you? I will. Did you write for money at all? I did, because it was owing to me; and you wrote to me, saying that I should apply to Mr. Hill for it. Why, you know that I had nothing to do with the financial department of the *Star*? You told me to write to Mr. Hill. Were you paid every week for your services? While I was under you I was paid for my services. And you did not write a letter for money to take you out of the country? Addressing the judge, "Your lordship has got enough; he has not denied having written to me for money to go to America, to take him out of Irwin's way." Griffin was most unmercifully cross-examined by counsel, and by several of the defendants, besides O'Connor, who kept him on his legs a considerable time.

When the evidence was concluded Mr. Dundas addressed the jury on behalf of Robert Brook, of Todmorden, and made a very able defence. Mr. Baines followed on behalf of James Scholefield, a dissenting minister, in whose chapel the Conference was held. Serjeant Murphy addressed the jury on behalf of Dr. M'Douall, Thomas Railton, and John Durham. He was followed by Mr. Atherton on behalf of James and William Stephenson. Mr. McOubrey was the last of the prisoners' counsel; he defended James Mooney and William Aitken. George Julian Harney then addressed the jury. He quoted from the *Sheffield Independent* a speech which he had delivered after the Conference at Sheffield in which he opposed the strike. The following pithy and truthful extract, we must do him the justice to quote:—

"He did not believe the majority of the trades were Chartists. They might carry a resolution here to cease work, and hundreds would cease; but would those who were not present be bound by it? He was sure they would not; but to-morrow morning the majority of the workshops and the wheels would be going. Those who had struck might assemble and turn them out; but would that make them Chartists? When they were out, would they stop out? Men who turned out, not for the Charter, but for fear of having their heads broken, when the turn-outs had left them, or when military protection was afforded them, would resume their labour in spite of the turn-outs. Even the *Northern Star* assured them that many of the men who had been turned out in other towns had resumed work. In Halifax they were turned out on Monday, blood was shed on Tuesday, but on Thursday the men returned to their work. Were the men of Sheffield going to make fools of themselves by passing a resolution for a strike, and then act as the men of Halifax had done? If they were going to strike, was it not worth while to spend a few hours in considering the subject? He hoped that some of the bold, fire-eating fellows who blamed him, would stand forth and give their reasons. Before he could consent to the strike, he must be satisfied of two things; 1st, that the trades of Sheffield were Chartist, and 2nd, that they would turn out of themselves for the Charter without coercion."

Harney then told the jury that his efforts to prevent the strike were successful; and after alluding to Cartledge and Griffin, he said:—

"Surely, gentlemen, you will not convict me upon the evidence of men so base as these. But if the verdict should be guilty, though the cold prison cell, though my consignment to the living tomb of crime and misery should be the consequence; yet believe me, gentlemen, I speak not the language of idle rant or bombastic folly, when I declare to you that I would not change my present situation for that of my accusers, to escape all that torture can inflict upon me. Though my march was from this court to the scaffold, there to exchange the embraces of love for the cold grasp of the executioner's red reeking hand, there to yield up life, with its heart-correcting sorrows, its hopes and joys, alas! too few, for that unfathomable futurity beyond the grave, I would not—I speak the language of calm reflection—exchange my lot for that of my accusers. Let them shrink from the light of day. Let them fly from the haunts of their species; and alone, cut off from the sympathies of their fellow creatures, and the love of their kind, feast on the reward of their treachery, and riot on the gains of their fiendish falsehood. Let them not forget their broken pledges and violated vows—vows of adherence to a cause they have so infamously betrayed; the remembrance of these will add a relish to their enjoyments, and zest to their pleasures. But, gentlemen, there will come a day when they will have their reward; when reflection's sting shall poison all; when the worm of memory shall gnaw at their hearts, and like the Promethean vulture, feast upon their vitals until the conscience-stricken wretches shall wither beneath the tortures of conscious guilt, and, dying, shall go down to the grave

without the love of wife or child, countryman or friend, to shed
a tear to their memories; remembered only to be execrated,
and thought of only with feelings of the utmost loathing and
disgust."

Harney delivered a long and effective address.   Samuel
Parkes was the next to address the jury.   He spoke at some
length, and was about to show that our social system was at
variance with the will of the Deity, when he was respectfully
stopped by the judge, and advised to keep closer to a consideration of the evidence, which he did during the remainder
of his address.   Richard Otley next entered on his defence.
He did not proceed at any considerable length; and before he
concluded, several of the defendants around him advised him to
use milder language, as by the course he was pursuing, he was
injuring his own cause as well as theirs.   Richard Pilling then
addressed the jury; and in the course of his defence gave
his personal experience of the degraded social position of the
working class.   His language was plain but forcible, and during
the time he spoke many of the auditors were affected to tears,
George Johnson followed, but before he had proceeded far he was
interrupted by the judge, who did not think the evidence against
him strong enough to warrant him in sending the case to the
jury, and with the consent of the prosecuting counsel, he was
accordingly acquitted.   Thomas Storah then rose and delivered
a short address.   He was succeeded by Bernard McCartney,
who applied himself to the evidence against him ; maintaining
that his conduct had been of a peaceable character.   He handled
the evidence in a very able manner.   John Allinson was
about to address the jury when the Attorney General gave up
the case against him.   William Beesley, the "North Lancashire Lion," as the Chartists familiarly called him, then entered
on his defence, and showed the jury that he had been opposed
to the strike, because he thought that to mix it up with the
Chartist movement was injurious to the latter.   He told his
prosecutors that if they hoped by the means they were taking
to crush Chartism, they would find themselves mistaken.   He
concluded :—

"Your verdict may consign me to a dungeon for a season,
but the time will soon pass over ; and when the gates shall be
again unbarred, and I am permitted to emerge once more into
the free air of heaven, I will be the same man.   Ten thousand
prosecutions cannot alter my principles ; for I am determined,
while life lasts, to sound the tocsin of the Charter as the death-
note of tyranny and faction.   Let ten thousand convictions be
obtained against me, and I will be a Chartist still."

C. Doyle was the next to speak.   In allusion to some of the defendants apologising for trespassing on the jury's time, he said, "I will not apologise for trespassing on your time. I have a good reason for doing so. In fact, I consider it no trespass. My liberty is at stake, and therefore I think you will bear with me, and hear me patiently." He then proceeded to show that he was no conspirator as had been alleged, and he defended his right to promulgate his opinions. He showed that many great men had advocated the same principles as himself, and he concluded by calling upon the jury to do him justice. Jonathan Bairstow then rose and entered into a very able defence. He complimented the judge and the Attorney General on the dignified and impartial conduct they had displayed during the trial. Albert Wolfenden delivered a short address, and was succeeded by James Leach, who entered into a lucid and masterly exposition of the social condition of the working class, showing how that condition had deteriorated within the short space of five years. He traced the recent agitation to that source, together with the machinations of the Anti-Corn Law League. Feargus O'Connor was the last defendant who addressed the jury. He was so elated with the conduct of his prosecutors, that he told the jury that he did not look upon the prosecution as an act of justice, or the leniency of mercy merely; but that he looked upon it, as regarded himself, as an act of grace. He analysed the evidence in a truly lawyer-like manner, and he then contrasted the conduct of the Government towards the Chartists with that shown towards O'Connell. He quoted Lord Brougham to show that the Anti-Corn Law League was at the bottom of the strike movement; Mr. Walter, of the *Times*, to show that it was owing to the New Poor-Law; the League and Mr. Cobden to show that it originated with the landlords; and others, he said, had charged it upon the Conservatives of Lancashire. He went on to say that the gentleman who got up the prosecution, reminded him of a fine old hunter which required a saddle wide in the gullet, full in the seat, and comfortable to ride on. The horse died, but the saddle was so good, that the hunting gentleman went down in the market with the saddle to find another horse that it would fit. So it was with the gentleman who got up the case for the prosecution. He went down into the manufacturing districts with his saddle to find who it would fit. He tried it upon the League; but finding that the Chartists had the broadest shoulders, and that it fitted them best, he placed the saddle upon their backs, and girthed it fast upon them. He went through the main portions of the evidence to show the flimsiness of the case; dwelt upon a variety of topics of a political nature, illustrating his case by numerous anecdotes, and every now and then raising a hearty laugh.   He sat down, after having addressed the jury for two hours and twenty minutes.

Several witnesses having been examined for the defence, the Attorney General replied at great length, but in a mild and temperate tone.   One could hardly avoid feeling that if there were any means by which the Government could get rid of the case and the defendants, they would gladly avail themselves of the opportunity.   There was no attempt to strain a single point ; as a public prosecutor, he made every admission in favour of the accused that he could possibly make.   On the following day Baron Rolfe summed up the evidence, wading through the voluminous notes before him with the patience and resignation of a martyr.   He evinced throughout a desire to give the prisoners every favour consistent with his position ; where it was possible to put a construction favourable to them it seemed willingly done.   The jury having retired to consider their verdict, returned in half-an-hour.   In the cases of twenty-one of the defendants they returned a verdict of not guilty.   Sixteen were found guilty on the fourth count, fifteen on the fifth, and seven were acquitted during the progress of the trial.   We shall give the names of all these in the appendix to this work.   Sentence was deferred, and counsel for the prisoners sued for a Writ of Error.   The Government never evinced a desire to follow up the prosecutions, although they, of course, went through the necessary forms.   When the defendants were brought up for judgment their counsel proceeded to show that the indictment was so drawn up that the whole proceedings against their clients must fall to the ground; inasmuch, as although the indictment stated the nature of the offences that had been committed, it did not state where the transactions had occurred.   The case was reserved for further consideration, and the defendants were liberated, each on his own recognizance of one hundred pounds to appear when called upon, and the Attorney General intimated that he would not require the defendants to appear during the arguing of the case.   From this time the proceedings were at an end.   The defendants were never called up for judgment; the Government saw that the objection was too clear to admit of argument.   Indeed, taking all the proceedings together, one can hardly escape the conviction that the whole trial was a farce; that the Government never intended to imprison the defendants, and that they purposely left a loop-hole in the indictment out of which their supposed victims might easily escape after an indulgence in the usual amount of legal jargon, for the purpose of saving appearances.

The authorities having thrown over the serious charge of arson against Cooper, he was tried at the Stafford March assizes for sedition, under two indictments, and on this occasion he proved a thorn in the sides of his prosecutors. There never was such a trial for a like offence in modern times. Cooper cross-examined the witnesses at such a length as to put all the officers of the court in a rage, which they could not conceal. It mattered little whether the questions put were of importance, so that they took up the time of the court, and gave annoyance to his prosecutors. When the evidence had been gone through he addressed the jury for ten hours. The trial lasted altogether ten days, and it threw the whole assize business for Stafford-shire, Shropshire, and Herefordshire into a state of confusion. As expected, the jury returned a verdict for the Crown, and the defendant was ordered to appear at the Court of Queen's Bench to receive sentence, when he inflicted another speech of eight hours duration in mitigation of sentence on his angry auditors, and would have continued longer only for the judge expressing a determination to conclude the trial that night. The result was that Cooper was sentenced to two years' imprisonment—the exact sentence that he had anticipated. This imprisonment was not without its fruits. One of its results was the production of a magnificent poem, entitled "The Purgatory of Suicides," which a large portion of the literary press declared to be equal to any poetical work of modern times. Another result was that Cooper was thoroughly cured of his O'Connor-mania, and before he was released from prison, he was denounced by his former idol through the columns of the *Northern Star*.

At the Stafford assizes John Richards was also tried, found guilty, and sentenced to twelve months' imprisonment; and Jeremiah Yates, of Hanley, underwent a similar sentence. We cannot forbear to mention one fact to Cooper's credit with reference to the first of these two persons. He became devotedly attached to Richards through this imprisonment, and as the old man was upwards of seventy years of age, and quite feeble in body, and therefore unable to perform any kind of labour, he allowed him a weekly stipend, which we believe was continued down to the time of Richards' death; and this was never bestowed grudgingly, but was often accompanied by a hearty wish for many years of life to the receiver.

At Liverpool and Chester many persons were brought to trial for offences connected with the strike. Lord Abinger presided at these trials, and in his charge to the Grand Jury went out of the way to make a most ferocious speech against the principles of Democracy, and all who held opinions favourable to those principles. He condemned the democratic institutions of America, and said all he could to excite the prejudices of his hearers against the prisoners, and expressed the deepest regret that the law was not more stringent with regard to offenders of that class. In sentencing some of the prisoners he told them that he entertained for them no other feelings than those of abhorrence and contempt. He also told them that the House of Commons would never allow members to sit in that House without a property qualification. He appeared ignorant of the fact that all the Scotch members were already sitting there without any such qualification. In short, this ferocious political judge threw all the opprobrium he could on the industrial orders, and all who advocated their cause. He set forth that the bulk of society were ever to remain the branded slaves of the few. This charge excited great indignation throughout the country. Even the middle class press denounced it; and it was made the subject of discussion and of a motion by Duncombe in the House of Commons; and although the motion was lost, it had a goodly number of supporters, and a very strong opinion was expressed against the brutal conduct of Lord Abinger, who not long after died, we believe unregretted, except amongst his private friends.

Almost immediately after the March assizes Duncombe also brought forward a motion for the appointment of a Select Committee to enquire into certain grievances complained of by White, Harney, Brook, Leach, Morrison, Skevington, and many others, in all about twenty-two persons. The petitions set forth a number of complaints as to a demand for excessive bail, harshness of proceeding when arrested, annoyances while in prison, and other similar matters. Duncombe, in a very lengthy speech, made out a strong case against the authorities, but of course his motion was rejected; only thirty-two voted in its favour, while against it one hundred and ninety-six recorded their votes.

We must just return to the latter end of the year 1842, a period memorable for the attempt to effect a union between the middle and working classes, under the auspices of Joseph Sturge. The Council of the Complete Suffrage Union had arranged for the sitting of a Conference for that purpose in the Autumn of that year ; but the Rev. William Hill, editor of the *Northern Star*, requested, in a letter publicly addressed to Sturge, the postponement of the Conference to a later period, in consequence of the confusion into which the Chartist body had been thrown by the recent arrests. Sturge and the Council at once acceded to the request, and the Conference was appointed to be held late in the month of December. It was arranged that the electors and non-electors should each return an equal number of members, except in cases where both bodies could mutually agree to elect the same persons. Towns with a population of less than five thousand were to return two members ; over that number they were to return four ; while London, Manchester, Liverpool, Birmingham, Edinburgh, and Glasgow, were each to return six. A fierce battle was now fought between the Complete Suffragists and the Chartists in the election of delegates. The Chartists were anxious to get their men elected if possible at the Complete Suffrage meetings, in order to avoid the expense falling on themselves alone, and in many cases they succeeded in so doing. At Leicester the electors held a separate meeting, but the redoubtable Cooper and his " Shaksperians " were at their posts, and effected an entrance, to the great discomfiture of the parties present. The fierce spirit of antagonism that raged between these two sections of reformers, augured but little for any union taking place between them at the Conference. All sections of the Chartists sent delegates to attend that body. Lovett, Collins, Parry (a barrister), O'Brien and many others, were deputed, and the Conference assembled at Birmingham on the 27th of December. Not less than from four to five hundred delegates were in attendance from all parts. Sturge was elected president of the Conference, and the work soon began in downright earnest. A motion was made by a member of the Complete Suffrage Union that the Bill of Rights, drawn up by the Council of that body, should be the basis of discussion. That document contained the six points of the People's Charter; but the motion made and supported by its friends was, to say the least, impolitic in the extreme. The Chartist body had long fought under the banner of the Charter. From the suffering that thousands of them had undergone, from the sort of living martyrdom that thousands more were undergoing at that very moment, the name of the Charter had become endeared to them; it had, in fact, become a household word. To endeavour, therefore, at one blow to set that name aside, was seeking to obliterate all the remembrances of the past. That past had been marked in many instances by folly, in some others by knavery; but with all its faults it had not been void of glory. Numbers of the Chartist body had exhibited a courage in the prosecution of their object which stamped them with the most indelible marks of man's true nobility. In the opinion of these, and thousands more who had not as yet drank so deeply the dregs of the cup of persecution, but who nevertheless admired the devotedness of their more unfortunate brethren, to give up the name of the Charter was a sort of political sacrilege.   Lovett took upon himself to represent this party.   Nothing could be more appropriate.   Lovett was one of the fathers of the Charter; now was the time for him to defend his offspring.   He rose amid the curiosity of the Chartist delegates, who expected that he was going to throw the weight of his influence into the scale of the Sturgeites, but in this they were agreeably disappointed, for Lovett announced that as the friends of the Bill of Rights had felt it their duty to exclusively move that document for the consideration of the Conference, he felt it his duty to move the People's Charter.   The Conference was taken by surprise. Both parties appeared confounded—the one in their joy, the other in their mortification.   The chairman and a few others only preserved their equanimity.   A tremendous cheer burst forth from the assembled Chartist delegates, who were almost frantic with enthusiasm.   O'Connor could not contain himself; he immediately rose to address the Conference.   Sometime previous he had stated that he had certain information that Lovett was one of a party to play the Chartist movement into the hands of the middle class; that such was not an opinion merely, but an undoubted fact.   Now he expressed his surprise that he should ever for a moment have doubted the political honesty of Lovett, on whom he bestowed the most fulsome flattery.   But if O'Connor intended by this gross adulation to win over Lovett to his party, he never made a sorrier mistake. All the time that he stood speaking the lip of Lovett was curled in scorn.   He thought of all O'Connor's antecedents, and his reflections only brought uppermost a feeling of contempt.   A   long   discussion   followed.   Mr.   Miall, Mr. Lawrance Heyworth, the Rev. T. Spencer, and others, ably advocated the Bill of Rights, and the Chartist leaders as ably advocated the Charter.   The combatants sometimes got to very high words, and were respectively hissed and cheered by the opposing parties.   Heyworth excited the indignation of the O'Connorites, by exclaiming, "It is not your principles that we dislike, but your leaders."   Mr. Summers, made the best and fairest motion, in the shape of a rider.   It was to the effect that both bills be the basis of discussion; but the Conference was now, with few exceptions, irrevocably divided into two parties, each resolved to stand by its own favourite resolution.   Had the Sturgeites proposed a motion similar to that of Summers, it might have commanded a large amount of support, even though unsuccessful in obtaining a majority, but it was too late; sides had been already taken, the ground was nearly all occupied, and the rider was almost unanimously rejected. The grand division followed, after which the chairman was compelled to announce that the Bill of Rights was lost, and that the Charter was carried by an overwhelming majority. Sturge immediately rose and stated that in consequence of the vote come to by the delegates, he and his friends felt bound to retire, and sit as a separate body ; and although the policy of the two bodies might be different, they could travel the same road, or at least move in parallel lines. Sturge and his friends then retired, and resumed their sittings in another place, where they discussed and adopted their Bill of Rights, and laid down plans by which they purposed to make its principles known to the country.

A few of Sturge's friends, however, conceiving that they were bound to remain with the majority, refused to quit their places. Among these were Mr. Pierce, a Quaker, from Newport, Isle of Wight, and the Rev. H. Solly, of Yeovil, whose unbending firmness in refusing to accompany their party, won for them the warm approbation of the Chartist delegates. The main body then proceeded to a consideration of the provisions of the Charter, in which some slight alterations were made, and they then considered a plan of organization for the Chartists of the United Kingdom. Cooper submitted a plan the basis of which was the appointment of an Annual Convention, which Convention should appoint a president, vice-president, treasurer, secretary, and vice-secretary, who were to constitute the Executive power of the Association, and to hold office from the day of their appointment until the ensuing annual meeting of the Convention. The members of the Convention were to be elected by public meetings in the respective localities. The Executive were to hold quarterly sittings in various places between the times of the meetings of the Convention, for the transaction of the business of the Association. The secretary of the Convention was to be the only officer in the receipt of a regular salary, the other officers and members of the Convention were to be paid only during the periods of their sittings. Sub-secretaries, sub-treasurers, and general councillors, were to be appointed by the members in their several localities. The Annual Conventions were to have the power of appointing general lecturers to propagate the principles of the Association, and the same power was to be vested in the Executive. Any officer of the Association found guilty of joining any association having for its object a less measure of justice than the People's Charter, was to be deprived of office by the members of the locality in which he might reside. In order to form a general fund, each member who could afford it was to subscribe one penny per week, and pay one penny every year for a card of membership, and make such other contributions as he might feel disposed to.   Out of the general fund the secretary was to receive three pounds, the vice-secretary, the treasurer, the president, and the vice-president fifty shillings each, and the other members of the Convention two pounds each per week, during the sittings of the Annual Convention.   During the presidential sittings, the secretary was to receive fifty shillings, and the other officers two pounds per week each out of the same fund, and at all other times during the year the secretary was to receive a salary of two pounds per week.   The members of the National Charter Association were also to earnestly recommend each other, by precept and example, to the practice of temperance and uprightness, to cultivate the intellect and moral feelings, to fulfil the golden maxim, " Do unto others as ye would they should do unto you," to trade with each other, and to assist each other in case of sickness or distress, and in finding employment.   This is an outline of the plan submitted to the consideration of the delegates, and it was agreed to by them that it should be submitted to the several localities, and that the first Convention should be held in London in the ensuing April, by which time the localities were recommended to   come   to   a   decision   on   it.   It   must   not,   however, he supposed that all was harmony and peace in the Conference. After the departure of Sturge and his party, Parry, the barrister, whom Thomas Cooper pronounced to be the best speaker of the Conference, moved a resolution in favour of conciliating and not opposing those who might feel disposed to go for the principles of the Charter, though pursuing a different mode of advocacy to that of the Chartist body.   Parry had been one of the strongest supporters of the Charter before the division.   George White opposed Parry's resolution, and met it with an amendment, when a long and stormy discussion ensued, which was at last ended by O'Connor rising, as he said, to throw oil on the troubled waters.   He proposed a rider, similar in every respect to Parry's proposition, and to which the latter gentleman, withdrawing his own resolution, gave his cordial support.   O'Connor's rider was adopted unanimously, the only reason for preferring it to Parry's resolution being that it was prosposed by Feargus O'Connor.   This factious spirit, however, by no means healed the dissensions of the Chartist body.   The party of Lovett soon after left the Conference, and although there were from three to four hundred Chartist delegates present at the commencement of the sittings of that body, they had dwindled down to thirty-seven by the time that it was agreed to submit the plan of organization to the localities. While the delegates were assembled the differences between some of the leaders came before them ; charges and counter-charges were made in quick succession. We do not care to enumerate these, but we feel bound to mention the fact that O'Connor appealed to Cooper, as to whether he or the editor at Leeds had conspired against the Executive, as stated in the letter to Mead ; when Cooper admitted that they had not, and that consequently, when he wrote to that effect, he did so without any authority from either. White and Harney had also previously denied being mixed up in any conspiracy of the kind. Harney showed a most inveterate spirit towards Campbell in giving this denial, finishing up his letter with "Avaunt, hell-fiend !" Now it strikes us, that this was a waste of his venom. If any one deserved his wrath it was Cooper, who had given very good cause for supposing that such conspiracy existed. We must here also observe that although no direct conspiracy might exist at that time against the Executive, neither O'Connor nor any of his salaried servants exhibited a good feeling towards that body. It was not sufficiently O'Connor-ridden to suit the purposes of the *Star* chamber ; and although but little was done openly against it, secret whisperings were at work to bring it into discredit, and thus to mar its usefulness. O'Connor never discountenanced any attacks made upon it, unless he saw that the wind of public support was blowing in its favour. This was almost always his public standard of right and wrong. He generally too, praised a man most enormously before he condemned him; thus leaving the more unreflecting to infer that his condemnation was a painful public duty. While his servants were whispering slanders against a man, O'Connor flattered him in the *Star*. When they came to attack him openly, O'Connor ceased to praise, and whatever policy he afterwards took depended upon the public. Some may ask—could a man act in this way and be honest? The answer to this question must depend upon what is meant by honesty. That O'Connor had a desire to make the people happier, we never in our lives disputed. He would have devoted any amount of work for that purpose; but there was only one condition on which he would consent to serve the people—that condition was, that he should be their master; and in order to become so, he stooped to flatter their most unworthy prejudices, and while telling them that they ought to depend upon his judgment, he at the same time assured them that it was not he who had given them knowledge, but that on the contrary, it was they who had conferred on him what knowledge he possessed. No other man ever stooped to flatter them so much. This was one of the secrets of his great popularity; but it was a popularity which was as unsettled as the waves. It swelled, and bubbled, and foamed for a while, only to recede, and be lost to its former possessor. He had a knowledge of the human heart, but it was only a one-sided knowledge. He knew that to flatter men, right or wrong, was the surest way to their affections ; but he forgot that men half-informed were never to be depended upon ; that they would cheer one day, and the next perhaps denounce or visit their former idols with the coldness of apathy. An excessive hankering after popularity, purchased at whatever price, was the great mistake of O'Connor's life. It led him to lend his influence, whenever the time arrived, to knock down every man who promised to rival him in the people's estimation. This was bad enough, but it was not the worst, for it led him not only to destroy the influence of men, but of measures, some of which were a thousand times as good as any ever proposed by himself. The consequence of such a policy was that the more intelligent, disgusted with such meanness and injustice, retired from the movement, thus taking from it all the real strength of which it could boast. They saw that there was no platform for honesty and independence, and they at length sank back in utter despair.

Soon after Cooper's plan was placed before the country, O'Connor also propounded a scheme of organization, the gist of which was, that a large hall should be taken by the Chartists of the metropolis, that there should be an Executive Committee chosen as formerly, whose members should hold their sittings in London ; that a body of thirteen Councillors should be appointed by public meetings, to whom the Executive should submit all documents before issuing them to the public. In case of disagreement, all such matters were to be put to the vote, the members of the Executive to vote as well as the Council. The Executive were likewise to attend, if they chose, all meetings of the Council, and to take a part in their debates, but not to have the privilege of voting. The Executive accounts were to be audited by ten members elected by the Council. A public meeting of the Chartists was to be held once in every month, when the minutes of the Executive and the Council were to be laid before them. O'Connor's plan appeared in the *Star*, after which a large number of letters were inserted on the subject of organization in the same journal. The only letter that attacked the principle of O'Connor's plan was one from R. G. Gammage, who briefly endeavoured to show the mischief .to which such a plan would lead ; that the existence of two such bodies as the Executive and the London Council of thirteen, the latter operating as a check upon the free action of the former, and from its superiority of numbers possessing a greater share of power, would lead to endless strife and bickering, in consequence of the jealousy and envy that would of necessity be created between the two bodies. The character of the London leaders at that time, with some few exceptions, strengthened this opinion. But he saw something beyond the differences that might arise from jealousy between two separate bodies; he saw that this was neither more nor less than a well-planned scheme on the part of its propounder to bring the Executive into subjection to his will; that every influence would be used to get a majority, if not all, of his creatures on the Council, in case of which the Executive would have been as much his own as though the power had been centred in himself.

Instead, however, of the Convention being held in April, 1843, as recommended by the Birmingham Conference, it was postponed until the 5th of September of that year, and in lieu of meeting in London, it met as before in Birmingham. O'Connor had by that time abandoned the plan of organization which he had previously propounded, and gave way to his editor and publisher, Mr. Joshua Hobson, who, together with Mr. Morrison, introduced a gigantic scheme for placing the working class upon the land, with a view to their social redemption. Of course the main portion of the plan was the joint production of O'Connor and his publisher; and it was one of the best schemes for dividing and breaking up the Chartist movement that could possibly have been invented by the genius or folly of man. Leaving out all other considerations for the present, the plan was in every sense illegal. In the first place, the title of the society was that of "The National Charter Association," which had for its object a political change. Now the law recognised no such thing as a political association. In the second place, the Association was composed of branches, and no society, even though the political part had been left out altogether, was legal under such circumstances. O'Connor knew these things very well. As a lawyer, he was bound to know them; and yet, despite this knowledge, he proceeded in the work he delusion. It was as if some of the leaders of the Chartist movement were resolved to try every means for bringing their principles to be abhorred by those not fully acquainted with their nature, and who therefore read those principles in the conduct of their advocates. The part they had taken in the late strike was, to say the least, a proof of their extreme folly;

for, extensive though the strike was, it was for the greater part forced, and could not therefore be successful, even as a strike for wages, in the districts where it had occurred. If the working class strike only from the mere compulsion of a number of their fellows, the richer class have merely to collect their forces, and the coerced workmen will resume work at the very earliest opportunity that a superior force enables them to do so with any degree of safety. But even though all the persons on strike in 1842 had voluntarily ceased labour, still that would have been no test of the feeling of the working class generally. A strike for a national object must be national in order to be successful. It was also clear from the evidence adduced at the trial, that a considerable portion of those most willing to strike were opposed to mixing up that strike with the political movement. The whole population inhabiting the districts on strike did not amount at the very highest computation to more than three-and-a-half millions of people. Supposing all of them to have been willing to engage in the struggle, still they would not have amounted to one-seventh of the population; but when we come to consider that the vast majority of those were either opposed to the strike, or felt but little interest in its favour, we must at once see how unfit were the leaders of that period for the task of pointing out to the people the glorious path to freedom and independence. The result was, as might have been anticipated, that the Chartists got the blame of all the follies enacted during the strike; and among a large portion of the men engaged in it they also got the blame of its failure, while not a single particle of good was achieved. The adoption of the Land Plan, illegal in its very foundation, and therefore destitute of that one essential where large funds are employed, security—was the next great folly which was to contribute to the disgrace of the Chartist movement. The plan found its supporters in the Conference at Birmingham, which was attended by thirty delegates, representing the following places:—J. Bairstow, Leicester; Thomas Clark, Cheshire; J. Cluer, Wednesbury; J. Dewhurst, West Riding of Yorkshire; C. Doyle and William Dixon, South Lancashire; H. Donaldson, Warwick; D. Ellis, Abergavenny; J. Eames and J. Mason, Birmingham; Squire Farrer and Joshua Hobson, Leeds; William Hosier, Coventry; G. J. Harney, Sheffield; J. Linton, East Riding of Yorkshire; S. Large, Marylebone; R. T. Morrison, Nottingham; R. Marsden, Saleden, Colne, and Clithero; P. McGrath and F. O'Connor, London; John Place, Burnley; J. Robins, Northampton; Henry Ross, Surrey and Kent; W. P. Roberts, Bath; W. Sale, Staffordshire Potteries; J. Shaw, Coggeshall;

J. W. Smyth, West Riding of Yorkshire; George Virgo, Brighton; T. M. Wheeler, London; R. H. Williams, Bristol. What made the matter worse there was another lawyer at the Conference besides O'Connor, in the person of Mr. Roberts, to whom the state of the law must have been also known, and yet he gave his support to the Land Plan. It would appear that the delegates themselves had their misgivings as to its legality when they passed the following resolution:—"That should the certifying barrister refuse to enrol the rules of organization adopted by the Conference, or any part of such rules, Messrs. Morrison, Hobson, and Wheeler apply for the legal advice of Messrs. O'Connor and Roberts, and if necessary, communicate with the delegates." The idea of taking the legal advice of two men who were either ignorant of the law, or knowingly gave their support to a plan that was illegal, is as rich a joke as ever was perpetrated on the public, and shows the sort of stuff of which the majority of the delegates were composed. Before the Conference separated Feargus O'Connor, Thomas Clark, P. McGrath, C. Doyle, and T. M. Wheeler were appointed to serve as the General Executive until the meeting of the Conference in the following April, and it was agreed that the secretary should receive two pounds per week, and the other members of the Executive thirty shillings each for their services, with the addition of travelling expenses when lecturing in the provinces.

O'Connor had up to this time refused to serve on the Executive, but circumstances had induced him to change his mind. He gave as his reasons for such change, that it had been disputed whether their Association was a legal one, and in case of its illegality, he desired to share the responsibility. That the delegates being limited in number, and many of them being but little known to the people, he thought that the whole country would not be satisfied with the appointment of a body, some of the members of which were little known, and in some of which all might not have implicit confidence; while he had, he said, the vanity to believe, that in his appointment as treasurer, with a seat on the Board, all would believe that he would see to the proper administration of the funds, and to the faithful discharge of their duties by the Executive. This was as much as to say that the country believed his colleagues to be rogues, and that his presence was necessary to keep them honest in their acts at least, whatever they might be in their intentions; and these men were servile enough to serve with him after this compliment to their integrity. His other reason for serving was, that being an unpaid servant, he might save thirty shillings per week to the Association. In the same address in which O'Connor gave his reasons for accepting office, he showed that if the paying members to the Association were only 25,000, their payments would make a weekly sum of £108 6s. 8d. ; while the payment of the Executive, twenty-six lecturers, and incidental expenses, would only amount to £46 10s.; leaving a balance of £61 16s. 8d. in favour of the Association, or £1,855 per annum, £600 of which he proposed should be swallowed up by the sitting of a Convention for a month in London (to do what, he did not explain), while £1,255 would remain in hand for a Law Fund, a Victim Fund, and a Carrying out of the Charter Fund. The Executive soon after their election appointed nine lecturers to agitate various districts; but instead of the funds pouring in for the payment of these, there was not even enough money to meet the demands of the Executive, and they consented to be paid out of O'Connor's pocket. The latter complained of this through the *Northern Star*, and his colleagues, ashamed at last of their dependent position, announced that they would not continue to serve the Chartist body unless they were freed from their degraded position. But no amount of badgering would bring in the funds. It was evident that great as O'Connor supposed the confidence of the country to be in himself, it was resolved that he should pay for the honour of being treasurer and guardian over the honesty of his colleagues; and notwithstanding their protest, they still continued to serve the public for the most part at O'Connor's expense. The plan of organization agreed to by the Conference, was laid before Tidd Pratt; but as might have been, and doubtless was expected, he expressed an opinion that the plan was not comprehended within the limits of the Acts of Parliament, and was consequently illegal. The plan was then altered to suit the emergency, but still not so as to place it under the protection of the law; but afterwards, that portion of it which referred to the Land and Building Fund, was entirely separated from the political part.

In the Autumn of 1843 O'Connor and Duncombe commenced a tour of agitation, principally through the North of England and Scotland. The former relied on this tour as a grand means of strengthening the Association, and wherever they went he enrolled members into it. Newcastle, Glasgow, Aberdeen, and many other places were visited by these chiefs of Chartism. At the latter place Duncombe took out his card of membership, and was enrolled as a member of the Aberdeen locality. At this beautiful city a great demonstration was made on the occasion. A procession was formed by the incorporated trades, which was led by the United Bakers in full regalia, and dressed in suits of rich pink muslin, and wearing splendid turbans. They were headed by three marshals on horse-back, two dressed in red and one in black silk velvet, and carrying broad-swords of polished steel, their horses being richly caparisoned. Chaplin in full canonicals, with powdered wig, marshals on foot, office-bearers carrying their batons, the master gorgeously dressed, with a train borne by five pages of beautiful appearance, all richly attired; the chaplain in his sacerdotal robes, bearing the Bible upon a crimson cushion suspended from his neck. Such was a portion of the paraphernalia used on this democratic occasion; and we ask, could the ranks of the aristocracy, or royalty itself, conceive anything more ridiculous than this excessive pageantry? Duncombe must have looked with a pitying smile upon men who could waste so much upon those gaudy trappings, at the very time that they were in the habit of denouncing their rulers for indulging in similar absurdities. As usual with O'Connor he exaggerated the results of this tour. The pro-ceedings at Glasgow will serve as a specimen. The two gentle-men were entertained at a soiree in that city, which took place in the magnificent City Hall. Messrs Moir, Adams, Paul, Duncombe, and O'Connor were the speakers. The latter sold cards of membership of the National Charter Association before the termination of the proceedings and disposed of more than five hundred. In addition to these he left a thousand with the secretary on speculation, and in the next number of the *Northern Star* it was announced, in O'Connor's letter, that he had disposed of more than fifteen hundred cards of member-ship at the Glasgow meeting. This exaggeration disgusted the leading Democrats of the city, and the National Charter Association never enjoyed much power after the evening of the enrolment. The very next day Moir, in our presence, ex-pressed his opinion in favour of a Local Charter Association, and his want of faith in the national scheme headed by O'Connor. All the lecturing and agitating powers of that gentleman were utterly unable to bring in the funds. He had got an Executive to his mind, but he had frequently to pay their salaries out of his own pocket.

The 8th and 9th of January, 1844, were marked in London by two festivals on the occasion of George White's liberation from prison, which were attended by some of the members of the Executive, and many of the metropolitan Democrats. At the latter of these festivals the toast of "Feargus O'Connor" was proposed, when White said, that it had got abroad that it was his intention to denounce Feargus O'Connor when he came out of prison. Here, then, was his denunciation :—

" He solemnly declared Mr. O'Connor to be in his opinion an honest man, and an indomitable patriot.   He believed if Mr. O'Connor had the wealth of a Rothschild, that he would apply it to the advancement of the happiness of the human family." " Yes," he again repeated, " Feargus O'Connor is a good and an honest man; and were he to denounce him, it would show him to be—what he trusted he never would be—one of the blackest of rascals."   Despite, however, this declaration, White did, some few years after, denounce the very man he had so warmly praised.

In the latter end of 1843, Mr Sharman Crawford, the radical member for Rochdale, addressed a letter to the radical reformers, through the *Northern Star* and the *Nonconformist.* In this letter he laid down the plan of a radical party in parliament, who should obstruct all business by making motions and speeches, and thus stop the wheels of the Government until the suffrage was extended to the whole people.   John Mason and some few others of the Chartist leaders expressed themselves in favour of the plan; but it was opposed by O'Connor.   The grounds he took were, that although Sharman Crawford was honest, he lacked energy and force, and if such a party was formed, it ought to be led by Duncombe, whose ability was undoubted, and who was the people's acknowledged leader.   Crawford's plan met with very little success. O'Connor's reasons were held to be conclusive by the Chartist body generally, and at a public meeting called by the friends of Crawford in London, Duncombe and O'Connor attended, and the plan was defeated by a majority of the meeting.   It appeared to be O'Connor's plan to establish a radical dictatorship inside, as he had pretty well succeeded in doing outside of the House of Commons.

In the summer of 1844 a plan was propounded for getting up a testimonial to Duncombe, in acknowledgment of his services to the working class.   O'Connor was for raising a very large sum, with which to purchase an estate; but Duncombe declined to receive anything in the shape of pecuniary reward, and the presentation consisted of a handsome piece of plate, worth about £700.   The Anti-Corn Law League had, for some time past, been making a-head of their opponents.   O'Connor had repeatedly challenged Cobden to meet him in discussion on the subject, which, however, the latter had always declined.   But on one occasion at Bradford, Cobden happened boastingly to ask, "Where was the man that would meet him in discussion, and maintain that the Corn Law was a just law?"   O'Connor at once accepted the challenge thus thrown out; still Cobden fought shy of O'Connor.   But speedily events so happened as to bring these two chiefs together upon the same platform. A requisition was got up by certain inhabitants of the county of Northampton to Messrs. Cobden and Bright, inviting those gentlemen to address a public meeting in the market square of that town. The requisition was signed by one thousand two hundred persons. The Chartists were immediately roused to action. A requisition was drawn up and presented to O'Connor, containing one thousand three hundred and fifty-three bona-fide signatures, soliciting him to meet Cobden and Bright in discussion on their favourite question. The requisition was gladly complied with, and both parties set actively to work to organize their numbers for the meeting. O'Connor, on the night preceding, and on the day of the discussion, appeared confident of a victory, and was in ecstacies at the chance of meeting the great guns of the League. "Whatever is in me," he exclaimed to his friends, "shall come out to-day." Towards the time of meeting numbers of people came into town from the country. The League endeavoured to keep the Chartist leaders from the platform by offering only half-a-dozen tickets for their admission. This would have been a miserable number on a spacious hustings crowded by their opponents. The Chartists were not to be thus baffled. Christopher Harrison, their secretary, a man of resolute energy, who had enjoyed many a platform battle with the League, and whose rough eloquence had often made them wince, set to work with several others to raise a hustings beside that of their opponents. When the members of the League saw the determination of the Chartists, they gave way, and allowed them a fair number of tickets, upon which they ceased their labours. At one o'clock, Messrs. Cobden and Bright accompanied by their friends, mounted the hustings amid the cheers of the League supporters. They were about to elect a chairman before the arrival of O'Connor and the other Chartist leaders, but a majority of the meeting warned them to desist. O'Connor, Wheeler, Clark, McGrath, and the local leaders shortly after arrived, amid the applause of the Chartist portion of the audience. A large part of the meeting appeared attached to neither party, but resolved to hear both, and judge for themselves. Mr. Grundy, iron founder, was proposed as chairman; the Chartists did not oppose, but voted for his election. Cobden was the first speaker, and he made out as good a case for the League as it was possible for man to make. Still it was felt that his position was a flimsy one, and that it would soon be dissipated by the sterner facts and reasoning of O'Connor; but those who had formed these expectations were doomed to be disappointed. That he delivered an eloquent speech, one of the most eloquent indeed that he had ever delivered, no one for a moment questioned; but as an answer to Cobden it was a miserable failure. He skimmed over the surface of every question, but below the surface he never ventured to dive. All the time he was speaking his friends imagined that he was only introducing the question, and when, after three-quarters of an hour's address he sat down, there was a look of blank disappointment. On his rising the cheers of the crowd had been loud and protracted, but when he resumed his seat they were comparatively faint, and speedily died away. What made matters worse, the speech had all the appearance of having been well prepared. A smile of triumph sat on the features of the leading men of the League as he concluded; they saw, that so far as O'Connor was concerned, the game was their own. McGrath followed O'Connor, to the evident delight of the Leaguers, as by that course Bright would secure the last speech. Harrison seconded O'Connor's amendment, which advocated an equitable adjustment between the various interests of the State in order to make Free Trade fair to all. He took that course so as to give McGrath the opportunity of reserving himself for Bright; but at O'Connor's bidding he went forward as soon as his chief had concluded. His speech was far better than O'Connor's, but he lacked the stentorian voice of the latter, and that fact, together with the disappointment the meeting had already experienced, made his words fall pointless. Bright followed McGrath, and levelled the most cutting sarcasm at O'Connor, which did not fail to produce an effect. Clark essayed to speak, but the meeting had become satiated, and the chairman proceeded to put the amendment and the motion, after which he decided that the latter was carried. Notwithstanding the failure of O'Connor's speech, it was our firm conviction that his amendment had the majority; but if so, that majority was a small one. Had the subject been properly handled, it would have been immense. The chairman, being one of the League, on finding the numbers so nearly equal, decided in favour of his friends. Thus did O'Connor on the 5th of August, 1844, give the League the greatest victory they ever obtained.

Only the month before O'Connor had pursued another piece of policy calculated to make the Chartist party appear ridiculous in the eyes of their enemies. An election was about to take place at Birmingham, in which Joseph Sturge was one of the opposing parties; and although, after the Birmingham Conference, O'Connor declared that should Sturge ever offer again to contest the borough of Nottingham, he would be there to oppose him, and although Sturge had not in the smallest degree altered either his principles or his policy, he no sooner issued his address than O'Connor journyed down to Birmingham and offered to assist in promoting his return. Whether he could reconcile it with consistency to oppose Sturge at Nottingham, and support him at Birmingham, we know not; we cannot, however, suppose that he drew any such distinction; but that in each case he acted from one of those unaccountable impulses which were ever the bane of his political movements.

In the Autumn of the same year a vigorous effort was made by the Chartist body to effect the release and return of Frost, Williams, and Jones. They were the more encouraged in this step by the fact that O'Connell and his party, through the issue of a Writ of Error after their trial and conviction had managed to break through the Government net, and issue from their prison after a confinement of three months. This movement of the Chartists was amongst the wisest they ever adopted. In all the principal towns requisitions were got up and presented to the authorities requesting them to convene meetings in aid of the object; and in Nottingham, Northampton, and a large number of other towns, these requisitions were complied with. Meetings were called, and petitions to parliament and the throne adopted. These were not without effect, for when Duncombe made his motion on the strength of these petitions for an address to Her Majesty, praying her to grant a pardon to the persons named, Sir James Graham, though opposing the motion on behalf of the Government, gave an intimation that at some future time it might be advisable to comply with the prayer of the petitioners. Very little, however, was done after this by the Chartist body in favour of the exiles, and it was not until 1850 that the Government gave them a pardon and that only on condition of their keeping out of the British dominions.*

We cannot refrain in this place from giving a specimen of the sort of motives which sometimes actuate political parties. Messrs. Bass and Gammage waited on the mayor of Northampton with a requisition signed by four hundred and sixty-three inhabitant house-holders. The mayor—a sort of Tory-Whig, rather more of the latter than the former—was quite agreeable to call the meeting, and was personally in favour of the object; but he must have the consent of a majority of the Town Council before he could accede to the wish of the requisitionists. Away they went to the most democratic member of

* An amnesty was granted to the Chartist prisoners on May 3rd, 1856, and Frost returned to England. He died July 29th, 1877, aged 96.

the Council, who refused to sign the requisition on the ground of the inutility of appealing to the Government.   The whig members were then waited upon, and after various journeys to and fro, three of them appended their names—one of them without any hesitation, another because he thought the exiles had been sufficiently punished.   The third grumbled, but gave no reason either for or against; he signed it, perhaps, because of the near approach of the municipal election.   From the Whigs they proceeded to the leader of the Tories, for they yet wanted seven names, and the Tories were in a minority.   The leader could not sign it without his colleagues, and his party always acted in a body.   He thought the mayor should at once have complied with the wishes of the requisitionists.   He was in favour of the object, and believed, as a lawyer, that they were entitled from the first to a free pardon.   There was a meeting of the conservative members of the Council in the evening; he should not be there, but they had better go and see what could be done.   Away they went to other tory members; they were all willing to sign if their leader did so. In the evening they attended the meeting at the George Hotel. The host, who was a member of the Council, never signed any of those things.   The others grumbled at the mayor for putting them to such an awkward test; but at last two of them signed it, on the ground that O'Connell had got clear.   They thought at the same time that Frost, Williams, and Jones, ought to have been hanged.   Another visit was paid to the leader of the Conservatives, with "Well, sir, all your colleagues are willing to sign, if you will set them the example." He smiled and signed, and then followed the signatures of his friends. Only one signature was now wanting.   Away they posted to the democratic member, with "Well, sir, the meeting now depends entirely upon you : only one is wanting to make a majority."   "Well, if that is the case, I will sign it."   He did so.   The meeting was called by a bill, on which appeared, next to the requisition, the names of the ten Councillors, as leaders in the movement; for the mayor concurred with the deputation that, for the sake of convenience, it would be better that the requisition should run, "We, the undersigned Town Councillors, together with four hundred and sixty three inhabitant householders, &c."   Great was the surprise of the whig and tory press at the appearance of the requisition; they could not understand it.   At the meeting the senior alderman, Mr. Sharp, took the chair, in the absence of the mayor, who was confined to his bed through illness; and so Democratic was he that, until Gammage had taken the sense of the meeting, he refused to occupy that post.   Then followed explanations from some of the Councillors as to their signing the requisition; Mr. Markham, the champion of the Tories, leading with a first-rate legal speech in favour of the object of the meeting. He was followed by Messrs. Marshall, Jeffrey, Gammage, Hanley, Hollowell, Munday, and others, and all the resolutions were carried unanimously; but on the following Saturday, both the local papers had the effrontry and the malignancy to oppose in their leading articles the object which so many of their townsmen had met to promote.

In the beginning of 1845 there occurred another of those unfortunate divisions which had so contributed to weaken the Chartist movement. M'Douall, finding that his return to England would compromise neither the safety of himself nor his fellow conspirators, had, after an absence of two years, returned, and almost immediately commenced a tour through the country. While in Scotland, finding dissatisfaction where-ever he went with the National Charter Association, and a desire for a separate Association for Scotland, he had suggested the latter at Glasgow, as most likely to conduce to the good of the cause. This gave offence to the Glasgow secretary, who wrote to the Executive, who, contrary to their expressed resolve on entering office, to send all letters of accusation to the parties accused before making them public, inserted not the entire letter, but an extract from it, in the *Northern Star*, without communicating a word to M'Douall himself. Near the same time a quarrel broke out between Leach and M'Douall; a fund had been collected for the latter in his absence, of which Leach was treasurer. The monies collected not being forthcoming, M'Douall complained through the *Northern Star*, when a paper war took place between the parties. At the same time, M'Douall was in a third encounter with O'Connor himself. When the question of the monies came before the Manchester Chartist Council, Leach made a statement before that body to the effect, that M'Douall had privately charged O'Connor with acting unfairly towards him in the affair of the Lancaster trials. O'Connor availed himself of the *Northern Star* on the following week to address a letter to the Manchester Council, appointing that body to try the case between M'Douall and himself; he never, however, consulted M'Douall as to the appointment of this tribunal, but treated him as though he had no right to any voice in the matter. The object in addressing the letter to the Manchester Council through the columns of the *Star,* was to get resolutions passed by the localities against M'Douall previous to the trial of the case. This course had its desired effect, at least in appearance, for such resolutions appeared on the following

week.   M'Douall did not recognise the Manchester Council
as a proper tribunal to try the case, so that O'Connor carried
everything his own way.   R. G. Gammage did not escape
from being mixed up in these squabbles—not from any desire
on his part to be engaged in them, but from an anxiety to see
justice done between the parties.   He was secretary to the
Northampton locality of the National Charter Association.
Mr. W. Hollowell, one of the oldest, most farsighted, and
consistent members of the Chartist body, brought forward a
resolution censuring the conduct of the Executive, for the
part they had acted towards M'Douall.   Gammage seconded
the resolution, on which a long discussion took place.   The
speeches of the O'Connorites were extremely amusing; their
logic may be summed up in an amendment made by one of
them:—"That this meeting exonerates the Executive from all
blame; but hopes that they will not pursue the same course
again."   With the aid of such logic as this, they succeeded
in defeating the motion by a majority of three.   When Gammage
saw the resolutions against M'Douall, and in favour of
O'Connor, in the *Star*, he felt disgusted with this premature
decision of the case.   One of the resolutions purported to be
from the Chartists of Kettering.   He had occasion to be at that
town on the Monday after the resolution appeared, and in a
conversation with the secretary, took occasion to reproach the
locality for its injustice in deciding on the case before the trial.
The secretary smiled and produced the minute book, which
showed that the resolution passed, and sent to the *Star*, was
very different to the one that appeared in that journal.   *That
the first called for a fair trial for both parties, whereas the last
contained a condemnation without a trial.*   It was thus that
Gammage came to know how business was managed in the
Star-chamber; that where resolutions did not square with the
views and interests of O'Connor, they were cooked, so as to
be rendered agreeable to his palate.   Gammage sent an
account of this affair to the Manchester Council, but instead
of thanking him, as any honest body of men would have done,
they, determined to have their master right, and his opponent
wrong, at any price, severely censured him for his pains.
This provoked a sharp retort from his pen, in which he freely
condemned their vile injustice, in sanctioning such forgery of
resolutions.   M'Douall, in a letter to Gammage, transmitted
a reputed extract from a letter from Smith, the Glasgow secretary, on whose letter the Executive had found fault with
M'Douall.   In this extract, Smith was made to say that his
letter, as it appeared in the *Star*, was different from the one he
sent to that paper.   Gammage wrote to Smith for the facts

of the case. His reply was, that his letter in the *Star* was correct. The reply was a long one, and Gammage sent a copy of it to the *Star*. The editor gave extracts, and tauntingly said, " Mr. Gammage doesn't like private letter writing ; will he produce the private letter on which he founded his queries to Mr. Smith?" Gammage sent the extract, but the inquiring editor never inserted it; thus leaving it to be inferred, that the Northampton secretary was ashamed of the part he had acted. Such was O'Connor-justice at that period, for we can only suppose the editor to have been a mere tool in his hands. About the same time, the *Northern Star* was removed from Leeds to London, O'Connor selling off his press and printing materials. The journal was now printed by Mr. McGowan of Great Windmill street, and was raised in price from fourpence-halfpenny to fivepence. This removal was made the occasion of a public festival in London, which was presided over by W. Clark, of the Charter coffee-house, Edgeware-road, one of the most earnest and enthusiastic Democrats of the metropolis, and withal an ardent admirer of O'Connor.

Another democratic journal was now in the field, under the title of the *National Reformer*, the property of O'Brien, and of which he was the editor. This paper enjoyed an existence of more than two years duration. Besides the advocacy of the political reforms set forth in the People's Charter, it laid down plans for the nationalization of the land, on the principle of compensation to existing holders. It went for a thorough alteration of our currency laws, condemning the Acts which fixed the price of gold, and made our currency to rest upon the plentifulness or scarcity of that metal. It advocated symbolic money, which should be based upon the real consumable wealth of the nation. Banks of credit, accessible to all classes, and which would therefore give to industrious sober men the opportunity, through the aid of loans, of becoming capitalists as well as workmen, was another of the reforms it propounded ; and the fourth great measure contended for, was that of equitable exchange, to be effected through the medium of national marts or stores, where producers might exchange their wealth for other wealth there deposited, or for symbolic notes representing the value of the wealth which they contributed, and which notes should be a legal tender throughout the country. Such were the great fundamental reforms set forth in the pages of the *National Reformer ;* but the editor always took especial care to impress his readers with the fact, that these reforms were only to be attained by the aid of political power. He combatted the notion which O'Connor was endeavouring to fasten upon the public mind, that the Co-operative Land Scheme of the latter would effect the social freedom of labour.   Week after week he sought by means of all the arguments it was possible for man to use, to show the utter absurdity of such plans, even though no law could be strained against them ; but seeing that such laws could be employed for their overthrow, he denounced as wicked and diabolical the means that were being used to excite hopes that it would be impossible ever to realize, and he predicted the utter failure of the whole Scheme, and the consequent retardation of the democratic cause.   For the manner in which O'Brien dealt with this question, he was denounced by O'Connor and his brethren of the Executive The former made the most extravagant calculations as to his power of placing the whole of his members in their cottages, on their own land, in an incredibly short time.   The period of six years was the utmost limit that he desired for effecting this great change in the social condition of his "dear children."

O'Connor had another antagonist at this time in the person of J. Watkins, who was formerly one of his most devoted disciples.   Watkins had denounced all O'Connor's opponents ; Lovett, Vincent, Philp, and the late Executive, had alike shared his wrath.   He now denounced O'Connor himself. The London Chartists had started a monthly magazine of which they made him editor.   In this publication he hurled his philippics at O'Connor, but the magazine soon ceased to exist. He afterwards wrote letters against O'Connor and the Executive in the *National Reformer*; but as O'Brien gave the parties aimed at the right of reply, he gave umbrage to Watkins, who soon denounced him also.   To damage O'Brien in the estimation of the public, O'Connor charged him with being in the pay of Spottiswoode and his gang, which was a society established professedly for the emancipation of industry, and which sought an alteration in the currency as a means of effecting that object.   Because O'Brien admitted the addresses of the society into his paper, and called attention to the subject treated of, O'Connor at once jumped to the conclusion that he must be in its pay.   O'Brien treated this charge as it deserved. He copied the whole of O'Connor's article from the *Northern Star*, and followed it with some satirical remarks, recounting many of the things O'Connor asserted, many others that he had promised, and some of the predictions he had made, and which had, he said, all been verified; from which facts, as O'Brien ironically styled them, they must believe O'Connor when he asserted that he (O'Brien) was in the pay of Spottiswoode and his gang.   This catalogue of O'Connor's absurdities, placed that gentleman in a very ludicrous light.   It would have been well for himself and the cause of the people, could O'Brien always have treated his enemies in a similar way.   O'Connor and his colleagues not only sought by every means personally to injure O'Brien, but they also attempted to ruin the character of his friends ; as an instance of which, O'Connor asserted that one Mozeley of Leeds, had been a spy for Lord John Russell in 1839, for the purpose of inciting the people to physical outbreaks, to tempt them to commit crime, and then betray them to the police.   For this it was said that he received the sum of seventy-two pounds.   O'Brien had a friend in Leeds by the name of Mosley, which name is pronounced in Leeds as Mozeley ; he was the only man bearing any such name among the Chartists, and believing the charge to be a thrust against himself, he wrote requesting the editor of the *Star* either to state that he was not the man alluded to, or to furnish proofs of his guilt.   The *Star* did neither the one nor the other.   As Mr. Hobson had been concerned in the charges against him, and was a member of the Leeds Town Council, Mosley got the subject brought before that body, when the veracious editor endeavoured to shift the responsiblity from his own shoulders, on to those of a brother member of the Council.   But even Hobson's version of the matter contra- dicted O'Connor's, for he charged the said member of the Council with informing him that the seventy-two pounds were given to put down the plug riots in 1842, whereas O'Connor fixed the date of the transaction in 1839.   But the member of the Council alluded to, gave the lie direct to Hobson, and told him that what he said was, that the seventy-two pounds was for the extra duty done by the police at that period.   The charge against Mosley, which was unsupported by evidence, and which was only trumped up because he was one of the sup- porters of O'Brien, produced a retaliation perhaps little antici- pated by its originators ; a retaliation, too, for which there appeared but too much ground.   It was no less than a charge against O'Connor, of having neglected to save Frost and his associates from the vengeance of the Government.   The charge was laid by William Ashton, of Barnsley, one who had for the Chartist cause suffered two years' imprisonment, and who had through a whole life been associated with the friends of labour and Democracy, having once undergone some years of transportation, in those days when for working men to combine was a very dangerous thing.   Ashton was a practical, bold, and determined Democrat, willing to make any sacrifices for the cause ; his past course was an earnest of what he was willing to suffer.   Ashton, disgusted at the conduct of O'Connor with regard to Mosley, with whom he was well acquainted, and of whose worth he was well aware, wrote a letter to his friend, with the view as he stated, of putting him in possession of the character of one of his accusers. Mosley sent this letter to the editor of the *National Reformer.* It appeared, from Ashton's statement, that a demonstration of the Chartists was in contemplation by some of their leaders, who met in London to arrange the same. The unfortunate affair that occurred at Newport, was the result of this arrangement. William Ashton was in London at the time, and met with these parties; but from private conversation with one of them, he soon learnt that he was not to be depended upon for the task he had undertaken to perform. Convinced of this fact, he was resolved, if possible, to save Frost from the snare which awaited him; but he was compelled to take ship at Hull, for France, in order to escape the clutches of the Government. The Rev. William Hill accompanied him to that port, and he communicated to that gentleman his suspicions that Frost would be betrayed, and urged him to see O'Connor, and get him to put a stop to the rash movement which was in contemplation. This Mr. Hill promised faithfully to perform. When Ashton returned from France, the Newport affair had taken place, and things had turned out just as he had predicted. He waited on O'Connor at Hammersmith, and asked him why he had not attempted to save Frost; when O'Connor denied that he knew anything about the affair, until after it had occurred. Soon after, Ashton waited on Mr. Hill, at Leeds, who declared solemnly that he had communicated the affair to O'Connor four or five days after parting with Ashton at Hull, and that he made the communication at the Bull and Mouth Inn, Leeds. George White afterwards went with Ashton to Hill, when he repeated his statement, and said further, that O'Connor started for Ireland soon after, where he remained until the mischief had been accomplished. Ashton further stated, that after these things had occurred, a Convention met in London, to devise means for rescuing Frost from the hands of the Government. O'Connor was elected a member of the Convention, but he never once attended their sittings. They however sent a deputation to wait upon him at the Tavistock Hotel, when he was in company with Geach, the attorney, who was, as our readers will remember, a relative of Frost. The deputation asked him for his advice. He told them that should Frost and his companions be convicted, and their lives endangered, he would place himself at the head of the people of England, and have a bloody revolution to save them; and Geach promised to head the people of Wales for the same purpose. Both

O'Connor and Geach urged upon the deputation the necessity of the people being prepared. The deputation gave in their report to this effect, at a secret meeting of the Convention at which Ashton was present. About the same time a delegate meeting was held at Dewsbury for the same object, from which a messenger was despatched to the Convention, for the purpose of learning their and O'Connor's decision. This messenger was sent back with the answer that they were determined to have a rising to save the victims; that O'Connor had promised to head them, and that Geach had pledged himself to head the people of Wales. The messenger was sent back to the Convention to say that the delegates had come to the same decision, and that they had fixed the 12th of January for the rising. If the members of the Convention approved of this decision, they were to return to their respective localities, and call upon O'Connor to perform his promise. O'Connor had the day before sent from Monmouth to Mr. Cleave an order for twenty-five pounds, to assist the Convention in any plan they might adopt. The members of the Convention returned to their localities to bring the people out; hence the risings at Sheffield and other places. But to the surprise of the men who had thus been led into the affair, the following number of the *Northern Star* contained a denunciation of the whole plan; and on the following week, O'Connor denounced it through the same organ. Such were the statements made in Ashton's letter to Mosley; and it is but right to add that, with regard to the first part of it, those statements were, as to the main facts, borne out by O'Brien. The latter affirmed that O'Connor was well aware of the intended rising at Newport; that it had been the subject of conversation between themselves; that he (O'Brien) had implored O'Connor to use his influence to stop it, as the inevitable consequence must be, in the unarmed and unorganized state of the country, the sacrifice of Frost and his companions. O'Brien has repeated the same statements to us in private. He offered, he said, to use what influence he possessed in order to prevent the intended rising, if O'Connor would not; but he begged of O'Connor to undertake the task on account of his greater influence, and therefore greater power, to effect the object. O'Connor solemnly promised to perform the task. "He would prevent it; the rising should not take place;" and on the faith of that promise, O'Brien left the matter in his hands. When, however, these statements came before the public, O'Connor denied them in toto; denied that he ever knew anything about the intended demonstration at Newport; that his first knowledge of the affair was after it had occurred. As impartial judges, let us discuss the probable truth on the sides of the respective parties.

In the first place, we ask—Is it probable that O'Connor, who had been the leading man in the Chartist movement, who had his agents everywhere, who had money at his command, and with these means in his hands had greater facilities than most men for learning every important step taken by his party, would remain during the several weeks that the matter was being discussed, in entire ignorance of the whole affair? Never was anything less probable. Why, the intended demonstration at Newport was not only known to almost every leading man in the Convention, but to numbers of men of minor influence in the movement; and we are to suppose, with these facts before us, that the man with greater influence than any other man, was almost the only one who knew nothing of the matter. The man who believes this must be possessed of a blind credulity which will for ever keep him groping in the dark. What above all confirms the statement that O'Connor had a thorough knowledge of what was going on, is the fact that, at that critical period, he left the scene of danger and embarked for Ireland. But he had another object in going to Ireland. What was that object, as stated by himself? Why, to persuade the electors of a single county—the county of Cork—to register their votes, so as to be prepared to return a Liberal member at the ensuing election whenever that event might occur. We do think, in all fairness towards O'Connor, that there is not a single man, whose judgment is worth one minute's consideration, but will without hesitation admit that the pretext was about as flimsy a one as could have been devised;—in fact, that it was, in the circumstances of the democratic party at that period, a most galling insult to the public understanding. His journey to Ireland, with his excuse for that journey, would almost of itself be a moral proof—if the term be admissible—of his perfect knowledge of the whole affair. Now, supposing this to have been the case, O'Connor acted a part, to use the mildest term, quite inexcusable ; and, considering his promise to O'Brien, a part most treacherous. Either O'Connor had faith in the contemplated rising, or he had not. If he had, it was his duty as leader of the people— which he assumed to be—to put himself at the head of the movement, or, at all events, to have taken a part in it. If he had no faith in its success, then there was no effort which he ought not to have made to prevent it. He did neither the one nor the other; and thus showed himself, with all his professions to the contrary, to be either cowardly or treacherous towards those whom he styled his friends. But, it may be asked—Was it possible that O'Connor desired the destruction of Frost? We do not suppose that he did, if his (O'Connor's) purpose could be served without it. But, as will be remembered by the men of that period, Frost was scarcely second to O'Connor in popularity. A love of popularity was the besetting sin of the latter. To win and retain that popularity, we conscientiously believe that with O'Connor all means were justifiable ; and that although he took no active part in organizing the Welsh movement, he quietly allowed the thing to go on, in order that his rival might be removed out of the way. O'Connor made a great merit of the sacrifices, pecuniary and otherwise, that he made to save the life of Frost. That he did not wish Frost to be hanged, we can readily believe. His blood might at some time or other have sat heavily upon his conscience ; but if ever it was the duty of one man to make sacrifices on behalf of another, it was O'Connor's duty to make sacrifices on behalf of Frost ; for he might, and he was the only man who could, have prevented the peril which endangered Frost's life. That O'Connor entertained no very generous feelings towards Frost, we have the evidence of Ernest Jones, who told us during a tour through the provinces in 1853, that O'Connor had told him that Frost was a scoundrel. "Of Frost," observed Jones, "I know nothing ; but O'Connor always told me that he was a d——d scoundrel." This was certainly a strange estimate of a man whom publicly he ever praised as one of the best of men, and whose fate he was ever professing to lament. O'Connor's conduct, with respect to the meditated attempt to save Frost, was equally reprehensible. Through his promises he led a number of honest and enthusiastic men into a snare, which might have, as in the cases of Holberry and Clayton, cost them their lives. O'Connor was by no means bound to join that movement, if he doubted of its success ; but having made a solemn pledge to place himself at its head, he was bound either to redeem that pledge, or to put a stop to the movement before his dupes had run themselves into danger, and it was heartless hypocrisy on his part, to publicly denounce that which he had privately encouraged.

We may be censured for these reflections. Honest but short-sighted men may think it better to let "bygones be bygones," and not to expose the treacheries and follies of the past, lest exposure should injure the cause of the people. Paltry, peddling, rotten demagogues, may seek to impress them with this mistaken notion. It is by no means a pleasant task to wade through the mass of treachery, falsehood, and folly, that engrafted itself on one of the noblest movements that ever engaged the energies of a people; but disagreeable as the task is, it must be performed. That which tended to lower and debase the democratic movement must be shown in its true colours, or the same errors will ever be repeated. The very desire to burke the truth, which we have witnessed, is a proof of the deep degradation to which we have been reduced. Fearless, vigorous honesty would say, "Out with the facts, and let us see from them if we cannot gather instruction for our future guidance." This is the policy upon which we will act, come what will; but in doing so, we take our conscience to witness, that we perform our task without any feelings of personal malevolence towards the objects of our strictures, and from a sense of duty alone. If the evidence already presented of O'Connor's knowledge of the Frost affair, previous to its taking place, be not deemed sufficient—though we believe that it will be conclusive enough to all impartial minds—we have yet further the statement of Lowery, a member of the first Convention. Wishing to have all possible evidence on the subject, we put this plain and straightforward question to him:—"Now, Mr. Lowery, you took an active part in the movement at the time of that unfortunate affair of Frost's; do you know whether O'Connor had anything to do with that affair?" Lowery's reply was, "O'Connor had nothing to do with getting up that movement; but he was perfectly cognizant of it, and was the only man that could have put a stop to it, had he been so disposed." Let the reader ponder the statements we have adduced, and then ask himself whether the evidence of all these parties is not more than sufficient, against the single denial of the party accused.

Nothing could be greater than the disagreements that existed amongst the old leaders, during the summer of 1845. While O'Brien, Watkins, and Carpenter, were pitted against O'Connor, all the latter three were in antagonism to O'Brien. O'Connor cast all the dirt possible on O'Brien's great principle of landed property, as upon his advocacy of a symbolic currency. O'Brien's views were the same as ever; the same as when O'Connor gave him the title of "schoolmaster." Watkins also attacked these principles, and denounced men who lived by political advocacy; the fact being, that Watkins himself had, until very recently, been dependent on the Chartist body, until the death of a relative put him in possession of a legacy derived from the public taxes, after which he took the title of an independent Chartist. Carpenter, then editor of *Lloyd's Newspaper*, also attacked O'Brien's principles and their advocate, although he had often propounded them, and had edited a political text book in which they were enunciated.

O'Brien in turn attacked these men for their inconsistencies, and showed up the fallacy of the Land Plan of O'Connor. O'Connor had calculated that with an original capital of five thousand pounds (the subscriptions of two thousand members at two pounds ten shillings each,) fifty members might be located, and a surplus remain of eight hundred and seventy-five pounds. He proposed to mortage the estate thus bought, together with the buildings, for four thousand pounds, with which another estate should be bought, and other fifty members located, adding to the four thousand pounds one hundred and twenty-five pounds of the surplus remaining of the original capital. The second estate was to be mortgaged in a similar manner, and a third estate bought with the money, and so on, until eight estates were purchased, and four hundred members were located. O'Connor calculated that these estates, which would more than double in value in three years, and would only cost thirty-three thousand pounds, would at the end of four years fetch at least sixty thousand pounds, thus gaining a profit to the society of twenty-seven thousand pounds. Other calculations were equally extravagant. Commenting upon these, O'Brien said :—

"In these calculations it is taken for granted that estates may be bought at the rate of £18 15s. per acre; that land at that price will be worth 15s. an acre per annum; that cottages can be erected on it at the average cost of £30; that working men bred in towns (for hardly any other are subscribers) will be able to pay £5 a year for their cottage and two acres, and yet continue to flourish on their bargain; that every man's holding will be more than double in value in three years; that as fast as fifty occupants can be located, monied men will be found to lend on mortgage nearly as much as the land and buildings cost; that fresh land may be purchased, and fifty more occupants be located in the same way; that there is no expense connected with the management of the society but what two shillings per head annually will pay; that all the purchases of land, and the mortgages effected upon it, will cost nothing for proving title, conveyancing stamps, &c.; that the treasurer, secretary, directors, &c. of this society will be all honest men, and charge nothing for their labour, (which it seems will be no sinecure) ; and above all, that landlords will never be wanting to sell land to the members, nor capitalists to advance them money upon pawning their title deeds. Such are a few of the very many strange things assumed in this curious table of calculations ; but if I mistake not, time will tell that the most of them are gratuitous assumptions. But the strangest of all is, that the philanthropic Feargus should have dragged millions of people after him to torch-light meetings, demonstrations, &c., all attended with great sacrifice of time and money, and caused the actual ruin of thousands through imprisonments, loss of employment, and expatriation, when all the while he had only to establish a ' National Chartist Co-operative Land Society ' to ensure social happiness for us all, and when, to use his own words in last week's *Star*, he had discerned that ' political equality can only spring from social happiness.' Formerly, he taught us that social happiness was to proceed from political equality ; but doubtless when his land-bubble has burst, he will have the old or some other new creed for us."

Shortly after these disputes O'Brien went on a tour, at the invitation of his friends in Birmingham, Sheffield, Rochdale, and other places. The O'Connorites did not let him pass without interruption. In Birmingham they were furious, but they were so few in number as to form but an insignificant portion of the meeting. In the other places they treated him with greater fairness. In Sheffield O'Brien threw out a challenge to O'Connor, at the public meeting, to meet him in discussion, when he would engage to prove that he (O'Brien) went for the whole rights of the people, and that Feargus O'Connor did not. This challenge was, however, never accepted. But O'Connor continued to ridicule O'Brien, and all the first principle men, whom he styled very great bores ; notwithstanding that three of his colleagues, Clark, McGrath, and Doyle, had been men professedly of that school. Meantime, O'Brien's caution was not without some little effect.

Near the close of 1845, a Land meeting of delegates took place at Dewsbury, when strong objections were made to many of the provisions of the Land Plan, and the practices of its managers, and resolutions were passed upon the subject. But all the important part of the report of such meeting was burked in the *Star* office ; notwithstanding which, the editor had the excellent taste to freely comment upon the proceedings of the delegates. David Ross commenced at this time to write, in the *National Reformer*, a review of the Chartist movement. Ross had been one of the Chartist lecturers since 1841 ; he was a teacher of elocution, and was accounted one of the best orators at that time in the movement, though not famed for any great grasp of political ideas. After his first letter, however, which was commented upon by O'Brien, he announced his intention for the present to discontinue the subject. While the Chartist body were ever squabbling amongst themselves, so much as almost to keep out of sight the great principles of their political faith ; while man-worship reigned supreme, and honest independence was almost laid prostrate at the feet of blind and unreasoning ignorance, the Anti-Corn Law League were moving forward with rapid strides. They began to show themselves at public meetings. They raised first £50,000 and afterwards £100,000, for the dissemination of their politico-economical doctrines. They scoured the country with tracts and missionaries, and it soon became evident that they were producing an effect upon the Legislature, and that victory must crown their gigantic efforts. In this emergency, O'Connor was true to his character, consistent in inconsistency. Sir Robert Peel, a statesman of the expediency school, and who was then at the head of the Government, announced a measure of so sweeping a nature, as to outstrip his old rivals the Whigs. Russell's last manifesto spoke of a four shilling duty ; Peel's scheme went for a total abolition of the Corn Laws. A great reduction was to be made at once, and in three years the duties were to expire altogether ; and Free Trade in many other departments was also planned in this Conservative measure. To the surprise of all parties (except it might be to those who were in O'Connor's secrets), Peel's plan no sooner appeared than that gentleman lauded it to the skies. There never was such a measure ; it was an " almighty measure " that would ' make the people great at home, and therefore great abroad ;" and he promised Peel, in the name of Duncombe and himself, the people's "undivided support." To some of those who had been accustomed to hear O'Connor call the League "the Plague," and who had often heard him style the Free-traders the "the free-booters ;" who had again and again heard him hold up the measure of that party, as nothing better than a scheme to make the producing class their slaves, and who had heard him say that that measure would be a positive injustice unless the people had control over its application; to some of those, we say, the conduct of O'Connor with regard to Peel's "Free-booting Plague" Plan appeared inexplicable. When the League was in bad odour, nothing but ruin was predicted by O'Connor in case of its success. Now it would make the Land Plan triumphant, by bringing down the price of land, and thus enable the people more freely to purchase. In short, his laudation of Peel's measure was the very antithesis of the amendment which he proposed at the Northampton meeting. We ask, Was not his whole opposition to the League a mere sham? and was there not a good understanding between himself and that body? We well remember one of our friends telling us, after the Northampton meeting, that such was his firm conviction. Our natural inclination to believe the best of all men, until their acts furnish proofs of their culpability, led us to doubt the correctness of this opinion; but it was not the opinion of a hot-headed man, but of a cool calculator (John Barker,) and on comparing notes, we found that opinion very strongly supported by evidence. O'Connor and Cobden went to Northampton by the same train; when they arrived at Blisworth, there were about twenty Chartists to meet the former. O'Connor told them that Cobden came into the same carriage; but as soon as he saw who was there, he had his luggage taken out, looked very black, and took his seat in another carriage. Now what seemed most strange of all was, that O'Connor should know Cobden, with whom he had not exchanged a word, and whom he declared *he had never before met in his life*, but whom he could point out to his friends easily enough. It is also worthy of notice, that O'Connor and Cobden met and conversed at Blisworth after the meeting, and that the former praised the latter enormously in the following number of the *Star*, though previously no language of reprobation was too strong for him to apply to the Corn Law repealer. Certain it is, that no speech was better calculated to give the victory to Cobden, than that of O'Connor at Northampton. A portion of the parties protested against the shifting policy of O'Connor : others were dissatisfied, and thought his conduct strange ; but he had so moulded the majority to his will that they yielded him a blind obedience, and charged the men who remained consistent with being in the pay of the Protectionists ; but as all candid men will at once see, if there were any pay in the case, it was more likely to be on the side of those who had turned apostates to their former professions, than on the side of those in whom no change had taken place. If O'Connor had stated his conversion to the principles of the Leaguers, the case might have been better for him ; but even after the measures of Peel had become law, in writing of Cobden and his connexion with the League, he said he was a good man, but had been bound to a bad system ; that very system to which he had given not only his own support, but the support of the Chartist body, before he even consulted them on the subject. The results of Peel's policy our readers all know. His measures became law ; but events occurred about the same and after that time, to prevent the mischievous effects which such a change must have worked to the productive interests of the country, by lowering prices, and raising the value of money. These effects were prevented by a vast emigration of the working class, which drained the labour market for the time of its surplus ;

but more especially were they prevented by the Californian and Australian gold discoveries, which under our gold currency laws increased the quantity of money at our disposal, kept the rate of interest low, and thus enabled the trading classes in a great measure to keep up prices, and prevent the usurers, tax-eaters, fixed income men, and idle classes generally, from reaping those golden advantages which otherwise they must have gained at the expense of the poor and industrious.

Before we quit this subject let us make a remark. It may be thought, from the question we asked a little further back, as to whether O'Connor's opposition to the League was not throughout a sham, that we meant to insinuate that he was, during all that period, in collusion with that party. Such is not our meaning. Our opinion on the subject is simply this ; O'Connor had an intense love of popularity, which often overcame every sense of duty. To have supported the League when they were unpopular, would have lost him that popularity which he enjoyed, he therefore opposed them ; but he cared very little for the question at issue, either one way or the other. When the League became so popular as to force their measures upon the Government, the Minister who proposed those measures became more popular still. To oppose any longer, would lose him a portion of his popularity ; he turned round, therefore, without any regard to principle or consistency. O'Connor was not a man without foresight, but it so happened that the things which he did really foresee he seldom revealed, while those which he pretended to see, seldom came to pass. He knew that Cobden's party would soon succeed, but he pretended to oppose them up to the hour of victory ; while there is certainly some ground for suspicion that there was, if not a direct, at least a tacit understanding between them, as they emerged from their weakness into strength. Let heartless demagogues who have stepped into his shoes say what they will, and let their dupes believe as implicitly as they may, an over-weening love of popularity was O'Connor's greatest curse. It cost him all that a man ought to value—consistency, principle, honour, reputation, real friends in exchange for soulless panderers who at last deserted him, and peace of mind. His other losses we have yet to notice. O'Connor was, however, at this time on the highroad to success—temporary, it is true, but still success. His flattering pictures of the speedy realization of his Land Plan, caused numbers to enrol under his banner. His lecturers scoured the country. M'Douall and he had become reconciled, and he again patronized the Doctor before the public.

O'Connor endeavoured, in the Spring of 1846, to get Thomas

Cooper to join him in the advocacy of his Land movement; but the latter refused, and expressed his conviction that it was a delusion, and would bury the Chartist movement. O'Connor got into a passion, and a quarrel ensued; upon which Cooper determined to quit him. We mentioned previously, that Cooper had become cured of his O'Connorism. When this was found out, his influence with the O'Connor-Chartists was speedily destroyed. A subscription had been started for the purpose of raising money for a testimonial, to be presented to him when the term of his imprisonment should expire; but a denunciation of him by O'Connor, at Manchester, caused the monies to be recalled. His denouncer afterwards withdrew his hostility, and it was proposed to start the subscription afresh; but Cooper very properly refused to receive any such aid, and sent back sums that had been subscribed at Rochdale, Nottingham, and other places. Cooper was liberated on the 5th of May, 1845; and when he reached London, by the per- suasion of McGowan, printer of the *Northern Star*, with whom he was on very friendly terms, he paid a visit to O'Connor, who apologized for his conduct towards Cooper, and obtained his forgiveness. In the course of their conversation "The Purgatory of Suicides," which was as yet in manuscript, came under notice, and O'Connor gave orders to McGowan to print it; but these he afterwards retracted, and left Cooper to find a publisher, and to pay the printer. He promised, before the work came out, to take two hundred copies; but that promise was never performed. He took neither two hundred copies, nor any part of that number. As, however, the work succeeded, Cooper's publisher took it on his own hands, and made an arrangement to pay the printer; upon which McGowan relieved Cooper from the responsibility. The publisher, however, soon after failed, and McGowan was thus minus the money; but the author never got a shilling by the first edition. O'Connor sought to make the public believe that he had befriended Cooper in this affair by becoming guarantor for the payment, and he got McGowan to write a letter to that effect, which was published. He could not, however, become Cooper's guarantor after the agreement had been entered into between McGowan and the publisher, and Cooper thus exempted from responsibility. We can well conceive that, as O'Connor promised in the first instance to pay for the printing, a sharp London tradesman, finding things had turned out unfortunate in other quarters, would seek to make O'Connor come back to his original promise; and that when it suited the latter to turn round upon Cooper, and use the affair of the "Purgatory" to his public disparagement, that with the hope of getting the money, the said London tradesman might furnish him with a letter which appeared to favour his cause.   This is not the History of Chartism, it may be urged ; but we are justified in referring to it, because this was one of the means of which O'Connor ever availed himself to destroy the independence of public men.   He aimed a blow at O'Brien through pecuniary agency.   When the latter was in Lancaster castle, without his knowledge, he ordered to be paid to his family the sum of one pound per week ; a fact which was industriously circulated throughout the country, so as to prevent subscriptions flowing in for O'Brien, as they would at that time have done from his numerous admirers, and above all, so as to convey a notion of O'Connor's generosity.   When O'Brien learned the fact, he offered to write weekly a letter in the *Star*, so as to give O'Connor value for his money, and many letters were so written and inserted ; O'Brien thus writing for a pound, what he had formerly received three pounds for writing from the very same quarter.   Yet when O'Connor found that O'Brien had a will of his own, and that he refused to allow himself to be destroyed without an indignant protest, the pound a-week was blazoned forth in the columns of the *Star*, and the term "ungrateful" was hurled at O'Brien, and the *Star*-chamber gave him the dignified title of "The Starved Viper."   As before stated, O'Connor could not get Cooper won over to his Land scheme.   A Chartist Convention was about to be held at Leeds ; Cooper was elected by the City of London Chartists to sit in that assembly.   After his election he gave public notice through the newspapers, that in the Convention he would move the following resolutions :—

"1st.—That the Executive do lay before the Convention minutes of all meetings of the Executive Committee held since their first election to office.

"2nd.—That the Executive do lay before the Convention a full account of their issue of the prepared sheets for quarterly returns described at page eleven of the Hand-book, and also a full and distinct account of the returns made by the several localities to the said prepared sheets.

If no minutes could be produced ; if it was ascertained that the issue of prepared sheets for quarterly returns had been given up, and if it was found from the facts that the Executive had not been able to attend to their duties, as described in page six of the Hand-book, he would move—

"3rd.—That the Executive Committee of the National Charter Association be chosen from members of the Association who are not directors of the Land Society.

If this motion was rejected, and a majority of the Convention decided that the Land directors be continued in the office of Executive Committee of the National Charter Association, before such decision was confirmed he would move—

"4th.—That T. M. Wheeler is not a fit and proper person to represent the body of Chartists as their General Secretary, for reasons which he had already expressed openly in conversation, by letter to Feargus O'Connor, the Leicester Chartists, and others, and at the public meeting at which he was elected as delegate to the Convention, and where his statements were corroborated by others.

" 5th.—That this Convention declares it to be most unfair and inconsistent with democratic principles, for members of one Chartist locality to offer themselves as members also of other localities, with the intent of opposing or carrying certain measures, as hath lately been the case in the City of London locality.

"6th.—That this Convention deplores the acts of violence which have filled the public mind with an aversion to Chartism, and hereby records its abandonment and disavowal of the doctrine of physical force, and its resolve to seek the establishment of the People's Charter as a statute of the realm solely by peaceable, moral, and constitutional means.

" 7th.—That this Convention proclaims its conviction of the paramount value of education, tolerance of the opinions of others, and morality of life, as constituents in Chartist character, and indignantly protests against the conclusion, that the low and vulgar abuse, and rash denunciating spirit of the *Northern Star* newspaper, is to be taken for genuine Chartism.

"8th.—That this Convention regards Feargus O'Connor as unworthy of the confidence of Chartists, and hereby earnestly warns British working men of the folly and danger of union with him."

As soon as Cooper's intentions became known, every effort was made to defeat them, and in the *Star* of July 25th, the attention of the Chartists was directed to the resolutions. Their author was denounced as a traitor ; the Chartists were called upon to speak out and to "settle" him at once and for ever, by instructing their delegates to vote for his expulsion from the Convention.   Clark and O'Connor had an interview, when the former said :—" Well, sir, I saw Cooper since I last saw you, and I don't know what he is about ; he said that we were all deceived, that you were not fit to be trusted with the funds,

or the management of the affairs. He asked in whose name
the estate was purchased ; and when I said in yours, till we
were enrolled, he said, " Good God ! why the man is over head
and ears in debt ! Do you know his liabilities? Do you know
that he is supporting the *Star* upon the Land Fund? and as
to settling his accounts at Manchester, did you count the
post-office orders that he produced ? or what security have you
for the money ? The country should be undeceived." This
produced two long letters in the *Star* of June 13th, from
O'Connor, together with two from Messrs. Cuffay and Knight,
giving an account of the state of the funds. The two latter
were auditors for the Land Society, and he had submitted his
accounts to their inspection, telling his readers that Clark and
McGrath, two of his directors, had examined them and found
them correct. In one of his letters O'Connor announced his
intention of resigning his office as deputy-treasurer to the
Land Society, as he was resolved to preserve his honour ;
he would, however, continue to be director and bailiff, and to
work for the people. Cooper sought admission to the columns
of the *Star*, but was refused ; and he then resorted to *Lloyd's
Newspaper*, and was taunted, by those who refused him
insertion, for writing in " *Lloyd's* refuge for renegades." One
of these letters O'Connor copied into the *Star ;* the following
is a portion of its contents :—

"It is now established, on his own confession, that
O'Connor has purchased the Herringsgate estate in his own
name, with the people's money. He is not a legal officer, no
deputy-treasurer being named in the rules, and where, then,
is his responsibility? The Land Society is not enrolled; the
trustees are a mockery, having never entered on office. I
neither believe his affirmation that he is not over head and
ears in debt, nor doubt that he has used, and still uses the
money paid by the shareholders in the Land fund, to keep up
the *Star*. I dare him to the proof, and he will have to meet
me sooner or later. I proceed on a tour to collect funds for
poor Frost, on Monday. In the country I shall speak my
mind to working men, and dare O'Connor to meet me anywhere, even in the Carpenters' Hall, Manchester, if he likes,
since he esteems that his stronghold, and I am almost a
stranger there ; or, if he prefers it, I will meet him publicly in
London, when I return. Why does he not call the Leeds
Convention together ? He knows he has broken the rules by
delaying it beyond the 20th of April. I dare him to call it.
Let me direct the attention of the Land shareholders to the 7th
rule whereby the trustees are removable yearly, and then ask
them whether they can for a moment suppose that O'Connor

intended the trustees to hold an estate for the shareholders. He knew that the society would never think of renewing trust deeds yearly and therefore must have purposed that the land should be purchased in his name only, from the first."

O'Connor, however, never accepted the challenge to meet Cooper before the public; but the latter thought he should get his turn in the Convention. Cooper went on his tour, but the influence of O'Connor prevented that tour from being successful in raising funds for Frost, though a considerable sum was sent in to other quarters for that purpose. In a letter inserted in *Lloyd's*, Cooper said in reference to the auditors' report:—

"The poor, unsuspecting auditors have been bamboozled with the Bank-book, &c. of the ' grand bailiff to paupers,' (this was a title bestowed on Feargus by himself). Rest satisfied with this ludicrous process of inspection, if you be foolish enough; but when you begin to think it is time to make a more common sense investigation (and you will begin to think so) how will you be able to unravel the difficulties that will arise from proper investigation having been deferred?"

Meanwhile, the object had been gained of obtaining a decisive verdict in O'Connor's favour before the Convention met. Resolutions from more than a hundred localities poured into the office of the *Northern Star*, most of them breathed unlimited confidence in O'Connor, and unbounded hatred of his accuser. By one body he was styled a "dog"; another discovered that he wanted a situation under the Government; a third designated him a needy political adventurer, courting popularity, imbued with jealousy, self-conceit, mischief, malice, and base ingratitude; a fourth, a chameleon, a mawworm, and a mean mischief-making tool in the Chartist cause; a fifth, a babbling fool; a sixth, a raving madman; a seventh, a slanderous scamp; an eighth, a convicted liar; a ninth, a double distilled imposter. Such were some of the choice flowers of eloquence used on the occasion. At one delegate meeting it was resolved to call upon the country to instruct the delegates to expel him from the Society, and to prevent him taking his seat in the Convention. All who alluded to the deputy-treasurership of O'Connor requested him to continue in the office, and he accordingly rescinded his resolution. One locality (Keighley) did, indeed, venture to suggest that in order to put a stop to such proceedings as those of Thomas Cooper, it was necessary to get the Society enrolled; but the tide of indignation, hatred, and denunciation of Cooper, was almost enough to overwhelm the strongest man. As Cooper was on a tour in connection with Douglas Jerrold's paper, it was asserted in the *Star* that he was going to have the political management of that journal, which was his reason for wishing to destroy O'Connor and the *Star*. This assertion brought a denial from Mr. Jerrold in the *Star* of the following week. At a meeting of the fraternal Democrats, David Ross had the courage to move an amendment to the resolution of confidence in O'Connor, and censure on Cooper, to the effect that they should suspend their judgment until those gentlemen met face to face before the public, but his amendment was over-whelmed. Cooper faced this storm of denunciation with a spirit of undaunted bravery. Secretary to the " Veteran Patriots', Exiles', Widows and Orphans' Fund," he threw up his office, and sent the following letter to Mr. John Skelton :—

" Having been denounced as a wolf in sheep's clothing, by the Chartists assembling at Carpenter's Hall, Manchester, who also desire that I may be discharged from the secretaryship ; I hereby discharge myself, hoping that some true sheep may be found, who will permit himself to be sheared, and succeed as cheerfully as I have done for the benefit of the sufferers.—THOMAS COOPER.

He also addressed two letters, one to the members of the Land Society, the other to the worshippers of Feargus O'Connor, through the medium of *Lloyd's Newspaper*. In the first letter he thus addressed the members:—

"Remember that no accounts, properly speaking, have been yet presented, either to your auditors, or your delegates in Conference. When has your treasurer, Mr. Roberts, acknowledged the receipt of your money? What proof have you that he is your treasurer? When did he present his accounts? They were not presented to the Conference of delegates, although O'Connor promised them, in Mr. Roberts' name. O'Connor's accounts are not, cannot be, under any circumstances satisfactory to you, without Mr. Roberts' declaration that he, as treasurer, has received the money subscribed by you. If Mr. Roberts were to make public acknowledgment that he has accepted the office of treasurer (for it is notorious that he refused it on a public occasion), even then you ought to direct that there be some investigation as to whether your 15th rule has been fulfilled :—' When the sum in his (the treasurer's) possession shall amount to £250, his duty shall be to deposit the same in the London and Westminster Joint-Stock Bank, to the names and credit of the trustees of the Society.' And again, whether your 16th rule has been fulfilled :—' The funds shall be invested in the London and Westminster Bank by the treasurer, in the joint names of the trustees, one of whom and the secretary, shall accompany

him to the bank for that purpose, and no money shall be withdrawn from the bank without an order from the directors,
stating the amount, and being countersigned by the trustees
for the time being.' Now remember, not one of the trustees
(as they are called in mockery), Mr. Duncombe, M.P., Messrs.
Sewell and Dron, of London, Mr. Titus Brooke, of Dewsbury,
and Messrs. James Leach, Dixon, and Sherrington, of Manchester, not one of the trustees has ever been to the bank
with Mr. Roberts, to deposit your money. Remember that
your money has never been invested in the London and Westminster Bank by your treasurer, in the joint names of the
trustees. Remember that not one of your trustees countersigned the order for drawing out money from the bank, to pay
the deposit on the Herringsgate estate."

In the letter to O'Connor's "worshippers" he said:—

"That responsible individuals in connexion with the *Star*
office had declared, that the paper was ten times in danger of
stopping altogether at Leeds, and its escape from absolute
annihilation since its removal to London, had been only averted
by O'Connor's resort to the Land money. O'Connor's whole
conduct in the purchase of the Herringsgate estate, with all
its sly and stealthy craft; his pretences that he had borrowed
£550 from Mr. Roberts; his silence as to whether that was
not really £550 of the Land money borrowed from the treasurer
(if he be one) on a mortgage of O'Connor's Herringsgate estate;
the bamboozlement about O'Connor's banking book, post-
office orders, bank orders, &c., without a syllable of acknowledgment that the treasurer had received the money; the fact
that Mr. Heywood's name was kept in the *Star* book, as a
debtor for upwards of £10,000, at a period when he was really
a creditor of O'Connor's, just as a blind to those who were
joining acceptances to the amount of £800 to keep up the *Star*:
I say all these, and other items in O'Connor's conduct, prove
his desperation, and corroborate the fact that he has been a
moneyless adventurer from the outset of his career."

As a reason why the conveyance of the Herringsgate estate
was not made in the name of the treasurer, O'Connor explained
that Roberts' clerk waited on him, and said:—"Sir, I can't
have the purchase made in Mr. Roberts' name; it will look
very strange now, after the affair being carried so far in your
name." He then consulted the directors, who advised him to
let the purchase be made in his own name. It would appear
from this, that Roberts was displeased with the treasurership
having been so long assumed by O'Connor. With regard
to the £550 borrowed from Roberts, O'Connor said it was the
product of some railway shares which that gentleman had

instructed him to sell, in order that he might purchase a small estate near Pinner, of which to make a model farm.

The Conference was held at Leeds on the 3rd of August. The reader will form a tolerably correct idea of the disadvantages under which Cooper would labour in attempting to make himself heard in such a body. After the credentials of the delegates had been read, he rose and asked for a report of Chartism, its numbers, funds, &c. Wheeler, the secretary, had no accounts of the kind to present; and McGrath, the president, declared that he knew nothing about it. Cooper persisted in addressing the delegates, when "rascal, scoundrel, liar, hypocrite," and many equally polite epithets were showered profusely upon him. He told them that they were perfectly aware that he had resolutions to propose, but still they clamoured. O'Connor tried to coax Cooper out of his resolutions, but to no purpose; when up started a man, almost new to the Chartist movement, and threatened if he did not desist he would move his expulsion. This person was no other than Ernest Jones. Cooper replied that he ought, as a man of genius, to be ashamed of announcing such a measure. Besides, he had only been a Chartist three months, and could not know what he was doing. Jones replied in the true style of the demagogue, viz., that while Cooper had been in the byways, he had been in the highways of Chartism, and had only the other day seen thousands of the veritable though not enrolled Chartists on Blackstone Edge, and heard the thunder of their cheers. Cooper told him that he talked like a child, and would sometime find out his mistake. Jones persisted in moving Cooper's expulsion on the ground of contumacy, and malicious resistance to the proceedings of Conference. The motion was seconded, and some held up their hands. Others remained neutral, doubtless from shame; but not a man had the courage to vote against it, though more than one had been bitterly hostile to Feargus O'Connor, and one of them had even professed to go with Cooper the day previous. The chairman declared Cooper to be expelled, but he refused to go. Some of them talked about forcibly ejecting him, but this put Cooper upon his metal: he dared them, and pointing to O'Connor, said:—"Why does not that great thundering coward, who has so often talked to me of physical force in private, come and put me out himself?" What, however, neither O'Connor, nor any of his subordinates, attempted to do by force, was effected by stratagem. Clark rose at four o'clock, and moved an adjournment to the following morning, which was carried. At the appointed time Cooper presented himself, but found three stout men barring his admission.

ERNEST JONES
FROM A WOODCUT

They produced a letter from the president as their authority. He tried to push past them but in vain. There was a crowd outside, whom Cooper addressed and denounced O'Connor. A few words of comment on these proceedings may not be out of place.

We by no means agree with all the resolutions which it was Cooper's intention to move. That the Chartists had acted foolishly, and some of their leaders worse than foolishly, with respect to physical force, we are free to admit, but we cannot accept the "peace at any price" doctrine. We believe that were it possible of adoption by the enslaved, that doctrine would preserve the system of slavery for ever; but we are firmly of opinion, that to render its adoption possible, human nature itself must be completely changed. But however this may be, Cooper was entitled to be heard in support of his views. More especially was he entitled to speak upon matters so gravely affecting the interests of the Chartist body as the public characters of their leaders ; and we appeal to all sensible men, whether it was honest or consistent with democratic justice, to put a gag upon his mouth, at the instance of a mere mushroom Chartist, when the parties accused were present, and had every chance of reply ? However partizans may excuse such cowardly injustice, common sense and common honesty will always condemn it. What, we ask, had the public a right to infer from such conduct, but that the parties in question were in dread of exposure ? The mover of Cooper's expulsion is here entitled to a brief notice. Ernest Jones, was the son of Col. Jones, aide-de-camp to Ernest, Duke of Cumberland, the late King of Hanover. Though of Welsh parents, he was, we believe, born and educated in Germany, and it was after the above royal personage that he was named. So fond was the King of the child of Col. Jones, that he honoured him (if honour it was) by becoming his godfather. It should also be mentioned, that Ernest Jones claimed to be descended from the great Emperor Charlemagne. At an early age Jones evinced an aptitude for rhyme, and a volume, for circulation amongst private friends, was printed ere he had reached the age of ten years. Of course these productions were sufficiently puerile, but they indicated the existence of a genius that would be more fully manifested at no distant day, and his natural capacities were assisted by all that education could be made to bestow. His friends destined the young poet for the profession of the bar, and being removed to England, he ultimately became a barrister of the Middle Temple, though we believe that his briefs, like those of many clever men, (and as a real lawyer no man could be cleverer) were never very numerous. His time was not, however, exclusively devoted to law, for besides his attendance at the courts, he yet found opportunity to court the muses. He produced the poem of "Lord Lindsay," the most poetical of his effusions, "My Life, on our Social State," and other pieces, as also the "Wood Spirit," a romance of the feudal ages, written in a beautiful, fluent, and fascinating style. With the press, Jones was highly successful, his works receiving the almost unqualified praise of the most aristocratic journals ; he was hailed by all of them as a great poet—one of the greatest of modern times. From some cause or other, Jones, in 1846, became a politician as well as a poet. Unknown previously to the working class, he came into their ranks under the patronage of Feargus O'Connor. An Aristocrat is always most acceptable to the working class, even to Democrats, and the young sprig of Aristocracy, promoted, as O'Connor would have said, to the ranks of the Democracy, was received with enthusiasm. He possessed exactly the qualities for captivating the crowd, with the single exception that, unlike his patron O'Connor, he was small in stature ; but his voice was stentorian, his delivery good, his language brilliant, his action heroic—and, above all, he had a concealed cunning, which had the advantage of bearing every appearance of the most extreme candour. In the art of flattery, no demagogue ever excelled him. He could in a breath transform a man who could scarcely string together five sentences in English, into a clever fellow, and a most accomplished orator ; and, what was stranger, he could get him to believe it. He was ever as ready to face the frowns of the elements of nature, as those of the enemies of Democracy. He would speak on a wild heath, amid the howlings of the pitiless storm, and dash aside the umbrella that was held to shelter him. How chivalrous ! In reality he was of a most social disposition, setting every one in his society at the most perfect ease—hence the poor exclaimed, "What a nice little fellow !" Above all, he reputed himself to be rich when he entered the movement ; and although Thomas Clark once declared that at that period he was "literally without a shirt," (a fact not in itself disgraceful), and although his own unintentional admissions go very far to confirm that declaration, a number of people are simple enough to believe that he had spent a fortune in their cause. In short, they believed everything that he chose to tell them. As a reasoner, Jones never attained, nor did he seek to attain a high standard ; but he had a happy method of making the most plausible sophistry appear to the unthinking like sound logic, and an unbounded assurance that could conquer every difficulty, and overthrow fact by assertion without a blush. This did all that was needful to establish for him a prominent position. Such was the man who moved the expulsion of Thomas Cooper from the Convention. It was utterly in vain that any man attempted to shake the confidence of the Chartists in O'Connor; that confidence became wider spread and firmer every day. In November, as much as £200 a-week came into the funds. "The Land and the Charter" now became the cry. Another Petition was projected, and the Executive held public meetings in many towns.

With the new year, *The Labourer*—a monthly magazine— was established in furtherance of the Land Plan, and was edited by O'Connor and Ernest Jones. Joshua Hobson having left the *Star* office, Harney became editor, and Jones and G. A. Fleming also contributed to its columns.

In the spring meetings to further the Petition were held in all parts of the country. On the 24th of May, 1847 the Herringsgate estate, which had now received the name of O'Connorville, was opened, and the members located on their allotments. A number of people, some on foot, others in vehicles, attended from various places near. O'Connor and the directors were of course there, also J. R. Cooper from Manchester, and Mr. Cochrane, the candidate for Westminster. Speeches were the order of the day at the public meeting, and afterwards at the meeting on the occasion. Doubtless this practical application of the Plan gave an impetus to the movement, for in one week in July, the subscriptions amounted to somewhere about £3,500, and soon afterwards more than £5,000 flowed in during a similar period.

In August came a general election, caused by a union of the Whigs and Protectionists to defeat the Irish Arms Bill which was brought in by Peel's Government, and on which they relinquished office to make way for the Whigs. Chartism had at this time the appearance of strength. Doubtless the numbers who had joined the Land Society desired to see some of their party in Parliament. A number of candidates came forward on Chartist principles. Duncombe and Wakley stood again for Finsbury; Fielden and Halliday for Oldham; Sharman Crawford for Rochdale; W. Williams for Coventry; D. W. Harney for Marylebone; Colonel Thompson for Bradford; Joseph Sturge for Leeds; Ipswich, H. Vincent; Worcester, J. Hardy; Norwich, J. H. Parry; Bolton, Dr. Bowring; Birmingham, Muntz and Scholefield; Macclesfield, J. Williams; Northampton, Dr. Epps; Nottingham, Feargus O'Connor;

Blackburn, W. P. Roberts; Halifax, E. Miall and Ernest Jones; Tower Hamlets, George Thompson; Derby, P. McGrath; Sheffield, Thomas Clark; Tiverton, G. J. Harney; Greenwich, S. Kydd; South Shields, T. Dickenson; Stockport, John West. Some of the candidates merely went to the hustings, made a speech, and took a show of hands. West was one of these, and he addressed the assembly for several hours in a really statesmanlike speech, which won general admiration, and gained him the show of hands. Dickenson also obtained a similar decision. Kydd, at Greenwich, maintained the cause with eminent ability, and was similarly elected, as was W. P. Roberts at Blackburn. But the speech which obtained, perhaps, the greatest celebrity, was that of Julian Harney, from the fact that he was the opponent of the clever, smooth, and wily Palmerston. The latter was so desirous of keeping a clear position, that he requested Harney to speak first, as he understood that he was about to attack his Foreign Policy. Harney acceded to the request, and entered into a long and masterly dissection of the noble Viscounts political career. That he gave his opponent something to reply to, may be judged from the fact, that the reply occupied a period of five hours. Notwithstanding the disadvantages of speaking first, Harney carried the show of hands, but declined going to the poll. Duncombe and Wakley were returned without opposition. Halliday retired from Oldham. J. M. Cobbett united with Fielden, but W. J. Fox came forward in opposition, and a union taking place between some of his friends, and some of the Tories, Fox and Duncuft were returned. There was no opposition to Sharman Crawford, at Rochdale; but at Coventry, W. Williams was ousted. D. W. Harney retired from Marylebone, but the renowned Robert Owen stood upon Chartist principles, and polled a single vote. George Thompson was more successful, for he was between 2,000 and 3,000 a-head of his opponent. At Halifax the friends of Miall and Jones united, and Sir Charles Wood's friends and the Tories did likewise. Edwards polled 511, Wood 507, Miall 349, and Jones 280. At Derby, McGrath polled 216, against 852 for Gower, who with Strutt was afterwards unseated for bribery. Colonel Thompson was elected for Bradford, but Sturge was not so fortunate at Leeds; he, however, polled 1,980 votes against 2,186, the influential Mr. Marshall being the candidate returned. At Sheffield, Thomas Clark polled 326 against 1,110. Vincent's friends contested the election boldly at Ipswich, and polled 546 votes, against 708; and at Worcester the battle was well fought, Mr. Hardy polling 927, against 1,121. At Norwich, the Radicals made a gallant stand, Parry polled 1,572 against 1,727; while at Birmingham, Muntz and Scholefield, and at Bolton, Dr. Bowring, were triumphantly returned. At Northampton, Dr. Epps polled 140, against 852. Macclesfield returned John Williams. But the election which surprised most of all, and which caused in some quarters the greatest joy, was that at Nottingham. When O'Connor announced himself a candidate, few were so sanguine as to expect that he would be returned; what, then, was the surprise and exultation, when it was found that he had defeated the Whig minister, Sir John Cam Hobhouse, polling as he did 1,257 votes, while Mr. Hobhouse polled but 893! This was the climax to O'Connor's temporary success. Everything appeared to go with him right joyously, and opposition seemed but the more to increase his power. At the nomination, his Irish drollery caused bursts of laughter at his opponent's expense. It should, however, be borne in mind, that this triumph was secured by a union of his friends with those of Mr. John Walter; but at any rate, Hobhouse must have gone to the wall.

At the latter end of August another Land Conference was held at Lowlands, a newly purchased estate of the Company being close to the spot; when the same directors were chosen with the exception of Wheeler, who had resigned, and was replaced by William Dixon. The same officers continued to constitute the Chartist Executive. By this time the total Land fund had reached the sum of nearly £50,000. O'Connor was all hope; he would bring out the *Democrat,* a daily paper, but he afterwards relinquished the idea.

On the last Monday in August there was a dinner in honour of George Thompson, at the Tower Hamlets. O'Connor, Vincent, and many others were present; the former delivered on that occasion one of his very raciest speeches. The same week there was a large public meeting in Edinburgh, to congratulate the Chartist electors on the stand they had made during the late election; and shortly after a public dinner, attended by two hundred persons, and a crowded meeting afterwards, were held at the Crown and Anchor, London, in celebration of the recent Chartist triumphs; but not one of the elected, save O'Connor, was present, and only one of the middle-class unsuccessful candidates, Dr. Epps, who got himself into disgrace before he left the meeting. W. P. Roberts, P. McGrath, Ernest Jones, Feargus O'Connor, and Julian Harney were the principal speakers. O'Connor made a great movement about this time, for the signing by the Land Members of the deed of settlement, with a view as he stated, to the Registration of the Company.

While Chartism seemed to be rising in England, the party of Mitchell was rising into activity in Ireland, and on the continent things began to assume a significant aspect. The course taken by Pope Pius, in Italy, filled the Democrats with hope, and in October 1847, a public meeting was held in the Eastern Institute, London, to congratulate the Pontiff on the popular course he was pursuing; which meeting was attended by Ernest Jones, Bronterre O'Brien, and other leading Democrats. Meanwhile, the signing of the National Petition went on vigorously, and O'Connor declared that he would have 5,000,000 signatures to that Petition by the time that it was presented to Parliament. "The Land, the Land, the Land," continued to be the cry of thousands, and that cry ran from mouth to mouth, till O'Connor appeared to be rising in invincibility. The agitation was not confined to the Chartist operatives; it found its way into rural parishes amongst men who before had never thought of their social elevation. The plan was fascinating; a beautiful cottage and four acres, with thirty pounds to work it, by a pre-payment of five pounds four shillings, how easily they might reach a social paradise! Men who had been vegetating with their families on nine or ten shillings per week were enchanted. It had taken a life of hard labour to enable them to raise five pounds; away went the poor result of this labour into the Land Lottery, in exchange for which they hoped to grasp the millenium. The directors pushed about the country. Dr. M'Douall, John West, and Samuel Kydd were appointed lecturers. The latter of these gentlemen was a native of Arbroath, in Scotland, and formerly followed, like Thomas Cooper, the occupation of a shoemaker. He first came prominently before the public about the time of the Sturge Conference, to which body he was deputed by the Chartists of Glasgow, at a public meeting. Young and enthusiastic, Kydd was at that time of the school of O'Connor. He was rendered more prominent after the Conference, by being the antagonist of James Williams, in a public discussion in Sunderland, on the policy of Kydd's great leader. Both gentlemen conducted themselves with great ability and tact; but Kydd vanquished his opponent in the estimation of the majority, and the following number of the *Star* heralded his victory by the heading of a report which ran thus :—" Defeat of all the robbers, by the whole-hog Chartist brigade of Sunderland !"—which at first sight led us to hope that the advent of the Charter was nigh at hand, and we were miserably disappointed, when on reading the report we found that the " defeat of the robber factions," was little better than a split between the Democrats themselves. Kydd, as a lecturer possessed great vigour and fluency of speech, and his lectures bore the traces of considerable intellectual force. There was, however, a kind of stiffness—an air of superiority in his demeanour, which did not leave the most pleasant impression on the minds of an audience. This was more in appearance than in reality ; for in the private circle there breathed not a more social, affable spirit, than Samuel Kydd.

But O'Connor was not allowed to go on smoothly with his Scheme. The *Dispatch*, *Lloyd's Newspaper*, *Manchester Examiner*, *Nottingham Mercury*, and *Nottingham Journal*, attacked him severely. The *Nonconformist* contained an answer to a correspondent, who enquired of the editor his opinion of the Land Plan. The answer was, that he could not see the practicability of the Plan ; but his columns were open to O'Connor's friends, if they thought they could show its practicability. This O'Connor called denunciation of his Plan, and in a long letter in the *Star*, which occupied about twelve columns, he lashed these editors furiously. Apostrophising the editor of the *Dispatch*, who had talked of giving him a caning, " Why," replied O'Connor, " Why, if it came to that, I would take the little knobstick priest, Miall, by the legs, and scatter you all to the winds of heaven." Still these journals kept levelling their artillery at the " pauper's bailiff." Week after week was the fire kept up. In the *Manchester Examiner* a series of letters appeared, under the signature of " One who has whistled at the plough." The writer was one Alexander Somerville, an old soldier, whose flogging case had some years before excited much sympathy. In one of his letters he had alluded to Hobson, the late editor of the *Star*, as having been in some measure connected with the Land Scheme. Hobson wrote an explanation in the *Manchester Examiner ;* but it contained besides, an attack on O'Connor's honesty, charging him, to use O'Connor's own words, with "plunder to the amount of £500." Among other things, he charged him with falsifying his books, so as to bring Cleave £2,000 in his debt, and that he was appropriating the Land money to his own purposes. Hobson asserted that O'Connor had often borrowed of Ardill, his clerk, and of himself, in order to keep up the *Star*. O'Connor summoned Hobson to a public meeting in Manchester. The other, however, would not consent to abide by the decision of such a tribunal, but offered to meet him before an audience, half of whom were to be admitted by each party. O'Connor would not agree to this, and with or without Hobson's consent, a public meeting he would have. A meeting was accordingly held at the Hall of Science, a building holding from three to four thousand persons. It was crammed, and thousands remained outside, who were addressed by M'Douall and West. How far such a tribunal was fit to try a question of accounts, may be gathered from the description of the *Star* reporter :—

"Neither pen nor tongue could describe his reception, when he presented himself upon the platform. It was not enthusiasm, it was madness, a frenzy that cannot be described."

While addressing the meeting, O'Connor hit upon every sentence calculated to rouse the hostility of his audience against his detractors, and to elevate himself; he told them that he had the evidence of a respectable gentleman (who he did not say,) and also that of a boy, that at the *Examiner* office they were in league with navvies to assassinate him, which led to groans and cries of "Oh, the villains!" If this statement was true, which we, however, by no means believe, it was certainly a poor return for O'Connor's past services to the League. Again, he said, "villains who quaff your sweat, gnaw your flesh, and drink the blood of infants, suppose that I too would crush their little bones, lap up their young blood, luxuriate on woman's misery, and grow fat upon the labourer's toil. No, I could go to bed supperless, but such a meal would give me the nightmare; nay, an apoplexy." O'Connor tested public confidence to the utmost. He said, " I have now brought money with me to repay every shareholder in Manchester." (Shouts of " Nay, but we won't have it !") "Well, then, I'll spend it all." (Cries of " Do, and welcome !") Again, he said, as an instance of his condescension, " It was related of the Queen, that when she visited the Duke of Argyle, she took up the young Marquis of Lorne, and actually gave him a kiss, and this was mentioned as a fine trait in her character. Why, he (O'Connor) took up forty or fifty children a-day, and wiped their noses, and hugged them. Did they think he was the man to wring a single morsel from their board, or to prevent their parents from educating and bringing them up properly? No, he was not : he loved the children, and their mothers also, too much for that." For more than three hours did O'Connor address the crowded and excited meeting, which was so densely packed before he commenced, that the reporters had to be pushed through the windows into the hall. He retorted the charge of dishonesty upon Hobson and Ardill, and read letters which he said he had received from Ardill many years before, charging Hobson with fraud, but of which he took no further notice. He declared that when the *Star* circulated forty-three thousand copies a-week, under the management of those gentlemen, it did not pay expenses ; and he said that while he was getting poor, they were getting

FEARGUS O'CONNOR

SHOWING THE FARMS OF HIS LAND PLAN

FROM A SCARCE LITHOGRAPH

rich.   He retorted on them the charge of falsifying accounts ;
and revealed the fact, that Hobson's salary was £520
a-year, which might well account for his growing rich, and
that Ardill received £100 per annum.   He called up William
Rider, who deposed to the frauds committed by these men on
O'Connor.   Rider was asked why he had not revealed these
to O'Connor before.   His reasons were—1st., Because nothing
could shake O'Connor's confidence in these men ;—2nd.,
Because O'Connor never would listen to any complaint of one
servant about another ;—3rd., Because as he was a subor-
dinate, it might have been thought that he wanted to step
into their shoes.   But surely O'Connor wanted no second-
hand evidence of fraud.   What man in his senses would suppose, that a journal like the *Northern Star* was not paying at
a circulation of forty-three thousand a-week?   O'Connor was
not simple enough to believe anything of the kind ; and we can
only set down his assertion that he received nothing from the
profits of the *Star*, and that these men brought him into debt
besides, as another of his gross exaggerations.   Even allowing
Hobson and Ardill to have been the rogues he represented them,
they would not have been guilty of roguery so transparent; and
if they had, O'Connor would not have been fool enough to
submit to it, and to have let his books run on for a period of
seven years without going through them, or employing some
one else for the purpose.   A statement of this kind could only
have satisfied a meeting of his most servile worshippers.
Hobson's version of the affair was, that O'Connor used to take
away the money and leave them to pay the bills.   That there
was some truth in this may be judged from the fact, that
when in 1839 he proposed to pay a second Convention, he
told the people they had furnished him with the means of
so doing.   Those means were only derived from the profits on
the *Star*.   If, however, he acted as foolishly as he himself
described, no public body should have entrusted large funds
into the hands of a man so evidently unfit to manage his
own affairs.   The large meeting voted confidence in O'Connor,
and as a proof that the vote was no sham, a thousand pounds
was paid down to him on the platform.   Not all the charges
of Hobson had the slightest effect in weakening the people's
faith ; they acquitted him before he broached a word in defence.
They did not attend his meeting to sit as impartial judges,
but to grace the triumph of one whom they already considered
a conqueror.   Of this O'Connor was well aware, and therefore
like a conqueror did he march to victory.   From Manchester
he journeyed to Nottingham, where a public meeting was held,
to which Tom Bailey, the editor of the *Nottingham Mercury*,

was invited. Bailey, like Hobson, declined on the ground that he would not be allowed fair play at such a meeting; but he also offered to meet him before an audience, one half of whom should be admitted by each party, which O'Connor would not however agree to. Of course the latter carried all before him. A letter from Hobson, in the *Manchester Examiner*, followed the public meeting, in which he endeavoured to prove O'Connor's poverty previous to establishing the *Northern Star*. O'Connor replied through his own journal, in some instances satisfactorily, in others not so. For the truth of some portion of his reply, he cited three persons as witnesses, whose names were appended. These were McGowan, his printer, and Fleming and Harney, two of his editors. In reference to the public meeting alluded to above, it is but too evident that no man would have stood the smallest chance of being impartially heard against O'Connor. He would have been served as William Ashton was served during one of O'Connor's visits to Barnsley. When Ashton rose to lay the charges against him, in reference to the Frost affair, before the meeting, O'Connor's worshippers rendered it impossible for him to obtain a hearing, and this was what O'Connor used to style "an honest public verdict."

CHAPTER XI.

DEMOCRACY IN EUROPE

We take our leave of the foregoing subject with feelings of
loathing and disgust, to dwell on matters of a more thrilling
interest.   It was evident, from the new life that seemed to
animate the people of almost every European country, that
great and stirring events were close at hand.   The *Northern
Star* of December 4th, contained accounts of Reform Banquets
held at Lille, Avesnes, and Valenciennes, in France.   About
the same time a meeting was held in London to commemorate
the Polish Revolution.   These events served to rouse the
Democracy of England.   Ireland was on the *qui vive*.   Organization was going on.   O'Connor brought the question of the
Union between the two countries, before the House of Commons, and made a motion for a Committee of Enquiry, for
which, though delivering a very able speech, he only found
twenty-three supporters.   A large public meeting was held in
London in favour of justice to England and Ireland, with a
view of forming an alliance between the Democrats of both
countries.   In the Commons, the Government proceeded
vigorously with another Coercion Act for Ireland, which
O'Connor opposed at every stage ; but which was carried,
being opposed on the third reading by a minority of only
fourteen.   Things progressed in Italy.   In the House of
Lords, Lord Minto, a member of the Government, was
accused of favouring the cause of Italian liberty at Rome,
an act which was acknowledged and defended by the Government.   Towards the latter end of December, 1847, large gatherings took place in London, and many of the provinces.   At the
former, Julian Harney, Ernest Jones, Carl Schapper (a
German,) and John Skelton, were the orators.   Scotland
began to move.   A large meeting was held in Edinburgh,
at which it was determined to start the *Weekly Express*,
a journal to be devoted to the furtherance of Democracy.
At Dublin, the Confederalists, or Mitchell party, began to
march with great vigour.   James Leach paid a visit to, and

addressed this body in January, 1848, and a union of sentiment began to grow up between them and the Chartists.   In
London, Cowper-street, John-street, and other large rooms,
were now the scene of frequent gatherings for the Charter,
and the signing of the Petition went on with great rapidity.
O'Connor visited Birmingham, where a large meeting took
place in the Town Hall presided over by Councillor Baldwin.
The meeting was very enthusiastic.   O'Connor seemed all
excitement at this period; he addressed letters every week
through the *Northern Star,* to the "Fustian Jackets, the
Blistered Hands, and Unshorn Chins," to the "Old Guards,"
and to the "Imperial Chartists," whom he would sometimes
treat as his subjects, and sign himself in his letters, "Feargus
Rex," in token of his royalty.

On the 2nd of February, a soiree was held at the National
Hall, Holborn, in honour of Messrs. Duncombe, Wakely, and
O'Connor.   The two former gentlemen were precluded by illness from being present, but the meeting was addressed by
the chairman (Ernest Jones), McGrath, Harney, Dixon,
O'Connor, and other speakers, who aroused their hearers to
enthusiasm.   About that time Jones addressed a crowded
assembly in the Odd-Fellows' Hall, Halifax, who loudly
responded to his exciting appeals.   The approaching
banquet at Paris, which was destined to be the precursor
of a revolution, was looked forward to with great interest
by the Democrats of England.   The French Government
were resolved on crushing the reform movement, and the
address, in answer to the royal speech, implied that fact.   The
opposition was however strong, and opposed 185 to 228 votes.
The news of this battle between the ministerialists and the
opposition caused immense excitement, for it was evident that
the struggle was fast approaching a crisis.   That crisis was
ended in a few days by the overturning of the throne, and the
establishment of a Republic.

The news of the French Revolution produced a panic in the
councils of despotism, and filled the Democrats with hope.
O'Connor's enemies had petitioned against his return, on the
ground of non-qualification.   A crowded meeting was held at
John-street, London, to defend his seat.   Mr. Sewell presided,
and the crowded assembly was addressed by Messrs. Clark,
Cuffay, Harney, Stallwood, and Jones.   About four hundred
pounds was subscribed for this object, and the petitioners
speedily gave up their suit.   The same week another large
meeting was held in London, to commemorate the Cracow
Insurrection.   Dr. M'Douall passed rapidly through Scotland,
haranguing large meetings.   Kydd traversed Yorkshire, and

Vest was rousing the Democrats in the neighbourhood of Newcastle-on-Tyne. An address, jointly adopted by the Executive of the National Charter Association, the Fraternal Democrats, the Chartist Delegate Council, and a public meeting at the German Society's Hall, Drury Lane, was ordered to be presented to the people of Paris. The following week's papers brought the news of the acceptance of the Republic by the people of France, and Chartism rose stronger than ever.

On the 2nd of March a tremendous gathering took place at the Circus of the National Baths, Lambeth. Thousands attended ; the place was so densely crowded that the Committee could only with great difficulty make their way to the platform. Messrs. Jones, Grassby, Harney, Szonakowski (a Pole), Clark, Dixon, O'Connor, and other speakers, addressed the meeting at great length. A resolution was adopted protesting against any English governmental interference with the French Republic. An address to the French people was read and carried, and Messrs. Jones, McGrath, and Harney were appointed as a deputation, to proceed to Paris and present the same to the Provisional Government. The meeting was succeeded by others during the week. Rooms were no longer of any avail ; they could not contain the thousands who attended. Stepney Green, Clerkenwell Green, and Bethnal Green, were the scenes of immense gatherings of the Metropolitans, who were addressed by the usual speakers.

On Monday, March 6th, a public meeting was held in Trafalgar Square, for the purpose of demanding the repeal of the Income Tax, or the immediate surrender of the reins of government by the ministers. It was a middle class meeting, convened by Charles Cochrane. The meeting was, however, proclaimed to be illegal, and Cochrane cautioned the people against attending ; but numbers did attend, tore the bills to pieces, and elected G. W. M. Reynolds to the chair. Reynolds had up to this time been unknown as a political speaker, though his fame was widely spread as the writer of several works of fiction. He had not, however, been dead to the world of politics, but had for many years been one of the contributors to the *Dispatch*. He conducted the Literary department of that journal, and also the Foreign News department. The readers of the *Dispatch* of that period will remember the severe articles on Louis Philippe, which appeared under the head of "Foreign Intelligence," those articles were the emanation of Reynolds's pen. They betrayed a pretty intimate acquaintance with French politics, and their tendency was Republican; for some time previous to the

French Revolution, the speedy downfall of Louis Philippe was predicted in those articles. Reynolds at length left the *Dispatch*, from the fact that some of the articles written by other contributors, were diametrically in opposition to his own, and he was fearful that, from their appearance in the same journal, they might be attributed to himself; he therefore gave up the lucrative situation which he held on that journal. Revolutions, and periods of political excitement, push many a man into prominence who might otherwise have remained in obscurity. The Trafalgar Square meeting was a golden opportunity for Reynolds. Charles Cochrane had turned coward and deserted his post; whoever should occupy it in the teeth of the Government proclamation would acquire a reputation for bravery which another occasion might never afford; and there was, besides, no knowing what might be the upshot of the tremendous movement then going on, not only in England, but throughout Europe. A bold and prominent position at the fitting moment, might lead to the highest honours in the State, supposing the English Chartists to follow in the footsteps of their Parisian brethren; and, in the excited state of the country, there was no guessing from one hour to another, whether the long pent-up discontent of the masses might not end in revolution. The distress that existed was terrible,—men could be scarcely worse off. Starvation glared from the eyes of thousands, who were reduced by poverty almost to despair. Reynolds occupied the chair without interruption, and several speeches were made against the Income Tax, on the French Revolution, and in favour of the Charter; and the speaking being at an end, the assembled thousands sent forth vollies of cheers for the People of Paris, and the People's Charter. The meeting dissolved peaceably. A great crowd followed the chairman up the Strand to his residence in Wellington-street, where amid loud cheers he addressed them from the balcony of his house. A portion of the people were, however, more unfortunate. Some well-fed son of the favoured class, got remarking on the idleness of the persons attending the meeting. This levity exasperated the parties attacked, and excitement ran rather high. This formed a pretext for the police, who attempted violently to disperse the crowd, and in doing so, exercised no little amount of brutality. The people attempted a defence, and drove the police back to their quarters; but that force receiving large additions from all quarters, the people were ultimately conquered, and many of them were taken wounded to the hospital. In the evening, however, a large number again rallied amid cries of " To the Palace !" and in the direction of Buckingham

Palace they proceeded. As in most assemblages of the kind, a number of disorderly persons joined the crowd, and broke the lamps and windows, and in some instances demanded bread of the bakers, and beer of the publicans. They found their way back to Trafalgar Square, and dispersed peaceably. On the two following days crowds again collected, and again came into collision with the police, but all ended without any thing very serious having occurred.

In the provinces, things began to look very threatening. In Glasgow the most dire distress prevailed. On the 6th of March a serious riot took place. The unemployed operatives had expected a distribution of provisions, which, however, did not take place. In a starving condition, and writhing under their cruel disappointment, they proceeded up Irongate and other principal streets, breaking into the provision and gun shops. It was only thieves and similar characters that helped themselves to anything more than necessity required. Business was suspended. The shops were shut. The people marched through the streets, crying "Bread or Revolution!" The police were almost useless, and the military were called out. The Riot Act was read, but in the meantime other bodies of people proceeded in different directions, entering the provision shops, and demanding bread. The excitement became so great, that the authorities sent to Edinburgh for more troops. On the following day, crowds again collected at Bridgeton, where the out pensioners were under arms. A boy threw a clod at one of these : he was arrested. A rescue was effected, when Captain Smart, Superintendent of Police, gave orders to fire. The result of this precipitate order was that five persons were shot, and some of them died upon the spot. The military continued to parade the streets, which were still lined with people, and all the public offices were strictly guarded. At Manchester, the people met in front of the Union Workhouse, Tile-street, and demanded the release of the inmates. The police marched in a strong body to the spot, but it was seven o'clock in the evening before they could disperse the crowd, having been engaged in the conflict for four hours. Later in the evening the people attacked the police station in the Oldham road, put out the lamps in that neighbourhood, broke up the stalls in Smithfield Market, with which they armed themselves, and attacked the police. The military were kept under arms, and the magistrates sat at the Town Hall, ready to act in case of emergency. O'Connor entered Hanley, in the Potteries, on the 6th of March. A tremendous procession escorted him into the town. Two thousand people sat down with him to tea in the Covered

Market, after which the people were admitted, when not less than seven thousand people were addressed by the great Chartist chief. Newcastle, Dumfries, Sunderland, Bath, Nottingham, and a host of towns were roused at the summons of the people of Paris. Public meetings were held, and the spark of Democracy seemed to light up every breast. At Carlisle, an election took place for the representation of the city. The Chartists put forward Dr. M'Douall, who was carried by a tremendous show of hands, went to the poll, and polled 55 against 414 votes. This mockery of representation must be noted, in order to show posterity the wide disparity between the electoral and non-electoral bodies in the enlightened nineteenth century. In Dublin, John Mitchell started a paper, under the title of the *United Irishman*. It breathed vengeance against the English Government, and gave plain instructions on street warfare, showing that every woman might be a soldier, by throwing bottles and other missiles, and even vitriol on the troops. The Chartist Executive summoned a Convention, to meet in London on the 3rd of April. The following week brought no cessation of agitation. A great meeting was held on Kennington Common, on the 13th of March. There were about twenty thousand persons present. Four thousand police were in attendance; eighty were mounted and armed with sabres and pistols, and amused themselves with riding about the Common. Numbers of the force were scattered through the meeting, dressed in plain clothes. Special constables were sworn in. The gun-makers were requested by the authorities to unscrew the barrels of their fire-arms, and the dealers in powder and shot were ordered to be cautious in the sale of those articles. The tri-colour waved from the hustings on which the speakers were assembled. Reynolds presided, and the mass was addressed by Messrs. McGrath, Williams, Clark, Dixon, and Ernest Jones, who delivered most thrilling speeches. The meeting unanimously adopted the Charter. On the same evening the South London Hall, Blackfriars Road, was the scene of another great gathering, presided over by Stallwood. Messrs. Clark, Dixon, Fussell, Rogers, McGrath, Captain Atcherley, and others, harangued the audience, and as at the previous meeting, the Charter was adopted. On the 14th, a densely crowded meeting was held at the John-street Institution to hear the report of the deputation to Paris. Harney was confined to a bed of sickness in Paris, but Jones and McGrath were present. J. Shaw presided. Jones, in the course of his speech, ridiculed the forces of the British Government, telling his hearers that there would be no fighting in England.

for there was nothing to fight with ; a man might as well fight with his own shadow. McGrath followed in a very exciting speech. Stallwood told the meeting that Barclay and Perkins had caused their men to be sworn in as special constables to break their heads, and called upon them to refuse to drink their beer. This was loudly applauded, and the meeting ended by giving cheers for the delegates to the French Republic, the People's Charter, and the *Northern Star*.

On the 15th March, a meeting was held on Blackheath, and although the magistrates tried every means of intimidation, and the rain poured in torrents during the time of meeting, the people stood firm, and pledged themselves to stand by the Charter. At Preston, O'Connor was entertained at a tea-party of six hundred persons on the 14th, whom he addressed chiefly on his Land Plan. At Birmingham, a large meeting was held in the Town Hall, in favour of the Charter. Baldwin presided, and speeches were delivered by Messrs. Blaxland, Corken, Weston, Sturge, Collins, Mason, and other speakers. A good spirit pervaded the meeting. On Sunday the 12th, Peep Green was visited by thousands of the inhabitants of the West Riding of Yorkshire, who were addressed by Messrs. Kydd, Shaw, of Leeds, and other speakers. The flag of the Republic was exhibited, and resolutions were passed pledging the meeting to stand by the Charter. Manchester, Bradford, Ipswich, Bath, South Shields, Stockport, Sheffield, and other places, were marked during the week by large gatherings of the people. At Shields two meetings were held, the last attended by ten thousand persons. West was the principal speaker. At Sheffield fifteen thousand persons were present. Ironsides presided. The yeomanry were under arms, but all was peaceable, and the chairman was appointed to visit Paris, to congratulate the Provisional Government. The same week O'Connor obtained leave to bring in a bill for the Enrolment of his Land Company.

On the 17th March, a great gathering took place in the Free-trade Hall, Manchester, to promote a fraternization of the Chartists and the Irish Repealers. Although charges of one shilling, fourpence, and twopence, were made for admission, a dense mass of people crowded the Hall, which was estimated to hold nine thousand persons. Smith O'Brien, M.P., and John Mitchell, were expected to be present, but did not attend; but the enthusiastic multitude was addressed by J. Leach, G. Archdeacon, F. O'Connor, W. P. Roberts, Michael Doheny, and T. F. Meagher, who spoke to resolutions in favour of the repeal of the union. The meeting enthusiastically adopted a congratulatory address to the people of France. This meeting was followed on the Saturday evening by a great soiree in the Town-Hall, which was decorated with banners, and all the other emblems of Democracy. The party sat down to tea, after which Mr. Dunn, chairman of the previous meeting, was called upon to preside, and spirited speeches were delivered by Messrs. Roberts, Finnigan, O'Connor, Doheny, and other speakers. The most democratic sentiments were responded to, and the meeting broke up, with deafening cheers for the Charter and Repeal.

On Sunday, the 19th, another meeting was held for the same object, on a wild spot of ground called Oldham Edge, about a mile from that town. Crowds of people flocked in from all the surrounding townships. O'Connor estimated the gathering at a quarter of a million. As soon as the meeting was assembled the clouds gathered, and the rain, driven by a sharp wind, began to fall; but presently the weather somewhat cleared, and Richard Pilling was voted to the chair. He told the meeting that if they intended to carry the Charter, they must be prepared to stand something more than rain. Messrs. Leach, Doheny, O'Connor, Donovan, Rankin, Webb, and J. R. Cooper each addressed the meeting. O'Connor said:—

"That was a sacred day, and a sacred cause, and let each man swear with him to high heaven, uncovered, never to abandon the cause until freedom had been obtained."

The whole multitude accordingly uncovered, when O'Connor resumed:—

"Was not that discipline? Was ever the word of command attended to more promptly? If there should come dark, and black, and sanguinary news from Ireland, he should not confine his defence of Ireland to the House of Commons."

Resolutions for the Charter and Repeal were unanimously carried.

In London the agitation was kept up with vigour. Another meeting was held on the 21st, in John-street, which was densely crowded, and was presided over by John Savage. Mr. Vernon made his first speech in favour of the Charter, and was followed by Ernest Jones, who advocated simultaneous meetings on the day for presenting the petition. Cuffay followed, appealing to all England, Ireland, and Scotland, to be up and doing. Alexander Campbell addressed the meeting in a speech which called for social emancipation before political power; but he was treated very coldly, and ultimately laughed down, and McGrath replied to him amid the cheers of the meeting. The Fraternal Democrats continued to hold

frequent meetings, which became more numerously attended
than ever. The Irish Confederates nightly enrolled numbers
in their clubs, which seemed to be the more augmented in
numbers in consequence of news having arrived of the arrest
of Smith O'Brien, Meagher, and Mitchell. Almost every
European country was now in the throes of revolution ; and as
each post brought news of the risings and triumphs of the people
in Austria, Prussia, the minor German, and many of the Italian
States, so appeared to increase the determination of the
Chartists and Irish Repealers to establish the long cherished
principles for which they had struggled. To assist the movement the trades' delegates met at the Bell Inn, Old Bailey,
London, and passed a resolution in favour of universal
suffrage.

John-street was, on the 27th March the scene of another
great gathering. W. J. Vernon presided over a densely packed
meeting. He expressed his disgust at the folly and farce of
petitioning, which he pronounced a mockery. He was for
giving the House of Commons only one hour to consider
whether they would grant the Charter. This sentiment was
loudly cheered. Dixon amid loud disapprobation, expressed
his dissent from the chairman's speech. John Skelton read a
written speech, urging the meeting to moral force, but was
compelled to leave off reading. Handley supported the views
of the chairman, and Ernest Jones also endorsed his sentiments,
and opposed the moral force speakers. He said :—

"Mr. Dixon tells us that we are not fit for this organization :
why not? Have we wooden legs, or cork arms? He tells us
that the people of England are not yet of that mind. Then all
England is one great lie. Then the men of Northampton lied
when they told me yesterday they were. Then it was a lie on
Oldham Edge. It is a lie in this Hall to-night, for they tell
us they are. Why all England must have entered into one
great conspiracy, for the sake of deceiving five or six unimportant individuals. No, sir; I believe the people are prepared to
pronounce the mighty fiat—to ring the inevitable knell of
slavery ! I should be a guilty man did I say so without a well
grounded conviction. For the evil that might come I should
in part be responsible. The widow and the orphan would have
a right to curse me. But, before heaven, I believe that we
stand upon the threshold of our rights. One step, were it even
with an iron heel, and they are ours. I conscientiously believe
the people are prepared to claim the Charter. Then I say—
take it ; and God defend the right !"

In conclusion he said :—

"We'll steer the right course. We wont be intemperate

and hotheaded, but we will be determined.   We'll respect the
law, if the law-makers respect us; if they don't, France is a
Republic !"
    McGrath followed Jones.   He did not adopt the sentiments of
the moral force speakers, but he was rather more cautious than
the ultra advocates of physical force.   The meeting ended with
cheers for the Charter, and groans for the Ministry.
    Reports continued to arrive of the march of Democracy in
the provinces.   Ten thousand people who afterwards marched
through the town in procession, were addressed by Dr.
M'Douall in Nottingham.   Newark, Plymouth, Tiverton, Merthyr, Padiham, Bradford, Northampton, Wigan, Southampton,
Dumfries, Dudley, Mansfield, Heywood, Bacup, Dundee,
Exeter, and other places elected delegates to the Convention,
adopted the Petition, and passed resolutions demanding the
Charter.   The week in which the Convention met, a vast number
of other places swelled the movement for the Charter, by the
holding of public meetings, and various other measures.   At
Leicester, McGrath addressed thousands in the vast Amphitheatre.   Twenty thousand people met on Nottingham Forest
on Sunday, the 2nd of April, and were addressed by M'Douall.
At Loughborough various meetings were held, which were
addressed by Messrs. Skevington and Dean; and M'Douall
spoke on Tuesday, the 4th, to four thousand people, who walked
in procession through the town.   The Chartists of Coventry
met in St. Mary's Hall, when Messrs Wood, Hartopp, Hosier,
Farn, Pritchard, and McGrath addressed them, and the
National Petition was adopted.   At Southampton, open-air
meetings were held every night amid increased excitement.
At St. Andrews, Fife, a public meeting was held in the City
Hall, where the Petition was also adopted.   At Macclesfield,
a great meeting was held on Parsonage Green, to promote
the union going on between the Chartists and the Repealers.
Messrs. Leach and West were the principal speakers ; the
spirit was enthusiastic.   At Staleybridge ten thousand persons
met and petitioned on behalf of Frost, Williams, and Jones.
At Stroud and Gloucester enthusiastic meetings were also
held.   Even Newport, where Chartism had never lifted its
head since the unfortunate riots, moved again for the Charter,
and a public meeting was held to forward that object.
Aberdeen elected its delegate at a large public meeting in the
Union Hall.   At Blackburn a meeting of four thousand persons
was held, who were most eloquently addressed by Kydd.
From scores of other places signatures to the Petition poured in.
Meeting upon meeting was held, speech after speech was delivered, and no means were left untried to fan the immense excite-

ment that seemed to threaten the existence of the Government. The long anticipated Convention assembled for business on Tuesday, April 4th, in the John-street Institution, the gallery of which was opened to the public. The following are the names of the districts represented, and of the representatives. Exeter, J. Prater Wilkinson; Ipswich, Samuel G. Francis; Bolton, Matthew Stevenson; Halifax, Ernest Jones; Wigan, James Hitchins; Leicester, George Buckby; Nottingham, George Julian Harney; Birmingham, Joseph Linney, and J. A. Fussell; Oldham, Samuel Kydd; Manchester, Daniel Donovan and James Leach; Liverpool, Edmund Jones and Henry Smith; Edinburgh, James Cumming and Dr. Hunter; Dundee, James Graham; Lancaster, J. T. Lund; Barnsley, Frank Mirfield; Newcastle-on-Tyne, James Watson; Northampton, W. Ashton; Bury, Thomas Tattersall; Stockport, J. West; Staffordshire Potteries, Samuel Bevington and Edward Sale; Aberdeen, James Shirron; Derby, G. W. M. Reynolds; York and East Riding, George Stevens; Paisley, Robert Cochrane; Glasgow, James Adams; Irish Democratic Confederation, C. McCarthy; Bath, Charles Bolwell; Bradford, D. Lightowler; Leeds, F. O'Connor and J. Shaw; Carlisle, John Lowery; Merthyr Tydvil, David Thomas; Ashton-under-Lyne, Robert Wyld; Worcester, Edward Walter; London, William Cuffay, Henry Child, and James Bronterre O'Brien; Plymouth, John Petrie; Norwich, William Dixon; Huddersfield, Mr. Murphy; Totnes, W. Tanner; Cheltenham, J. P. Glenister. McGrath was elected president, and Doyle secretary. The first question raised was as to McCarthy's qualification, he being elected by a society called the Irish Democratic Confederation. Messrs. Cuffay and O'Connor opposed his admission; Ernest Jones supported it. The matter was referred to a Committee, who decided in his favour, thus making the Convention an illegal body. A discussion followed on the rights of the Executive Council to its vote, Wheeler reminding O'Connor that he had been elected delegate for Leeds. O'Connor waved his right to vote. O'Brien said, as O'Connor appeared there as an elected delegate, he should not be allowed to escape from his share of the responsibility. O'Connor declared that he did not wish to shake off one particle of the responsibility. He then announced that he had received a letter from Duncombe, in which he stated that his health was much better, and that he hoped to be with them by the following month. The discussion on the rights and responsibilities of the Executive was resumed, and four motions were made upon the subject. O'Brien moved that all elected delegates should sit and vote. West moved that members of the Council should sit *ex-officio*, and that they should be allowed to speak and vote. For West's motion there were eighteen ; for O'Brien's four. The former was carried. A Committee was appointed to fold and arrange the Petition. The delegates then gave in their reports. Wilkinson reported that his constituents were opposed to physical force. Matthew Stevenson said there was no use in preaching patience to the starving masses. He described his constituents as being in a most wretched and horrifying condition. Ernest Jones said that his constituents wished to conduct the movement, if possible, on moral force principles, but if necessary, they were ready to fight to a man. They were ready, if necessary, to rush down from the hills of Yorkshire, in aid of their brother patriots of London. James Hitchin described the people of Wigan as suffering a great amount of oppression and misery. They were ready to try one more Petition, but if that were rejected, they would "go to work," let the consequence be what it might. Buckby had received no instructions, nor was he prepared with any report. The people had told him that they would get the Charter by moral force if they could ; if they could not, they were determined to have it by other means. Harney said that his constituents had resolved that this Petition should be the last presented to the House of Commons, as at present constituted. Whatever other instructions he might receive, he would enforce them to the best of his ability. Linney's constituents were tired of meetings. The people of Wolverhampton, Bilston, and Dudley were ready to obey the Convention. He felt determined to have the Charter before he left London. Fussell said the people of Birmingham were better off than in former years. The middle class had declared for the Charter. The Chartists had the use of the Town Hall. They hoped the questions of physical and moral force would not be introduced into the Convention to destroy its unanimity. Kydd said that in Oldham there was a general feeling of discontent. So long and so continuous had been the misery, that the people began to feel reckless. They entertained the idea that constant starvation was worse than death. Donovan said ten thousand of the people of Manchester were out of work. They wished to attain their ends without physical force, but they wished for the Charter at all risks. The shopkeepers felt the necessity for a change. Their trade had fallen off more than one-half, while their rents and outgoings were the same : six thousand summonses had lately been issued against poor-rate defaulters. Edmund Jones said that in Liverpool ten thousand river porters had been out of employment for twenty weeks. Liverpool saw bankruptcy on the one hand, and revolution on the other. H. Smith believed that if no other town commenced a revolution, Liverpool would. The feeling was, that if the Petition was granted, they must obtain it at the point of the bayonet. There was a great body of the trades, who had by destitution become Democrats. James Cumming said that in Edinburgh they were not poverty-stricken Chartists; they were Chartists from principle, and were ready to support that principle on the field, in the dungeon, or at the stake. James Graham was not instructed to say so, but his firm conviction was that the people of Dundee would indignantly resent any attempt to coerce the Irish, and that they would be ready by every means to support the People's Charter. Lund said the Chartists of Lancaster were ready to join in extreme measures, if there were any probability of success. Mirfield said that his constituents, at a large public meeting, had instructed him to say that if the Government let the military loose upon Ireland, something else would be let loose here. If the Petition was rejected, they hoped the Convention would not break up, but that they would take into their hands the government of the country; that they would divide the land into small farms, and give every man an opportunity of earning his living by the sweat of his brow. James Watson said, come what might, the people of New-castle-upon-Tyne were resolved to have the Charter.

On the following morning the delegates re-assembled. Ashton described the destitute condition of the Northampton shoemakers. He was justified in stating that the working men were determined to have the Charter at all hazards. They thought the man who would not fight for it was unworthy of it. He was instructed to support any measure that would insure the adoption of the Charter in the shortest possible time. James Leach said his report was much the same as his brother delegate's. He should say nothing of physical or moral force, but leave that to the chapter of accidents. Tattersall said the state of the people of Bury was most frightful, trade was so bad that they could scarcely keep body and soul together. Such a state made the people reckless. The Charter was the all-absorbing topic. At no previous time was the feeling so intense or so enthusiastic as at present. He could say emphatically, the men of Lancashire were up to the mark; but thought they should not destroy the labour of years by any act of rashness. West said the people were starving on less than half wages. The people of Stockport had deter-mined that this should be the last Petition. He, like Tattersall, was opposed to a precipitate movement, but he was equally opposed to cowardice. Bevington said poverty and destitution prevailed to an alarming extent, and he never witnessed such a state of uneasiness and restlessness. The people were determined to accomplish their rights at all and any risk. Sale coincided with his colleague. The authorities had refused to issue any more summonses for poor-rates, and had, at the suggestion of an open air meeting, taken twenty acres of land on which to employ the destitute poor. Excitement in favour of the Charter ran very high. James Shirron said the people of Aberdeen were not well organized, but on great occasions the people had always come out in large numbers. They had procured ten thousand signatures to the Petition. If that did not succeed, they would recommend the adoption of an address to the Queen, and leave any further steps to the Convention. Reynolds said that in the district of Derby the best feeling prevailed. He thought this should be the last Petition to the House, and that its refusal would be a declaration of war against labour. A few drops of blood were as nothing in the scale ; and if moral means failed, the people were prepared for any means. The people of Derby agreed fully in his sentiments. G. Stephens' constituents wished a deputation to wait on Lord John Russell, and represent to him the condition of labour. A company of the 57th Regiment were quartered at Hull, and before they left for Ireland thirty seven attached their names to the Petition. The people of Hull wished the Convention to continue its sittings until the Charter was gained. Cochrane's constituents were in favour of the delegates waiting on the members of parliament, to reason with them before the Petition was presented ; and that the several members should be written to by persons residing in their districts. If the Petition was rejected, they recommended simultaneous meetings all over the country, to decide on what was next to be done. Adams had brought up a hundred thousand signatures to the Petition, and another thirty thousand had since been forwarded. The middle class had begun to fraternize. Publicans were the only ones that refused them aid. Poverty prevailed to a great extent, and discontent kept pace with it; and so strong was the feeling, that at any rate they could manage to keep all their soldiers to themselves. He had no particular instructions, but he should oppose any precipitate movement as being calculated to injure their cause. As regarded the late riots in Glasgow, the Chartists had no connection with them except to oppose them. Lightowler represented a hundred thousand persons, and he should have seventy thousand signatures to the petition. The opinion of his constituents was, that life under present circumstances was a burden, and they were resolved to have their rights at all hazards. The people were in a starving condition, and the time had arrived when a change should take place; this was the opinion of a great majority of his constituents. O'Connor looked on that Convention as a fair and faithful representation of the people. Chartism was increasing. He believed that he should have five million four hundred thousand signatures to the Petition. The events in France had given an impetus to the movement. Thrones were crumbling and tumbling on the Continent; and was it to be expected that England would remain in slavery under such circumstances! On Monday they would go down to the House. He was not prepared to destroy the movement he had been mainly instrumental in raising by precipitation, nor was he prepared to allow the people to remain in bondage one moment longer than they could obtain their freedom. Look to Ireland at the present moment! He thought he might say with the delegate from Glasgow, that they would be at least able to keep all the military there. He was now becoming a *quasi* minister, and doubtless would be asked what they intended to do on Monday. On the faith of that Convention he should reply, that not one pane of glass, nor one pennyworth of property, would be injured. That peace and good order would prevail, while their grievances were under discussion. An Alderman had told him in the House, that he would be shot on Monday. He told the Alderman that were he shot, shooting would take place all over the country. He would be in the procession, in the front row of the front rank, and now they might shoot away. If the Petition was rejected, he recommended simultaneous meetings all over the country, to address the Queen to dismiss the Ministry, and call to her councils men who would make the Charter a cabinet question. If that were unavailing, he would never flinch, but would sooner die than not win the Charter. He meant to wait no longer than the time when the majority of the people demanded it, and were prepared to establish their rights. He thought they now had power to obtain it. When O'Connor had concluded his speech, O'Brien rose to make some remarks, believing that it was calculated to mislead as to the preparedness of the people ; but O'Connor rose to leave the Convention, on the ground of having to attend the House to support Sharman Crawford's bill relative to Ireland. O'Brien remarked, that as O'Connor had declared that he had no confidence in the parliament, that it would in a very short time cease to exist, and that the Convention was the only body that he looked to to solve the great difficulty of the country, he thought his attendance there of more importance than his attendance in a parliament, which, according to him, would soon cease to exist. Several of the members raised objections to O'Brien's proceeding, and the general feeling appeared against it. He rose to leave the Convention, but was at length persuaded to remain. Lowery said the condition of the Carlisle people was most fearful. They were not in favour of physical force. They thought the Charter would be gained without it. Wigton, Dalston, and other towns, thought that it would never be gained without physical force. John Shaw's constituents believed their condition could not be worse. They were prepared to risk their all on the attempt to gain the Charter. His instructions were not to return until the Charter was the law of the land. D. Thomas's constituents were desirous of having a procession in their district, at the same time as the procession went to the House with the Petition. They were prepared to carry out the views of the Convention. Robert Wyld represented a hundred thousand unenfranchised workmen, and had brought up seventy thousand signatures to the Petition. The district had authorized him to say that collision with the authorities would be premature, until one more step had been first taken. They were tired of petitioning, and if London did its duty, Lancashire would not be behind hand. M. Walter thought that petitioning under any circumstances was humiliating ; he should, however, go with it on this occasion. Some of his constituents were in favour of physical, others in favour of moral force. Cuffay said the middle class of London were opposed to them, but the working class were up to the mark. In the Westminster district they increased thirty or forty a night. The Confederates were with the Chartists, and would march under their own banner on Monday next. The trades were also coming out. He was prepared to carry out all he had said. H. Child said his constituents were determined to have their rights, peaceably if they could, but forcibly if they must; but the people would keep peaceable until their prayer was either granted or rejected. Reynolds announced that the Government had sent two reporters to take a report of their proceedings, an announcement which was loudly applauded. Petrie's constituents were peaceably inclined, but wished, nevertheless, energetic measures to be taken to obtain the Charter. Dr. Hunter said Edinburgh was not so Democratic as he could wish. He had no instructions from his constituents. He thought the Charter could be made the law by moral force alone ; for when the people said, We will the Charter, it must become law. Glenister could not say, as others had done, that his constituents were prepared for such and such things, but they desired agitation, and a long pull and a strong pull for the obtaining of their rights. William Tanner's instructions were to remain until the Petition was presented. Marsden had brought with him sixty-five thousand signatures. Unless something was done, he sincerely believed it would be impossible to keep North Lancashire quiet. They were prepared to wait some time for it to be done, but a change must be had. Dixon's constituents were little better off than those of Marsden. Should the Petition be rejected, they were for simultaneous meetings all over England, at one day and at one hour, and never to desist until the Charter was law. McCarthy's constituents were determined to achieve their liberties, and they had rifle clubs. Should a single shot be fired in Ireland, forty thousand Irishmen in London were ready to avenge their brethren. Murphy's constituents were resolved to have the Charter, morally if possible, but to have it any road. Harney had received a letter from his constituents, to the effect that the Convention should continue their sittings until the Charter became law. A meeting was called for Monday next. The Mayor had refused the use of the Hall, and said he had received a letter from Sir George Grey, setting forth that a great number of pikes were being manufactured and distributed in Nottingham. O'Brien did not think the people of London generally were with them, nor did he think they were prepared for ulterior measures at the present moment. He would not go against the law, so long as he thought the law would do them justice ; but as soon as he found that the law would not do them justice, and that the people were stronger than the law, that moment he snapped his fingers at it.

Such were the reports given in by the delegates, and it will at once be seen that the country was suffering under an enormous load of misery ; that such misery had given rise to a vast amount of discontent, which, together with the excitement on Continental affairs, had produced a very threatening state of things. But these were not alone the elements necessary to carry a successful revolution. They might have been auxiliaries, but for the groundwork it required something more. It required a well-grounded, intelligent public conviction, formed in the minutes of deliberation,—of the truth, the justice, the value, and necessity of the people's political and social rights. That intelligent conviction was, after years of agitation, yet to be achieved. Kydd submitted a very important motion, relative to the issuing of an address, setting forth the condition of the country. Messrs. Wheeler, Wyld,

Ashton, Cuffay, McCarthy, Stephens, and Cochrane opposed the motion ; some on the ground that it was premature, others on the ground that it was unnecessary. It was, however, supported by Messrs. Cumming, West, Fussell, Ernest Jones, Clark, Glenister, Hitchins, and Petrie, and ultimately was carried unanimously ; when Messrs. Kydd, West, Adams, Wyld, Graham, Marsden, and Leach were appointed to draw up the address. This document reflected great credit on its authors ; it contained a great amount of information, and it even received the praise of some portion of the press opposed to the Charter. Clark read a programme of the Executive Committee. Among other clauses was one for the Convocation of a National Assembly, for the purpose of presenting a National Memorial to the Queen. Reynolds moved an amendment :—

" That in the event of the rejection of the Petition, the Convention should declare its sittings permanent, and should declare the Charter the law of the land."

He had hoped, after O'Connor's speech of yesterday, that they should have no more temporising, yet they had the temporising policy of the programme. Cuffay was opposed to any further petition or memorial, and he was opposed to a body declaring itself permanent, that represented only a fraction of the people. He said that he was elected by only two thousand out of the two million inhabitants of London. He moved that the Convention should confine itself to presenting the Petition, and that a National Assembly should be called instead. Then come what might, it should declare its sittings permanent, and go on, come weal or come woe. Lowery seconded the amendment, as his constituents were not yet in favour of violent ulterior measures. Tattersall moved that simultaneous meetings should be held on the 12th of April, and that such meetings should decide what should be the future steps of the Convention. Linney seconded the amendment. Ernest Jones moved that simultaneous meetings be held, in case of the rejection of the Petition, to adopt the memorial, and to elect delegates to a new Convention ; the present one to sit until such new Convention should assemble. James Watson supported the amendment of Ernest Jones. He was satisfied that their constituents would not warrant them in taking rash steps, and Jones's amendment, while it was determined and fair, at the same time avoided rashness. A long discussion ensued on the various motions, but ultimately the Executive embraced Jones's amendment; and the other amendments having been withdrawn, the following programme was adopted :—

"1st.—That in the event of the National Petition being rejected by the House of Commons, this Convention prepare a National Memorial to the Queen to dissolve the present Parliament, and call to her council such ministers only as will make the People's Charter a cabinet measure.

"2nd.—That this Convention agree to the convocation of a National Assembly, to consist of delegates appointed at public meetings, to present the National Memorial to the Queen, and to continue permanently sitting until the Charter is the law of the land.

"3rd.—That this Convention call upon the country to hold simultaneous meetings on Good Friday, April 21st, for the purpose of adopting the National Memorial, and electing delegates to the National Assembly.

"4th.—That the National Assembly meet in London on April 24th.

"5th.—That the present Convention shall continue its sittings until the meeting of the National Assembly."

When these resolutions were adopted both delegates and audience rose and loudly cheered.

The Convention did not confine itself to its Conventional sittings. Some of the members attended public meetings in the Metropolis. On Tuesday, the 4th, the Fraternal Democrats called a meeting in Farringdon Hall, which was crowded. Ernest Jones presided. The meeting was addressed by Messrs. Harney, West, Kydd, Adams, Cumming, and others. Among other resolutions passed was one calling upon the Convention, in case of the rejection of the Petition, to declare its sittings permanent. Besides this meeting, others were held on Kennington Common and in John-street. The former was addressed by Messrs. Fussell and Ernest Jones ; the latter by Jones of Liverpool, Clark, Tattersall, Leach, Bolwell, Linney, Donovan, Ernest Jones, and Vernon. The spirit displayed was enthusiastic. A large crowd were unable to gain admission to the John-street meeting. A meeting was also held in the St. Pancras Vestry Rooms on behalf of Frost, Williams, and Jones. Henry Hetherington was in the chair. Watson, of Newcastle, in an energetic speech, moved a resolution for the Charter, which Wyld seconded. Messrs. Walter, Arnott, Kydd, West, Glenister, Jones, Fussell, and others spoke, and the resolutions were all unanimously carried. A meeting on Kennington Common, and a procession from thence to the House of Commons, to accompany the Petition, was determined on by the Convention ; but the Government issued a proclamation, declaring such procession illegal, and warning all persons not to attend. The subject was talked of in the House of Commons, when Sir George Grey announced the resolution of the Government. O'Connor condemned it, but Sir George was inflexible, and amidst the loudest cheers he announced, that it was his intention to move for leave to bring in a bill for the better security of the Crown and Government. The Convention issued an address setting forth their peaceable intentions, but all in vain. Preparations went on, and special constables were sworn in by thousands. O'Connor had now a difficult game to play. In the same number of of the *Northern Star* appeared two letters from him. In the one he condemned the mouthing patriots, who talked of attending the demonstration armed, and charged them with causing the Government proclamation. He wrote of the folly of raw recruits, and cautioned the people against them ; and backed up his letter with one that he had received from Duncombe, on the same subject. In the other letter he said :—

" If I had trafficked in your confidence, and made merchandise of your credulity, I might perhaps be induced to cry—*wait, wait, wait!* But your poverty, your destitution and misery, and my own feeling and sense of humanity, the love of truth and justice, would not allow my lips to utter the delusive words ; and therefore it is that I tell you, that in my soul I believe the propitious hour has arrived, when our long suffering and martyrdom may be crowned with the laurels of victory."

On the Friday, the question of the procession was again brought before the House by Drummond. O'Connor announced his intention to take part in it. Several members spoke, some censuring the Government for their interference, others commending them, and urging O'Connor not to attend, but to do his best towards stopping the procession. Sir George Grey moved for leave to bring in his Crown and Government Security Bill, which made open and advised speaking of seditious language, a felony in all parts of the United Kingdom, punishable with transportation. It was stoutly opposed by O'Connor, George Thompson, Hume, Muntz, Bright, and others ; but the first reading was carried. It went through its several stages, and passed the Commons on Wednesday, the 12th, and the Lords on the following day. In the Commons the numbers were : for, two hundred and ninety-five ; against, forty. In the Lords it passed unanimously. John Mitchell immediately changed the name of the *United Irishman* to that of the *Felon*, and wrote as strongly as ever. The Government did not stop with the Felony Bill, but also proceeded with an Alien Bill, which, like the preceding, was of course carried through both Houses and passed into law. Sir George Grey was asked in the House whether the meeting on Kennington Common, would, as well as the procession to the House, be illegal? Sir George replied that that would depend on the character of the meeting. As soon as the Government proclamation appeared, the subject was brought before the Convention. T. M. Wheeler moved :—

"That they should issue a proclamation, declaring their determination to hold the meeting on Monday next, notwithstanding the foolish proclamation of the Government, and notice of the police."

This motion made no mention of the procession to the House; but in the debate which followed, and which was joined in by Messrs. Cuffay, West, Child, Adams, Stevenson, Cochrane, Shaw, Bolwell, Watson, Wilkinson, O'Connor, Kydd, E. Jones, McCarthy, Frances, Reynolds, Clark, Ashton, Lightowler, Wyld, Dixon, Fussell, Donovan, Harney, Shirron, Buckby, Walter, Cumming, and Tattersall, an unanimous resolve was manifested to join in both meeting and procession, and the motion of West was carried. Harney read an article from the *Times*, to the effect that it was the intention of the Chartists to attend the meeting and procession armed. A deputation was appointed to wait on Sir George Grey, stating that no such intention existed. Messrs. Wilkinson, Reynolds, and Clark were appointed for that purpose, and they accordingly proceeded to the Home Office. Sir George Grey could not be seen, but they had an interview with the Under-Secretary, Sir Denis le Marchant, and also the Attorney General. The former told them that he did not think that anything they could say would alter the determination of the Government. Before they left, they wrote a note to Sir George Grey, to the effect that it was their resolve to hold the procession to the House peacefully. On the motion of West, deputations were appointed to wait on members of the Government, to represent to them the state of the country ; and deputations were accordingly appointed who performed that mission. On the motion of Ernest Jones, it was resolved that the country should be requested to hold public meetings on the 10th of April, for the purpose of pledging support to the Convention ; that the result of such meetings be sent to the chairman of the Convention, and that the said meetings should adjourn to the 12th, to hear the report from the Convention relative to the presentation of the National Petition. Harney informed the Convention that one man in London had got an order for thirty thousand staves ; an announcement which was received with groans. On the motion of Harney, a committee was appointed to report concerning the Electoral Districts, and delegates to

the new Convention ; so that in the event of the present Con
vention being mowed down in the streets of London, or swept
into Newgate, there would be others to take their places.
On Saturday O'Connor was in the Convention; and
having spoken on the Crown and Government Security Bill,
it was resolved that deputations should wait on the Liberal
members, to solicit their opposition to and obstruction of
the measure.   These attempts were fruitless ; for, as before
observed, the Bill speedily became law.   It should, however,
be noted, that the opposition secured its enactment for a
period of two years only.   Harney suggested that the
members of Convention should appoint their successors, in
case of their being absent against their wills on Tuesday.
Ernest Jones seconded the motion. Messrs. Watson, Wheeler,
Reynolds, West, Kydd, and others, supported it.   Clark
moved as an amendment, that the simultaneous meetings
should appoint the next Convention in the event of such a
contingency.   The motion received fourteen, and the amendment twenty-eight votes.

On Sunday, the 9th, Bronterre O'Brien appeared before his
constituents at the Chartist Hall, Lambeth, to tender his
resignation as a member of the Convention.   He gave as his
reason the fact, that the delegates from the country seemed
likely, on account of the distress of their constituents, to go
faster than prudence warranted; finding which he could no
longer act with them.   He had not attended their sittings for
the last three days.   It was deemed advisable that all their
measures should be unanimous, and as he could not go with
them, he had resolved not to throw the apple of discord
amongst them.   He believed they were actuated by the best
motives; but their convictions were different to his, and had
been so from the first.   O'Brien was received with strong
marks of disapprobation, and was eventually compelled to sit
down.   He had been advised not to attend the meeting, but
he was resolved, he said, to act up to principles which he had
always publicly avowed, and to which he considered himself
unalterably pledged.

The ever memorable 10th of April arrived, and vast preparations were made by the Government.   Beside the regular
troops quartered in the metropolis, others poured in from
Windsor, Hounslow, Chichester, Chatham, Winchester, and
Dover.   The marines and sailors of the Royal Navy at Sheer-
ness, Chatham, Birkenhead, Spithead, and other government
towns, as well as the dockyard men, were kept under arms.
The Thames police kept watch upon the mercantile marine,
lest they should show any leaning towards the Chartists.

Heavy gun-batteries were brought from Woolwich, and placed at various points. The marines were stationed at the Admiralty. Many of the troops were disposed of secretly, to be ready in case of necessity. The mounted police were armed with broad swords and pistols. All the public buildings were put in a state of defence. Two thousand stand-of-arms were supplied to the general post-office, for the use of the clerks and officers of that department, who were all sworn in as special constables; and the officials at other public places were equally well provided. All the steam vessels were ordered to be ready for any emergency, in order to convey troops. At the Tower the guns were examined, the battlements strengthened by barricades, and the troops held in readiness to march at a minute's notice. The labourers at the docks were sworn in as specials. The city prisons were guarded by military, and the churches were converted into barracks. The public vehicles were generally withdrawn from the streets. In the city seventy thousand persons were sworn in as special constables, and military officers commanded them. The royal carriages and horses, and other valuables, were removed from the palace. The military force amounted to nine thousand men. It being believed that the procession would go from Kennington Common, over Blackfriars Bridge, to the House of Commons, great preparations were made in that quarter. At Stepney Green, Finsbury-square, and Russell-square, bodies of the Chartists met with bands and banners, and paraded the streets on their way to Kennington Common, where six thousand police, and eight thousand specials were in attendance. Before eleven o'clock Trafalgar-square was filled with police. The approaches to Westminster Bridge were, on the Surrey side, guarded by strong bodies of that force, and the Bridge was placarded with bills, announcing that no procession would be allowed to accompany the Petition to the House. Every commodious place in this vicinity was filled with military, police, or specials. The artillery was also present. Various bodies continued to arrive on the Common with music and banners, bearing various inscriptions, such as " Liberty, Equality, Fraternity ;" " Ireland for the Irish." The Convention assembled at nine o'clock, Reynolds occupying the chair. The delegates' names were called. When the name of Bronterre O'Brien was called, McCarthy said he understood O'Brien had resigned, and he wished to know when he attended last. Doyle said they had no notice of his resignation officially, and he had not attended since the day before the proclamation was issued from the Government. Doyle also announced that he had received a letter from the

Commissioner of Police, in reply to one sent by him that the route of procession was altered. The latter stated that the contemplated procession would on no account be allowed to take place. O'Connor delivered a precautionary speech ; took the blame off the Government for the preparations they had made, and charged it upon those who had talked of an armed demonstration. He said he was prepared to ask the meeting "in the name of courage, in the name of justice, in the name of God, not to hold the procession, and thus throw their great cause into the hands of pickpockets and scoundrels, and give the Government an opportunity of attacking them." He then stated that preparations had been made for shooting from certain windows on the leaders of the movement. He was told this by Alderman Humphery in the House of Commons, by the police, and others. The delegates started from the Convention Room at ten o'clock. The procession was headed by a car, decorated with various banners, and drawn by four horses. This car was to convey the National Petition. This was followed by a second car, drawn by six horses, and containing the delegates. On the front seat were Feargus O'Connor, Doyle, McGrath, Jones, Wheeler, and Harney. This car, like the preceding one, was profusely decorated. As the delegates left a body of people fell into procession behind them, eight abreast. Having arrived at the National Land Company's office, the procession stopped to take up the Petition. This accomplished, the procession resumed its march through Holborn, Farringdon-street, and New Bridge-street, to Blackfriar's Bridge. Two or three hundred pensioners were on the Steamboat Pier, who, on being recognised, were loudly cheered by the people in the procession. Quite as many police were on the other side of the Bridge, and a little further on were fifty mounted police with cutlasses. As far as the Blackfriar's-road most of the shops were open, but from the Bridge they were mostly closed. The procession at length reached the Common, where the several bodies of men, with their bands and banners, formed into a dense mass, estimated at from one hundred and fifty thousand to one hundred and seventy thousand, and who burst into loud cheering as the delegates' car came upon the Common.

No sooner had the car reached its destination than O'Connor was sent for to the Horns' Tavern, where Mr. Mayne, Commissioner of Police, was awaiting him. A report soon spread that O'Connor was arrested, but this was an idle rumour. Mayne informed him that the Government would not interfere with the meeting, but that the procession would not be allowed. That the Government had the means of preventing it, that those means would be used, and that O'Connor would in that case be held responsible for the consequences. O'Connor promised that the procession should be abandoned. Having returned to the car, he was greeted with loud cheers and waving of hats, which continued for a considerable time. O'Connor had to conquer a difficulty. He had led the people to believe that he would head the procession to the House of Commons, and he had pledged himself to the police that it should be abandoned ; he must therefore proceed by cautious steps. "My children," he commenced, "you were industriously told that I would not be amongst you to-day : well, I am here !" and the crowd burst into a loud cheer. He told them that he had received one hundred letters urging him not to attend, as his life would be sacrificed ; but he replied, "I would rather be stabbed to the heart, than resign my proper place among my children." Here shouts of "Bravo !" burst from the meeting. "Yes," he continued, "you are my children. These are your horses, not mine. This car is yours, made of your timber. I am only your father and your bailiff, but your honest father and your unpaid bailiff !" and again was he saluted with a shout of applause. He now commenced to implore them not to injure their cause by any act of folly. He would go down on his knees to implore them not to do so. He pointed to the Petition, which he said contained the voices of five millions seven hundred thousand of their countrymen, who would be looking for good conduct from them that day. He spoke of the blessings he had in store for them from his Land Plan, and said he could not spare one of his children from the feast. He told them that his physician had forbidden his appearing amongst them ; that he had spent six sleepless nights, and that his breast was like a coal of fire. He then told them that the Executive would accompany the Petition, and urged them not to accompany it. He called on those who were determined to act like prudent, sensible men, and to see the Charter speedily the law of the land, to hold up their hands ; when a forest of hands were raised. He said, "So help me God, I will die upon the floor of the House, or get your rights for you. I love you better than my own life. Last week I offered to the Convention the profits of the *Star* to carry out the movement." He made the meeting laugh by a humorous allusion to the feeding of the Land Company's horses, which had drawn the Petition, and said he had confidence in their sense and wisdom, and their resolve to carry the contest to an early issue ; he declared that now he was assured of their discretion he breathed freely, and the pain had gone from his breast. "If you want to kill me," he continued, "my life is at your command; but to others, I will not surrender it without a struggle. Then there is another thing I wish you to remember,—I don't think you could well spare me just now. I will go with you steadily and peacefully and resolutely, and I will present your Petition to-night. On Friday there will be a debate upon it, and nothing can prevent our success, if the people do not destroy themselves by intemperance and folly." He called upon those who thought the Convention had acted wisely in preventing a flow of bloodshed among the people, to raise their hands; and again a forest of hands were raised. He congratulated them again and again upon their good sense and repeated his exhortations respecting the procession; and concluded by saying, "that though I may be stretched on the rack, I will smile terror out of countenance—go on conquering and to conquer, until the People's Charter had gloriously become the law of the land;" whereupon enthusiastic applause burst from the vast multitude.

Ernest Jones followed O'Connor; he said before the Petition reached the House, it would contain six million of signatures, and reiterated the advice which had just been given. He called on them, however, to continue their exertions, and if the Petition were rejected, to carry their prayers respectfully to the foot of the throne. Clark moved the adoption of a petition against the coercive measures before parliament, which Kydd seconded, and Reynolds supported. While O'Connor was recommending this petition, there were cries of "No more petitioning;" but the resolution to petition was carried. Messrs. McGrath, Wyld, Edmund Jones, Daly, Reynolds, West, and Harney addressed large bodies of people on other parts of the Common, during the time that O'Connor was speaking to the main body. The meeting being at an end, the Petition was placed in three cabs, and the Chartist Executive accompanied it to the House of Commons. The police guarded the bridges, and for upwards of an hour after the meeting, prevented any approach on the part of the people. Some endeavoured to effect a passage, but the police used their staves, often with very little moderation. The masses did not, however, risk a collision with the police, and considering the excitement previously existing, the day passed off in a singularly peaceful manner.

On the same day O'Connor presented the Petition to the House, which he stated was signed by five million seven hundred thousand persons. He also presented one for the same object, signed by thirty thousand persons. He moved that the first Petition be read by the clerk at the table, which was accordingly done. Lord Morpeth, stated that Sir

George Grey, was unavoidably absent on account of business; but he might say for him, that whatever might be his sentiments on the prayer of thc Petition, he would not wish to appear wanting in respect to that or any other petition, signed by a large number of his fellow-subjects. The Petition being rolled out of the House, Bright presented a petition from delegates at Manchester, representing six thousand persons, praying for the six points of the Charter; the abolition of the law of entail and primogeniture; a limitation of the hours of labour; and local boards for the regulation of wages. Lushington gave notice that on Friday next he would ask whether it was the intention of the Government to introduce any measure of parliamentary reform during the session.

The Convention re-assembled on Tuesday the 11th. Jones moved the appointment of a committee to draw up a report of the previous day's proceedings, for distribution in the metropolis, and throughout the country. Cuffay opposed the motion on the ground of expense, but it was ultimately carried. Clark moved the appointment of a committee of three to prepare a petition to the House of Commons for the impeachment of the Government. Lundy, because he thought it would lead to no practical result, moved the previous question, which Cuffay seconded. After a long discussion, in which nearly every member took part, the motion was carried almost unanimously. O'Connor having offered to give the profits of the *Star* to the Convention, it was opposed and declined; but a resolution was carried, that the Convention would have no objection to receive a donation from O'Connor towards its expenses. O'Connor made a speech, and told the delegates that he estimated the number at Kennington Common at from four to five hundred thousand persons. Harney moved the appointment of a committee to select delegates to visit the various districts, to prepare the people for the meetings on Good Friday for the election of the National Assembly. The motion was carried with one dissentient, and the committee was appointed. On the motion of Leach, the Convention, by a large majority, disapproved of any resolution denunciatory of the middle-class as a body. A resolution was then adopted on the motion of Kydd, condemning the Alien Bill, introduced by the Marquis of Lansdowne in the House of Lords. Shirron made a motion which was adopted, that the Convention call upon the trades to adopt the Charter.

On the same day that the last three motions were adopted, an important scene occurred in the House of Commons on the

subject of the National Petition.   Thornley brought up a report
from the Committee on public petitions.   He stated that with
the assistance of thirteen law stationer's clerks, the petition
which O'Connor had said contained five million seven hundred
thousand signatures, had been examined, and it was found to
contain only one million nine hundred and seventy-five thousand
four hundred and ninety-six, and amongst the rest were signatures such as Victoria Rex, the Duke of Wellington, Sir Robert
Peel, Colonel Sibthorpe, &c.   There were also a large number
of fictitious names, such as Pugnose, Longnose, Flatnose,
Punch, Snooks, Fubbs, and other obscene names, which he
would not offend the House—or its dignity by repeating.
O'Connor denied that it would be possible for thirteen clerks
to count one million nine hundred thousand signatures in the
time, and moved for a committee to enquire into the subject.
He attributed the fictitious names to Government spies.   He
believed the number of signatures he had stated was correct.
He did not believe he should have any difficulty in
obtaining fifteen million or double or treble that number.
Thornley said the Committee was not appointed specially to
examine that Petition, but it was appointed in the early part
of the session, to examine all petitions presented to the House.
O'Connor had stated that the Petition was contained in four
large bundles, and it took himself and four other persons to
lift the largest.   The Petition had been weighed that morning,
and was found to weigh 5cwt. 84lbs.   The Committee was, he
trusted, too well known to render any further statement necessary.   Lord John Russell expressed himself satisfied with the
report.   The Earl of Arundel and Surrey, Maurice O'Connell,
and Sir R. H. Inglis having spoken, Cripps, one of the Committee, got up and confirmed the statement of Thornley, and
stated that out of ten thousand signatures, eight thousand two
hundred were those of women.   He made some strong remarks
upon O'Connor, who replied that he could not be answerable
for every signature contained in the Petition.   He had palmed
no falsehood upon the House, nor had he charged the Committee with practising a deception.   After he had spoken
O'Connor left the House.   Colonel Sibthorpe denied that he
had signed the Petition.   After several other members had
spoken, Lord John Russell moved the arrest of O'Connor, and
the Speaker obtained an assurance from Cripps, that he would
not leave the House.   O'Connor had conveyed a challenge to
Cripps through the medium of Ernest Jones.   He was soon after
taken into custody, and brought before the House of Commons, and after explanations and apologies between him and
Cripps, the affair was allowed to drop.   O'Connor afterwards

announced that after what had occurred he should not, for the present, persevere with the motion of which he had given notice.

Another public meeting was held at John-street Institution on Tuesday, the 11th. Skelton moved a resolution, approving the steps taken by the Convention to prevent the shedding of blood. Churchill moved an amendment, not condemning the Convention, but couched in terms of faint praise. Vernon seconded the amendment, but it was withdrawn, and the resolution was carried. Fussell moved a resolution condemning the Crown and Government Security Bill, which Walter seconded, and it was supported by Jones, who observed "that a Gagging Bill was about to be passed, at the instigation of Sir George Grey, but that was a reason why he should speak stronger and louder." Great applause followed this announcement. The resolution being carried, the crowded meeting separated. In the Convention on Friday, the 14th, O'Connor stated his intention not at present to bring the Charter before the House, and he recommended more petitioning. A resolution was passed approving of O'Connor's resolution, also a vote of thanks to, and sympathy with, that gentleman. Kydd moved that a return should be made from every delegate, of the number of signatures from his district. Harney believed the signatures from his district were genuine, but he suggested that the men of Nottingham should form themselves into a National Guard, as the most convincing answer they could give to those who denied their numbers ; until that was done, he would never risk his life. Ernest Jones believed the number of signatures was under estimated, rather than otherwise. There were two hundred thousand signatures now lying at the office, and he had been advised of forty-seven thousand from Halifax, which had never arrived. Adams moved that the Convention would undertake to procure a greater number of genuine signatures to the Petition than it was reported to have had, if the Government would consider that an argument in favour of its consideration. Both motion and amendment were got rid of, by the Convention voting the previous question. Ernest Jones moved a resolution for the distribution of tracts, not for the purpose of showing what the Charter was, as it would be too late, now that they expected to have the Charter in a very short time; but to show the benefits it would confer. The motion was carried, and two pounds eighteen and sixpence subscribed by strangers present towards carrying it out. On the motion of Jones a memorial to the Queen was also agreed to ; and it was resolved to send that gentleman to Scotland to prepare the way for the National Assembly. Stevenson moved a resolution, denouncing the press for its unfair and one-sided proceedings. Some of the delegates objected, that the only remedy was the people supporting their own press; but the motion was carried by a large majority. In the course of the discussion, Cuffay said they should call the publisher and printer to the bar, as they did in another House. This remark caused loud laughter, which was renewed when Cuffay read a letter to the Convention, purporting to be from Colonel Sibthorpe, inviting him to dinner on Wednesday next. The memorial to the Queen having been brought up, it was resolved to submit it to the simultaneous meetings, to be signed by the respective chairmen, on their behalf.

Meetings still continued to be held throughout the country. At Aberdeen, six thousand persons passed a resolution in favour of forming a National Guard. On Thursday, the 13th, a crowded meeting took place in Adam-square Hall, when confidence was voted in the Convention, and an open air meeting was held on the following Monday evening. It was intended to walk in procession, but a request from the authorities induced the meeting to abandon its intention. On the 19th, a crowded meeting was held in the City Hall, Glasgow, when a similar resolution to that passed at Edinburgh was carried, and also a resolution to support the Convention by every lawful means. At Greenock and Dundee large meetings also took place, and similar resolutions were passed. On the 17th, Jones arrived at Aberdeen, where a meeting of ten thousand persons was held in the open air, at which resolutions were passed against the House of Commons and Ministry, and in favour of the formation of a National Guard. McPherson presided, and the meeting was addressed by Messrs. Henry, Macdonald, Wright, Smart, Lindsay, Findlay, and Jones. At nine o'clock the crowd dispersed, a portion adjourning to the Union Hall, which was crowded to excess. The meeting was again addressed by Messrs. Henry, Wright, Smart, and Jones, and at last broke up with cheers for O'Connor and the Convention. At Ayr, and many of the smaller towns in Scotland, similar meetings were held, and resolutions passed. At Manchester, meetings of shopkeepers, of special constables, of trades' delegates, and of the Chartists generally, were held in support of the Charter. A meeting was held on the Sunday in Smithfield, Manchester, said to have been attended by a hundred thousand persons, who pledged themselves to support the Convention in any emergency. At Newcastle, North Shields, Hull, Bury, Liverpool, Whitehaven, Loughboro', Bilston, Worcester, Tiverton, Bristol, Heywood, Sutton-in-Ashfield, and other towns, large and spirited meetings were also held. At Bilston the mail was guarded by mounted police. Meetings and processions took place almost every day, and the utmost enthusiasm was manifested. In Mitchell's paper the articles on Street Warfare were continued with increasing spirit, and they breathed a tone of defiance of the Government. At Dublin a crowded meeting of Repealers was held in the Music Hall, Abbey-street, which was addressed by Mr. Stritch, the chairman, Fraser, O'Donnaghue, Barry, Smith O'Brien, Meagher, Dunne, Mitchell, McGhee, and Doheny. An Irish tri-coloured flag was displayed in the meeting, with an enormous pike blade shining over it. The strongest determination was manifested by the meeting. O'Connor was invited to attend a meeting in Dublin, to support the Charter, on Easter Monday.

On Monday, the 17th, the Convention again met. Clark again brought forward the question of the Petition, stating that petition sheets were received from Leeds, with fifty-four thousand signatures, and from Manchester, with one hundred and seventy thousand. He had no doubt a great error had been made in the number of signatures to the Petition, and therefore they ought not to be ashamed to acknowledge it. A Committee on the subject was appointed. Harney read a paper from Nottingham, which stated that the Chartists had formed themselves into an Armed Life and Property Protection Society. Clark, on Wednesday, reported from the Committee appointed to enquire into the signatures to the Petition, that they could not ascertain whether the numbers stated by the House of Commons' Committee were correct, or those given by the persons entrusted with the getting up of the Petition, they therefore declined to make any report. On the motion of Clark, the meeting of the National Assembly was postponed till the 1st of May. During the discussion Reynolds alluded in strong language to the Bill of Sir George Grey, declaring that if the people would support them, he would go in defiance of such a law, even though he might be transported for life. Harney made a motion, that instead of the Memorial being signed by the chairmen of the public meetings, it should be signed by all males from eighteen years of age upwards. Seven voted for the motion, and seven against, and the Chairman gave his casting vote against it. A letter was read from Ernest Jones in which he stated that a National Guard, six thousand strong, had been formed at Aberdeen, and that processions took place nearly every night; and that Glasgow and Edinburgh were preparing to follow the same course.

In the *Star* of April 22nd a letter appeared from O'Connor, in which he aimed a blow at the coming National Assembly, proclaiming it illegal.   He also denounced the folly and indiscretion of some members of the Convention, for whose acts he had had to suffer contumely and reproach in the House of Commons, and towards whose expenses he had paid a hundred and fifty pounds.   He ridiculed parties being ready to " tuck up their sleeves and go at it," which was evidently intended for Julian Harney, these being the words once made use of by him years before.   He quoted a letter he had received from a shorthand writer, whose name at his own request was withheld, stating that the daily papers had all been requested to put down the meeting on the 10th at fifteen thousand, which was the cause of the numbers being so stated by all those papers.   Was this letter a hoax ?   O'Connor knew, from his own paper, that the numbers stated by the *Morning Post* were from eighty thousand to one hundred and fifty thousand, and by the *Sun* at one hundred and seventy thousand.   O'Connor also related, in the same letter, that an Irish policeman in disguise followed him on the 8th of April, and informed him that if he attended the meeting on the 10th, he was to be shot.

The following week was famous for meetings.   A crowded meeting of the trades was held at the National Hall, London, at which resolutions were carried for the Charter, and Repeal of the Union.   O'Connor visited Manchester, where a crowded meeting took place in the Hall of Science, which was addressed by that gentleman and several others.   On Easter-Monday, he visited his constituents at Nottingham, where a huge procession was formed; O'Connor, with Messrs. Sweet, Mott, and Roberts, being seated in a triumphal car, drawn by four horses, with postillions dressed in green silk velvet jackets and caps.   From the Railway Station they proceeded through the streets to the Market-square, where it was estimated from twenty to twenty-five thousand persons were assembled. Sweet occupied the chair.   Roberts moved, and G. Harrison seconded, a resolution of confidence in Feargus O'Connor, who then addressed the vast assembly at considerable length.   In the evening seven hundred sat down to tea in the Exchange Rooms.   Roberts read an address to O'Connor, and Harrison spoke a few words; after which O'Connor again addressed the meeting.   At the meeting in the Market-place Dr M'Douall and the Rev. Thaddeus O'Malley were elected to the National Assembly.   At Liverpool an immense meeting was held in the open air, when Messrs. Thomas and Edmund Jones were elected to that body.   At Glasgow a large gathering, said to number a hundred thousand persons, took place on the Green, over which Moir presided.   Messrs. Paul, Duncan, Fraser,

Murray, Davies, Clough, Adams (of the Convention), Harley, and Ross, addressed the assembled thousands. Resolutions were passed against the Gagging Bill. At a previous meeting, Messrs. Adams, Harley, and Murray, of Dublin, were elected to the Assembly. At Dundee, a crowded meeting assembled in Bell-street Hall, at which R. Kydd took the chair. J. McCrae having proposed a resolution, Ernest Jones delivered a thrilling address, and asked the meeting if they were determined to back up the National Assembly in any measure they might adopt to gain their rights? There was a loud response in the affirmative. Ernest Jones visited Edinburgh, where a densely packed meeting was held in the Waterloo Rooms. J. Grant, of the *Weekly Express* presided. Adams, delegate for Glasgow, spoke at some length, and was followed by Jones, who electrified the audience with his eloquence. After Dr. Hunter had addressed the meeting, and cheers had been given for Feargus O'Connor, the people dispersed. Greenock was visited by Messrs. Jones and Adams. The Chartists formed a procession, though forbidden by the authorities, and met the delegates who were accompanied by Messrs. Burrell and Nelson, from Port Glasgow, at the east end of the town. There were about seven hundred people in the procession. They drew up in Delingburn-square; Campbell was called to the chair, and Messrs. Jones and Adams delivered addresses. Afterwards some of the people, again walking in procession, came into contact with the police, and met with some severe blows.

On Good-Friday a West Riding meeting took place on Skercoat Moor, Halifax. Great preparations were made by the authorities. The special constables, the yeomanry cavalry, the pensioners, and the military were in readiness. Processions, with music and flags, poured in from Bradford, Huddersfield, and other places. An immense concourse of people assembled on the Moor. B. Rushton, the veteran Democrat, presided. Harris, of Leeds; Lightowler, of the Convention; Shackleton, of Halifax; Emmott, of Keighley; Shaw, of the Convention; Clisset, of Halifax; Joseph Barker, of Wortley; and other gentlemen addressed the meeting. The usual resolutions were passed. It was estimated that eighty thousand persons attended. Besides the meetings already named large numbers were held in various towns, at which delegates were elected to the Assembly. At Dublin, a great meeting was held in the Princess' Theatre, for the purpose of forming a league between the Irish Repealers and the English Radicals. Richard O'Gorman, Esq., was in the chair, and the meeting was addressed by J. Mitchell, Patrick O'Higgins, and many other gentlemen, and resolutions were passed in accordance with the object of the meeting. Another meeting was held on the 24th of April, presided over by Mitchell, and addressed by Messrs. Leach and Kydd; after which a resolution was passed in favour of the principles of the Charter. In Drogheda, and other towns, similar meetings were held.

At a meeting of the Convention on the 23rd of April, it was resolved that, despite the letter of O'Connor, the Assembly would meet on the 1st of May. On May the 1st, 1848, that body met accordingly, and the following gentlemen handed in their credentials :—J. Shaw, Tower Hamlets ; W. Dixon, Norwich ; W. J. Vernon, West London ; T. Clark, Sheffield ; J. Crossley, Staleybridge ; T. Briggs, Sheffield ; J. Matthews, Bury ; A. Sharp, Tower Hamlets ; M. Stevenson, Bolton ; E. Candelet, Hyde ; Dr. M'Douall and T. O'Malley, Nottingham ; J. Basset, South London ; T. Firts, Lynn ; J. Pebody, Northampton ; R. Cochrane, Paisley ; J. McCrae, Dundee ; J. Peacock, Greenock ; S. Bartlett, Bristol ; T. M. Wheeler, South London ; J. Shaw, Barnsley ; H. Mitchell, Rochdale ; J. Arkell, Swindon ; W. Brook and J. Barker, Leeds ; S. Kydd, Oldham ; J. Adams, and A. Harley, Glasgow. Dixon was appointed chairman, and Shirron secretary. A discussion took place on the legality of the Assembly, on account of the number exceeding forty-nine. Some strong remarks were made on O'Connor ; Shirron observing that they could place no dependence on the word of a man who told them one day that the Assembly was legal, and the next that it was illegal. Ultimately it was resolved, on the motion of Ernest Jones, that all delegates duly elected should be summoned forthwith to take their seats. Captain O'Brien attended from the Irish Confederates, as a mark of respect, but did not sit in the Assembly. McCarthy presented his credentials ; but although Ernest Jones urged his admission, it was decided that he should not be admitted, not having been elected at a properly convened meeting. West took his seat for Stockport ; Hargreaves for Warrington ; G. Abbs for Longton ; R. Mirfield, Keighley ; W. Insoll, Dudley ; S. Bentole, Macclesfield ; J. Hoy, Salford ; H. Roden, Birmingham ; C. B. Henry, Aberdeen ; McIntosh, Newcastle-on-Tyne ; Carver for Birmingham District. The delegates commenced giving in their reports on Monday evening, and did not finish until Wednesday morning. It was evident, from these reports, that a great majority of the districts were opposed to physical force. The Northampton delegate was elected on the moral force principle, although the delegate to the Convention had said his constituents were ready for fighting. Leeds had elected two moral force delegates. Shaw of London, Sharp, E. Jones, McLean, Henry, Shirron, McIntosh, and T. Jones, with their constituents, were in favour of physical force, if necessary. McCrae said his constituents had formed a National Guard. Wheeler said the same of his. E. Jones said his constituents wished to observe the laws that protected life and property, but determined to break those that restricted liberty and justice. At Aberdeen, he said, a National Guard of one thousand persons was formed, and they were ready to support the Assembly, should it declare itself a Parliament. Meetings were held at Edinburgh thirty thousand strong, and they had commenced talking of a National Guard. The magistrates there had handed over the safety of the town to the Chartists. At Paisley, where he had attended a meeting and procession of thirty thousand persons, with one hundred banners and twelve bands of music, fire-arms were discharged along the line of procession in token of rejoicing. At an overflowing meeting in the City Hall, Glasgow, the people pledged themselves to support the Assembly, whatever it might decree. Kydd reported his mission to Ireland, and stated his belief that if the proper means were taken, the Irish people would receive the principles of the Charter. Peacock, Shaw, of Barnsley, and Rankin of Edinburgh, censured O'Connor for his letter. On the motion of Jones, the Assembly by a large majority adopted the following as its programme :—Means of enabling the Assembly to give increased vigour to the movement ; the organization and policy of the Chartist body ; the presentation of the Memorial to the Queen ; the best practical method of making the Charter law. Doheny took his seat as delegate for Salford, T. Jones for Liverpool, and Messrs. Churchill and McCarthy for Finsbury. A great deal of time was then wasted upon the question of how the Assembly should proceed. The delegates generally seemed to have no settled policy. Moral and physical force came under discussion, when M'Douall strongly condemned the promulgation of the notion that the people were prepared to resort to physical force. Ultimately, the delegates adopted a motion by Candelet, that all discussion on the questions of moral and physical force were highly impolitic, and that an address to the country to that effect be drawn up. Letters were read from Barnsley and Liverpool—one for, the other against, O'Connor. A discussion ensued, in the course of which the *Star* was charged with unfair reporting. Not one delegate defended that journal. It should here be stated that Ernest Jones was no longer employed on the *Star*. Both he and Harney had had notice from O'Connor, that they could no longer be employed on the *Star* if they sat in the National

Assembly. Harney retained his post as editor, and declined a seat in the Assembly; but Jones resigned his trust into O'Connor's hands, and took his seat amongst the delegates. O'Connor addressed a letter in the *Star* to the Assembly, in which he sought to defend his conduct.

On Saturday, the 6th, it was resolved to call upon the country to raise the sum of ten thousand pounds for purposes of agitation. A new party for household suffrage, and other measures, had been formed under the auspices of Hume. Dr. M'Douall moved a resolution that the Chartists should attend meetings called by other bodies of Reformers, not for purposes of obstruction, or moving factious amendments; but for showing calmly and rationally the superiority of the Charter over other measures of reform, and to defend it if attacked. Ernest Jones thought the Chartists should attend public meetings, and move amendments to anything short of the Charter. He should be opposed to attending meetings of electors for purposes of obstruction. Ultimately, M'Douall's motion was carried, with an addition by Brook that they would stand by the Charter. On Monday Place took his seat for Blackburn, and Marsden for Preston. Shaw reported that his constituents had passed a vote of confidence in O'Connor, and McGrath said a large and enthusiastic meeting, at the South London Hall, had done the same. Adams said if this course was persisted in, he should rake up the meetings at which votes of no confidence had been passed. Dr. M'Douall brought up a report from the Committee on organization. The report recommended the division of the country into districts, localities, wards, and sections. That an Executive of five be appointed for the current year by the Executive; district and local officers to be appointed by the localities. The Executive to have two pounds each weekly, and when travelling, second-class fare, and two shillings and sixpence per day. Ten Commissioners to be also appointed by the Assembly, to be under the control of the Executive, and to be paid the same when employed. The district officers were to keep an active superintendence over the localities, and to furnish weekly a report to the Executive, as to number of members, state of trade, feeling of the people, and movements of public bodies. A Liberty Fund of ten thousand pounds to be raised by voluntary subscriptions; an office in London to be at once taken by the Executive. This plan was adopted, with the exception of the members electing the Executive in six weeks; the Assembly appointing a Provisional Executive in the meantime, and twenty Commissioners instead of ten. Ernest Jones expressed himself in favour of a Permanent Executive, appointed by the Assembly, and subject to the approval or rejection of the people. The Assembly then elected Messrs. McCrae, Jones, Kydd, Leach, and M'Douall as the Executive. Tuesday, May 9th, Mitchell took his seat for Rochdale, and T. Adams, Wheeler, Brook, Rankin, Pilling, Stevenson, Sharpe, Cochrane, Peacock, Shaw, Harley, Bassett, Cumming, Child, Donovan, Shirron, Henry, Lightowler, and West were appointed Commissioners for six weeks, similarly to the Executive. At the outset of this day's proceedings, Vernon and others complained that nothing had been done and that if such a state of things continued, the agitation must die. Some other delegates expressed the same opinion. Child confessed, as one of the organization Committee, that they had not done their duty.

On Wednesday, the 10th, Kydd brought up a very sensible address to all classes on the labour question, which after being discussed, was unanimously adopted. M'Douall read a letter from the Associated Trades' delegates of Glasgow, complaining of the differences of the Assembly and O'Connor, of their frittering away their time in petty debates on matters comparatively unimportant, and of their neglect of business. They urged union amongst the leaders. In answer to this letter, resolutions were passed to the effect, that the Assembly had not as a body entertained any question about O'Connor, and that it repudiated all personalities. In a discussion on the duties of the appointed Commissioners, considerable ill-feeling was manifested; Child expressing a hope that when they went out to lecture they would confine themselves to plain common sense, give themselves no airs, and if they had any sarcastic powers, would keep them at home, carefully locked up. The chairman stated that he had received an insulting letter, calling upon the Assembly to disperse. On the motion of Rankin, a resolution was adopted :—" That a standing army is contrary to the British constitution, and inimical to the liberty of the subject."

A deputation appointed to wait on O'Connor respecting his motion, stated, that having done so, that gentleman replied that Hume had given notice of a motion for universal suffrage, based on a three years' residence (this was false, it was household suffrage); vote by ballot; triennial parliaments; and equal electoral districts (this last was also false). He thought it advisable not to bring his motion forward until that was decided, and he recommended more petitioning. Adams, amid cheers and laughter, said they had been talking of a conciliatory policy, but this was a perplexing policy. M'Douall said the correspondence from the country was very cheering, organization was going on. In Newcastle district they expected to have twenty thousand members in two or three weeks, and in Cornwall the Chartists were very strong. It was then agreed that a large metropolitan demonstration take place for the adoption of the Memorial to the Queen. Marsden and Vernon were in favour of a procession to accompany the Memorial. Ernest Jones said if he ever took part in another procession, it would be one from which he would not draw back. He would not, if the people were ready, shrink from the responsibility ; but it would be time enough to talk of the procession when they had the meeting. Kydd, though ready to act with the people in a mass, if they resolved on a procession, made some judicious remarks against the suggestion, as did several other delegates.

While the Assembly was discussing the provinces were not idle. O'Connor visited Leicester, May the 8th, and was welcomed by a procession. Two meetings were held, one in the open air, the other in the Amphitheatre, at both of which O'Connor spoke, and was received with great enthusiasm ; and at more than a hundred places, meetings were held, and resolutions passed of confidence in Feargus O'Connor, some of them denouncing his assailants. A proposition was started at Ashton for commencing the *Democrat*, daily paper, to be under the management of O'Connor. It was proposed to raise twenty-five thousand pounds as a start. Some other localities voted in favour of the proposition, which was also encouraged by O'Connor.

At the next meeting of the Assembly, a motion by West, for a repeal of the union between Great Britain and Ireland, and another by Carver against the connection of Church and State, were adopted. Kydd moved a resolution on the Poor-laws, advocating the employment of the poor on the public lands. He went ably into the subject, and the resolution was carried. Ernest Jones moved a resolution, recommending the people to arm, which was supported by all the delegates who spoke, excepting Arkle, who thought they should content themselves with merely asserting the people's right to do so. Jones' motion was adopted. The chairman read a letter from Harley, resigning his post as Commissioner, and his seat in the Assembly, in consequence of being requested to do so by a committee at Glasgow, for his sentiments respecting O'Connor. A long discussion now took place upon the question of presenting the Memorial. The Lord Chamberlain had been written to, to know when a deputation might wait upon the Queen, and that functionary had referred them to Sir George Grey.

Adams moved that the great meeting about to be held to adopt the Memorial, should proceed from the place of meeting to Buckingham Palace, and demand an audience of the Queen and that the Executive Committee march at the head of the procession. The latter part of the resolution seemed to be aimed at Ernest Jones, who, when at Glasgow, had said that the people could get immediate access to the Queen's presence. No very amiable feeling was manifested during this discussion, and Adams' motion, though strongly supported by some of the delegates, was rejected. McIntosh moved a similar resolution, the debate on which took place on Saturday, the 13th. It was a long wrangling discussion, in the course of which almost every delegate found fault with somebody else, and ultimately an amendment by Cochrane, to leave the matter in the hands of the Executive, was agreed to. West moved that the Assembly at its rising should dissolve. Pilling seconded the motion. Shaw, of Barnsley, moved the adjournment of the Assembly for six weeks, which was seconded by Bassett. Ernest Jones supported the motion, and said :—

" He did so with peculiar feelings, because they had now heard the funeral oration for that Assembly pronounced by its own members. Several members had joined their eloquence for that purpose : there was a division amongst them. When that Assembly met, it was then that the Chartist body saw the elements of popular power gathered together and concentrated. It was then that that power might have been wielded for the mightiest objects ; but amid the desertion of friends, and the invasion of enemies, the fusee had been trampled upon, and the elements of their energy were scattered to the winds of heaven. Resolutions had been received from different parts of the country, but how got up, or in what sort of meetings, he would not say, abusing, some of them, certain members of the Assembly, and others, the whole Assembly itself. Under these circumstances then, he decided within himself, that if they started again, as start they must, they must start afresh, start with new power, with new energy, with new confidence ; they must start afresh from the fountain head of Democracy. As for that Assembly, they were but sixty in number. They had waited for the remaining forty delegates from the other districts. They had not gone forward with the Memorial, and that was the reason. The best thing they could now do was to dissolve, and return to their constituents. Their meeting had not been in vain ; *they had gained two triumphs— first, union, and second, independence.* These were triumphs they had achieved, and which it was worth meeting to achieve."

What the orator meant when he talked of union, it is impossible to conceive. He set out by stating that there was a division, and ended by stating that their meeting had produced union, a most glaring contradiction. Perhaps he knew not himself what he meant. The motion of West was carried by a large majority. A long discussion ensued on a motion by Donovan, recommending the *Northern Star* to the people; in the course of which Vernon said the 10th of April was a defeat, and he could not vote for the motion. Adams could not vote for it, as the *Star* had called him a wolf. McLean charged the *Star* with making him to say, that there were eight hundred riflemen in Alva. This false report had provoked a complaint against him from his constituents; the fact being that he had never stated any such thing. Several delegates spoke more or less in defence of the *Star;* but ultimately the motion, and an amendment by Adams, were withdrawn. Thus ended this Assembly.

CHAPTER XII.

DECLINE OF O'CONNOR'S POWER

It is scarcely worth while to dwell at any length on the state of parties at this period. It is evident that the spirit of unity was wanting in the Chartist body. O'Connor's policy, on the 10th of April, 1848, had been the main cause of the disunion. The physical force party were evidently at loggerheads with the Chartist chief. They endeavoured to conceal it as much as possible ; but their feelings were too strong to remain long pent up. Ernest Jones, though exercising more caution than some of his colleagues, was well known to be disgusted with O'Connor's policy. But the latter was right in the course he took in abandoning the procession : the people were anything but prepared for a physical encounter with the Government. O'Connor was wrong, not in abandoning the procession, but in having encouraged so long the empty braggarts, and enthusiastic but mistaken men of the Convention, and in inducing them, almost to the last moment, to believe that he would head the procession to the House of Commons. The boasting which took place on this subject, and the miserable result, inflicted a wound on Chartism from which it has never recovered. After the 10th of April, and the exposure of the National Petition, the Assembly should never have met. It was powerless for good, and made itself simply ridiculous by wasting most of its time in mere talk. With the exception of Kydd, and a few others, there were no statesmen in that Assembly ; hence the wordy warfare, which lasted more or less from its beginning to its close. Although such a number of resolutions of confidence in O'Connor poured in from all quarters, his power declined from the 10th of April. As men reflected they perceived that he was not the man they had fondly imagined him to be, and step by step they withdrew from him their support. The meeting on Clerkenwell Green to adopt the Memorial, was not, according to the *Star*, attended by more than three or four thousand persons—though it was said to have been an enthusiastic meeting.

At Bradford a tremendous gathering took place. The Executive had despatched M'Douall to that town, in consequence of a rumour of an intended outbreak. Thousands attended from Halifax, Keighley, Bingley, and other places. Numbers brandished their pikes in the Halifax procession. The various bodies marched in military order, and paraded the streets of Bradford. They were addressed by Messrs. Lightowler, Shaw, White, Smith, and M'Douall. The latter pledged the immense mass to keep the peace—to respect life and property—to arm, but to discountenance any premature outbreak. Not the slightest interference took place by the authorities. Bradford was that day in possession of the Chartists.

Hume's new movement began to be agitated out of doors. In some places it was met with approval; but at several meetings the Chartists attended and moved and carried amendments for the Charter. O'Connor denounced the "four-legged animal," as he called Hume's measure, through the columns of the *Star*.

Great excitement now reigned, in consequence of the news from Ireland that juries could not be got to convict O'Brien and Meagher; and that Mitchell had been arrested, under the New Felony Act, for his articles in the *United Irishman*. A few days brought news of Mitchell's conviction, and sentence to fourteen years transportation. He hurled defiance at his prosecutors; declared that he had been tried by a partizan judge, and perjured jury; and that the sheriff was a juggler. Almost as soon as convicted, Mitchell was hurried out of the country. Intense excitement reigned in Ireland, the manufacture of pikes going on briskly. Physical force still appeared to be organizing too in England. At a Chartist delegate meeting for Lancashire and Yorkshire, held on the 28th May, a resolution was passed in favour of the formation of a National Guard. Meetings in London for the Charter and Repeal, and to sympathise with Mitchell, were held on the 29th and 30th, on Clerkenwell Green. The first meeting was addressed by Messrs. Beezer, Jones, McCrae, M'Douall and others. It afterwards formed in procession, and traversed several streets of the metropolis. A collision took place in Redcross-street between the people and the police, and a proclamation was issued against the processions. The second meeting was addressed by Messrs. Williams, Sharp, and Daly. Just as the people were dispersing, the police interfered, and drove them from the ground. Another meeting was held on Wednesday night; a disturbance was anticipated. Specials, police, and military were in attendance, and the meeting was dispersed by force.

In Yorkshire things appeared threatening. Training and

drilling went on at Bradford, and the several towns in the district. Three thousand men drilled openly at Wilsden. They marched in military array, preceded by black banners, surmounted by pike heads, and a resolve was manifested to resist by force any attempt to arrest the leaders. At Bingley, two of such leaders were rescued by a body of two thousand persons. The magistrates of Bradford issued a proclamation against such proceedings, and an attempt was made to arrest Lightowler, and a person called " Wat Tyler," who had manufactured a large number of pikes. The attempt failed, and a severe fight took place between the people and special constables, and afterwards the police. The military were at last called out ; the Chartists still fought with their bludgeons, but at last they retreated before the military force, happily without loss of life. George Copley, W. Stott, G. Ainley, W. Connor, F. Hatslead, W. Bairstow, W. Smith, J. Downe, H. Whitecombe, T. Glennan, S. Ratcliffe, J. Heaton, F. Vicary, W. Winterbottom, J. Darwin, J. Wood, W. Sagar, and Mary Mortimer, were arrested, and charged with drilling and threatening to shoot the constables when captured. At Bingley, Issac Ickersgill, J. Hallings, T. Bottomley, H. Shackleton, R. Slater, J. Smith, F. Whone, I. England, T. Rawsthorne, T. Whitaker, E. Lee, J. Crabtree, J. Taylor, W. Smith, R. Atkinson, and J. Quinn, were captured in the mills, while at work, for assisting in the rescue of T. Kilvington and W. Smith. They were sent by special train to York castle. In Leeds meetings were held, arming recommended, and drilling carried on, against all of which the magistrates issued a caution. In Manchester a meeting was announced in Stevenson-square, which was forbidden by the Magistrates. At the time appointed, police, specials, and military, were under arms. A body of the Chartists left Oldham for the meeting, armed with pikes, bludgeons, and various weapons ; but on hearing of the military preparations, and being persuaded by some of their leaders, they returned home. Large numbers of the people, after the closing of the mills, crowded Ancoats Lane, Swan-street, Oldham-road, and its neighbourhood, and took up the pavement, which they threw at the police ; but nothing serious occurred, and the streets were soon cleared.

Meetings of Chartists and Repealers were announced early in June, to be held at Bethnall Green, London Fields, Victoria Park, and Bishop Bonner's Fields, London. Every preparation was made by the authorities, and the meetings were dispersed by force. In Bradford men continued to be arrested while training to arms. In Leicester clubs were formed and arming went on extensively. In Newcastle a large meeting was held on the Moor, to sympathise with Mitchell, and strong language was used by many of the speakers. The London tradesmen got up memorials to the Queen for the suppression of the meetings, and the arrest of the leaders. Their wishes were speedily gratified. Ernest Jones, John Fussell, Alexander Sharpe, Joseph Williams, and W. J. Vernon, were arrested, and examined on charges of sedition for speeches delivered at Clerkenwell Green, and Bishop Bonner's Fields. Jones had been arrested at Manchester, after addressing a large and excited meeting on the previous night. He expressed his surprise before the magistrates at being arrested for the speech given in evidence; but he was told that it was seditious, and the whole of the prisoners were committed for trial. Another grand demonstration was announced to take place in Bishop Bonnor's Fields, and great determination was evinced. The Government redoubled their preparations to prevent it. Large forces was stationed in the neighbourhood. Dr. M'Douall arrived in a cab; and having ascertained that the authorities would put down the meeting by force he prevented the people from assembling. At Croydon, Manchester, Loughboro', (the latter visited by O'Connor), meetings were also prevented from taking place; but at Liverpool a meeting was held on the sea-beach, and addressed by Messrs. McLean, T. Jones, Smith, Lloyd, and Dr. Reynolds. At Birmingham Kydd addressed an open-air meeting in Loneday-street as did also G. J. Mantle. On Blackstone Edge thousands assembled, notwithstanding the wet weather, and were addressed by Messrs. Clarke, G. White, G. Webber, and James Leach. A policeman in disguise was detected, and roughly handled, and would probably have been killed, but for the exertions of White. Thousands of the Yorkshire Chartists assembled on Toftshaw Moor, presided over by Harris of Leeds. Resolutions were passed in favour of the Charter, and in condemnation of Mitchell's conviction. At Nottingham, a large meeting was held in the Market-place, addressed by Kydd, and others; and at Sheffield a procession welcomed O'Connor to the town, where he addressed the assembled thousands in the Cattle Market, and afterwards at a soiree attended by five hundred persons. At the June session of the Central Criminal Court, several persons were tried, and found guilty of assaults on the police, riot, &c., and sentenced to various periods of imprisonment.

The much talked of Memorial was abandoned because an audience with the Queen was not allowed. The Executive and Commissioners were in due time elected by the localities. O'Connor, McCrae, M'Douall, Jones, and Kydd, were elected on the Executive; the Commissioners were A. Fussel, C. McCarthy, J. Leach, J. West, R. Pilling, T. Tattersall, J. Adams, J. Sweet, I. Ironside, T. Wheeler, A. Sharpe, J. Shirron, D. Lightowler, W. J. Vernon, D. Donovan, W. Brook, G. White, J. Linney, W. Cuffay, R. Burrell. Hume brought forward his motion for Reform in the House of Commons, when after a long debate, eighty-four voted for, and three-hundred and fifty-one against, the motion.   At the July session of the Central Criminal Court, Messrs. Fussell, Sharpe, Williams, Vernon, Jones, and Francis Looney, were put upon their trial.   Every obstacle had been thrown in the way of Jones and others obtaining bail after their committal. They were all defended by counsel at great length; but there seemed a predetermination to convict them, and they were all found guilty.   Before sentence was passed upon Fussell the prisoner denied most indignantly what had been attributed to him by one of the witnesses, namely, the recommendation of private assassination.   He was twice stopped by the judge, (Mr. Justice Wylde) but persisted in his denial, and was then sentenced to two years and three months imprisonment, and afterwards to find sureties, himself in one hundred pounds and two others in fifty pounds each, to keep the peace for five years.   Williams, in reference to a remark made by the judge that hard working men would not attend the meetings, said he was a working man, and had toiled twenty hours out of the twenty-four, for sixteen shillings a-week.   Williams was a journeyman baker. He was sentenced to two years and one week imprisonment, and required to give the same sureties as Fussell to keep the peace for three years.   Vernon, on being called up, declared that had Fussell made use of the expressions on private assassination, attributed to him, he would have thrown him from the van.   He was sentenced to two years imprisonment, and to find the same sureties as in the preceding cases.   Sharpe was sentenced to two years and three months imprisonment, and the like sureties. He commenced a reply to the attack of the Attorney General; but the officials, with the most indecent haste, hurried him from the bar.   Looney was sentenced to two years and two months imprisonment, and the same sureties to keep the peace for two years.   Jones addressed the court at some length, being several times interrupted by the judge, who sentenced him to two years imprisonment, and to find sureties, himself in two hundred pounds, and two others in one hundred and fifty pounds each, to keep the peace for five years.

In Ireland arrests continued.   The *Felon* newspaper was seized, and Mr. John Martin, its editor since Mitchell's conviction, surrendered himself on learning that a warrant of arrest had been issued against him. Mr. Gavan Duffy, of the *Nation* newspaper, O'Dogherty and Williams of the *Tribune*, T. F. Meagher, and Mr. Doheny were also placed under arrest, and committed for trial. Most of the persons arrested having been admitted to bail, continued to address public meetings ; clubs increased in number, and excitement grew every day. In England the Liberty Fund progressed but slowly. In the *Northern Star* of the 15th of June, 1848 the secretary to the Executive announced that they were without funds, and must cease to work unless the means were supplied. The same number of that journal furnished the country with a specimen of the value of the statements of mere blusterers on physical force. A meeting took place at Aberdeen, when Mr. Henry, the late delegate, said :—

" He had told the men of London that the Chartists of Aberdeen were up to the mark, and procuring arms; but he was ashamed to say that the men of Aberdeen had made him a liar. As a proof of this, he would ask all to hold up their hands who had obtained arms. (Here one hand was held up amid loud laughter.) Ernest Jones had announced to the Assembly, that there were in Aberdeen six thousand Chartists, all good men and true, armed to the teeth, and waiting for the fray. He knew at the time that Jones was mistaken, but he did not contradict the statement, as he thought that if it were sent abroad, it might do good, and induce others to be up and doing."

On Sunday, the 18th of July, a delegate meeting at Blackstone Edge, passed a resolution that all movements for the Charter had failed, in consequence of the Chartists opposing moral force to the physical force of their oppressors. In the *Star* of August the 5th, a letter appeared from Mr. Smart, the Chartist secretary, Aberdeen, denying that they (the Chartists of Aberdeen,) had ever told Ernest Jones that their National Guard amounted to six thousand. They had told him that they had six hundred names on the books, that they hoped to get three thousand, and that then they meant to apply to the Government for arms. The arrests continued. M'Douall was apprehended at Ashton; John Shaw and others in London. In Edinburgh Messrs. Rankin, Walker, and Cumming were arrested for attending an illegal meeting. At Greenock, Messrs. Burrell and Neilsom, and at Glasgow, James Smith, were also arrested. The Legislature passed a Bill for suspending the Habeas Corpus Act in Ireland, and a large number of persons were placed under arbitrary arrest. This drove Smith O'Brien, Meagher, and others, to insurrection; which, however, proved futile, the Catholic clergy using all their influence against it and ultimately the leaders were arrested on charges of treason. At the York assizes the prisoners were tried for drilling, &c. John Quin, Joseph Hollings, Thomas Bottomley, H. Shackleton, and eleven others, for riot and rescue at Bingley, were discharged on entering into security in fifty pounds to keep the peace, and about thirty others were discharged on similar conditions. J. J. Johnson and W. Sagar, for riot and assault at Bradford, were sentenced to two years imprisonment with hard labour. W. Connor, J. Heaton, W. Winterburn, W. Smith, H. Whitcombe, J. Downes, and F. Vicary, were sentenced for the same offence to eighteen months imprisonment. A. Tomlinson, a youth, convicted of sedition, was sentenced to eighteen months' imprisonment, without hard labour. J. Ramsden, B. Plant. D. Holroyd, and T. Fell, for drilling, were sentenced to the same term of imprisonment, with hard labour. J. Cockerham, H. Butterfield, R. Bradley, and A. Bowler, for a similiar offence, were sentenced to twelve months with hard labour. J. Leeming, for drilling, received a similar sentence. The rioters at Bingley, were sentenced, I. Ickersgill, six months with hard labour, Crabtree two months, Kilvington one month, and J. Bland, a special constable, was fined ten pounds for neglect of duty. Arrests continued. The authorities of Manchester and neighbourhood had information of secret meetings of the Chartists and Irish Confederates, and Messrs. James Leach, T. Whittaker, H. Ellis, G. Rogers, H. Williams, G. Webber, D. Donovan, J. J. Finnigan, P. Deolin, M. Carrigan, J. Leaman, G. White, J. Dowlan, S. Cairns, and T. Rankin, were placed under arrest, and speedily committed for trial.

At Ashton a more serious affair occurred. A body of the Chartists met on Monday, August the 14th, and sallied forth from their room, having encountered some of the police, one of that force, named Bright, was shot dead, and others were pursued but escaped. The military were called out, and attacked the Chartists, some of whom were taken prisoners, and the rest took to flight. Messrs. Grant and Hamilton were arrested at Edinburgh, and with the other prisoners were charged with high treason. In London the police arrested a large number at the Angel Tavern, Webber-street, the Orange Tree, Orange-street, and at another public-house in Moor-street. At all these places they found a number of loaded pistols, pikes, daggers, spear-heads, and swords, and some of the prisoners wore iron breast-plates, while others had gun powder, shot, and tow-balls : three hundred ball-cartridges were found secreted in St. James's Churchyard, Clerkenwell.

In the quieter districts, the authorities were equally busy. R. G. Gammage had been agitating for a month in the rural counties of Buckingham, Bedford, and Northampton. Wherever he went, the Superintendent of Police followed to watch the proceedings. At last, for delivering a lecture explanatory of the Charter at Towcester, and because he would persist in maintaining the right of meeting by refusing to leave off speaking at the bidding of the police, he was arrested and committed for trial; but the prosecution was afterwards abandoned. W. Cuffay, and a number of others, were charged with the offences named above. A hideous wretch named Powell, doubtless employed by the authorities, was the principal witness. In giving his evidence he admitted entering the Association for the purpose of getting information, and communicating it to the Police Commissioners. "*I encouraged,*" he said, "*and stimulated these men, in order to inform against them. I gave the men some bullets. I gave balls to Gurney. I gave him half-a-pound of powder. I also cast some bullets and gave them to him.*" Eternal infamy rest on the heads of a Government that could make use of such a vile instrument! The trials of the various parties arrested speedily followed. George Shell, James Maxwell Boysan, Robert Crowe, and J. J. Beezer, were all tried and found guilty of sedition, sentenced to two years imprisonment, and to find heavy sureties to keep the peace for five years. At the Lancashire assizes M'Douall was tried for sedition, conspiracy, and riot, found guilty, and sentenced to two years with hard labour, in the gaol of Kirkdale. He remonstrated against being confined there, as his constitution would not bear it in the present state of the gaol; but he was told by Justice Cresswell, that he should have considered that before he made himself amenable to the law. Most of the prisoners traversed to the following assizes.

Arrests continued. John West was apprehended, as was also the celebrated Joseph Barker, editor of a penny publication called *The People*. In September the London Chartists were brought to trial. John Shaw, for sedition, was sentenced to two years imprisonment. William Ritchie, Alfred Able, William Gurney, J. Shepherd, J. Snowball, J. Richardson, G. Greenslade, H. Small, E. Scadding, W. Burn, P. Martin, W. Lacey, T. Jones, C. Young, W. Dowling, H. Argue, W. Cuffay, and Fay, were indicted for conspiring to levy war against Her Majesty. A number of witnesses were called, the principal being the spy and informer, Powell. Messrs. Kenealy, Huddlestone, Ballantine, and Parry, were counsel for the prisoners. Cuffay objected to being tried by a middle-class jury, and demanded, according to the provisions of Magna

Charta, to be tried by a jury of his peers. Of the villany of the spy, Powell, the following will serve as a specimen. R. Fennell, one of the witnesses for the defence, deposed as follows:—

"Had known Powell for the last thirteen or fourteen years. From what he knew of him, he would not believe him on his oath. Had heard him called "Lying Tom" to his face, in Mr. Smith's shop, hundreds of times. Had heard him say that he would send the Queen, the b——y Foreigner, her family, Lord John Russell, and Sir George Grey, to hell in no time. Had asked witness to join the Chartists at Cartwright's about ten days before the 10th of April. He told him that he was not a Chartist, and that the Chartists would not get that measure by the way they were going on. Powell said they would get it in a month. Also asked him (witness) to propose him as a delegate, after he (Powell) had proposed him as a member, as he could thereby get two or three pounds a-week, which would be better than working at old Smith's at carpentry. Told him (witness) that the Government was a weak and a b——y Government, and said, Look at the Queen expending her hundreds of thousands a-year in idleness, and here we are obliged to work at the bench for a bit of bread. He said, if he would come to his house, he would show him materials enough to blow London to hell in half-an-hour."

On being cross-examined by the Attorney General, as to why he would not believe Powell on his oath, he said :—

"Is it likely that I would believe a man, when I have heard him swear times out of number, that he would swear anything if he was paid for it. Had heard him read the scriptures, and when he came to the name of Christ or the disciples, seen him tear the part out, and say of either, 'Let us burn that b——. The disciples were the biggest scoundrels I ever heard of.' When he came to the name of Judas, he heard him once say, 'He was a capital fellow. He got well paid. I would have done it for half.'"

Many other witnesses corroborated the statements of Fennell. Another villain, named Davis, deposed to secreting himself in a room at Greenwich where the Chartists and Confederates met. That he reported these meetings to Mallalien, the Superintendent of Police, who told him that the meetings might go on, and that he would send a policeman to attend them. Davis said, "After this I advised people to go to these meetings, and the landlord used to give me half-a-sovereign or five shillings now and then, in return for my friendship." On the evidence of these villainous spies of a more villainous Government, Dowling, Cuffay, Fay, and Lacey, were found guilty. On being brought up for judgment, Fay said, "It must be evident to everybody that Powell was committing perjury in all he stated. It is useless to say more." Dowling said, "Tyrants may declare patriotism to be felony, but they cannot make it felony." Lacey declared that he never had the slightest intention of carrying out the Charter by violence. Cuffay said :—

"I say you have no right to sentence me. Although the trial has lasted a long time, it has not been a fair trial, and my request to have a fair trial—to be tried by my equals—has not been complied with. Everything has been done to raise a prejudice against me, and the press of this country—and I believe of other countries too—has done all in its power to smother me with ridicule. I ask no pity. I ask no mercy. I expected to be convicted, and I did not think anything else. But I don't want any pity. No, I pity the Government, and I pity the Attorney General for convicting me by means of such base characters. The Attorney General ought to be called the Spy General, and using such men is a disgrace to the Government ; but they only exist by such means. I am quite innocent. My locality never sent any delegates at all, and I had nothing to do with the luminaries. I have a right to complain of the other spy, Davis, being kept back till the last moment. It is to my having a loaded pistol—I only carried it for my protection, as my life had been threatened. This, however, is what I have always expected. I am not anxious for martyrdom, but after what I have endured this week, I feel that I could bear any punishment proudly, even to the scaffold. This new Act of Parliament is disgraceful, and I am proud to be the first victim of it, after the glorious Mitchell. Every good Act was set aside in Parliament. Everything that was likely to do any good to the working class was either thrown out or postponed ; but a measure to restrain their liberties would be passed in a few hours."

Baron Platt then sentenced the prisoners to be transported for life, upon which Fay exclaimed :—"This is the baptism of felony in England." Ritchie pleaded guilty, and received a similar sentence. Able, Gurney, Snowball, Scadding, Martin, Winspere, Prowton, Conway, Morgan, Young, Jones, Argue, Poole, Herbert, and Irons, pleaded guilty to an indictment for misdemeanour. With the exception of Poole, Herbert, and Irons, who were sentenced to eighteen months, the prisoners were sentenced to two years imprisonment, with hard labour, a fine of ten pounds, and to enter into securities to keep the peace for five years. Shepherd, Richardson, Greenslade, Burn, Taylor, Cox, Gibbs, Alexander Harby,

Samuel Harby, Martin, and Small, were discharged on entering into their own recognizances to appear if called upon to do so.

Feargus O'Connor was not idle during the time that the Chartist trials were going on. He sought out the best counsel for the prisoners, and had to pay a large share of the expense. He addressed letters through the *Star* every week to the Chartists, praising his own prudence, and censuring the folly of others, which folly had led to such lamentable results. He continued to fire away week after week at the defunct Assembly. In the *Star* of September the 9th, he thus wrote :—

"Then came the National Assembly, consisting of delegates not elected by the people, because the people were not allowed time for reflection ; and that Assembly, awed by the galleries —a large portion of the audience consisting of detectives and spies sent by the Government—spent three mortal weeks* in abusing me, because I would not be a party to destroy the triumph we had gained, and which might have been turned to good account, if sufficient time had been given to organise the mind of the country for a fair representation of the Chartist body; and I must do Bronterre O'Brien the justice to say, that he enforced the doctrine over and over again in the Convention, of the necessity of having a full and acknowledged representation of the whole people. I unhesitatingly declare, that the base and shameful falsehoods told by numerous members of that Assembly, as to the state of preparedness and resolution of their several districts, was treason and treachery of the rankest kind."

On September the 18th, O'Connor addressed his constituents in the Market-place. Great was his triumph about this period, for a committee of the House of Commons, though declaring his Land Plan illegal and impracticable, and that the accounts had been very improperly kept, many of the balance-sheets not being produced—at the same time reported that the Company was indebted to O'Connor, according to the evidence, in the sum of three thousand four hundred pounds.

Samuel Kydd appeared at this time to be the most useful of the leaders yet at large. He travelled and lectured in many important towns, not in the usual style of bombast, but on questions connected with the great cause of labour, on which he spread a large amount of information. He even visited the University City of Oxford, and lectured in the Town Hall, the Oxford papers reporting his lectures.

In Ireland the State Trials went on under a Special Commission, lasting for a considerable period. The evidence was voluminous. O'Brien was first put on trial. He was defended

*The Assembly sat only eleven days.

by Mr. Whiteside, who moved every eye to tears by his eloquence; which, however, was ineffectual in securing a verdict
for his client.   Messrs. McManus, Meagher, and O'Donoghue,
were also tried for the same offence of high treason, and a
verdict of guilty was returned against all.   On receiving
the sentence of death, all the prisoners behaved with the
greatest calmness and dignity.   Their punishment was afterwards commuted to transportation for life.   The Attorney
General, during some of the Chartist trials, declared the new
plan of organization to be illegal.   The Executive therefore
recommended its abandonment, and the adoption of the old
plan.   The old Executive had been displaced by Messrs. T.
Clark, W. Dixon, H. Ross, P. McGrath, E. Stallwood, and G.
J. Harney, with S. Kydd as Secretary.   The latter stood candidate at the West Riding election in December; but though
acquitting himself ably, the show of hands went against him,
and in favour of the Liberal candidate.   O'Connor made himself busy with going on a tour in Lancashire, Yorkshire, and
Scotland, where great meetings assembled to hear him.

Special assizes were held in December at Chester and
Liverpool, for the trial of Chartist prisoners.   At the former,
G. J. Mantle was tried on a charge of conspiracy, and found
guilty.   Amos Armitage, J. Brown, J. Cheetham, J. Hall, J.
Hindle, J. Ralph, J. Shore, J. Shawcross, J. Done, P. Collier,
R. Markland, P. Matlocks, T. Schofield, S. Shaw, E. Wylde,
and C. Sellers, were charged with seditious conspiracy.   Most
of the prisoners were found guilty, and sentenced to various
terms of imprisonment.   Mantle was sentenced to confinement
for two years.   At Liverpool there were sixty-five persons
charged with conspiracy and sedition.   Joseph Radcliffe and
Joseph Constantine were indicted for the murder of Bright at
Ashton.   The Attorney General prosecuted, and Mr. Pollock
conducted the defence.   The trial occupied two days, and
although witnesses swore that Radcliffe was not the man who
killed Bright, he was found guilty and sentenced to death.
The evidence, however, was so doubtful, that the capital
sentence was never executed.   J. Constantine, T. Kenworthy,
J. Walker, J. Sefton, J. Statt, and T. Tassiker, were charged
with levying war against the Queen.   With the exception of
Sefton, who was sentenced to ten years, all the other prisoners
were sentenced to transportation for life.   Winterbottom,
E. Harrop, Healey, Bolton, J. Harrop, Jesson, and Fetlow,
for conspiracy, were sentenced to various terms of imprison-
ment, varying from three months to one year.   W. Grocott,
W. Chadwick, E. Clark, Cropper, John West, George White,
J. Nixon, T. Rankin, M. McDonough, D. Donovan, and J.

Leach, were charged with seditious conspiracy. A spy, named Ball was the principal witness, but his evidence was so contradictory on cross-examination, that it rather damaged the prosecution than otherwise. The prisoners, most of whom defended themselves, were however found guilty. Rankin, Leach, Grocott, Cropper, Donovan, West, and White, were sentenced to one year's imprisonment, and to enter into sureties to keep the peace for two years. Leach, nine months imprisonment. McDonough and Chadwick six months, and Nixon four months imprisonment. G. J. Clark, J. Dowlan, Patrick Devilen, H. Ellis, J. J. Finnigan, J. Foyle, M. Hume, W. Heap, S. Cairns, J. Lenion, T. Roberts, G. Rogers, G. Ramsden, F. Spooner, T. Whitaker, W. Burton, and Joseph Barker were offered their discharge on condition of entering into their own recognizances to appear when called upon. All agreed except Barker, who refused, and demanded to be tried, having got about fifty witnesses ready for the defence. His refusal enraged the judge, who charged him with morbid vanity, but in vain ; Barker was immovable. The Attorney General fumed and fretted, and the judge insulted ; but at last they gave up the task, and Barker was discharged. Charles Bowker was found guilty of delivering a false, scandalous, seditious, and blasphemous speech at Heywood, and sentenced to two years imprisonment.

It is impossible to leave unnoticed the rabid and unjustifiable conduct of Justice Erle at these trials. He lost all the dignity of the impartial judge, and showed himself a political partizan of the worst class. He lectured upon the folly of universal suffrage, and went so far as to compare Frost, Williams, and Jones, to Barrabas. He was evidently unfit for his important office.

At the York assizes Henry Hunt, W. Angus, Isaac Jefferson, Nathaniel Frith, and D. Lightowler were severally tried for drilling, found guilty, and sentenced,—Hunt to eight, Jefferson four, Angus ten, Frith eleven, and Lightowler nine months imprisonment. J. R. Tomkins, and seven others named Lilley, Kershaw, Farrell, Radcliffe, Lees, Pogson, and Neal, all mere youths, were charged with conspiracy, and, with the exception of Radcliffe and Lees, were found guilty. D. Linden, A. Stratton, T. Wilkinson, T. Ibbetson, E. Wilman, J. Riddelholgh, J. Helliwell, W. Wood, E. Power, and James Smyth, were charged with conspiring to destroy the Bradford gas-works, seize the magistrates, and detain them until the enactment of the Charter. No less than three spies, named Shepherd, Flynn, and Emmet, were produced as witnesses. The prisoners were found guilty, and the sentences were afterwards passed upon them. Tomkins and his fellow-prisoners were each imprisoned for one year, and bound to find security to keep the peace for one year more. Farrell and others were sentenced to six months imprisonment, and to find security to keep the peace for one year. Linden and others were discharged on their own recognizances.

The Victim and Defence Fund was much required at this period, and a meeting on the subject was held at the John-street Institution, at which, notwithstanding past affronts, Thomas Cooper presided, and was most warmly received. Other meetings were also held in London, which were addressed by Kydd, Clark, and other members of the Executive ; and Feargus O'Connor and Kydd continued to lecture in many important districts. The Hall at John-street was filled on the occasion of the first anniversary of the French Revolution. A tea was served upon the occasion. Julian Harney presided, and the meeting was addressed by G. J. Holyoake, J. Bronterre O'Brien, T. Clark, Walter Cooper, R. Buchanan, C. Keen, W. Dixon, E. Stallwood, and others, in thrilling speeches.

The result of the Edinburgh trials was wonderfully favourable to the prisoners, considering that they were committed for treason. Only Ranken and Hamilton were tried, and the offence had so dwindled down, that they only received four month's imprisonment each. They were welcomed at a splendid soiree by their friends on their release, and spoke as boldly as ever in favour of the Charter.

O'Connor now began to fall out with his editor, Julian Harney. The latter had written a series of articles in the *Northern Star*, in which he had advocated Republicanism, and which he had principally devoted to Foreign Politics. This displeased O'Connor, who wrote in the *Star* as follows:—

"But latterly, every line of this writer which has appeared in the *Star*, so far from keeping the Chartist movement distinct, has been devoted to Foreign Policy, and the anticipated glories of Republicanism. I have often told you how easy it was to tickle the fervid imagination of brave and suffering millions with exciting appeals, which may drive the feeling, the enthusiastic, and the brave, to face death in any shape; while the exciter may shelter himself under the mantle of irresponsibility, and smile at the woe that he has created. What would you say of me if I appeared before an enthusiastic and excited audience, in a garb descriptive of nationality and valour, and said:—'When you see me next, I will come to proclaim the Charter, or this National badge shall be saturated with the blood of the martyr?' And what would you say if I did not make my appearance before the same audience, although the Charter was not proclaimed, although blood was not shed in the struggle to achieve it? What would you say to me now, if in 1839 I had appeared before you with the cap of liberty, and declared that I was ready to 'tuck up my sleeves and go at it,' and if, when the struggle came, I was *non est inventus?* What would you say, if during the Lancaster trials, when rampant Toryism and Whiggism looked for a large Chartist sacrifice, I had turned a puling spooney, with my face bathed in tears, lest I should suffer the penalty consequent upon my struggle for freedom? What would you say if upon the 9th of April, when I was assured by scores that I was to be shot upon the 10th, I had called a secret meeting of delegates, and if I had proposed to that meeting that the meeting on Kennington Common should not take place? Oh, in such a case, how poor and pitiful are the strictures now written by enthusiastic Democrats, compared to what their denunciation, their just reviling, and reproach would then have been."

Harney replied to this side-attack in the *Star* of the following week, and besides quoting two letters from Beezley and Leach, testifying to his " manly " conduct at the Lancaster trials, he quoted the following from O'Connor's pen :—" The friends of Chartism rejoiced at the standing, the bearing assumed by the conspirators, during the whole trial. It may appear trivial to notice the details of such a matter, but they operated most powerfully in extorting an amount of respect and attention, which in its turn supported the cause, of whose humanising operations it was itself the result. It would perhaps be invidious to point particular attention to the address of any individual, where all acquitted themselves so well ; but the speech of Harney will be read with peculiar interest, and fully justifies the position which he occupied as the first speaker." Harney might have retorted upon O'Connor his expressed determination to have the Charter by the 29th of September, 1839, or to give the Government "Michaelmas Goose" on the 30th, and his expressed resolve to head the people in the case of Frost, and the non-fulfilment of those pledges; but he was too prudent to allude to these matters.

We cannot here refrain from noticing, that one effect of the movement of 1848 was, that of bringing a large number of democratic papers of various shades into the field. After O'Brien retired from the Convention—from which he saw no good would arise, and that the delegates were boasting of a power they did not possess, which boasting would end in defeat and disgrace, as it assuredly did,—he started a newspaper in the Isle of Man, called *The Reformer*. The size of this paper was afterwards doubled, and ultimately a third and smaller series appeared. In these papers he set forth his old doctrines on the great social and political questions then agitating society. He endeavoured constantly to show how the revolutions on the Continent must fail, and how the leading Democrats would be sacrificed, unless they mastered the great social problem, and put an end to the reign of landlords and usurers of every kind. These things were not attended to, and exactly the results that O'Brien predicted, happened. *The Reformer* rose under O'Brien's management to fifteen thousand weekly. When the Government abolished the privilege of the Isle of Man papers, and prevented them circulating out of the island without the stamp, an end was put to the *Reformer*. *The Power of the Pence* was another of the papers edited by O'Brien and devoted to the same cause. *The Spirit of Freedom,* edited by Gerald Massey and J. B. Leno, was started in the little town of Uxbridge, and existed for a considerable time; it was full of fire, and breathed the spirit of Republicanism. In the little town of Buckingham was started the *Progressionist*, edited by Mr. John Small of that town. It was first a monthly, but afterwards came out weekly; it changed hands, and R. G. Gammage became its editor. One of its most powerful contributors was Mr. John Rymill, of Northampton, from whom letters appeared every week, full of enthusiasm and hope for the future of Democracy. Altogether there appeared forty-eight numbers of this periodical. In Cambridge the *Operatives' Free Press*, and in Wisbeach the *Voice in the East*, were started, and enjoyed a short existence. *The Public Good*, a monthly, advocating Democracy on peace principles, was edited by Passmore Edwards; and on the same principles was started, and existed for a considerable time, the *Standard of Freedom*, a weekly newspaper, published by J. Cassell. Afterwards came *Reynolds's Political Instructor*, a large penny publication issued weekly, which rose to a sale of fifty thousand copies. It was the best of all the works ever issued by Reynolds. It contained able letters from the pen of Samuel Kydd, on the important question of Labour; a popular History of England, by E. T. Roberts; a series of remarkable articles on the Origin, Progress, and Phases of Human Slavery, by J. B. O'Brien; and talented articles from other writers. Thomas Cooper issued a weekly periodical, justly entitled *The Plain Speaker*, full of the usual vigour of its editor. While on a mission, in connection with this paper, Cooper came again into collision with O'Connor. A correspondent wrote from Bolton that he had been finding fault with the Land Plan. O'Connor inserted the letter in the *Star*, together with the following remarks :—

"Tom is a most comical genius.   He has been protestant, dissenter, and infidel; puritan, saint, and atheist; total, teetotal, abstemious, and boozy.   He is the very impersonation of trinity in unity.   He has been all things to all men, and God only knows what he may be next.   But I sincerely hope that he never will be my Poet Laureate, or the advocate of the Land Plan, as in such case I should suspect myself, and fear the sterility of the soil.   This poet did more to paralyse Chartism in the Midland Counties than any other man.   He confessed himself a physical-force Chartist, but relapsed into moral-force resistance; and as confession is half way to repentance, I hope the soul of the Suicide may escape Purgatory."

Cooper replied to this letter through the *Star*, denying most of O'Connor's assertions as to his character, and bringing many things to the latter's recollection which had occurred formerly; and announced that he would immediately return to London, and test O'Connor's power by waiting to see whether the Chartists, in the several towns to which he had been invited, would renew their invitations.   The same paper contained a letter from O'Connor, which concluded thus:—

"I am sure there is no one whose co-operation in the good cause I hail with greater pleasure than that of Thomas Cooper, whose works will live when I am no more; and therefore in perfect sincerity, and without the slightest reserve, I bury all past differences in the tomb of insignificance.   I tender you the right hand of friendship, and subscribe myself your faithful and affectionate friend, Feargus O'Connor."

Cooper took no further notice of O'Connor; but the invitations to lecture were renewed, and he visited a number of towns in various parts of the country, where he was enthusiastically received.

The party of Mr. Hume now came more publicly before the people ; and at a public meeting held at the London Tavern, on the 16th May, 1849, to inaugurate the movement, which meeting was densely crowded, T. Clark, of the Chartist Executive, attended, and made the first step towards a union of the Chartist party with the Middle-class Reformers; but the very paper which contained a report of this meeting, contained also a letter from Feargus O'Connor, warning the "Old Guards" against the new movement.   The Chartists continued to hold frequent meetings in various parts of the metropolis.   One very crowded meeting was held in Milton-street Theatre, on June 4th, and was addressed by Reynolds and O'Connor. At this meeting a resolution was proposed by Clark, and seconded by O'Connor, and carried, inviting the Hume-party to a consideration of the Charter.   The same week Hume renewed his motion, which only met with eighty-two supporters in the House of Commons.   O'Connor brought forward in the House the case of Ernest Jones, who, for refusing to pick oakum, was confined in a cell 6ft by 4ft., and kept on bread and water for three days and three nights; and although he was in a bad state of health, his bedclothes were removed by day, and he was compelled to lie on the iron bars of his bedstead. This treatment was afterwards altered, through O'Connor paying five shillings per week to save Jones from the picking of oakum.   The Chartist prisoners in Kirkdale—Leach, White, and others—were not idle.   They were treated as first-class prisoners; and being allowed pens, ink, and paper, they wrote several Chartist tracts, which were published to the world.

On July 3rd, 1849, O'Connor's long-delayed motion for the Charter was brought forward in the Commons, and after a debate, just fifteen, including tellers, voted in its favour.   The names of these were, W. J. Fox, J. Greene, L. Heyworth, J. Hume, C. Lushington, Lord Nugent, J. O'Connell, C. Pearson, W. Schofield, H. W. Tancred, Col. Thompson, Geo. Thompson, Sir J. Walmsley, F. O'Connor, and Sharman Crawford.   Such was the result of this motion, after all the bluster of 1848, after all that excitement which converted London into a military fortress, and sent the Royal Family to the more peaceful shades of the Isle of Wight.

Although above three hundred pounds had been subscribed for the defence of the Chartist prisoners, O'Connor was summoned to appear in the Queen's Bench, at the suit of an attorney whom he had charged with the defence of Ernest Jones and the other Chartist prisoners, and had to pay one hundred and one pounds, being the balance of three hundred and sixteen pounds due for services rendered.

O'Connor now drew towards the Hume-school of Reformers. He attended a meeting in the Standard Theatre, and held out the olive branch, telling the meeting that the only object the Chartists had, was to make the rich richer, and the poor rich. O'Connor appeared so disappointed in various ways, that he now announced his intention of retiring into private life. Whether the Chartist body really wished him to do so is uncertain; but instead of hundreds of resolutions imploring him to remain—although there were a few individual Chartists who wrote to that effect:—not one locality sent a resolution to the *Star* upon the subject. O'Connor, however, was not going to retire yet.   The Foreign question excited great interest at this time.   The invasion of Rome and Hungary by Foreign troops, created sympathy with the invaded in England. A meeting was held in Hall's Riding School, Marylebone, which was crowded, to sympathize with Hungary. Mr. Hume M.P., J. Cassell, Mr. Moncton Milnes, M.P., Sir De Lacy Evans, M.P., Dr Rogers, Mr. Headham, M.P., Colonel Thompson, M.P., H. Hetherington, J. Williams, M.P., and J. Wyld, M.P., were the speakers; there was, however, on the part of these gentlemen nothing but lip sympathy. Julian Harney was called on by the meeting, and amid thunders of applause advocated armed intervention, and tested the meeting on the subject, when almost every hand was uplifted, and again the applause was renewed. Sheffield, Glasgow, Manchester, Exeter, Birmingham, Westminster, Carlisle, and all the principal towns followed the example of London, in declaring sympathy with Hungary.

O'Connor again figured side by side with the Hume-party, at the first aggregate meeting of that body at Drury Lane, and Thomas Clark was there to support him. O'Connor, who had kicked overboard so many men, not for dereliction of principle, but on points of policy, who would not have even the name of the Charter altered, who had collected thousands to defeat schemes for Household Suffrage, now gave in his adhesion to a Household Suffrage Association. Lord Nugent was the boldest of the Reform party at this meeting. He went so far as to say, that were he to vote for a tax, and at the same time refuse to vote for Universal Suffrage, he would look upon himself as a thief and a robber.

This period was marked by two events, which in certain circles caused great regret. One was the death of Henry Hetherington, by cholera; the other, the emigration of John Mason to America. Hetherington was followed to the grave by a large number of friends. Five hundred walked in procession, and not less than two thousand were at the grave. G. J. Holyoake delivered an appropriate address on the occasion, as did James Watson, one of his oldest political associates. Mason was entertained at a tea-party in Birmingham, which was attended by Messrs Muntz, Douglas, George Dawson, and other gentlemen. A purse containing forty pounds was presented to Mason, as a testimonial of respect. Other deaths of a more lamentable kind occurred. They were those of Joseph Williams and Alexander Sharpe, two of the imprisoned Chartists. The all-devouring cholera took off these victims; but the whig Government prepared their bodies for the reception of the fell disease, by the harsh, cruel, and starvation treatment to which they subjected them. At their funeral not less than twenty thousand persons were present. Addresses were delivered by Messrs. Clark and Stallwood, and afterwards a monument was raised to the memory of these Chartist martyrs. Williams, before his death, in allusion to the cause of his

disease, said—"It is not cholera, but cold and starvation."
These events led to an attempt to obtain a general amnesty
for political offenders. A large meeting was held at John-
street, London, on September 25th, for that object, which was
addressed by G. J. Holyoake, W. Dixon, T. Clark, Tindall,
Atkinson, Lloyd Jones, H. Ross, and Feargus O'Connor,
when a memorial to her majesty was adopted. These cases
excited considerable sympathy, and other meetings were held
for the same object, both in town and in the provinces.
O'Connor became every day more in love with the Financial
and Parliamentary Reformers. A few months ago and their
movement was nothing but an artful dodge, now he not only
approved of the scheme, but had every confidence in its
promoters, and he travelled to Norwich, Aberdeen, and other
distant towns in order to render them his support.

In the *Star* of October 27th, a letter appeared from Samuel
Kydd, resigning his office on the Executive. Kydd had been
the hardest worker on that body. Scotland, the North of
England, the manufacturing districts, the Midlands, and almost
every other quarter of the kingdom, had received his services in
the shape of lectures on the question of Labour and Capital.
He now complained that no effectual organization had been
realized, and that the Association was in his debt to the amount
of sixty pounds; and he said his brethren of the Executive were
of opinion with him, that it was not desirable to retain the name
of an Association, if not efficiently supported. An attempt
was made to revive the agitation, and two meetings were held
in London, attended by O'Connor, Reynolds, McGrath, Dixon,
Harney, Clark, and others. It was decided to call a Metropolitan delegate meeting, consisting of twenty-eight delegates,
to consult upon the subject. A large meeting was held at John-
street to elect delegates, which was addressed by McGrath the
chairman, G. W. M. Reynolds, S. Kydd, F. O'Connor, Bronterre O'Brien, and D. W. Ruffy. O'Brien attributed the failure
of past agitations to a neglect of the doctrines of social right.
O'Connor denounced the nationalization of the land.
O'Connor, Dixon, Clark, and Utting were elected delegates.
Westminster, Tower Hamlets, and the other districts, also
held meetings, and elected delegates. Lambeth elected E.
Mills, Collins, Pattinson, and Hobden; Finsbury: Messrs.
Townshend, Allnut, Lee, and Blake; Westminster: Harney,
Grassby, Arnott, and Milne; Tower Hamlets: Reynolds,
McGrath, Davies, and Drake; Southwark: Langor, Percy,
Wilkins, and Percy; City of London: Stallwood, Brown,
Bentley, and Fowler. At this Conference a plan of organi-
zation was agreed to, very similar to others previously adopted;

the number of members of the Executive being altered to five instead of eight. A Provisional Executive was appointed until the regular election could take place by the members. A rather warm discussion took place between Messrs. Harney, O'Connor, Clark, and Reynolds. The three latter had attended the meetings of the Parliamentary Reformers, and O'Connor had done so as the representative of the Chartist body. Harney objected to O'Connor taking upon himself to represent that body without their consent. A resolution was passed by the Conference against obstructing other bodies of reformers; but Harney persisted in criticising the middle-class politicians through the *Star*.

A new association had lately sprung into existence under the auspices of J. Bronterre O'Brien, under the title of the National Reform League. It was inaugurated at a public meeting, presided over by G. W. M. Reynolds, which was addressed by O'Brien, Lloyd Jones, and other speakers. This League was founded on the principles long advocated by O'Brien. Besides seeking the political reforms embraced in the People's Charter, it sought to spread instruction on the people's social rights, and laid down, as a means of securing these, nationalization of land, mines, and fisheries; a currency based on the consumable wealth of the nation, instead of the present false monetary system; nationalization of credit, so as, by the aid of state loans, to enable the poor to rise by industry to comfort and independence; and national marts, in order to effect exchanges of wealth upon terms of equity and justice. O'Brien lectured weekly at the John-street Institution, on the principles of the League, which were speedily embraced by the *elite* of the London Democracy. Shortly after, this body took the Eclectic Institute, Denmark-street, Soho, where O'Brien lectured twice or three times a-week, on his cherished principles.

The Chartist party became more divided than ever, in consequence of the attempted union with middle-class reformers. O'Connor, who until recently had denounced Cobden, followed him to Aylesbury, where a public meeting was held in the County Hall, and bespattered him with the most fulsome praise as he had previously with the foulest abuse. Kydd and Clark fell out at a meeting in London, called for the Protection of Native Industry. Clark was with the Free-traders, whom he had always so bitterly denounced. He made some offensive remarks toward Kydd, who challenged him to discussion on the merits of Free-trade and Protection. The challenge was accepted, but the discussion never came off.

At a great meeting on the 14th of January, 1850, there were

more signs of disaffection. It was called by the Provisional Executive. O'Connor presided. Julian Harney took occasion to make some strictures on the new reform movement, and expressed a hope that when the continental people again got the upper hand of their tyrants, they would treat them to that mercy they had received at their hands. Clark denounced the speech of Harney on both points; but the sympathies of the majority were with the latter. At this meeting W. J. Vernon, who had been liberated, addressed the audience, and was received most cordially. Reynolds, McGrath, O'Brien, and Dixon also addressed the meeting; O'Brien defending Harney against the attack of Clark. The latter in company with Reynolds and O'Connor, visited Leeds, Bradford, Manchester, and other large towns, where great numbers attended. Reynolds also visited the Potteries, Newcastle-upon-Tyne, Glasgow, and other towns, where he addressed densely crowded meetings. Harney replied to Clark through the pages of the *Northern Star*, in no very measured terms; which provoked a rejoinder still more abusive, in which Clark charged Harney with cowardice, and with proposing, while pale and trembling, at a secret meeting of delegates, to abandon the meeting on Kennington Common, though no one had been so forward to boast of his determination to defy the Government. Harney admitted the fact as to his wish to give up the meeting; but said it was owing to the fact of not finding Clark and his friends in a fighting mood, and thinking it better to abandon the meeting, if the procession was not also to take place. A resolution having been passed at Birmingham, calling on Clark to resign his office on the Provisional Executive, he did so; and his example was followed by Messrs. Doyle, McGrath, and Dixon. On the other side Messrs. Kydd, Harney, and Grassby, resigned office.

Meetings were frequently held about this time to review the proceedings in Parliament, which were addressed by Reynolds, Harney, O'Brien, and other democratic advocates. O'Brien carried his principles into company little prepared perhaps to receive them. A society had been started under the auspices of Luke J. Hansard, called the National Regeneration Society, who called public meetings to discuss various measures of reform. O'Brien attended one of these meetings, and proposed his measures on land, credit, currency, and exchange, as well as three other propositions, preliminary to the establishment of the fundamental points of national reform. These three propositions were, a repeal of the new poor-law, and a restoration of the Law of Elizabeth, with the employment of the poor at remunerative industry on the public lands; equitable adjustment between debtor and creditor in consequence of the fall of prices; and the payment of the interest on the National Debt by the owners of property, in whose interest the debt was contracted. O'Brien carried these propositions by an immense majority. Clark and his party started a National Charter League in opposition to the old Association, and appealed to the public for support. Harney proceeded on a tour to counteract the doings of Clark, and addressed large meetings at Manchester, Rochdale, Stockport, Macclesfield, and other places, where votes of confidence in him were passed. O'Brien at this time began to wield more influence at public meetings. There was scarce a meeting that he did not attend, and propound his principles. Every week he was at John-street, where he was rapturously applauded; and he was invited to Greenwich, and other places in the neighbourhood.

On the 30th of April, 1850 a meeting was held at John-street, addressed by Milne, Kydd, and Ruffy. Messrs. Beezer and Looney, two of the liberated prisoners, made their appearance amid an enthusiastic greeting. The South London hall was also the scene of numerous gatherings. On Monday, April 28th, O'Connor was present at the opening of the People's Hall at Hanley,—a splendid building purchased by the Chartists and Secularists,—which was crowded on the occasion. He was received during the delivery of a long address, with the wonted enthusiasm of the men of the Potteries for their chief. The destruction of Universal Suffrage in France called forth a crowded meeting on the 3rd of June at John-street. O'Brien, Reynolds, and Harney delivered soul-stirring addresses on the occasion. O'Connor paid a visit to Scotland. At Glasgow James Adams came forward to oppose him; but during an attempt for two hours-and-a-half to obtain a hearing, the meeting was one continued scene of uproar, and Adams was at length dragged from the platform by the police, whose services had been called for by the O'Connorites. The chairman left the chair and the people were dispersing when, at the invitation of O'Connor a portion remained, whom he addressed. O'Connor also visited Paisley, where Cochrane appeared and spoke against him; but a vote of confidence in him was unanimously carried. Edinburgh and Gorgie Mills were also visited by the energetic agitator; and on his return he addressed large meetings in Carlisle and Newcastle-upon-Tyne.

The Executive—which now consisted of Thomas Brown, William Davies, James Grassby, G. J. Harney, Thomas Miles, John Milne, E. Stallwood, G. W. M. Reynolds, and John Arnott,—began to take their stand upon social as well as political rights; and at John-street on the 18th of June, a resolution approving of those rights, as propounded by O'Brien, was brought forward by them, and adopted by the meeting. At the next meeting held in the same place, John Shaw, who had been released from prison, attended, and met with a warm reception; and it was announced that Dr. M'Douall was also at liberty. Harney and O'Connor had parted company, in consequence of the latter not allowing him liberty to write in the *Star* certain strictures on Clark and his party. He had started a penny paper under the title of the *Red Republican;* and Reynolds had merged his *Political Instructor* into a newspaper, of which for a short time Bronterre O'Brien was the editor. On the 11th of July, Ernest Jones and J. Fussell were entertained at a soiree in the John-street Institution. After tea the hall was crowded. Harney occupied the chair. Walter Cooper, Reynolds, Wheeler, Vernon, Beezer, Shaw, W. J. Linton, O'Brien, and Stallwood, severally addressed the meeting,—some of them in eloquent and energetic speeches. Jones and Fussell were greeted with deafening cheers. The former said they must now teach the people their social as well as their political rights; and he congratulated them on the appearance of Harney's *Red Republican.*

O'Connor again brought forward a motion for the Charter on the 11th of July, 1850, but the House was counted out. Chartism seemed reviving out of doors. Blackstone Edge was visited by thousands on the 14th of July, and resolutions for the Charter were spoken to by Rushton of Ovendon, Williams of Stockport, Shackleton of Halifax, Leach, George White, Dr. M'Douall, Harney, Bell of Heywood, Roberts, and O'Connor. It was estimated that not less than thirty thousand persons were present. In the evening of the same day O'Connor visited his stronghold, Manchester, where he addressed a crowded meeting in the People's Institute, for which he received, on the motion of Dickenson, the thanks of the meeting.

On the 15th of July, Ernest Jones entered Halifax, accompanied by a grand procession of people who had met to welcome him once more to their town. The people rent the air with their cheers. Shackleton, Harney, and Jones, addressed the multitude in West Hill Park, and the meeting was then adjourned till the evening, when thousands again assembled. Gaukroger presided. An address was presented to Jones, and speeches were again delivered by the same gentlemen. On the following day another meeting was held, when Jones was presented with a purse containing fifty sovereigns. Ernest Jones addressed, through the *Northern Star*, a letter, in which he repudiated the Middle-class Movement. O'Connor, about the same time, had a letter in the same paper, in which he sneeringly alluded to the "poor gentleman" who spoke against his policy at the London meetings. There followed another letter from Jones to Harney, in opposition to Clark's recent attack upon his courage, this was, of course, also an answer to O'Connor. Jones and O'Connor attended a great demonstration at Mountsorrel in Leicestershire, on Sunday, the 10th of September. It was estimated that twenty thousand persons were present. Jones also spoke in Leicester to a large meeting on the following night. At Bingley, Jones was met by a procession with music. He was escorted into the town in a carriage with greys, and conveyed to the Market-place, where he addressed the people. Afterwards three hundred persons sat down to tea in the Odd Fellows' Hall, where they were addressed by Messrs. Jones, Robinson, Hornsby, Holt, and Lightowler. Jones was presented with eleven pounds by the Chartists of this little town. On the following morning (Sunday,) he addressed an open-air meeting at the "Druid's Altar," one of the most romantic spots in Yorkshire. Doncaster, Sheffield, Hebden Bridge, Holmfirth, and Bradford, were also visited by Jones; at Sheffield and Bradford, Beezer was also present. At the latter place Jones was met at the railway, where a carriage was in waiting to receive him; and he was escorted through the streets by thousands of persons to the Temperance Hall, where upwards of seven hundred persons sat down to tea. A public meeting followed, and the room was so crowded that the great orator addressed the crowd from the steps of the Hall.

What increased the excitement at this time was the visit of the Austrian General, Haynau, to London, who was assailed by Barclay and Perkins's draymen, and driven into a dust-bin for his merciless cruelties inflicted on the brave Hungarians. Votes of thanks were passed to the draymen at every meeting, for the personal chastisement inflicted on this monster of despotism, who had presumed to pollute the shores of England with his presence. A crowded meeting, addressed by O'Connor, was held at the Cowper-street Hall, on the 17th of September, on behalf of the Refugees, when the very mention of the draymen called forth the most tremendous cheering. At Leeds, Jones lectured in the Bazaar to a numerous audience, by whom he was heartily welcomed. At Newcastle-upon-Tyne the Nelson-street Lecture Room was filled, and when he made his appearance he was greeted with enthusiastic and protracted plaudits. At South Shields, Bristol, and Sunderland, as well as numerous other places in England, he lectured, and was equally well received. From England, he crossed the border and journeyed into Scotland.   At Hawick he lectured to a crowded and enthusiastic audience, as also at Kirkaldy.   At Aberdeen the Union Hall was crowded, and Jones was hailed with the warmest enthusiasm.   Resolutions for the Charter, and complimentary to the lecturer, were proposed and seconded by Messrs. Smart, Deans, Wright, and McDonald, and then Jones on rising to speak was again enthusiastically applauded.   After his speech a festival was held in honour of the guest of the evening.   He delivered a lecture in the same place on the 28th of September, and had again the pleasure of speaking to a crowded audience. Glasgow, Kilmarnock, Cumnock, Hamilton, Tillicoultry, and a number of other places, testified to the popularity of Jones. In all of them he received that welcome to which his sufferings justly entitled him.   On returning to England he lectured at Staleybridge, Rochdale, Padiham, Coventry, Northampton, Manchester, the Potteries, and many other places.   At Manchester he addressed a numerously attended open-air meeting in Camp Field, and afterwards one in the People's Institute, which was densely crowded.   In the Potteries the People's Hall was crammed, and the loudest applause greeted the lecturer.   At all these Barclay and Perkins's draymen were tremendously applauded.

An attempt was made about this time to unite the several democratic societies, and for that purpose a conference was held in the metropolis, to which were invited delegates from the National Charter Association, the National Reform League, the Social Reform League, the Fraternal Democrats, and the Trades.   Harney, O'Brien, Delaforce, Thornton Hunt, Holyoake, and many other leading men attended.   They sat in deliberation many times.   A union was attempted to be formed which should embrace all under the name of the National Charter and Social Reform Union, but it turned out a signal failure.   A new source of grievance arose.   O'Connor, in a letter to the Chartist body, recommended a conference to be held in Manchester, and that locality fixed New Year's Day for the purpose.   To this the Executive demurred.   Ernest Jones opposed it.   A West Riding delegate meeting denounced it, saying that the Executive was the proper authority for calling such a conference together.   Jones addressed a letter to the Chartists, through the *Northern Star*, urging them not to agree to O'Connor's proposal, and expressing a hope that the minority would abide by the majority, which was evidently opposed to the conference.   Notwithstanding this, O'Connor persevered, and attended a meeting in the People's Institute, Manchester, on the 17th of November, in support of his proposition. G. J. Mantle opposed the calling of the conference, but he could not obtain a fair hearing ; and a resolution to call the conference was almost unanimously adopted. O'Connor at this meeting turned round upon his middle-class allies, the Financial and Parliamentary Reformers, and stated his belief, that had they the casting vote to give for or against the Charter, they would vote against it. In consequence of the position taken by O'Connor and the men of Manchester, the Executive, to test the Chartist body, resigned office. Jones addressed another letter to the Chartists in strong terms of reprobation of the proposed conference. In writing of it he said,—" Perhaps an attempt may yet be made to uphold the perishing spirit of faction in our ranks, by meetings, cheers, rhetoric, and clap-trap ; take it for what it is worth." The Manchester Council replied to Jones's letter through the *Star*. The general feeling appeared to be in favour of the Executive, the localities approving the policy pursued by that body. Week after week Jones followed up the charge, by writing letters in *Reynolds' Newspaper* and the *Northern Star*. "The Charter in Danger," was the title of one in the *Star* of December the 21st, in which he replied to the Manchester Council, and whom he attacked without reserve, not, however, so with respect to O'Connor, although he was the head and front of the schism. Jones, though pretending to be very candid in his remarks upon that gentleman, generally wrote of him with dignified respect, however severely he might lash the Council of Manchester, who were but doing O'Connor's bidding. He criticised the plan of action which those gentlemen had laid before the people. They professed to desire to labour for the Charter, " pure and simple," without regard to questions of social reform ; and yet one of the objects of the conference was the establishment of Co-operative Stores. On this subject Jones wrote as follows :—

"If this is not the 'jog trot' system, it is something worse. They will have the Charter pure and simple, and in the very next line they tack the grocery business to it. They tell us when we have a universal organization of meal-tubs, we shall find that a considerable help towards getting up the agitation for the Charter. How many years shall we be, good heaven! with low wages, short time, panics, and misery coming on (according to their own showing),—how many years shall we have to wait before a few working men have become shopkeepers and fine gentlemen, and condescend to help us in obtaining the Charter? How many Aristocrats of labour shall we make before we have learnt that we have been only increasing the ranks of our enemies? Oh my friends, that proposition might have come from the camp of the enemy. This is keeping the Charter 'pure and simple' with a vengeance. No one can appreciate the value of the principle of Co-operation more than I do. It is what we must carry out when we have the political power—that is, the Charter; but if you think to get the Charter by means of commercial co-operation, you are bad coachmen, for you are putting the cart before the horse."

Jones did not content himself merely with writing, but he journeyed to Manchester, and thrust himself into one of the meetings called by the Council, and denounced their conduct most severely. Harvey fired heavy shot at the same party every week in his *Friend of the People*, which was now the title of his penny periodical. Meantime the election of the Executive proceeded. There were 21 candidates, O'Brien, Cooper, Massey, and others declining to stand. The result was as follows:—Reynolds, 1805; Harney, 1774; Jones, 1757; Arnott, 1505; O'Connor, 1314; Holyoake, 1021; Davies, 858; Grassby, 811; Milne, 709; Hunt, 707; Stallwood, 636; Fussell, 611; Miles, 515; LeBond, 456; Linton, 402; Wheeler, 350; Shaw, 526; Leno, 94; Delaforce, 89; Ferdinando, 59; Finlen, 44. It will thus be seen that the once-popular idol, O'Connor was only fifth on the poll and nearly five hundred below the more popular Reynolds; and perhaps it was compassion more than approval of the man, that dictated the number of votes still recorded in his favour. The nine highest on the poll were the successful candidates.

CHAPTER XIII.

DISAFFECTION AMONGST THE CHARTIST LEADERS

We mentioned previously, that Jones maintained publicly an attitude of dignified respect towards O'Connor; but it was only the prudence of the hypocrite which dictated his conduct. In secret he hated O'Connor, and would have used any means to crush him, could he have done so without risking his own popularity, but some sort of reserve was yet deemed necessary. If he wrote strongly against the Manchester Council, the blind O'Connorites would scarcely regard that as an attack upon their chief; but it was an attack—the attack of a coward who dare not strike direct, and chooses a roundabout course to assail his antagonist. While Jones had not the courage to write or speak openly his real sentiments, while in the very letter in which he denounced the Manchester Council so unreservedly, he professed that no man had a greater regard for O'Connor than himself, he went about plotting in the dark to secure his overthrow. When the struggle was taking place between the Executive and Clark and his party, Jones waited on O'Brien at his residence in Lowndes Court. There was present on the occasion Mr. Leslie of Edinburgh, a friend of O'Brien's. The conversation turned upon the squabble between the party of Clark, McGrath, &c., and that of Harney and Jones, (for Clark and his party were still in the field with their National Charter League, and were doing all in their power to push forward the Manchester conference.) Jones in the course of conversation was quite in a fury against O'Connor, and said he was exercising a despotic power over Chartism, utterly incompatible with Democracy. He said that at any cost that power must be put down, or it would put down the Charter; and then mustering all his power of persuasion, which to weak minds was by no means inconsiderable, he continued:—

"You, O'Brien, are the only man who can put it down. You hold the balance of power in the scale of Chartism. Whatever scale you throw your weight into will preponderate, and the more readily now, as the contending parties are nearly equal.   Do then, I pray write some articles for the *Star*—some letters to the people, which I will engage to get inserted; and in those articles or letters, you can at once break up the conspiracy of Clark and Co. to hand over the Chartists to the Manchester School, and O'Connor's treacherous support of Clark's scheme, while he alternately bullies or cajoles the people's honest leaders.   O'Connor has established a vulgar despotism by lies and bluster, which you, O'Brien, owe it to yourself and the cause to help us to crush."

But O'Brien's mind was not so weak as to be unable to see through Jones's selfish scheme.   He had opposed O'Connor—none more bitterly.   He knew the truth of Jones's accusations —bitter experience had taught him their truth ; but he despised the man who was afraid to declare in public his real sentiments respecting O'Connor, and who, while professing to have the greatest regard for him, could have the cowardly meanness to be plotting against him in the dark.   Under these feelings he replied that O'Connor was a falling man, and that he never cared to assail the weak or tottering; that he exposed and opposed him in the days of his strength, to his own injury and disquiet; but now that more dangerous enemies than O'Connor were in the field, it would be folly to single him out and spare the others.   That for the rest, he cared little which of the contending leaders got the upper hand, as he had no cónfidence in any of them.   "For instance," said O'Brien, "can I have confidence in you, Jones, when I find you write in this manner of O'Connor (here O'Brien put his finger upon the paragraph in the *Star*, in which Jones professed to have so much regard for O'Connor) one week, and the next ask me to help you to put him down through his own paper—the paper in which you yourself are bolstering him up."   Leslie, who was present during this conversation, and who afterwards related it publicly at the Eclectic Institute, smiled and looked Jones in the face, till even he was confused and compelled to blush ; but making the best of the dishonourable situation in which he had placed himself, he sought to justify that dishonour by an apology more dishonourable still.   "*My dear fellow,*" he rejoined, addressing O'Brien, "*we must sometimes hold the candle to the devil.*" Yes, the "noble" O'Connor, "the man of whom Democracy ought to be proud," was a "devil" in the estimation of his aspiring pupil, Ernest Jones—the chivalrous Ernest Jones, who has "no secrets," whose whole conduct is "open to the world."   Of course Jones will deny all this, for there is nothing he will not deny if it suits his purpose.   But there are collateral proofs of this opinion of O'Connor entertained by the secret plotter, Ernest Jones.

Sometime after the above conversation, he published a weekly periodical called *Notes to the People*, in which was a very cleverly written romance entitled, " The History of a Democratic Movement, compiled from the journal of a Democrat, the confessions of a Demagogue, and the minutes of a Spy." The character of the Demagogue is sustained by one Simon De Brassier, and in the greater part of the portrait there is an unmistakable resemblance to O'Connor ; so much so, that at the time every one who read it at once recognised the likeness. Jones was still fearful of attacking O'Connor fairly, but he could conveniently give him a thrust in the side through the tickling pages of romance ; so that if it became convenient to deny that the portrait was intended for O'Connor, the denial could be made, for no one could positively swear that the artist did intend him. The conjecture might in the mind amount to a positive certainty ; but where was the proof, in face of the author's unblushing denial ? In introducing his hero on the stage of politics, he describes him as the younger son of a far-descended though untitled family. He is described as possessing a " noble form," a " commanding figure, with calm dignity and self-possession graven on his magnificent features, and waving his arm for silence." He tells his audience that " he has hitherto been the child of pleasure, and made one among the rich herd of idlers and tyrants who disgrace the name of man." He says "Working men, birth nobles, by the patent of your labour, I have made my choice this day ; I cast my lot with yours." He goes on to describe himself as " a man of wealth, but that wealth is now dedicated to your cause. It is true I have kept my hounds and hunters ; there are two of them—pointing to his horses—grown fat on your starvation. God forgive me, to think that what has fattened those horses might have sustained those babes I now see starving at their mother's breast." He then declared his intention to sell off his horses. Those who remember how O'Connor used to boast of his wealth, of his hunters, of the useless life he had exchanged for the more useful one of serving the people, of the sale of his stud, and his renunciation of pleasures, for the purpose of devoting himself to their cause, will at once see the intention of the author. Jones describes his hero as a high-bred beggar, brought up to the profession of the bar ; but having few briefs, extravagant without the means of supporting his extravagance, living on his relations, and at last having wearied them with his calls for money, he enters into a scheme with a usurer named Bludore, a jobber in the funds. De Brassier was to bring the people to the verge of revolution; Bludore was to take advantage of the slackness of the money market induced by the agitation, and buy up shares and funds for De Brassier, who was afterwards to check the movement he had created, when the said shares and funds would go up, and the Demagogue thus reap a fortune by the ruin and misery he created. Further on he depicts the Chartist Movement in 1848, with of course a little colouring. At the head of a great movement which threatens to overwhelm him, and being afraid, or not having principle enough to push that movement to a successful issue, De Brassier exclaims :—" I must check this movement without losing my popularity and I must alter its tone and temper, for it is growing too democratic for De Brassier." He then determines to get up a series of processions, and demonstrations, which the author describes as "ridiculous parades;" remarking that "a great meeting on Tara, Clontarf, Kersal Moor, or Kennington Common should never be held, except it is intended that it shall result in immediate action of some kind or other." The author goes on to make his hero search for the means of unseating those who were his rivals in popularity, and for this purpose he calls a convention. The convention assembled. Two hundred delegates—the choicest, noblest, boldest, aye, perhaps wisest spirits of Democracy,—assembled, and De Brassier, amid the general plaudits of that gallant band, assumed his place at the head of the people's council. The delegates give in their report —a most cheering one as to the state of public feeling—upon which De Brassier challenges their statements ; tells them they are weak, and at last makes some of them believe so. He is opposed, upon which he rises and says :—

"Gentlemen, a horrid conspiracy is afloat ; it is concocted by Government ; a plot to destroy us. They are thirsting for our blood. There," he continued, throwing down a letter— "there is a warning I have received, by a member of the police itself, that I am to be shot as soon as a movement is made. The leaders are to be picked off ; I have the list of names. There is a file of picked marksmen in every battalion, who are to concentrate their fire on given individuals, instead of random volleys. There is no escaping. A member of the detective police will accompany them, and point out the devoted men. I repeat, I have the list of names ; I won't read them gentlemen ; but in now looking round this board, my eyes rest on several of their number."

A large part of the above is O'Connor's almost word for word. He was constantly talking of letters that he had received from the police and others informing him that he was to be shot ; and he told Leach on the morning of the 10th, that both of them were marked for assassination ; that he was certain of it. There can be no mistake here as to who is intended, if O'Connor's speeches in the *Star* of April the 15th, be referred to.

" De Brassier rose again. 'I have told you that a deep plot is at work. I have hitherto kept the movement clear. I have prevented all violence. I have not given the Government a handle. I have prevented all bloodshed, —I will do so still. I will save the movement from fools and traitors. I know them. I now tell you that some of the people's most trusted leaders are in the pay of the Government, and some of them are seated in this room'. In opposition to the assertion of the movement's weakness, and the want of sympathy entertained for it by the working-class themselves, the delegates appealed to the enthusiastic meetings and demonstrations in the country, and the excitement caused by the assembling of the convention in the town in which it sat —nay, the crowded state of the Hall, and the cheers of the audience. ' Spies and traitors, paid by Government,' cried De Brassier, 'do not let those cheers mislead you. There are men sent into this Hall in the dress of working men, ordered to applaud and cheer the most violent sentiments. They are detectives. They are marking you and every one that applauds. Fools, they cheer you just to get you to commit yourselves.'"

In the *Star* of April 22nd, O'Connor, after a story about an interview with an Irish policeman, says :—

" Now old Guards, I did not require this statement to convince me that spies were sent to John-street ; and for this reason, having a sharp eye and a sensible ear, I always found that the most ridiculous speeches were cheered by those wolves in sheeps' clothing, while the sensitive working-men shook their heads, and hung them down."

The author also makes De Brassier throw suspicion on the integrity of some members of the Convention. In a letter in the *Star* of April 29th, O'Connor says :—

" I hold the man in utter contempt who was capable of holding one language in the Convention and another language out of the Convention, and what will you say to a delegate of that Convention, after having elicited the boundless cheers of an excited audience by an exciting speech, saying to another delegate of the same Convention on their way home—' *Did you hear the damned fools how they cheered me?*' "

Again :—

"The constituencies that had sent the delegates saw the time wasted in bickering and in the most disgraceful strife.

De Brassier trumpeted to the world that the Convention was full of paid spies and traitors; that he being the only man to save the movement, was being made the victim of a conspiracy among the delegates; that the public time was wasted in a personal attack on him; and called upon the country to protest against the suicidal policy of its would-be representatives. The effect may be imagined; funds ceased to flow in for the support of the delegates.   De Brassier then turned round upon them and said—' Did I not tell you so?   I said public sympathy was not with you ; if it is, where is the money ?   That is the barometer of the movement.   Now you see who is right.' Alas! it was De Brassier who had destroyed the confidence— it was De Brassier who had thus prevented the supplies—it was De Brassier who had stifled the enthusiasm—it was De Brassier who had divided the movement—it was De Brassier who had sown distrust and set every man against his neighbour: and now De Brassier called the effect the cause. He turned the tables, and made the mischief he had created appear to be the result of the incompetency, folly, envy, and treachery of those whom he was ruining.   In vain the latter protested.   They had no means of access to the people.   De Brassier monopolised all the channels of communication. They had none.   They had no papers to report them ; they had no money to travel about the country as he did, and reason with the people who condemned them.   Soon the delegates began to get into debt.   Money not arriving from the country, the Convention was obliged to break up in dis-grace, covered with liabilities ; and the delegates hung like paupers about the town, unable even to get back to their homes.   Then De Brassier came forward, and offered the money out of his own private purse ; dire necessity forced most of them to accept it.   The Demagogue took good care to publish the fact with stentorian force, and the delegates, if they dared to defend their own characters, were accused of being ungrateful wretches, whose base little envy had tried to destroy the great leader of the people, who, notwithstanding had extended the noble hand of unexampled generosity to the jaundiced traitors who had tried to sting him."

It will be borne in mind that O'Connor in 1848 was con-stantly in the habit of setting forth in his letters, how fools and knaves were destroying the movement, and how he was the only man to save it from their knavery and folly, and how he accused the delegates of personally attacking him.   It will also be borne in mind that the Convention was precisely in the state Jones described, over head and ears in debt ; that this was the cause of quarrelling in the Convention, because some of the delegates were taunted by others with their dependent position ; that O'Connor did come forward and pay the debts ; and that in the *Star* of April 22nd, he thus alluded to that subject :—

" I bore without a murmur the indiscretion and folly of some members of the late Convention, and my reward was the payment of one hundred and fifty pounds towards their expenses, and insults, contumely, and reproach in the House of Commons for every act of indiscretion."

This is pretty conclusive as to whose portrait Jones was painting. But again :—

" De Brassier now rushed off into the country ; post, rail, steamer—all were put in requisition to make him almost ubiquitous. Everywhere he shrieked forth—' Spies and traitors ! I have saved the movement from a pack of knaves. I have prevented the shedding of torrents of blood. I have taken you out of the hands of villains. Peace, law, and order ! What a victory we should have had if it had not been for those spies and traitors ! But we have baffled the Government ; we have destroyed their plot. I have saved you—I have saved you !' and the tears of exultation ran down his smiling cheeks."

In the Convention on the morning of the 10th, O'Connor said :—

" Had it not been for the folly of some persons out of the Convention, and of a few in it, there never would have been any opposition to their demonstration, and it would have been the grandest thing of the kind ever seen in England."

In the *Star* of the following Saturday, he writes to the " Imperial Chartists ":—

" When the announcement of our intention to hold a meeting on Kennington Common, and there to form a procession to escort the National Will to the Senate House was made, that announcement was allowed to pass unnoticed by the Government for many weeks ; and now that we have triumphed in our moral strength, I assert, without fear of contradiction, that that intention would never have been interfered with by the Government, but for the folly of some, the indiscretion of some, and the treachery of some of those professing to belong to our ranks."

The following passage, which is taken from an earlier chapter, should be well studied. Taking O'Connor's conduct in 1839 and 1848 in conjunction, and comparing it with this passage, the reader may see at once the author's intention :—

" Well did he (De Brassier) know there would be partial insurrection and rioting,—blood would be shed—convicts would be exiled—thousands would be ruined—hearts would be broken: but what cared he for that?   He would gain doubly. On the one hand, the most ardent, the most popular, the most upright, would be sure to get transported for life.   He would have so many rivals—rivals whom he began to fear—removed out of his path, and it would afterwards make good stock-in-trade to talk of the glorious exiles, or to vituperate the rashness and folly of those who did not follow his advice, and who therefore paid the penalty of their presumption and vanity."

The writer goes on to describe secret conspiracies as the result of De Brassier's policy which the Government gave instructions to their agents to let proceed, until they had attained a certain pitch; which was exactly the policy of the Government in 1848, as will be seen from the evidence of Davis, the spy.   In fact, throughout nearly the whole of this very clever and brilliant romance, the circumstances and events narrated by the writer, are almost exactly similar to the circumstances and events with which O'Connor was so long mixed up.   A large portion, if not the greater part of the language used by De Brassier, is to be found almost sentence for sentence in the speeches and writings of O'Connor. So conscious was Jones of the effect his romance would be calculated to produce, that in the introduction he took care to caution his readers against supposing that the tale contained any personal allusions; an assurance which sometime after he was obliged to repeat, in consequence of pointed interrogations by the friends of O'Connor, who could not do otherwise than recognise the portrait.

Despite the opposition of the Executive as a body to the proposed Conference at Manchester, it assembled on the 26th of January, 1851.   There were, notwithstanding all the previous influence of O'Connor, only four localities represented. The so-called National Charter League (a small society in London) elected Messrs. McGrath, Clark, and Ambrose Hurst, as delegates.   Beside these, O'Connor and Leach represented the Chartists of Manchester, a number of whom had, however, split off and formed a separate locality in opposition to the new policy.   Lawson represented Lower Warley ; North, Bradford ; and Mantle, Warrington.   Hurst was appointed to preside.   After some time spent in debate, as to the state of Chartism, McGrath moved a resolution, which was seconded by Clark, attributing that state to the folly and extravagance of a large portion of the people's advocates. Mantle moved that, "As the Conference represented only four localities, it should dissolve, and leave to the people themselves the choice of the time and place for a conference."

Messrs. Mantle and North voted for the amendment, and O'Connor, Leach, Clark, McGrath, and Lawson, for the motion. Clark then moved, "That this Conference recommend, that when Chartists attend meetings of other political bodies, reformers favourable to the extension of the franchise, or other progressive reforms, that it shall be for the purpose of lending aid and support," which was seconded by Leach. O'Connor, notwithstanding all his previous support of the Middle-class Movement, now turned round upon his new allies, and opposed the motion.

"He would remind them of the deceit practised on the people in former times by the middle-classes. The people had no more chance of getting justice from this class, than they had from the man in the moon. They must rely solely on themselves. The Financial Reformers would use them for their own purposes. They came there to unite the public mind, and in doing so they must not be considered puppets in the hands of the middle-classes, which that resolution would show to be the fact."

Again, he said :—

"He would tell them, that although Cobden and Bright might now vote for the 'Little Charter,' still, if there was any chance of ever making that measure law, they would bribe some of their own party to prevent it.   The aim of these men was to juggle for their own benefit.   He told them in conclusion, to place no confidence in any other class of the community but the working-class.   For his own part, he would never confide nor co-operate with any other.   He had spent upwards of one hundred and thirty thousand pounds in their cause, and he would never desert them."

Clark showed that O'Connor had done more than any other man in the Chartist Association to aid the Parliamentary Reformers, and read extracts, shewing that he had, at an expense of twenty pounds, travelled nearly six hundred miles to Aberdeen, to attend one of their meetings; and that when it was proposed in Committee to alter the rules of the Association, and go for Universal Suffrage, instead of the Household Scheme, O'Connor opposed it, and would not throw the smallest obstacle in the way of the Middle-class Reformers. That he went to Norwich and supported them, had done so in his letters in the *Star*, and advised others to do the same, and had strongly condemned all opposition.   The reading of these extracts was a heavy blow to the supposed consistency of O'Connor; but he only reiterated his last expression of opinion, which he supported with additional observations to the same effect.   Clark consented to somewhat modify his resolution;

but still O'Connor opposed it, and moved an amendment, which though excellent in itself, sought to get rid of the motion by a side wind. His amendment was—"That the people shall offer no opposition to any party who will honestly join with them for the establishment of the People's Charter, whole and entire." Clark and party ultimately fell in with the amendment of O'Connor, and it was carried unanimously. Clark's was also carried, O'Connor, North, and Mantle voting against it. A resolution was then come to, to abide by the Charter whole, entire, and alone; but immediately after, the Conference stultified itself by recommending the establishment of Co-operative Stores, which O'Connor at first opposed, but afterwards voted for, Mantle alone dissenting. But now came the finishing blow to this Conference, which was to have accomplished so much. Mantle moved a resolution in favour of sending delegates to the coming Conference in London, called by the Executive. Clark, McGrath, Hurst, and Leach, had all along acted as though such a body as the Chartist Executive did not exist, and, as they could not therefore now recognize their claims, they opposed the motion. O'Connor, however, supported it, declaring that he would guarantee that the Conference should not be the tool of the Executive. He declared that if he had studied for a whole month, he could not have penned a better or a more timely resolution. He declared also, that he would not surrender his political principles whatever trafficking politicians might say or do. This called up McGrath, who said he thought that when O'Connor made use of the terms "trafficking politicians," he should distinctly state whom he meant, that the people might be on their guard against the deceivers. O'Connor, however, remained silent. On the motion being put, O'Connor, Mantle, North, and Lawson, voted for, and Clark, McGrath, and Leach against it; after which the three latter, with the chairman retired, completely discomfited; the whole proceedings having, as they declared, become null and void by the passing of the last resolution. A public meeting was afterwards held in Manchester, which confirmed all the proceedings of the Conference, except the last resolution. Not even the support of O'Connor at the Conference could induce the meeting to agree to it. A quarrel arose out of the proceedings of the Conference, in consequence of O'Connor insinuating that Harney was dismissed from the *Star* office for recommending private assassination. The question was brought before the Executive. O'Connor endeavoured, but in vain, to shirk its discussion. The Executive passed a resolution, exonerating Harney from blame, and a public meeting in John-street Institution, confirmed the decision of

the Executive, by passing a resolution as follows :—
"This meeting having heard the report of the Executive
Committee, and Mr. Harney's explanation, resolves that Mr.
Harney is exonerated from all charges and imputations said
to have been made by Mr. O'Connor against him at the
Manchester Conference ; and that the conduct of Mr. Harney,
through all the circumstances connected with his secession
from the *Northern Star*, was that of a true and honourable
Democrat, worthy of the people's love, nobly contrasting with
the servile baseness too often characteristic of journalists.
Furthermore, this meeting having considered the sentiments
of Mr. Harney on which his enemies have grounded their
charge of his having recommended private assassination,
hereby repudiates the accusation as a vile calumny, and
denounces the accusers as slanderers and moral assassins,
worthy of the execration of all honest men."

An amendment, moved by Holyoake, as containing in his
view a more dignified expression of opinion, met with many
supporters.   It ran as follows :—
"This meeting, having heard Mr. Harney's defence in
reply to the accusations brought against him, hereby expresses
its satisfaction thereat, and reassures Mr. Harney of its
confidence."

The original resolution was, however, carried by a large
majority, amid loud cheering.   O'Connor had denied the
report containing the charge said to have been made by him
against Harney at the Conference, but a letter was read from
the reporter to Reynolds' newspaper, affirming the correctness
of the report.   Ernest Jones was one of the strongest
supporters of the resolution.   He denounced the amendment
as "namby pamby," and stigmatised some persons who had
issued an anonymous placard against Harney, as "dastardly
ruffians."   While O'Connor was attending the Conference
he visited a number of the manufacturing towns, and addressed
large meetings at Stockport, Rochdale, Oldham, Ashton,
Bolton, and other places, in all of which he was well received.

The Executive—which now consisted of O'Connor, Harney,
Jones, Reynolds, Arnott, Holyoake, Thornton Hunt, Grassby,
and Milne,—put forth its programme of principles and plans,
to be brought forward in the Convention.   Considering the
former professions of its members, the programme was a
very meagre affair.   The great fundamental principles of social
right were overlooked ; the principal point noticed in relation to
the question was that of an alteration in the law of partnership,
so as to more effectually protect the interests of members of Co-
operative Societies.   O'Brien attended the first meeting held

at John-street, at which the programme was brought under public notice, and denounced that document for its short-comings, pronouncing it to be a ferrago of unadulterated humbug. A large portion of the meeting sympathized with his remarks. At the next public meeting Holyoake commented upon the speech of O'Brien, and compared him to the late William Cobbett, who was said to wield a flail, and who, when he had no enemies to lay it on, laid it on his friends. Benny and Pettie addressed the meeting; the latter finding fault with O'Brien, amid great interruption. D. O'Connor endeavoured to show the fallacy of supposing that working men could, as a class, free themselves from social bondage merely by means of co-operation; and Rogers defended O'Brien, and said that the only point in the programme which would benefit the people, was the Charter. Finlen addressed the meeting, stating his belief that the people must have their political before they could get their social rights.

The Convention met at the Parthenium Rooms, St. Martin's Lane, London, on Monday, March the 31st, 1851. There were thirty delegates from the following places :—Greenwich and Kent, Reynolds ; North Lancashire, J. Gray ; Portsmouth and Edinburgh, Thornton Hunt ; Westminster and Marylebone, A. Hanniball ; Lambeth and Southwark, G. Shell ; Tower Hamlets, J. Shaw ; City and Finsbury, J. Finlen ; Bradford District, A. Robinson ; Exeter and Tiverton, T. M. Wheeler ; Manchester, F. O'Connor and G. J. Mantle ; Worcestershire and Gloucestershire, G. J. Harney ; Bristol, T. Savage ; Halifax District, E. Jones ; Paisley District, Rev. A. Duncanson ; Nottinghamshire, William Felkin ; Staffordshire Potteries, J. Capewell ; Sheffield and Rotherham, J. J. Beezer ; Cheshire, W. Benfold ; Coventry and Birmingham, A. Yates ; Northampton, John Barker ; Leicester, G. Wray ; South Shields, D. W. Ruffy ; Edinburgh, W. Pringle ; Huddersfield District, T. Hirst ; Dundee, J. Graham ; Derby District, J. Moss ; Newcastle-on-Tyne, J. Watson ; Dudley District, D. Thompson ; Glasgow District, D. Paul. The delegates having given in their reports, the policy of the Chartist body was brought before the Convention. A few of the delegates were still in favour of agitating for the Charter, and nothing but the Charter. Among these were the delegates from Manchester, Derby, the Potteries, and Northampton ; but the great majority were in favour of agitating for the social as well as the political emancipation of the people. It was also agreed that, while the Chartists should not oppose the Financial and Parliamentary Reformers, they should form no alliance with that party. Holyoake, and two or three others, spoke against the latter part of the resolution, but it was carried almost unanimously. It was then resolved —only six delegates dissenting—to alter the Charter so as to make it deprive of the vote, criminals, only while undergoing their sentence. The adoption of such a resolution shows how very imperfectly men observe the movements in which they are engaged, for the principle contained in it had been adopted by the Conference at Birmingham nearly nine years previous, at which time that part of the Charter was altered accordingly. Resolutions were agreed to for another National Petition for the Charter, to be adopted at simultaneous meetings, and signed by the chairman of each meeting ; for bringing forward Chartist candidates at the forthcoming election ; in favour of the Chartists seeking municipal influence, and for issuing addresses on that subject ; for carrying the agitation for the Charter amongst the trades, through the agricultural districts, amongst the colliers, miners, and railway labourers, and the appointment of special missionaries to Ireland. Although the Executive had in their first programme left unnoticed the fundamental principles of social right, they introduced into the Convention, day by day, propositions regarding those principles. A clause was introduced and adopted in favour of the nationalization of the land by the establishment of a Board of Agriculture ; the restoration of poor, common, church, and crown lands to the people ; and the empowering of the State to gradually purchase up other land, until all of it should become national property. Another clause went for the separation of Church and State ; the existing church property to become national, with a due regard for vested interests. A third clause laid down the principle of national, secular, gratuitous, compulsory education. A fourth asserted the right of Co-operative Societies to registration and enrolment, and expressed an opinion that the co-operative bodies should all be joined in a national union, the profits to be paid into a general fund ; the State to open a Credit Fund for advancing money to bodies of working men desirous of associating together for industrial purposes. A fifth clause asserted the right of the poor to substantial relief when out of employment, and to be employed where possible on the land ; the aged and infirm to be entitled to relief, either at their own homes, or in special buildings erected by the Government, as they themselves might choose. The sixth clause asserted that all taxes ought to be levied on land and accumulated property. The seventh provided for the extinction of the National Debt by means of the interest being applied as repayment of the capital. The eighth set forth that standing armies were contrary to the principles of Democracy, and dangerous to the liberty of the people; but that it was necessary that a standing force should be maintained for a time, and that a reform in the army was necessary, as also in the navy. The ninth clause asserted the right of every individual to bear arms, and to be afforded the opportunity of military training. The Convention also passed a clause in opposition to capital punishment. The whole of these propositions underwent considerable discussion, and were spoken to by some of the delegates most ably. The discussions too, were generally free from acrimony, nearly every man expressing his opinion in a calm and dignified spirit. The programme adopted by the Convention was vastly superior to any adopted by previous Conventions. Many parts of it displayed good statesmanship. Principle was combined with practicability in the discussion on the Land Question. There were only two delegates who spoke in opposition to the Executive clause, namely, Harney and Finlen, who were for nationalizing the land without any compensation to existing owners. They did not, however, persevere much in their opposition. While laying down the principles of social right, the Convention voted a great social wrong, by the adoption of the clause on the opening of a Credit Fund. It was the communistic element, which was strong both in the Executive and in the Convention, that obtained the passing of that clause. It received, however, a vigorous opposition. Graham opposed it very ably, maintaining that as the Credit Fund would be national, people ought not to be forced into co-operative bodies in order to be entitled to its benefits ; but that they ought to be allowed to participate in those benefits as much, if they chose to work upon the individual principle, as though they had joined others in the scheme of co-operation. Ernest Jones was the special pleader in favour of the clause : he maintained that men could work best in co-operation, and affirmed that they did not force men to co-operate ; they could please themselves. Graham rejoined, " Yes, they can please themselves, as the people who pay to support the church. The clergy say, ' We don't compel you to come to church, but you shall pay whether you come or not.' In like manner Mr. Jones says, ' You can do as you please about co-operating, but if you don't you are not to receive your share of the national funds, though they equally belong to you as to the co-operators.' " This apt illustration of the shrewd Scotch workman astonished the sophistical lawyer, who shook his head amid the laughter of the Convention. Others, however, came to the rescue, and the clause was carried ; but the numbers were nearly equal.

During the sittings of the Convention Hanniball introduced a resolution in favour of a reform in the Currency, as advocated by O'Brien. There were several speakers on the question. Holyoake said they had better not discuss the question as there was no telling where the discussion would end. Reynolds made one of the best speeches on the subject. The majority of the delegates did not, however, appear to understand the bearings of the question, and ultimately, on the motion of Wheeler, a resolution was passed pledging the Executive to direct public attention to a consideration of the subject. The only thing that led to any sort of acrimonious feeling amongst the delegates, was a letter of O'Connor's in the *Northern Star*, in which he endorsed a statement made by the *Times*, Lord Lyndhurst, and Stuart Wortley, to the effect that the foreign refugees intended to make a physical demonstration on the opening of the Great Exhibition of All Nations, in London. A resolution was passed by the Convention repudiating the statement. O'Connor did not often attend the sittings of the Convention; he did not, indeed, appear to possess much influence in that assembly. When present he was very little noticed; and many of the delegates appeared to view him with a kind of contempt. This remark will apply to some who had fawned upon him in the days of his power, but who deserted his cause when they perceived it was sinking. He did not, however, forget to remind them that he had spent one hundred and thirty thousand pounds in the cause, and that he had never travelled a mile, nor eaten a meal, at the people's expense. O'Connor's appearance at that time, indicated that a great change had come over him. There was not that buoyancy of spirits that formerly characterised the great leader of the "Imperial Chartists." It was evident, to a close observer, that the mind of the once vigorous agitator was shaken. All his speeches and letters were incoherent, and his eye lacked its usual lustre. He generally appeared as if in a dream. The letters he wrote in the *Northern Star* week after week, in which he cautioned the people against the foreigners that were coming to the Exhibition, and urged them by no means to take a part in the contemplated revolution, were additional evidences of his weakness. Harney and Jones were at that time endeavouring to start a stamped paper, entitled *The Friend of the People*, to act as a counterpoise to the *Northern Star*, and a subscription was started for that purpose, but the amount subscribed did not reach more than twenty-two pounds after defraying expenses, and the project was abandoned. Harney, who had so often aided O'Connor in the days of his prosperity in destroying so many others, now turned round upon his former master with unrelenting hostility. In the 24th number of his *Friend of the People* was an article headed "The Revolution come at last." The article bore reference to the affairs of the Land Company. O'Connor had established in connection with the Company a Bank in which some thousands of pounds had been deposited; and a letter appeared from the manager, informing the depositors that, pending the decision of Parliament upon the liability of the Land Company to repay the advances of O'Connor, the payment to depositors was suspended. The letter of the manager stated that this decision was come to with the full concurrence of the Land Company's Directors. O'Connor now found that every plank was falling from his sinking ship. There was a time when some of these men allowed him to issue addresses in their name, without his ever asking their consent; but the day of prosperity was gone, and that of bitter adversity had set in. Clark, Doyle, McGrath, and Dixon, addressed a letter through the *Daily News*, to the depositors in the Bank, and the members of the Land Company, in which they repudiated the notice of the manager, and stated that in 1848 O'Connor assumed the whole proprietorship of the Bank, and that from that time they had not interfered in its management; until, on the introduction of the Bill for winding up the affairs of the Land Company, they discovered that it was intended by O'Connor to defray all the losses of that establishment out of the Land Company's property, whereupon they protested against anything being done to increase the liabilities of the Company. This protest O'Connor construed into a warranty for refusing to meet the demands of the depositors in the Bank. They objected, too, that the amount which O'Connor made the Company to be indebted to him was not the true amount. That since August, 1849, he had received several thousand pounds of the Land Company's monies, of which neither they nor the shareholders knew anything. They also showed that any amount due to O'Connor by the Land Company could not be touched by either the depositors or himself, inasmuch as he had assigned all such monies on the 31st of March, 1851, over to one Marshall Turner, his solicitor, and they quoted a legal document to that effect. They disclaimed all connection with the closing of the Bank, and refusing payment of the depositors. O'Connor attempted a reply to these statements through the same journal in which they appeared. He said he had paid the directors out of his private purse for several months past, and that the account between himself and the Company stood thus ;—Paid on behalf of the Company £11,926 14s. 11d., received £4,921 10s. 8d. ;

due to O'Connor £7,005 4s. 3d. But O'Connor made no
allusion to the charge of the directors, that he had assigned
all monies due to him by the Company, to Marshall Turner.
Harney commented severely on these matters, and thus concluded his article :—

"As yet, we are only at the beginning of the revelations.
O'Connor alieniated from himself the affections of all honest
men, surrounded himself with none but sycophants and
traffickers, and now he begins to meet his well merited
reward."

In the following number Harney followed up the attack in
an article headed, " Rogues All ;" followed by portions of a
letter from the directors, taken from *Lloyd's Weekly Newspaper*,
which contained a second attack on O'Connor's honesty.
This letter was also addressed to the depositors in the Bank,
and the members of the Land Company. The directors
showed that when the committee of the House of Commons
made its report, there was a balance in hand of £7,659 14s.
2d. ; that O'Connor had since received several sums, and made
several disbursements, which left the Company in his debt
£899 17s. 1½d., instead of £7,005 4s. 3d. as stated by himself.
That in order to make out a larger claim, he had set down £3,606
which he had lost by his own Bank, £2,000 for travelling
expenses, and interest which he declared due to him at 4 per cent.
They charged O'Connor with omitting in his account of receipts,
£409 18s. 4d. paid over to him by themselves, from August,
1849, and they showed, according to his own letter in the
Daily News, that the £3,606 which he had lost by his own Bank,
and which he charged to the Company, was not money out of
his own pocket as asserted, but that it proceeded from the sale
of land and other property belonging to the Company. They
further showed that he had held monies in his possession
belonging to the Company, on which interest was due to a
larger amount than the sum lent by himself. That while the
interest due by the Company amounted only to £96, at the
same rate of interest he owed the Company for the monies held
by him £121 2s. 4d. ; thus leaving a balance in the Company's
favour.   They declared that out of £5,331 9s. received by him
since October, 1848, the only sums he had paid were two—
one amounting to £216 10s. 5d. the other £1,000 paid to
meet current expenses, so that he had to account for the
principal and interest upon £4,114 18s. 7d., and they also
demanded that he should pay interest on the £3,606 paid into
his own Bank. They stated that they had the strongest
reason to believe that O'Connor had effected sales of the
Company's property at a ruinous sacrifice, to enable him to

carry on his Bank. They further stated that a mortage had been effected on O'Connorville estate, amounting to £1,383 15s. 7d. That the mortgagee was W. P. Roberts, solicitor to the Company, a knowledge of which they had only just gained, whereas such a transaction ought not to have taken place without their consent and concurrence. They objected to the large amount charged for travelling expenses, and denied that they had for the past eighteen months obtained more than a fourth part of their salaries, although O'Connor had received large sums from the sale of the Company's property, which he had devóted to propping up his Bank, and another sinking property, the *Northern Star,* which, without the aid derived from the sale of the Company's lands, would have been long ago extinct. These men who had been so long the sycophants of O'Connor, thus finished up their address :—
" O'Connor, acting upon the principle that possession is nine points of law, and having all the property of the Company in his own name, has withheld or paid at his pleasure ; and by converting a trust proprietorship into a personal one, he has mistaken the exchequer of the Company into his own pocket, otherwise it need hardly be remarked, that little indeed could be obtained from this latter source for any purpose whatever. We are bound, in justice to ourselves, to expose the falsity of the ostentatious bounty of O'Connor ; and have to assure the members, that his statement in reference to us is totally untrue."

Harney, however, would not let the directors pass for honest men. He thus commented in his article :—
" Let them not lay the flattering unction to their souls that they can redeem themselves by destroying O'Connor. On the contrary, the more they succeed in blackening his character, the lower they sink themselves in the slough of infamy. They shared the spoil with him when the money came rolling in, and now they must share with him the execration of their long-confiding, but at last enlightened, dupes and victims."

Clark was not content with firing at O'Connor through the *Daily News* and *Lloyd's,* but journeyed to Manchester, and called a public meeting, where Leach, Donovan, and himself, impeached the honesty of O'Connor and W. P. Roberts. O'Connor retorted upon Clark that he had in his possession a clock, belonging to the Land office. Clark replied that he bought the clock, and held a receipt for the money. The Land Company was going to wreck more and more every day, many of the allotters refused to acknowledge O'Connor as their landlord, or to pay him any rent, some of them declaring that such was their condition, that they could not pay.

The Executive continued to work as well as their limited

means would permit. They frequently issued circulars enunciatory of Democratic principles, and Ernest Jones took an extensive tour through the country and delivered lectures. A public meeting, presided over by Wakley, was held in the metropolis, to demand an enquiry into the prison treatment of Ernest Jones. Messrs. Holyoake, O'Brien, and others addressed the meeting in favour of its object, and a petition was adopted unanimously. The Council of the National Reform League called a meeting in the Eclectic Institute for an enquiry into the treatment, not only of Jones, but of all other prisoners sentenced at the same time. The meeting was addressed by Feargus O'Connor, Bronterre O'Brien, Beezer, Fussell, Boyson, and Gurney, and a petition to Parliament was agreed to.

Letters still continued to be written in the newspapers against O'Connor. He replied to them, or rather noticed them; but there was now very little fire in his pen. He seemed almost to have lost his power of vituperation, and he wrote very little of any kind. On the 19th of July, notwithstanding this denunciation of him, a demonstration in his honour was held at O'Connorville, when he was presented with an address, expressing sympathy and gratitude. On the 7th of August the Bill for winding up the Land Company received the royal assent.

The meetings of the Executive did not continue long to be largely attended. Jones was on a tour; Harney was visiting Scotland and delivering lectures as, also, was Holyoake. At a meeting on the 24th of September, 1851, the secretary read a letter from Reynolds, announcing that in consequence of illness, he could no longer attend to his duties on the Executive. He, therefore, resigned his office, and made the Association a present of twenty pounds, in which sum they stood indebted to him. He gave a similar reason for declining to contest the borough of Bradford, for which place he had pledged himself to stand as a candidate. At the next meeting of the Executive, at which Messrs. Arnott, Grassby, Hunt, Jones, and Milne were present—it was unanimously agreed to thank Reynolds for his services in the Chartist cause. Harney now began to find fault with Holyoake for his praise of the Manchester Reformers, and said he did not see how he could consistently remain a member of the Executive. LeBlond was elected on the Committee in the place of Reynolds.

O'Connor's intellect was now evidently on the decline. M. Kossuth, the great Hungarian leader, landed in Southampton on the 20th of October. There was a grand demonstration to welcome him to our shores, and this was followed by a banquet got up by the corporation.   O'Connor was present, and very abruptly went up to Kossuth, seized him by the hand, and declared that he loved him, &c.   He was expostulated with by the Mayor; when, looking contemptuously, he asked, " What's the matter?" and sat down.   At the great demon-stration of the working men of London, in honour of Kossuth, the committee refused to admit O'Connor to the Hanover-square Rooms.   Thornton Hunt was the principal actor in the affair, but a remonstrance from Reynolds procured O'Connor admission.   Bronterre O'Brien could not be excluded, as he was a member of the Committee for getting up the demon-stration, but he was refused a personal introduction to Kossuth. Ernest Jones did not attend the demonstration, because the Charter was not to be mentioned by the speakers at the meet-ing.   The treatment of O'Connor called forth resolutions con-demnatory of the conduct of the Committee, from a number of the Chartist localities.   The Committee defended itself, on the ground that their wish was to secure an effective and orderly demonstration, and that the recent conduct of O'Connor had shown that he was not master of his own actions.   They also stated that Kossuth refused to receive the address if O'Connor took any part in the proceedings.

Dissatisfaction now began to be manifested at the Executive on account of the apathy of the Chartist body.   A public meeting was held at the Cowper-street rooms on the 12th of November, over which Mr. Cudden presided.   It was addressed by Messrs. Dick, Rogers, Stratton, Bryson, Osbourne, and Swift, against the Executive—while Mr. Slocombe and Mr Farrow defended that body.   O'Brien addressed the meeting, but only to expose the *Globe* newspaper for having misrepresented his speech at the Kossuth Banquet.   He had written to the *Globe* and inser-tion was promised, but only an unimportant paragraph was inserted, while a long article appeared in reply to it.   The meet-ing broke up without any resolution having been come to.   In the *Star* of November the 15th, a letter appeared from Ernest Jones in which he called attention to the forthcoming election of the Executive.   He found fault with some of his colleagues, and called upon the Chartists to beware of playing the Chartist movement into the hands of any other party, by having a majority on the Executive more identified with other move-ments than with that for the Charter.   He advocated the abolition of the unpaid Committee of nine, to be substituted by a paid Committee of three persons.   On the 23rd a public meeting was held at John-street, to consider the question of Chartist organization, when the meeting resolved itself into a Committee for considering the subject.   Ernest Jones moved the reconstitution of the Metropolitan Delegate Council, which after considerable discussion, in which Messrs. Osbourne, Nicholls, Lee, Leno, Cudden, Wheeler, Hunt, Murray, LeBlond Dick, Beezer, Bligh, and others took part—was carried with two dissentients.

The Executive grew weaker every day. Messrs. Holyoake, Hunt, and LeBlond sympathised with the Middle-class Reformers, and the split between them and some of their colleagues became inevitable. Julian Harney who was lecturing at Newcastle, Shields, and other places, sent a letter to the secretary of the Executive, declining to stand for re-election. Want of time, and the weak state of his health, were the reasons alleged. He found fault with his more moderate colleagues for remaining on the Executive when they were giving their support to other movements, and he condemned Jones's plan of a paid Executive without a sanction of the Convention. In the *Star* of December the 13th, LeBlond addressed a letter to the Chartists in opposition to the sentiments of Jones, in which he defended his own line of policy in reference to the middle class. Jones rejoined in the following number of the *Star*.

The *coup d'état* of Louis Napoleon called forth an expression of opinion in the metropolis. A public meeting was held at the National Hall, and was presided over by G. J Holyoake. J. Pettie proposed the following resolution:—

"That this meeting protests against the political changes in France—against the arbitrary and heartless means by which they have been effected, and deems it a duty to raise a public voice on behalf of a friendly people, crushed under a military rule. Also to call earnestly upon our government to use its political influence on behalf of the restoration of the liberties of the people, destroyed by the indefensible aggressions of organised despotism."

G. Hopper seconded the resolution, which Mr. Tasenall supported, as did also Messrs. Birch, of Oxford, Goodfellow, and Ellis ; upon which O'Brien moved an amendment, couched in stronger terms :—

"That this meeting contemplates with abhorrence and disgust the triumphant usurpation of Louis Napoleon—an usurpation accomplished by a continuation of crimes, including perfidy, violence, and organised murder, unparalleled in the history of Europe. That we deeply sympathise with the great and generous French people, in seeing their hard-won constitutional rights and liberties so foully trampled upon by military force, and we earnestly hope, in common with all good men, that Europe will speedily see a termination of this usurper's power, worthy of his reign, worthy of his crimes, and of his ingratitude toward the French people."

O'Brien justified, by reference to facts, the strong terms of his resolution, which was seconded by Charles Murray, and on being put to the vote was carried by a large majority.

On the 3rd of January, 1852 the *Northern Star*, which had been under the proprietorship of Feargus O'Connor since the latter end of 1837, changed hands, passing from that gentleman, into the hands of Messrs. Fleming and McGowan, his editor and printer, who purchased the sinking and losing property for one hundred pounds. For some time before this event the paper appeared to be entirely under Fleming's management; all the articles were written with the seeming purpose of handing over the Chartist body to the Middle-class Reformers, and very little of Chartism appeared in its columns.

Meanwhile, the election of the Executive proceeded. Notwithstanding that O'Connor was evidently incapable of even managing his own affairs, having manifested repeated signs of derangement, six hundred persons recorded their votes for him. The nine elected were: Ernest Jones, John Arnott, Feargus O'Connor, T. M. Wheeler, James Grassby, John Shaw, W. J. Linton, J. J. Beezer, G. J. Holyoake. The first polled only 900 votes—just half of what were polled by Reynolds at the previous election—while the last polled but 336. These numbers revealed the weakness to which the Association had become reduced. But a still greater source of weakness lay in the incongruity of the elected Executive. O'Connor was unable to serve. Ernest Jones resigned his seat, declaring that he could not serve on such an Executive, and he implored the Chartist body to elect a Convention without loss of time. Wheeler likewise resigned. His grounds were, that the Executive were unable to pay a secretary, that he had been objected to by Holyoake on the ground of inebriation, and that no one else would serve gratuitously. W. J. Linton could only serve conditionally. He believed the Chartist body to be dead, and that the old policy would not bring it to life. There were but two ways for the working-classes to gain the Charter—one was by force, the other by a union with the middle-classes. For the first, they were no more prepared than they were in 1839 and 1848. The only alternative, therefore, was the second; and he advised a union, having for its object universal suffrage, and the abolition of the property qualification. Only on conditions like these, could he consent to serve the Chartist body, which he was anxious to do. The resignations brought forward an address from the remaining members, who censured Harney and Jones for leaving the Executive with a debt of thirty-seven pounds, contracted during their term of office, and for which they ought to hold themselves in part responsible. The Executive gave up the office in which they had hitherto met, in order to lessen the expense, and save future debts. The *Northern Star* now openly advised the abandonment of the Charter, and recommended an agitation for universal suffrage and the ballot. It proclaimed that the word Chartist was "offensive to both sight and taste." Ernest Jones attended the meetings of the Delegate Council, which appeared to be a body antagonistic to the Executive, and seeking to lessen its influence. Jones replied to the Executive on the money question, and stated that his resignation of office did not shift the legal responsibility of the debt from his shoulders, he was just as liable as before. Jones now denounced the *Northern Star* for its abandonment of Chartism. The editor replied that his attacks proceeded from a feeling of revenge, because he had sought to be connected with the proprietors of the *Star,* and was rejected. Jones's allusions to O'Connor were at this time very gratifying to the admirers of that gentleman. He spoke of him in terms of fulsome praise. The reason for this course is obvious. When he wanted O'Brien to plot with him the destruction of O'Connor, the latter was standing in the way of his leadership. He was in the way no longer; and as it was chiefly on the O'Connorite section that he depended for the formation of a party, it was necessary to forget his antecedents, and in order to conciliate the O'Connorites, to praise their fallen chief. Jones blamed the proprietors of the *Star* for wresting that paper out of the hands of O'Connor. Whatever might be the demerits of the *Star* itself under their management (and it was certainly anything but a Chartist paper), certainly no blame was attached to them on this score; for that paper was a losing concern before they purchased it for one hundred pounds, and there was therefore nothing dishonourable in such a bargain. It was decidedly more than it was worth. A writer in the *Star* of January 24th, alluding to Jones's attack, thus wrote :—

" He talks of undue advantage having been taken of 'the worn out warrior,' when no one has done more to wear him out than he has. He has lived on O'Connor's bounty for years. O'Connor was compelled to pay the costs of this learned gentleman's defence, and the costs of the Macnamara action to enforce it. O'Connor paid a large amount of money during his imprisonment, to exempt him from oakum-picking, and for other purposes ; and ever since his liberation, he has been his greatest slanderer and calumniator."

Jones replied to this through his *Notes to the People*, that he had never lived on O'Connor's bounty, that he only received his salary as editor of the *Star* and *Labourer*, and that he told the Defence Committee in the presence of O'Connor, that he wished to conduct his own defence, and that if one farthing was to come out of O'Connor's pocket he refused to have counsel.* Ernest Jones now denounced the system of Co-operation which had become adopted by bodies of working men, and he and Lloyd Jones held two discussions on the subject, one at Padiham and the other at Halifax. Ernest Jones maintained the proposition,—"That Co-operation cannot be carried out successfully, without first obtaining the political rights of the people." To shew Ernest Jones's opinion of all co-operative schemes, previous to the political enfranchisement of the people, we cannot do better than quote from one of his speeches during the discussion ; merely premising that he had no objection to co-operation, even at present, if conducted on a right principle ; although, even then, he was clearly of opinion that it must end in failure. He said :—

" They required the co-operation of the many for the starting in business of a few. They might co-operate to buy land, but the land bought by the many, would locate only a few ; so in the other branches of production. Now they next looked for the reproductive principle. Where was it ? Let them take the case of the Amalgamated Iron Trades, the co-operative money of the many goes to buy a business for the few. All those who subscribe will not be those who are set up in business. But for the ten thousand pounds subscribed by twelve thousand people, only two or three hundred will be at work. The reproduction of the capital again would be stopped by the competition of the capitalists, to meet which would require all the resources of the co-operative concern. Thus the reproduction of the capital of these few, was prevented from this circumstance ; they have got to compete with the capitalist, who lowers the price in competing with the co-operative manufacturer. The capitalist compels all his wage slaves to work for less, and the co-operative manufacturer is obliged to lower his profits in order to compete with the monopolist who lowers his wages. Thus, there are two insuperable difficulties for the present co-operator. It requires the capital of the many to set up the few ; the few cannot reproduce that capital, owing to the resources being crippled by the competition of the rich ; and that very competition, by lowering wages in the labour market, prevents the remainder from repeating the experiment. But suppose they had political power ; by trying co-

* He had counsel notwithstanding, and O'Connor had to pay.

operation before they got political power, they were putting the cart before the horse. The co-operative cart was very good when laden, not with profitmongering, but with christian co-operation. It was very good for piling their sugar, tea, and coffee in ; but they would stick in the mud of competition and misrule. Their's was the cart, but political power was the horse that must pull them out of the mire. With political power, they could secure the poor lands, which had so long been in the possession of the porpoise bishops and pastors. They might club their pence together till eternity before they would be able to get one capitular estate from one fat bishop ; but by a people's parliament, they could do it in an hour."

In a series of letters inserted in his *Notes,* Ernest Jones enforced the same views.

A split now occurred between Jones and Harney, who, until lately, had been most intimate friends, and political associates. Jones kept urging on the importance of a Convention, and resolutions were passed in many localities in favour of his views. He also propounded a plan for establishing a people's paper, to be conducted by himself, which, after realising two pounds per week, was to divide its profits with the editor and the Chartist body—that body of course to find the capital ; and he pledged himself to accept any other gentleman the Chartist body might select, to edit the paper with him on equal terms, if they saw the necessity of such a course. Harney, in conjunction with Gerald Massey, had brought out another *Friend of the People,* price three-halfpence —his former periodical bearing that name having ceased to exist. Twelve numbers of the new paper had appeared. In the latter numbers Harney held up the Chartist movement to scorn, maintaining that it was next to dead, and that it was, on the old policy, incapable of revival. He alluded to Ernest Jones as attempting to establish a new dictatorship for himself, and severely condemned the past policy of Chartism. The *Star* being for sale, Jones made a bid ; but Harney making a larger bid, got possession of the paper. Then Jones became furious, and Harney, in replying to him, displayed all his old vindictiveness,—pouring upon Jones a volley of denunciation, scorn, and biting satire. Jones replied in characteristic style, and these two leaders of the people, who formerly had held up each other as "chivalrous, disinterested, and patriotic," accused each other of the most mercenary motives. Harney compared Jones to the originators of Californian Gold Companies, South Sea Bubble Companies, Railway Bubble Companies, and the like ; in short asserted him to be the veriest stage trickster : and Jones retorted upon Harney that he had selfishly sought to appropriate to his own use the monies subscribed for the *Friend of the People* newspaper, by sending a circular immediately after the one announcing the abandonment of the projected paper, stating that the periodical, to be conducted by himself and Massey, was about to start, and calling for support, with the view of getting the money already subscribed for the abandoned journal. The great grievance appeared to be, that Harney had secured the *Star* from Fleming and McGowan, whom Jones declared to be two of the greatest enemies the Charter ever had. He accused Harney of outbidding him step by step. A letter from McGowan, however, showed that Jones was twice offered the paper, and a certain time given him to make up his mind. Not hearing from him by the stated time, McGowan wrote to Harney, and the bargain was concluded. He denied that there was any attempt on his part to drive a bargain, or that there was any "bidding" in the case on the part of Harney. Jones, however, sought to throw discredit on McGowan's statements, and quoted, not his letters, but very puny extracts from them, in support of his position. During this controversy, Harney prided himself on always having contended for fair play and justice in his connection with the movement. He certainly did seek that fair play and justice for himself when O'Connor assailed his freedom of expression; but no man ever did more than himself, in the days of O'Connor's power, to prevent the principle of fair play being extended to others.

The Executive had continued to decrease in numbers. A Conference was held in St. Martin's Hall called by the Financial and Parliamentary Reformers. Jones, Shaw, and Beezer attended to move and support an amendment to the resolution brought forward by that body. Holyoake, on this occasion, spoke against the policy of his colleagues, and supported the Middle-class resolution. Of course, there had all along been no mistake as to his sympathies being with that body. He revealed as much in the Convention of 1851, and he was re-elected on the Executive after his oft-repeated expression of feeling in their favour ; but we cannot help thinking, that when two resolutions were before a meeting—one for the Charter, the other for a smaller measure of reform—that it was the duty of a member of the Chartist Executive to speak and vote for the Charter, and if he could not do that to at least resign his post. At a public meeting, too, held after the Conference, Holyoake repudiated the policy of Shaw and Beezer, and the consequence was the resignation of those gentlemen ; so that the Executive now consisted only of Holyoake, LeBlond, Hunt, Arnott, Linton, and Grassby, all but the last two being in favour of the scheme of the Middle-classes. Under these circumstances Jones urged more strongly than ever the calling of a Convention, and appealed to the Manchester Council to take the initiative by calling one. That body at once responded to the invitation.

Harney entered on his office of editor of the *Star of Freedom* —the new name of his paper. He was assisted in his labours by Messrs. Massey, Kydd, Linton, and Alexander Bell. The first number was issued on the 1st of May, 1852, and the following week, despite all obstacles, there appeared the first number of the *People's Paper*, edited by Ernest Jones.

CHAPTER XIV.

The Conference, to consider the re-organization of the Chartist body, assembled at Manchester on the 17th of May, 1852. There were present William Grocott and E. Clark Cropper for Manchester, Ernest Jones and James Finlen for London, Robert Bell for Oldham, Charles Cittee for Stockport, William Hosier for Coventry, and William Cockroft for Halifax. Many other places were represented by letter. About thirty localities had pronounced in favour of the Conference, while not more than about four had pronounced against it. The delegates sat five days. They adopted the system of voluntary contributions for members of the Association—agreed to the appointment of a paid Executive of three persons, and fixed their salaries at thirty shillings per week, with travelling expenses when lecturing,—the Executive to be appointed provisionally by the Conference for three months, and afterwards elected every six months by the members. Ernest Jones proposed, and William Cockroft seconded, R. G. Gammage as one of the Provisional Executive. Clark Cropper bore testimony to Gammage's political and moral worth, and he was unanimously elected. Cittee moved, and Cockroft seconded, the appointment of Finlen. Jones, after asking if Finlen would devote all his time to the movement—declared that he knew him well, and knew that there was not a more truthful Democrat, or a more talented man in the movement. He hailed the acquisition of such an advocate with delight. Finlen having answered satisfactorily, was elected unanimously. Finlen proposed Robert Crowe, who was seconded by Hosier. Crowe had suffered two years' imprisonment for a speech delivered in 1848. Finlen bore testimony to his worth, and he was also elected unanimously. Abraham Robinson, of Wilsden, was also proposed ; as was Ernest Jones, who however objected, on the ground that editors of papers had other work to do, and he was of opinion that they were not fit persons to be on the Executive ; but should the number of three not be completed, by any of those elected declining to serve, he would act provisionally, for three months. Jones had, when denouncing the old Executive, always objected to editors serving on the Executive of the Charter Association. Crowe and Robinson declined to serve, and Jones was therefore a member of the Provisional Executive.

R. G. Gammage was a native of the town of Northampton. At 12 years of age he lost his father, and was brought up under the guidance of an affectionate mother, who had a severe struggle with poverty in bringing up a family of five children. He served a seven years' apprenticeship to the trade of a coach trimmer. It was in the establishment of his master, where, from hearing the conversations of the workmen, he first imbibed the principles of Democracy; and at the age of seventeen he became a member of the Working Men's Association. He had, during the battle of the unstamped, been a reader of several of the papers edited by Bronterre O'Brien, which occupation speedily settled his political creed. When, therefore, the Charter came before the country, he was quite prepared for its adoption. He afterwards resided, while in business, at Sherborne, Dorsetshire, Chelmsford, again at Northampton, and for a short time at Leeds, and Harrogate,—in all of which places he endeavoured to spread knowledge of democratic principles. He speedily found, however, that this course was anything but in accordance with his personal interests, in the particular line of business which he followed. In 1842, when on a visit to Newcastle-on-Tyne, at a time when almost every leading Chartist was under prosecution, he was induced to offer himself as a lecturer, and for nearly two years he visited most parts of England and Scotland. After his tour had ceased, he resided about twelve months at Northampton, and succeeded in getting the Chartists of that town well organized; there being about eighty paying members in the locality of which he was secretary. Things went on smoothly enough until he had occasion to censure the conduct of O'Connor, of whom he had been more or less an admirer; but his plain speaking upon the conduct of that gentleman brought him much ill will, although a vote of confidence in him was afterwards carried unanimously at a general meeting of the members. His friend Hollowell was the mover of the resolution, which the O'Connorites could not directly oppose; but which some of them wished withdrawn, on the ground that they considered "a vote of confidence tantamount to a vote of censure." Hollowell, however, persisted, and no one voted in opposition, while with one exception, every hand was held up in favour. After this Gammage removed to Stony Stratford, where for a short time he carried on the business of a hawker; but afterwards exchanged this for the humble occupation of a shoe-maker, preferring it, with the personal independence which to a large extent exists among the "gentle craft," to a better paid business under greater restriction.   He did not, however, find himself so independent here as he desired.   All was well enough until 1848, when, from the active part he took in the Chartist movement, he lost his employment after repeated warnings, and then removed to Buckingham, where, working for Mr. Holland, the principal shoe manufacturer of the place, he enjoyed that liberty of action, which he above all things desired.   It was in this place he resided when elected on the Executive.   When solicited by the Conference to allow himself to be elected on that body, he consented, on the ground that he would not be expected to interfere with any meetings of the Middle-class Reformers, unless such meetings were, in the strictest sense, public—that is, unless the public were appealed to, when he thought it quite legitimate to set forth the claims of the Charter.   It should be known that, although he had not always agreed with the policy of Ernest Jones, he then believed him to be honestly devoted to Democracy.   The crafty and insidious policy of the barrister blinded him to his ambition. There was such an apparent frankness in all that he wrote, that, having had but the most slender personal acquaintance with him, he believed him to be, though with many errors, a thoroughly honest man.   He was mistaken, as many had been before him.   It must be borne in mind, too, that Jones remained faithful to the Charter, while others, though still declaring themselves favourable to its principles, were weakening the Chartist body by allying themselves with the Middle-class Reformers.   He was, therefore, almost the only leading man with whom Gammage, holding the opinions he did as to all Middle-class schemes of reform not founded on the rights of man, could consistently work.   Gammage was a mem-ber of the National Reform League, presided over by O'Brien, and was heart and soul with that body ; but its operations being principally confined to the metropolis, he had but little opportunity of pushing its principles in the provinces.   Ernest Jones, too, had professed to be in favour of those principles. Gammage prepared the first address of the Executive, in which were set forth the principles of O'Brien on Land and Currency, which his colleagues, especially Jones, pronounced to be excellent.

The new Executive did not find its path altogether smooth. Shaw and Beezer resumed their seat on the old Executive, who appealed to the country to rally to their support.   The

R. G. GAMMAGE
FROM A PHOTOGRAPH

appeal was but little responded to, except in so far as the money was subscribed to clear off the debt.   At the first meeting of the Metropolitan Delegate Council there was quite a storm.   A resolution was moved approving the policy of the Manchester Conference.   Messrs. Wheeler, Stratton, Massey, Beezer, Brisck, Ferdinando, and Snaggs, stoutly opposed it. On a division the numbers were, for the resolution in favour of the Conference, sixteen; against, twelve.   At the following meeting there were forty-five delegates present— so brisk had been the creation of localities, some real, others only nominal.   Beezer and others again attended, and raised a warm opposition to the new Executive.   This meeting was followed by an aggregate meeting of the Metropolitan Chartists which was well attended.   Messrs. Hagges, Loomes, Grant, Osbourne, Wood, Morgan, Bilbin, Longshaw, Jones, Finlen, and Bronterre O'Brien, supported a resolution in favour of the policy of the Conference.   O'Brien thought that as long as the Executive acted up to the spirit of their address they would deserve most cordial support.   Charles Murray argued against the right of the Conference to elect the Executive, and moved an amendment in accordance with his views, which was supported by Messrs. Farrah and Stratton; but the resolution was carried, with few dissentients, amid loud applause. A West Riding delegate meeting was held at Bradford, to consider the policy adopted by the Conference.   Geo. White headed a formidable opposition, and a scene of the utmost disturbance ensued; ultimately the opposition left, and resolutions were passed approving of the Conference policy.   The mass of localities—most of them small in number it is true— approved the appointment of the new Executive and very few resolutions appeared against it.   The *Star of Freedom* sought to turn the whole of the proceedings into ridicule, and denounced the new Executive collectively, and two of them individually. Jones was continually held up to reprobation, and Finlen was compared to an actor at a penny theatre.   Before Harney had written thus, he should have reflected on his own position in former times; for certainly, in the early stages of the movement, his many antics on the platform were the sport of the more sober leaders of the people: but like a ruined debauchee, who has indulged in pleasure to satiety, and shut himself up in seclusion from the world, Harney was the bitterest in denunciation of those faults in which he had formerly indulged.   It should be stated, moreover, in justice to Finlen, that allowing Harney's assertion as to his being a mere actor to be true, he was an actor that always laboured under a considerable share of feeling and was enthusiastic in all that he advanced.   His enthusiasm was a reality, not a sham,—which is more than can be said for some political stagers.

O'Connor had now arrived at a lamentable state of mind. In the Spring he had been cruelly imprisoned for seven days for an assault, when it was evident that his mind was in an unsound state. Reynolds laid his case before the magistrate who committed him, but the statement produced no influence on his decision. O'Connor afterwards went to America, but returned to London, and attended the law courts, interrupting the business by wild but humorous remarks, which caused him to be removed. In the House of Commons his conduct was equally strange. He threw the House into confusion, by accosting a large number of members, and shaking hands with every one he met. He was committed at length to the custody of the Sergeant-at-Arms, and medically examined. It having been proved beyond a doubt that he was insane, he was ordered to be discharged ; and in a few hours the once powerful, energetic leader of the Chartists,—the man who seemed as though he could defy every blast of adversity, and set at defiance the assaults of the sternest foe, was an inmate of a lunatic asylum. The complications of his Land Plan, and the loss of that popularity, to gain which had been the labour of his life, but of which he had been stripped by the machinations of Jones, Harney, Clark, Doyle, Dixon, McGrath, and Leach, amongst his whilom followers, led to the loss of his reason. Alas ! how fleeting is the breath of the multitude, when that multitude is uninformed. One day the vault of heaven rings with their cheers, the next day the applause may be exchanged for groans or apathy, if they find not their idol all they had anticipated. One day " Hosanna ;" the next " Crucify him." When sometime after O'Connor's removal to Dr. Tuke's Asylum, Mr. Sweet and the men of Nottingham attempted a national subscription on his behalf, they could raise no more for their fallen champion than the miserable sum of thirty-two pounds, most of which was subscribed in Nottingham alone.

The new Executive proceeded with its labours. Gammage started almost immediately for the West of England and Wales, where he addressed public meetings, and sought to extend the organization. He was invited to stand as a candidate for Exeter at the general election in 1852 ; but his friends afterwards abandoned their design. He travelled and spoke at Bristol, Tiverton, Torquay, Totness, Ashburton, Plymouth, St. Austle, Truro, Redruth, Penzance, and many other towns in the West of England,—as well as visiting Merthyr Tydvil, Llanidloes, Newtown, and Swansea, in Wales.

Finlen issued an address to the electors and non-electors of

Coventry, and he would doubtless have obtained the show of hands, but the Whigs persuaded the Chartists that if they took their candidate to the hustings, they would have to bear a share of the expenses, so Finlen withdrew. His exertions were not confined to Coventry ; he visited and lectured at Hanley, Manchester, Staleybridge, Halifax, Newcastle-on-Tyne, and many other places. Ernest Jones again contested the borough of Halifax. At the nomination twenty thousand persons were in attendance. Jones delivered what was considered by good judges to be one of the most powerful and magnificent orations ever listened to. He held that heaving mass at one moment breathless, and silent almost as the grave ; then he excited a burst of frantic cheering ; and again he drew from the meeting terrific groans for the whig candidate, Sir Charles Wood. Out of that immense multitude only about five hundred held up their hands for Sir Charles, while thousands upon thousands declared for Jones ; but the poll reversed this decision, for Jones polled but thirty-eight votes. What a miserable farce of representation.

The election of the new Executive by the members showed, for Gammage 922, Finlen 839, Jones 739, Bligh 95, M'Douall 51, Cropper 20. The Executive elected as their secretary William Grocott, who had been previously appointed by the Conference. It was on this election of the Executive that Gammage began to see the real design of Jones. After all that he had urged on the impropriety of electing editors on the Executive—after writing upon that impropriety week after week, he consented to be a candidate for the office, though there were five other candidates in the field. As soon as Gammage saw that he was put in nomination, he immediately wrote, strongly urging him for consistency sake not to consent to election. Jones never replied to this letter ; but remarked to Grocott, " Gammage is perfectly right in his argument, but he is a bad general ;"—the bad generalship consisted in urging him to a course of consistency. When will Democrats learn that consistency is at the very foundation of good generalship ? Jones consented to serve on two conditions,—one was, that he should be master of his own time, and the other that he be unpaid. There was no necessity for imposing the latter condition—Jones knowing well that such was the drain upon the Chartist body for the support of the *People's Paper*, that there were not likely to be any funds to pay him. Only twenty-seven pounds was subscribed to the Charter Fund for the first quarter ; thirteen pounds of this went to pay the secretary his salary, and all that Gammage got for his three months' hard work, was little more than two weeks' salary. Jones could, then, very well exact the condition of working without pay. After he was elected he told his constituents that, remembering his former advice about the election of editors on the Executive, he should have felt most distressed and pained had they not honoured him with their suffrages, as he felt convinced that the greater part of his ability to serve them would have been neutralised. He aspired to greater usefulness and activity than to sit at a desk as the recording machine of the movements of others. He would be a voice, not an echo—the actor of deeds, not the scribe of others' actions. But he forgot to explain how it was that he objected to serve when proposed at the Conference, except for a limited period, until another could be obtained. The simple truth is, that his objection was nothing but a sham. It was not long before thirteen of the members of the *People's Paper* Committee, including some of the oldest Democrats of the metropolis, separated from Ernest Jones, and charged him with reckless mismanagement of the funds of the paper. He called a public meeting, and read a statement respecting the matter at issue, amid great confusion; and he afterwards published his defence, which was deemed satisfactory by the majority of the Chartist body. The price of the 20th number of the *People's Paper* was raised to fourpence—it still being carried on at a loss. The thirteen seceders from the Committee availed themselves of an opportunity to oppose Jones at a public meeting held at the John-street Institution, to hear addresses from the Executive. They, in conjunction with others, had issued a bill calling on the "friends of truth" to attend. Messrs. Straight, Parker, Ruffy Ridley, Athol Wood, Gerald Massey, and many others, were in attendance; and when Ernest Jones made his appearance, he was much groaned at and hooted, though loudly cheered by the great majority of the meeting. Charles Murray was called to the chair, and first introduced R. G. Gammage, who was received with almost unanimous applause. When Jones went forward, he was again met with a volley of groans and hisses, which were responded to by loud cheers from the majority. He spoke at some length. Richard Hart moved a resolution:—

"That this meeting is of opinion, that no confidence can be placed in the success of any democratic movement, while Mr. Ernest Jones is connected therewith."

The speaker went considerably round about his subject, and was frequently interrupted. At last he made way for O'Brien, who was loudly called for, and who moved a resolution to the effect, that no democratic movement could succeed, that had not for its object the destruction of landlordism, usury, and profitmongering—which could only be brought about by the nationalization of land and credit, and the establishment of a sound system of currency, and equitable exchange. Ernest Jones seconded O'Brien's resolution, which was carried with one dissentient amid loud cheering. O'Brien argued during his speech, that the Paper Committee had no right to foist the disputes between Jones and themselves upon a meeting called for another purpose. A vote of thanks to the chairman concluded this stormy meeting.

Gammage proceeded on another tour through Coventry, North Wales, Manchester, Halifax and neighbourhood, and Newcastle-on-Tyne, where he addressed a meeting in company with Ernest Jones, who had been on a tour through Edinburgh, Glasgow, Dundee, Aberdeen, and many other Scottish towns, and who lectured on his return at Shields, Sunderland, Barnsley, Rochdale, and other places. Gammage succeeded Jones in Scotland, going as far as Dundee and Blairgowrie. He stayed a month in Scotland, lecturing nearly every day during the time. Returning to Newcastle again he addressed meetings in that district for nearly three weeks, and then returned to the South, lecturing on his way through, and arriving in London about the middle of May. On the 18th of June he commenced a tour in company with Ernest Jones through the provinces. They confined themselves chiefly to the North and the Midlands, but visited some of the Western towns as well. The Executive had, before starting, prepared the draft of a petition to Parliament for the Charter, which was adopted at all the meetings they attended. There were six open-air demonstrations made during this tour—on Blackstone Edge; Westhill Park, Halifax ; Newcastle Town Moor ; Mountsorrel, Leicestershire; Nottingham Forest; and Kennington Common. In-door meetings were held at Manchester, Staleybridge, Rochdale, Oldham, Bradford, Todmorden, Bacup, Newcastle, Shields, Darlington, Leicester, Barnsley, Northampton, Coventry, Birmingham, Worcester, Cheltenham, Bilston, Newton, Llanidloes, Hanley, Longton, and many smaller places. Several of the meetings were held in Town Halls. At Rochdale, Thomas Livesey (chief constable,)—a gentleman who had for many years been a warm and untiring friend to the Chartist cause—occupied the chair. This tour continued over a period of six weeks.

While Jones and Gammage were at work in some places, Finlen was lecturing at Exeter, Torquay, Cheltenham, and other places in the West ; and after their return to London, Gammage proceeded, with his brother Thomas, to Exeter and Torquay, where they addressed meetings in favour of the petition, which in both places was adopted. The whole of the petitions were presented by Apsley Pellatt ; but neither he, nor any other member, could at that time be prevailed on to make a motion on the subject. J. M. Cobbett was the only one who promised to second a motion if made. Scholefield was of opinion that nothing short of a great national movement would make any impression on Parliament.

After Messrs. Jones, Finlen, and Gammage had attended meetings in the metropolis, the latter proceeded to Scotland, and lectured in several places, returning to and lecturing at New-castle, and other towns in the North of England; after which he spent six weeks lecturing to the miners of North Stafford-shire. Towards winter Ernest Jones started on a tour, com-mencing with the Eastern Counties, afterwards taking the Midlands, and then journeying towards the North. At that time thousands of the working class in the manufacturing districts were locked out from the mills because they had asked for a rise of wages. Jones had excellent meetings wherever he went, and applied himself assiduously to a discussion of the Labour Question, taking up an idea, which had been broached in *Lloyd's Paper*, for the meeting of a Labour Parliament. Gammage supported the calling of the same, as did Finlen, the other member of the Executive. But the former did so on the understanding that the parliament was to meet to discuss the question of political and social rights, which Jones had assured him was his object. Gammage's sur-prise, therefore, as well as his disappointment was great, when Jones propounded a scheme of co-operation in land and manu-factures, in utter opposition to the views laid down by him in the discussions with Lloyd Jones, and on many other occasions. Before, he had always held up to ridicule the idea of the people gaining social amelioration without political power;—now in imitation of O'Connor when propounding his Land Plan, he laid down that his co-operative scheme would get the political power which was wanted. If they adopted it, the people would "get the Charter laid at their feet before they had time to ask." He supported his plan with a piece of the veriest special pleading ever used by a trafficking lawyer. Despite Jones's inconsistency, nearly forty delegates assembled at Man-chester; and adopted his plan ; and an Executive, consisting of Finlen, George Harrison, Abraham Robinson, James Williams, and Mr. Hoggs, with Ernest Jones as an honorary member, was appointed by the Labour Parliament. The people had, however, been too much warned by the occurrences of the past, to fall into the scheme of a man who had always previously pronounced such schemes as worthless, so long as

the people were without political power ; and who, it was
evident, had only "jumped Jim Crow" to serve some purpose
of his own; for these sudden conversions are always suspicious.
The plan did not take. ·The contributions—which, according
to Jones, were to amount to five million pounds a-year —were
not sufficient to pay the salaries of the Executive, who were
involved in a debt of eighteen pounds, which rested upon the
shoulders of a single individual. When Jones found that his
bubble was not sufficiently attractive, he blew it to nothing,
and advised the people to send no monies but what were sufficient to pay off the debt ; and he instanced the failure of his
own scheme, which was going to lead the people into paradise,
as a proof of their growing intelligence, as they were becoming
more convinced that political power was the only means to the
great end they had in view. Matchless impudence! was ever
trickery more transparent?

Gammage's connection with the Chartist Executive was
now about to draw to a close. While he was at Newcastle
the following resolution was passed by the Chartist body.
John Robson in the chair. Moved by James Watson:—

"That it is the opinion of this locality, that in order to make
the *People's Paper* a paying organ the time has come when
another talented and popular editor must be joined with Mr. E.
Jones, upon equal principles."

This resolution was sent to the *People's Paper*. Another
resolution was passed, which was moved by Andrew Foggon
Bain, to the effect that O'Brien be written to, to know if he
would consent to write in the *People's Paper*. The sin of these
resolutions (and it was a mortal sin in the eyes of Ernest Jones),
was at once placed upon the shoulders of Gammage. Just at
that time an event occurred which favoured Jones's wish for
Gammage's destruction. John Days, secretary to the National
Reform League, had written to a friend—and in his letter had
made some allusion to sums of money held by Jones, which he
had received towards a testimonial on behalf of O'Brien. The
friend alluded to construed Days' letter into an attack on
Jones's honesty, and the latter was heartily glad of this occur-
rence, to aid him in defeating the Newcastle resolution. A
paragraph appeared on the subject in the *People's Paper*:
Gammage was in Rochdale, and the paragraph was pointed
out to him by one of Jones's friends. Guessing at Jones's
motive, he expressed his disbelief in the statement, and said
that he had particular reasons for not believing it, and that
those who were in the secret knew better than to believe it
without further evidence. On these words a false and scandalous document was sent from Rochdale to Jones, who used

it to his own advantage.   It was signed by five persons, whereas
only one of them was present at the conversation in question.
Malignity breathed in its every line.   Gammage wrote to the
person to whom Days' letter had been addressed, for a sight
of it, just for his satisfaction; but he never got his wish complied with.   Then came a series of articles from Jones, week
after week, endeavouring to make his readers believe that
O'Brien, Days, Gammage, and Co., were in a conspiracy to
ruin his character, so as to wrest the paper from his control.
A letter from Days was mutilated, and just such extracts inserted as suited the honest editor's purpose.   Gammage's letters
in defence, were either inserted so as to spoil the sense or
kept back until the editor's poison had had time to circulate;
and all this time honest Mr. Jones professed to be giving all his
opponents fair play.   His first comment on a letter from Gammage was a mixture of cant and low cunning.   He was anxious,
he said, for the breach to be healed; but it was only on the
condition that his victim should be his abject despicable tool;
and when he found his plan did not succeed, his malignity
knew no bounds.

The election for the Executive was about to take place, and an
effort must therefore be made to prevent Gammage's election on
that body.   To that end every nerve was strained by his unscru-
pulous enemy.   When he found that Gammage would only serve
on the Executive as being responsible to his constituents alone,
and that he refused the degrading patronage of the vile schemer
who was belying his character, there was no alternative but to
get him off; calumny therefore was heaped upon calumny, and
he was made responsible, not only for what he was himself made
to say and do, but also for all that Jones in his reckless assertions sought to father upon O'Brien.   At Jones's solicitation, resolutions poured in from the localities denouncing the co-editor-
ship.   He left them no alternative ; for he told them that if they
were favourable to it, he would retire from the paper.   He
placed the names of other men prominently before his readers,
and they were proposed as candidates for the Executive.   He
delayed announcing the time for nominating the Executive until
after his poison had taken deep root.   But despite all these
things, votes poured in for Gammage rather more numerous
than Jones desired.   At the time for closing the poll, the votes,
as was shewn by the *People's Paper*, placed Gammage in a
majority of 17 over Mr. Shaw.   Contrary, then, to the rule
of the Association, which says the election of the Executive
shall take place every six months, the Committee postponed the
closing of the lists for a week ; but though Gammage was of
course one of the Committee, he was never consulted.   Still

this did not succeed, for the following week 501 votes appeared
on his behalf, while Shaw had but 456.   But as the votes were
being summed up, in stepped Mr. Antill, one of the London
shoemakers.   "Well," said he, "is Gammage out?"   "No,"
said Jones, with apparent unconcern, "I think he has the
majority."   "What majority has he?" rejoined Antill.   "I
believe about 19," replied Jones.   "Oh, then," said Antill,
"he is out, for I have 64 votes against him from the ladies'
shoemakers;" and he pulled a paper out of his pocket to that
effect.   This man was one of the scrutineers of the votes.
"Well, I must confess that I am glad," said Jones, "it will
save all further trouble; for if he had been elected, Finlen and
I would have resigned."   These sixty-four votes looked very
much like a juggle.   The ladies' shoemakers had not been heard
of for a long time in connection with the Chartist movement,
and it appeared from the above, that these votes would never
have been given in, if the object could have been gained without
them.   So ashamed was Jones of these votes, that he did not
insert them in his next paper; but in the following one, a week
after the decision of the scrutineers had been published, he
published among a list which he said had arrived too late, these
same sixty-four votes; the fact being that they were the very
votes which decided the election.   Numbers of other votes
which were accepted by the scrutineers, Jones had too much
discretion to publish; while those that were published, were in
many instances published twice, so as to confuse the reader in
examining the lists.   The difference between the published lists
and that decided as genuine by the scrutineers, was as follows:

PEOPLE'S PAPER LIST.

Jones.	Finlen.	Gammage.	Shaw.	Williams.	Royall.
759	637	435	361	194	28

SCRUTINEERS' LIST.

Jones.	Finlen.	Gammage.	Shaw.	Williams.	Royall.
942	829	501	520	195	28

DIFFERENCE.

Jones.	Finlen.	Gammage.	Shaw.	Williams.	Royall.
183	192	66	159	1	0

It will be seen in what quarters the greatest disparity lay.
These numbers were given in a printed circular issued by the
Soho Locality of the National Charter Association.   J. Murray,
a scrutineer appointed by that locality, was so convinced of the
juggle, that he moved:—
      "We, the scrutineers, appointed to cast up the votes for
the Executive, request that all the votes for the Executive,
not already published, be published in next week's *People's
Paper*."
      This straightforward resolution did not meet with a seconder,

and Murray refused to sign the report of the scrutineers; a course which met the hearty and unanimous approval of those by whom he was appointed, and who refused to recognize the new Executive. Twenty-three of the Cheltenham Locality sent a protest against the postponement of the election, and declared that they would not recognize the new Executive; and a similar protest was sent from Ripponden, by Messrs S. Moores, H. Holland, J. Simpson, C. Sutcliffe, and J. Whiteley. Gammage also sent a protest against the postponement; but Jones replied, that as it was decided on by two members of the Executive, the protest would have been better reserved. This however, was a falsehood, for Finlen declared that he alone took that responsibility—that Jones had nothing to do with it. Jones acted the part of a vile schemer throughout the affair. The way in which he treated two resolutions sent him for insertion, is an instance of his love of justice ! When the affair of the paper broke out, two public meetings were held in the Eclectic Institute, with regard to his letter, and were addressed by O'Brien with reference to the whole case ; and the following resolution was unanimously adopted:—

" That the conduct of Mr. Ernest Jones, as evinced by the *People's Paper* of the last three weeks, is disgraceful to that journal and to himself; that his pretended charges and insinuations against Messrs. Days, Gammage, and O'Brien, are wholly unprovoked, and without a shadow of fact to stand upon,—the real object of such charges being, manifestly, to excite sympathy and subscriptions for his newspaper. That Mr. Days' correspondence has been foully misrepresented— he having written no secret letters to Chartist secretaries, nor said aught of Jones, in secret letters or otherwise, but what he desires Jones to publish ; and that the whole of what Jones has uttered about a pretended conspiracy against his newspaper, is a tissue of wretched fictions and deliberate falsehoods, known to be such by the London Democrats. This meeting, moreover, is fully satisfied—not less from Jones's general character, than from the editorial articles in question,—that the whole affair has been got up by Mr. Jones from purely mercenary and ambitious motives, in order to get rid of men whose integrity he fears, and to extort more money from the Chartist public intelligence under false pretences, agreeably to his habitual practices."

The members of the Soho Locality of the Charter Association, adopted the following :—

" That this locality views with feelings of indignation Mr. Jones's conduct towards Messrs. Gammage and O'Brien, in this week's paper. We know that such remarks and assertions are totally uncalled for and unfounded ; for, after dispassionate and unprejudiced consideration of all the evidence at present before us, we are firmly convinced that Mr. Gammage is an injured man ; and as for the assertions about Mr. O'Brien, we cannot, in justice to that gentleman, do otherwise than declare their entire falsity,—for owing to our proximity to the Eclectic Institute, it is a fact that some or other of our members are present at all Mr. O'Brien's discourses.   We are thereby in a position to state, and bound in justice to assert, that the imputations cast upon Mr. O'Brien publicly in the *People's Paper*, are gross misrepresentations and falsehoods ; and we say, in conclusion, we consider Mr. Jones bound, in common honesty, to give the gentlemen concerned, every opportunity to publicly defend their injured characters, and that his determination to exclude so important a subject after next week, is premature, unjust, and unwise."

The first of these resolutions was entirely burked, and of the second, just four lines were inserted.   Gammage was invited by the Soho Democrats, and the members of the National Reform League, to London.   At a public meeting in the Eclectic Institute, he laid the case of the *People's Paper*, Ernest Jones, and himself, before a numerous audience, among whom were some of Jones's supporters.

Jones took another tour in the summer of 1854, and displayed the most unpardonable extravagance of speech.   At Newcastle-on-Tyne he delivered two lectures.   His largest audience consisted of three hundred and seven persons, whom he told that the Charter was all but obtained—that nothing could prevent it becoming law in less than twelve months; and he repeated the same at a meeting of friends after his lecture. Miserable deluder!   When will Democrats learn that these empty boasters are their veriest foes—that they keep away thousands of sensible men by their reckless extravagance and impudent assumptions!   We admire honest enthusiasm, but we despise the miserable boasts of an artificial patriot.   Jones had lately been attempting to resuscitate the movement by sympathy for the refugees, and he actually succeeded in carrying an amendment for the Charter, at a meeting called at the London Tavern.   There was also a great meeting held at St. Martin's Hall, to promote the alliance of the people when Mr. Herzen, the Russian and several other refugees, spoke in the language of their respective countries, and their speeches were afterwards translated into English.   Ernest Jones presided at this meeting, and Finlen and G. J. Holyoake were the English speakers.

The National Charter Association had ceased to exist, for it was without any elected head. After Jones, Finlen, and Shaw were declared elected on the Executive, the latter only attended two or three meetings, not through any fault of his own, but because there were no funds to enable him to lecture ; but though without funds, the London Chartists had the liberality to reprimand him for not performing his duties as a member of the Executive, and they got reprimanded in turn by Jones, for not furnishing the means of agitation, a rather bitter reproach, coming from such a quarter ; for such was the never-ending drain upon the resources of the body for the support of his paper, that it was next to impossible to find funds for anything else. As that paper showed, not much short of eight hundred pounds had been subscribed up to that time to keep it in existence, exclusive of all the gifts which Jones dignified by the name of loans. Among the latter was sixty-one pounds ten shillings lent by the Chartists of Newcastle, who had some difficulty in getting a receipt from that gentleman, acknowledging the debt. The paper was a mystery, which puzzled even some of Jones's friends. For instance, when the affairs of the paper were under discussion, in alluding to Watson's offer, Jones said that Gammage might have known that the paper was printed nearly at cost price by McGowan ; yet, after McGowan's death, the paper being twice removed, a reduction of two pounds in the cost of printing was effected on each occasion ; so that if McGowan printed it nearly at cost price, it must have been printed for under cost price afterwards. For nearly three years that paper existed, and it was nearly always at paying point. Jones once announced that it actually paid its way, still the cry was " money to clear off arrears ; and unless money is speedily found, the circulation will fall once more." Nothing more probable than this ! Ernest Jones was not the man to lead a great movement ; he had intellect and energy, but he was ambitious and mercenary. He must command the movement, or he would reduce it to nothing. He might have got up a little ephemeral excitement, but a substantial movement, never. If, perchance, he temporarily rallied a power, it would only be to inflict the same misfortunes as were suffered under the reign of O'Connor, of whom he was a ridiculous imitator. Excitement, persecution, imprisonment, transportation—and then another relapse into apathy. Surely we ought to work for better results than these, after all our years of agitation. Finlen had been in the country lecturing, but with no great results in the large towns, where the stillness of apathy reigned among the people. He was the only lecturer who was actively working with Jones.

Thomas Cooper joined the body in the beginning of 1853, a difference, however, on the question of social rights, expressed by Gammage in respectful terms, and by Jones in very strong language, caused him to leave the Association. While the National Reform League existed in the metropolis O'Brien lectured twice a week at the Eclectic Institute. A Democratic Association, for the establishment of political and social justice, was formed in Newcastle, of which R. G. Gammage was the secretary. Julian Harney was secretary of the Republican Brotherhood, which was started in the same town. There was then no Chartist Executive.

We conclude our task, which has often been a painful one. In doing so, let us sum up the names of some of the men, who in past days guided the Chartist movement; and, as far as we know, state their fate. O'Connor died insane in a lunatic asylum, in 1855. John Collins sank into physical weakness and imbecility, and died, we believe, in 1850. Atwood, after the follies of 1839, retired from Parliament into private life. William Lovett was proprietor of the National Hall, Holborn, and died in 1877. Vincent became a lecturer on Civil and Religious Liberty, the Commonwealth, and other subjects. Douglas became editor of the *Birmingham Journal*, and Edmonds was town clerk at the same place. Mr. Doubleday, one of the talented writers in the *Northern Liberator*, died in Newcastle in 1870, respected by all classes and parties. The Rev. Wm. Hill became editor of some trade journal at Edinburgh. The Rev. Dr. Wade died before 1854. Dr. Taylor, as before intimated, died in Ireland. Robert Lowery was engaged in lecturing on Temperance and Education. James Williams was a bookseller, and member of the Sunderland Town Council. His young and earnest friend, Binns, emigrated to New Zealand, where he died of consumption. Hetherington died of cholera. Moir carried on the business of a tea-dealer in Glasgow, and was a member of the town council. Ebenezer Elliott, the poet, died in 1849. Abraham Duncan emigrated to America. John Fraser devoted his life to music. The Rev. J. R. Stephens was in 1854 still a preacher in the neighbourhood of Ashton ; while the Tory Oastler, lived at Norwood, and though full of years, conducted a periodical called *The Home*, which took for its motto, "The Altar, the Throne, and the Cottage." Dr. Fletcher practised as a surgeon at Bury. R. J. Richardson carried on the trade of a bookseller at Manchester. Peter Bussey emigrated to America in 1839, where he has ever since remained. John Fielden died soon after his defeat at the Oldham election, in 1847. M'Douall emigrated to Australia in the summer of 1853, where he died. R. K. Philp resided in London, and was, we believe, proprietor of some periodicals. Bairstow, Campbell, and Mason emigrated to America. James Leach carried on the trade of printing at Manchester. Doyle, we believe, was agent to an Assurance Company at Birmingham. William Beesley carried on the business of an auctioneer at Accrington. William Jones, of Liverpool, emigrated to America, but returned, and we believe resided in his native town. John West was, the last time we heard of him, residing at Manchester. Arthur O'Neill was minister of a baptist chapel at Birmingham. Clark, McGrath, Wheeler, and Dixon were, we believe, connected with Assurance Companies, and except the latter, who resided at Wigan, were living in the metropolis. Reynolds carried on business as a journalist, his newspaper circulating 50,000 copies weekly. Beezer emigrated to Australia in 1852. Thomas Cooper died in 1892. Besides these, there are a host of men once active in the Chartist Movement, who are resting in the tomb; and a large host of others, who emigrated to other lands. This vast emigration has doubtless, among causes already pointed out, tended to weaken the Chartist body, by depriving it of its leaders. We cannot contemplate the past movements of all these men without deep and sometimes painful feelings. May we never be slow to imitate their virtues; and above all, may their failings serve as beacons to warn us off the rocks on which they were so often wrecked, and on which they wrecked (though but temporarily) the noble cause which they espoused.

APPENDIX A.

Mr. William Ryder has written us a letter containing some explanations and denials. He says that he did not address the meeting at which he was elected; only two of the candidates (O'Connor and Pitkeithly) addressed the meeting. He only reached the outskirts of the meeting when it terminated, and though secretary to the Radical Association of Leeds, he never pushed himself into notoriety; nor was he aware that he had been elected, or even proposed, until the meeting had concluded. He wishes to know what meeting we refer to at page 107, attended by himself, Harney, and Marsden. It was the meeting which was publicly made the subject of complaint in the Convention. Mr. Ryder states that he tendered his resignation before the meeting was held on Peep Green, referred to in page 113, at which meeting he was not present. On more particularly referring to our notes, we find that the resignation of Mr. Ryder was read at the meeting in question, and was accepted. He says, in reference to physical force :—

"For thirty-five years I have belonged to the same school, and still believe it to be the bounden duty of every man to possess arms, and to learn their use ; but while propounding this doctrine, I have invariably opposed partial and premature outbreaks, contending that a want of unity incapacitated us from compassing our object; and that we lacked this unity in consequence of man-worship, and the treachery and bickerings of self-constituted leaders, and idle adventurers. I repeat, that I still hold the same doctrine of the necessity of man being armed and trained to enable him to cope with domestic enemy, or foreign foe. I never thought your moral force, your rams horns, or your silver trumpets would level the citadel of corruption. When I see a bold united people,
            'With banners unfurled,
            Resolved for their freedom to die,'
Then, and then only, shall I have hope of my country's salvation. I glory in being of this good old school, and if on the brink of starvation, I would prefer the bullet of a physical force opponent to the speech of a moral force comforter."

LETTER OF THOMAS COOPER.

We have received the following letter from Mr. Cooper, to which we gladly give insertion :—

10, Devonshire Place, Stoke Newington Green,
DEAR SIR,   February 26th, 1855.

I wish to correct part of the statements concerning myself in your 'History.' I do not blame you for want of their correctness. It must be expected that misstatements will arise out of such a warfare as ours has been. You say I was 'O'Connor-mad' in 1842, and while heading the Leicester Chartists. I do not controvert the phrase, for I think we were all mad, more or less, at that time. I only want to shew that there was *method in my madness;* and that my course in Leicester was not so utterly unlike the rest of my life, as to be altogether that of a *blackguard:* for really, if your statement be left uncontradicted, such must be the impression with the majority of your readers.

I was about to return to London, on leaving my employment on the *Leicestershire Mercury,* in the early part of 1841, when the Chartists entreated me to stay, and conduct the little periodical they had just started, the *Midland Counties Illuminator.* I had already written for them, and they believed my heart was with them. I consented to stay ; and if I know my own heart at all, my consent sprung from the purest and most devoted self-sacrifice for the poor and oppressed. The little paper would have stopped because they could no longer raise funds to carry it on ; but they gave it into my hands entirely, and I borrowed and begged money to carry it on. I also began to deliver Sunday evening addresses in the market-place, in the form of sermons, partly religious and partly political ; and these discourses were attended by thousands. When the general election of 1841 approached, the Whigs— knowing the Chartists would oppose the return of Easthorpe and Ellis—intimidated the printer of our little periodical, and it had to be stopped. Nor could I find any other printer in Leicester who dared to print it. At last one was found who had only a small collection of poor types ; and, rather than be beaten, I started a small halfpenny paper, and—as it was a tiny light compared with the *Illuminator*—I called it the *Chartist Rushlight.* This was carried on weekly, until the election took place, when I was proposed on the hustings as the Universal Suffrage candidate. While I was addressing the crowd, one of the Whig party approached me with a huge tin extinguisher fixed to a pole and attempted to place it on my head—*to extinguish the rushlight!* The Whigs laughed, and their members were returned ; but now I changed the title of our weekly halfpenny paper, and, to shew that I would not be ' put out,' called it the *Extinguisher*. The paper in that form continued to the end of 1841.

Just before the election I had succeeded, though with some difficulty, in getting a house and shop, in a tolerably central situation, and here I published my little paper, sold the *Northern Star* and other periodicals, opened coffee-rooms, and also commenced the sale of bread. I still continued my Sunday night addresses in the market-place, divided Leicester into districts, began to press the enrolment of Chartist members ; and the consequence was that I grew popular, and I may say powerful, in a certain sense.

You observe (on page 203 of your ' History ') that there was another party of Chartists in Leicester, too intelligent to bow to my dictatorship. Now the most intelligent men of the body were with me : witness my beloved and most faithful friends up to the day of their deaths—the two poets, John Bramwich and William Jones. I do not like even to mention old quarrels, much less to revive them. I and John Markham (whom you name on the same page) have long ago renewed our friendship ; but if I must state the truth, it was not their ' intelligence,' but their friendship for Markham (their old leader, whom they considered I had supplanted) which made the other party of Chartists arise. They were never more than few in number, and remained at the old meeting place,— a very little room,—while we, when the winter came on, and I could no longer talk in the market-place, hired a large room attached to the Amphitheatre, and which (from the time of its being built, years before) had always been called the 'Shake-sperean Room.' As there were now two societies, and I liked the name of Shakespeare, (for which I trust I shall be excused) I proposed that our society should be called the ' Shakesperean Brigade of Leicester Chartists.' Thus, it was from the room in which we met, that we took our name. The term 'brigade' was very commonly used by Chartists, in lieu of ' society;' and as for the title of ' General,' it was given me by admiring and loving working men. I adopted it in sport, at first, but afterwards it was not easy to lay it aside.

With midwinter, 1841-2, the severest distress commenced in Leicester. I had seen wretchedness enough before ; but now, when employ ceased for thousands, and that for months, the distress was appalling. You say (on page 202) that when the people followed me through the streets, they halted at the doors of the shopkeepers to receive their charitable contributions. I assure you that is a great mistake. I never led a begging procession ; but I gave away bread, and gave credit for bread to many who were never able to pay me—until I owed my baker sixty-six pounds. I claim no praise for so doing. It was rather a part of my 'madness.' I ought to have been 'just before I was generous.' I know it; and yet *that* is the lesson I have, all my way through life, found the most difficult to practise; and I am afraid it is now too late for me to alter—unless I could get a new nature.

Amidst the discouragements of that winter, I ventured to start a Sunday School for adults, men and boys. Many scores attended, and our lesson books were the Old and New Testaments, Channing's Self-Culture, and two or three of his Essays besides, Campbell on the Corn-Laws, &c., &c. Bramwich, Jones, and others of our most intelligent members, assisted me in the conduct of this school. It was broken up when the spring came and discontent grew more rife; but, if I had remained another winter in Leicester, I purposed to revive it. The spring of 1842 was fearful. The lack of employ continued; and the people grew either despairing or threatening. I continued to enrol Chartist Members, old and young, till we had three thousand names on our register. I also began to address the people on week-nights, and on Sunday mornings and afternoons, as well as on Sunday evenings. On some fine evenings we would sing through the streets, to shew our numbers, and also to vex our middle-class opponents. But these were not '*daily tasks,*' as you term them; and they were always harmless, for we never committed any violence. I was greatly puzzled and astonished when I read (on the same page of your 'History'), that 'when Cooper was unable to head these processions, another man took his place, dressed in a military suit;' for I never saw or heard of such a man. Yet a Leicester friend reminds me that something took place in the spring of 1842, which your informant (whoever he may be) has distorted into the raw-head and bloody-bones shape of a 'man taking my place, dressed in a military suit.' The crowds of poor applying for relief at the Board of Guardians became so great, that a mill was set up at the Union-House, as a test of willingness to work. The mill had to be worked in a very laborious way and the poor men, feeling they were degraded because they were poor, formed a band with a man at their head who sometimes wore an old cast-off soldier's cap—and so used to beg, when the day's degrading labour (for which they received the most miserable pittance) was over. But this was no Chartist affair: the men were not connected with us; and the man with the soldier's cap never 'took my place,' nor was he ever a Chartist.

I said that my paper, called the *Extinguisher*, was carried on to the end of 1841. For a few weeks I published no paper, hoping work would begin again to be given out to the men, and distress would lessen. But I was wearied with waiting, and soon commenced the *Commonwealthsman,* a weekly three-halfpenny paper. This succeeded well for a short time, but I was compelled to give it up when the summer drew near. This succession of little papers, I should observe, was a source of strength to Chartism, and also to the cause of Labour—for the papers afforded the working men a means of exposing their wrongs, in the matter of wages, stoppages, &c. Moreover, there was always a 'Poet's Corner,' to which Bramwich and Jones were regular contributors; and their contributions (usually in the form of Chartist Hymns) were afterwards collected into the 'Shakespearean Chartist Hymn Book,' and were sung at our meetings.

This reminds me to correct another passage on page 203 of your 'History.' You say,—'On the release of his great idol, Cooper composed a song, to which he gave the the title of the Lion of Freedom,' &c. I did not compose the song nor any line of it, nor did I give it a title. The song first appeared in the columns of the *Northern Star,* and was understood to be the composition of a Welsh female Chartist. A Leicester working man (Valentine Woolley) first set it to an air (or rather to a fragment of the melody of a glee); we adopted it; and, it is perfectly true, that I usually introduced it at our meetings—nay, I spread it wherever I went, either into the Leicestershire villages, or into such towns as Sheffield, Nottingham, &c.

And now a word or two respecting my attachment to O'Connor. The people taught me this attachment. I did not teach it to them. I was assured they had no hope in Chartism, but in him. He won me also, by his letters, and by his conversation, in the few interviews I had with him, during my Leicester chieftainship. I saw reason in the after time to alter my opinion of him; but during the period I am referring to, I held that *union* was the absolute requisite for Chartist success; and as the people cleaved to O'Connor as their leader, I became a foe to all who opposed him as the fomenters of *disunion.* For this reason I opposed O'Brien. And I regret that my opposition was not enacted in the fairest spirit. I have since apologised to him; and have also publicly intimated to the Leicester people that I considered we did wrong towards him. Whether O'Brien can forgive a wrong when it is acknowledged, I am not sure. I must be allowed to correct one of your sentences, in reference to my treatment of O'Brien. You say (on page 203) 'He had well trained and drilled his soldiers, and had made them understand the doctrine of passive obedience to his decrees.' Depend upon it, if I had attempted to make the people 'understand' anything of the kind, they would have stoned me in the street. If I had the 'power of a king' in Leicester, as you say, be assured it was by teaching and practising a very different kind of doctrine. No: the truth is, I was the people's instrument, rather than their director, even in those stormy contests with O'Brien and others. And it is thus, in all ages and in every country, whether on a large or small scale, that a popular leader keeps the lead: his temperament, nature, and powers fit him, by quick sympathy, and strong, energetic will, to become the people's mouthpiece, hand, and arm, either for good or evil.

With regard to Mr. Sturge, I think it is pretty generally known that I long ago confessed my regret at being misled to say one word against him. I have lived to receive proof of his kindest personal friendship; and believe him to be one of the best human beings. To Vincent I never apologised: I still think that, under the circumstances, he deserved what he got. I am sorry you stained your pages with the name of a man who called himself 'William Dean Taylor.' Taylor was not his name: he only assumed it to hide himself from the law, which would have punished him for his own crimes. He was one of the vilest and most immoral men that ever found his way into the Chartist ranks. As for little Philp, I dare say I might call him 'a boy;' for his appearance was so delicate that many called him the 'lady Chartist.' Depend upon it, I never 'almost went down on my marrow bones' to such a jackanapes. When you talk about his 'calm and *dignified* tone,' you remind me of the man who talked of the 'majesty of a magpie.'

I have written you at a greater length than I had intended; but hope you will, nevertheless, find room for this letter in your Appendix. I do not ask it as a favour. I never saw you but once in my life; but our meeting (it was at Leicester, in that troublous time,) left an impression of your intelligence and uprightness on my mind. The impression has been confirmed by what others have reported of you; and I confide that you will not only be willing, but anxious, to correct any misstatements into which you may have been unavoidably led, in the compilation of your 'History of the Chartist Movement.'—I am, dear sir, Your's truly,

Mr. R· G. Gammage.   THOMAS COOPER.

Cooper did quite right in claiming as a matter of justice insertion for the above and also in presuming that such insertion would not be refused. To defend oneself from attack, is the right of every man and we should be worthy only of being despised, did we refuse that right to another which we claim for ourselves; but which we regret to say, we have seldom obtained at the hands of our ruthless detractors, who disguise themselves with the cloak of Democracy, but who appear to know as much of real Democratic justice as an Emperor of Russia or a King of Naples.   We are quite willing to bear our testimony to Cooper's disinterestedness in his connection with the Chartists of Leicester.   We have had other evidence than his own, as to his sacrifices while residing in that town.   We never regarded him, in his connection with the Chartist movement, as a mercenary agitator; we always understood him to be the very reverse of that.   Our not noticing his periodicals and schools, was an omission, though not intentional.   With regard to the processions in Leicester about that period, it appears that we have confounded two different bodies of men—the Chartists and the unemployed,—though in many instances, doubtless they were the same persons.   Let us briefly explain what we know of the subject.   We were in Leicester in the spring of 1842, and called at the house of Cooper, a circumstance forgotten by that gentleman; but we actually walked with him to the first of the two meetings which O'Brien was advertised to address, and were on the platform during the evening.   At that time we had no acquaintance with O'Brien; but we were about to expostulate with Cooper in the course of the evening, when we were stopped by Beedham, who addressed us in no very courteous manner with "Leave him alone; he knows best what to do."   On that evening, while in Cooper's, we saw a large procession of half-starved men come up to the door, where they separated.   Cooper appeared very busy that evening.   The procession was headed by a man in a soldier's cap, and a red jacket.   Of course we did not mean that the military suit was anything but a mock one. It was these processions that stopped at the houses of the shopkeepers to receive their charitable contributions; and it appears from Cooper's letter, that with these processions he had nothing to do; a great number, however, of the men engaged in the one we saw, entered Cooper's house, including their mock military leader.   With regard to the "Lion of Freedom," it was the the general impression that the song was Cooper's. This doubtless arose from the fact, that Cooper published it in his hymn-book; and as most of the songs and hymns had the authors' names attached, and that had not, it was concluded that he was the author, as he sung it oftener than anything else at the meetings he attended.   When we said that Cooper had well trained and drilled his soldiers, and made them understand the doctrine of passive obedience to his decrees, we did not mean that he had literally told the people that they must in all instances obey him; but that, by his commanding manner, he had so influenced them that he could always be sure of their support. We had no intention of injuring Cooper by any observations we made. We would not do an injustice to any man if we knew it; and if our language upon some men appears hard, it is chiefly because of the injustice with which those men have treated others. Our intense and never slumbering hatred of injustice is the cause of our apparent harshness, and not any vindictive feelings towards the individuals. We look upon all injustice, done by one Democrat to another, as an obstacle in the way of Democracy; against such injustice we will, whatever be the issue, wage unceasing war. We congratulate Cooper and our readers upon the admirable spirit displayed generally in his letter, which is quite sufficient to assure us of the generosity of his nature.

APPENDIX B.

"THE PEOPLE'S CHARTER.

"BEING A BILL TO PROVIDE FOR THE JUST REPRESENTATION OF
THE PEOPLE OF GREAT BRITAIN AND IRELAND IN THE COMMONS
HOUSE OF PARLIAMENT. REVISED AT A CONFERENCE OF THE
PEOPLE, HELD AT BIRMINGHAM, DECEMBER, 1842.

" Whereas, to insure, in as far as it is possible by human
forethought and wisdom, the just government of the people,
it is necessary to subject those who have the power of making
the laws to a wholesome and strict responsibility to those
whose duty it is to obey them when made.

"And whereas, this responsibility is best enforced through
the instrumentality of a body which emanates directly from,
and is itself immediately subject to the whole people, and which
completely represents their feelings and their interests.

"And whereas, the Commons House of Parliament now
exercises, in the name and on the supposed behalf of the people,
the power of making the laws, it ought, in order to fulfil with
wisdom and with honesty the great duties imposed on it, to be
made the faithful and accurate representation of the people's
wishes, feelings, and interests.

"BE IT THEREFORE ENACTED:—

"That, from and after the passing of this Act, every male
inhabitant of these realms be entitled to vote for the election
of a member of Parliament; subject, however, to the following
conditions:—

"1. That he be a native of these realms, or a foreigner who
has lived in this country upwards of two years, and been
naturalized.

"2. That he be twenty-one years of age.

"3. That he be not proved insane when the lists of voters
are revised.

"4. That he be not undergoing the sentence of the laws at
the time when called upon to exercise the electoral right.

"5. That his electoral rights be suspended for bribery at
elections, or for personation, or for forgery of election certificates, according to the penalties of this Act.

"Electoral Districts.

"I. Be it enacted, that for the purpose of obtaining an equal representation of the people in the Commons House of Parliament, the United Kingdom be divided into three hundred electoral districts.*

"II. That each such district contain, as nearly as may be, an equal number of inhabitants.

"III. That the number of inhabitants be taken from the last census, and as soon as possible after the next ensuing decennial census shall have been taken, the electoral districts be made to conform thereto.

"IV. That each electoral district be named after the principal city or borough within its limits.

"V. That each electoral district return one representative to sit in the Commons House of Parliament.

"VI. That the Secretary of State for the Home Department shall appoint three competent persons as Commissioners, and as many Sub-Commissioners, as may be necessary for settling the boundaries of each of the three hundred electoral districts, and so on from time to time, whenever a new decennial census of the people be taken.

"VII. That the necessary expenses of the said commisioners sub-commisioners, clerks, and other persons employed by them in the performance of their duties, be paid out of the public treasury.

" Registration Officers.

" Be it enacted, that for the purpose of procuring an accurate registration of voters, for finally adjudicating in all cases of objections made against persons claiming to be registered, for receiving the nominations of Members of Parliament and Returning Officers, and declaring their election ; as well as for conducting and superintending all matters connected with registration, nomination, and election according to the provisions of this Act, the following officers be appointed :—

"1. Returning Officers for each electoral district.

"2. Deputy-Returning Officers for each district.

"3. A Registration Clerk for every parish containing number of inhabitants, or for every two or more parishes if united for the purpose of this Act.

"Returning Officer, and his duties.

"I. Be it enacted, that at the first general election after the passing of this Act, a Returning Officer be elected for every electoral district throughout the kingdom, and so in like

* There are, say, 6,000,000 men eligible to vote. This number, divided by 300, gives 20,000 to each member.

manner at the end of every year.

" II. That, at the end of every such period, the returning officer for each district be nominated in like manner, and elected at the same time as the Member of Parliament for the district ; he shall be eligible to be re-elected.

" III. That vacancies occasioned by the death, removal or resignation of the returning officer, shall in like manner be filled up as vacancies for Members of Parliament, for the unexpired term of the year.

" IV. That every returning officer shall appoint a deputy-returning officer, for the day of election, for every balloting place within his district, and in all cases be responsible for the just fulfilment of the duties of such deputies.

" V. That it be the duty of the returning officer to appoint a registration clerk for every parish within his district containing   number of inhabitants, or for every two or more parishes if united for the purposes of this Act ; and that in all cases he be responsible for the just fulfilment of the duties of such clerks.

" VI. That he also see that proper balloting places, and such other erections as may be necessary, be provided by each parish (or any number that may be united) and that the balloting boxes be made and provided according to the provisions of this Act.

" VII. That he receive the lists of voters from all the parishes in his district, in which lists shall be marked or specified the names of those persons who have been objected to by the registration clerks or any other persons.

" VIII. That between the first of April and the first of May in each year, he shall hold *open* Courts of Adjudication at such a number of places within his district as he may deem necessary, of which courts (place and time of meeting) he shall cause due notice to be given in each parish of the district, and at the same time invite all persons who have made objections and who have been objected to.   And after hearing the statements that may be made by both parties, he shall *finally adjudicate* whether the voters' names be placed on the register or not.

" IX. That the returning officer shall then cause to be made out alphabetical lists of all the registered voters in all the parishes within his district; which lists, signed and attested by himself, shall be used at all the elections for the district. Such lists to be sold to the public at reasonably low prices.

" X. That the returning officer receive all nominations for the member of his district, as well as for the returning officer of his district, and shall give public notice of the same according to the provisions of this Act ; he shall also receive from the Speaker of the House of Commons the orders for any new election, in case of the death or resignation of the member of the district, as well as the orders to superintend and conduct the election of any other district, in case of the death or resignation of the returning officer of such district.

"XI. That the returning officer shall also receive the returns from all the parishes within his district, on the day of election ; and on the day following the election he shall proclaim the state of the ballot, as directed by this Act, and perform the several duties appertaining to his office, as herein made and provided.

"XII. That the returning officer be paid for fulfilling the duties of his office, the sum of   per annum, as hereinafter mentioned.

"XIII. That, upon a petition being presented to the House of Commons by at least one hundred qualified electors of the district, against any returning officer of the same, complaining of corruption in the exercise of his office, or of incapacity, such complaints shall be enquired into by a committee of the House, consisting of seven members ; and, on their report being read, the members present shall then determine whether such returning officer be or be not guilty, or he be or be not incapacitated.

"XIV. That, for conducting the first elections after the passing of this Act, a returning officer for each district be temporarily appointed by the Secretary of State, to perform the duties prescribed by the Act. He shall resign his office as soon as the new one is appointed, and be paid as hereinafter mentioned. *See Penalties.*

"DEPUTY RETURNING OFFICER, AND HIS DUTIES.

"I. Be it enacted, that a deputy returning officer be appointed by the district returning officer to preside at each balloting place on the day of election, such deputy to be subject and responsible to his authority, as well as to the provisions of this Act.

"II. That it be the duty of the deputy returning officer to provide a number of competent persons, not exceeding   , to aid him in taking the ballot, and for performing the necessary business thereof.

"III. That the deputy returning officer shall see that proper registration lists are provided, and that the ballot begin at six o'clock in the morning precisely, and end at six o'clock in the afternoon of the same day.

"IV. That the deputy returning officer, in the presence of the agents of the candidates, examine and seal the balloting-boxes previously to the commencement of the balloting; he shall in like manner declare the number of votes for each candidate, and shall cause a copy of the same, signed by himself, to be forwarded to the returning officer of the district, and another copy to the registration clerk of the parish.

"V. That the deputy returning officer be paid for his services as hereinafter mentioned. *See Penalties.*

"THE REGISTRATION CLERK, HIS DUTIES.

"I. Be it enacted, that a Registration Clerk be appointed by the district returning officer for every parish within his district containing   inhabitants; or for every two or more parishes that may be united for the purposes of this Act; such clerk to be responsible to his authority, as well as to the provisions of this Act.

"II. That for the purpose of obtaining a correct registration of all the voters in each electoral district, the registration clerk of every parish as aforesaid throughout the kingdom shall, on or before the 1st of February in each year, take or cause to be taken round to every dwelling-house, poor-house, or union-workhouse in his parish, a printed notice of the following form:—

"Mr. John Jones, you are hereby required, within six days from the date hereof, to fill up this list with the names of all male inhabitants of your house, of 21 years of age and upwards; stating their respective ages, and the time they have resided with you; or, in neglect thereof, to forfeit the sum of one pound for every name omitted.

"A. B., *Registration Clerk.*

Name.	Address.	Age.	Time of Residence.
John Jones.	6, Upper North Place.	21 years.	3 months.

"N.B.—This list will be called for at the expiration of six days from this date.

"III. That, at the expiration of six days, as aforesaid, the registration clerk shall collect, or cause to be collected, the aforesaid lists, and shall cause to be made out from them an alphabetical list of all persons who are of the proper age and residence to qualify them as voters, according to the provisions of this Act.

"IV. That if the registration clerk shall have any just

reason to believe that the names, ages, or time of residence of any persons inserted in the aforesaid list are falsely entered, or not in accordance with the provisions of this Act, he shall not refuse to insert them in his list of voters, but he shall write the words 'objected to' opposite such names ; and so in like manner against the names of every person he may have just reason to consider ineligible, according to the provisions of this Act.

"V. That on or before the 8th of March in each year, the registration clerk shall cause the aforesaid alphabetical list of voters to be stuck against all church and chapel doors, market-houses, town-halls, session-houses, poorhouses, union-work-houses, and such other conspicuous places as he may deem necessary, from the 8th of March till the 22nd. He shall also cause a copy of such list to lie at his office, to be perused by any person without a fee, at all reasonable hours ; and copies of the said list shall be sold to the public at a reasonably low price.

"VI. That, on or before the 25th of March, the registration clerk shall take, or cause to be taken, a copy of the aforesaid list of voters to the returning officer of his district, which list shall be signed by himself, and be presented as a just and impartial list, according to his judgment, of all persons within his parish who are eligible according to their claims, as well as of all those who have been objected to by himself or other persons.

"VII. That the registration clerk shall attend the Court of Adjudication, according to the notice he shall receive from the returning officer, to revise his list, and shall perform the duties of his office as herein provided.

"VIII. That the registration clerk be paid for his services in the manner hereinafter mentioned.

"ARRANGEMENT FOR REGISTRATION.

"I. Be it enacted that every householder, as well as every person occupying or having charge of a dwelling-house, poor-house, or union-workhouse, who shall receive a notice from the registration clerk as aforesaid, shall cause the said notice to be correctly filled up with the names, ages, and time of residence of every male inmate or inhabitant of his or her house, of twenty-one years of age and upwards, within six days of the day of the date of such notice, and shall carefully preserve the same till it is called for by the registration clerk, or his proper officer.

"II. That when the list of voters is made out from these notices, and stuck on the church doors and places aforesaid, any person who finds his name not inserted in the list, and who believes he is duly qualified as a voter, shall, on presenting to the registration clerk a notice in the following form, have his name added to the list of voters:

> "*I, John Jones, carpenter, residing at———in the district of———being twenty-one years of age, and having resided at the above place during the last three months, require to be placed on the list of voters as a qualified elector for the said district.*

"III. That any person who is qualified as a voter to any electoral district, and shall have removed to any other parish *within the said district*, on presenting to the registration clerk of the parish he then resides in, his voter's certificate as proof of this, or the written testimony of any registration clerk who has previously registered him, he shall be entitled to be placed on the list of voters as aforesaid.

" IV. That if an elector of any parish in the district have any just grounds for believing that any person disqualified by this Act has been put upon any parish register within the said district, he may, at any reasonable hour, between the 1st and the 20th day of March, cause the following notices to be delivered, the one at the residence of the registration clerk, and the other at the residence of the person objected to ; and the registration clerk shall, in like manner, send notice of the grounds of objection to all persons he may object to, as aforesaid :—

"To the Registration Clerk.

> " *I, William Smith, elector of the parish of———in the district of———object to A.B. being on the register of voters, believing him to be disqualified.*

" To the person objected to.

> " *Mr. A.B. of———I, William Smith, elector of the parish of———in the district of———object to your name being on the register of voters for the following reasons :* (here state the reasons) *and I will support my objections by proofs before the returning Officer of the District.*

> " Dated this   day, &c.

" V. That if the person thus objecting neglect to attend the court of the returning officer at the proper time, to state his objections, he shall be fined ten shillings for every such neglect, the same to be levied on his goods and chattels, provided he is not prevented from attending by sickness or accident ; in which case his medical certificate, or a certificate signed by ten voters certifying such fact, shall be forwarded to the returning officer, who shall then determine whether the claim to be put on the register be allowed or not.

" VI. That if the person objected to fails to attend the court of the returning officer at the proper time, to substantiate his claim, his name shall be erased from the register, provided he is not prevented by sickness or accident; in which case a certificate shall be forwarded, and the returning officer shall determine as before directed.

" VII. That if it should be proved before the returning officer, in his open Court of Adjudication, that any person has frivolously or vexatiously objected to any one being placed on the list of voters, such person objecting shall be fined twenty shillings and expenses, the same to be levied on his goods and chattels, and paid to the person objected to.

"VIII. That, as early as possible after the lists are revised as aforesaid, the returning officer shall cause a copy of the same to be forwarded to every registration clerk within his district.

"IX. That the registration clerk of every parish shall then correctly copy from such lists the name, age, and residence of every qualified elector within his parish or parishes, into a book made for that purpose, and shall place a number opposite each name. He shall then, within——days, take, or cause to be taken, to all such electors, *a voter's certificate* of the following form, the number on which shall correspond with the number in the aforesaid book:—

> "*No.* 123. *This is to certify that James Jones, of*——*is eligible to vote for one person to be returned to Parliament (as well as for the Returning Officer) for the district of*——*for one year from the date hereof.*
> "Dated.
> "Registration Clerk.

"X. That if any person lose his voter's certificate by fire, or any other accident, he shall not have a new certificate till the next registration; but on the day of any election, if he can establish his identity on the testimony of two witnesses, to the satisfaction of the registration clerk, as being the qualified voter described in the registration book, he shall be allowed to vote.

"XI. That the returning officer is hereby authorised and commanded to attach any small parishes within his district for the purposes of this Act, and not otherwise; and in like manner to unite all extra-parochial places to some adjacent parish. *See Penalties.*

Arrangement for Nominations.

"I. Be it enacted, that for the purpose of guarding against too great a number, who might otherwise be heedlessly proposed, as well as for giving time for the electors to inquire into the merits of the persons who may be nominated for Members of Parliament, as well as for Returning Officers, that all nominations be taken as hereinafter directed.

"That for all general elections of Members of Parliament a requisition of the following form, signed by at least one hundred qualified electors of the district, be delivered to the returning officer of the district between the first and tenth day of May in each year ; and that such requisition constitute the nomination of such persons as a candidate for the district :—

"*We the undersigned electors of the district of recommend A. B. of   as a fit and proper person to represent the people of this district in the Commons House of Parliament, the said A. B. being qualified to be an elector according to the provisions of this Act,*

"Dated, &c.

"Signed.

"III. That the returning officer of every electoral district shall, on or before the 13th of May in each year, cause a list of all the candidates thus nominated to be stuck up against all church and chapel doors, market-houses, town-halls, session-houses, poor-houses, and union-workhouses, and such other conspicuous places within the district as he may deem necessary.

"IV. That, whenever a vacancy is occasioned in any district by the death, resignation, or other cause, of the Member of Parliament, the returning officer of that district shall, within three days after his orders from the Speaker of the House of Commons, give notice thereof in all the parishes of his district in the manner described for giving notices, and he shall at the same time request all nominations to be made as aforesaid, within ten days from the receipt of his order, and shall also appoint the day of election within eighteen days from the receipt of such order from the Speaker of the House of Commons.

"V. That if, from any circumstances, no person has been nominated as a candidate for the district on or before the 10th of May, persons may then be nominated in the manner described as aforesaid at any time previous to the 20th of May, but not after that date.

"VI. That, at the first election after the passing of this Act and at the expiration of every year, the nomination of candidates for the Returning Officer be made in the same manner as for Members of Parliament, and nominations for vacancies that may occur in like manner.

"VII. That if two or more persons are nominated as aforesaid for members to serve in Parliament for the district, the returning officer shall, at any time, between the 15th and 31st of May, (Sundays excepted) appoint such times and places (not exceeding   ) as he shall think most convenient to the electors of the district for the candidates to appear before them, then and there to explain their views and solicit the suffrages of the electors.

"VIII. That the returning officer see that the places above described be convenient for the purpose, and that as many such erections be put up as may be necessary; the same to be paid for by the returning officer, and charged in his account as hereinafter mentioned.

"IX. That, for the purpose of keeping good order and public decorum, the returning officer either take the chair at such meetings himself, or appoint a deputy for that purpose.

"X. That, provided only one candidate be proposed for Member of Parliament for the district by the time herein before mentioned, the returning officer do cause notice to be given, as hereinafter mentioned, that such a candidate is elected a member for the district; and if only one candidate be proposed for the Returning Officer, he shall in like manner be declared duly elected.

"XI. That no other qualification shall be required than the choice of the electors, according to the provisions of this Act; providing that no persons, excepting the cabinet ministers, be eligible to serve in the Commons House of Parliament who are in the receipt of any emolument derivable from any place or places held under Government, or of retired allowances arising therefrom.

" ARRANGEMENT FOR ELECTIONS.

" I. Be it enacted, that a general election of Members of Parliament, for the electoral districts of the United Kingdom, do take place on the first Monday in June in each year; and that all vacancies, by death or otherwise, shall be filled up as nearly as possible within eighteen days after they occur.

" II. That a general election of Returning Officers for all the districts take place at the expiration of every three years on the first Monday in June, and at the same time Members of Parliament are to be elected; and that all vacancies be filled up within eighteen days after they occur.

" III. That every person who has been registered as aforesaid, and who has a voter's certificate, shall have the right of voting in the district in which he has been registered, and in that only; and of voting for the Member of Parliament for that district, and the Returning Officer for that district, and for those only.

" IV. That, for the purpose of taking the votes of the qualified electors, the parish officer in every parish of the district (or in every two or more parishes if united for the purposes of this Act) shall cause proper places to be provided, so as to admit of the arrangements described in Schedule A, and so constructed (either permanently or temporarily as they may think proper) that the votes may be taken with due despatch, and so as to secure the elector while voting from being inspected by any other person.

" V. That the parish officers of every parish in the district provide a sufficient number of balloting boxes, made after a model described in Schedule B (or made on one plan by persons appointed to make them, as was the case with weights and measures), and none but such boxes, duly certified, shall be used.

" VI. That, immediately preceding the commencement of the balloting, each ballot-box shall be opened by the deputy returning officer (or otherwise examined as the case may be), in the presence of an agent appointed by each candidate, and shall then be sealed by him and by the agents of the candidates, and not again be opened until the balloting has finally closed, when notice shall be given to such of the agents of the candidates as may then be present, to attend to the opening of the boxes and ascertaining the number of votes for each candidate.

" VII. That the deputy returning officer preside in the front of the ballot-box, and see that the balloting is conducted with strict impartiality and justice ; and that the various clerks, assistants, and parish constables properly perform their respective duties, and that strict order and decorum be preserved among the friends of the candidates, as well as among all persons employed in conducting the election ; and he is hereby authorised and empowered to cause all persons to be taken into custody who interrupt the proceedings of the election, seek to contravene the provisions of this Act, or fail to obey his lawful authority.

" VIII. That during the time the balloting is going on, two agents of each candidate may be in the space fronting the ballot-box, and immediately behind the deputy returning officer, in order that they may see that the election is fairly conducted ; such persons to be provided by the deputy returning officer with cards of admission, and to pass in and out by the entrance assigned them.

" IX. That the registration clerk of every parish in the district, who has been appointed for the purposes of registration, be at the balloting place, in the station assigned him, previously to the commencement of the balloting, and see that no person pass on to the balloting place till he has examined his certificate, and seen that it corresponds with the registration list.

"X. That the parish constables and the officers stationed at the entrance of the balloting place, shall not permit any person to enter unless he shows his voter's certificate, except the persons employed in conducting the election, or those persons who have proved the loss of their voter's certificate.

"XI. That at the end of every year, or whenever the Returning Officer is elected at the same time as the member for the district, a division shall be made in the balloting places, and the boxes and balloting so arranged as to ensure the candidates the strictest impartiality and justice, by preventing the voter from giving two votes for either of the candidates.

"XII. That on the day of election, the balloting commence at six o'clock in the forenoon and terminate at six o'clock in the afternoon of the same day.

"XIII. That when any voter's certificate is examined by the registration clerk, and found to be correct, he shall be allowed to pass on to the next barrier, where a balloting-ball shall be given him by the person appointed for that purpose ; he shall then pass on to the balloting box, and, with all due dispatch, shall put the balloting-ball into the box of the candidate he wishes to vote for, after which he shall, without delay, leave the room by the door assigned for the purpose. *See Schedules A and B.*

"XIV. That, at the close of the balloting, the deputy returning officer, in the presence of the agents of the candidates and other persons present, shall break open the seals of the balloting-boxes and ascertain the number for each candidate; he shall then cause copies of the same to be publicly posted outside the balloting place; and immediately forward (by a trusty messenger) a copy of the same, signed by himself and the agents present, to the returning officer of the district; he shall then deliver a similar copy to the registration clerk, who shall carefully preserve the same, and produce it if necessary.

"XV. That the persons employed as assistants, for inspecting the certificates and attending to the balloting, be paid as hereinafter mentioned.

"XVI. That all the expense of registration, nominations and elections, as aforesaid, together with the salaries of the Returning Officers, Registration Clerk, Assistants, Constables, and such other persons as may be necessary, as well as the expense of all balloting places, balloting-boxes, hustings, and other necessaries for the purposes of this Act, be paid out of an *equitable district rate*, which a District Board, composed of one Parochial Officer chosen by each of the parishes in the district, or for any two or more parishes if united for the purposes of this Act, are hereby empowered and commanded to levy on all householders within the district.

"XVII. That all expenses necessary for the purposes of this Act incurred within the district be paid by the district board as aforesaid, or their treasurer; that the salaries of all officers and assistants required for the purposes of this Act be fixed and paid by the said board, according to the expenses and duties of the various localities.

"XVIII. That all accounts of receipts and expenditure for electoral purposes shall be kept distinct, and be audited by auditors appointed by the district board, as aforesaid; copies of which accounts shall be printed for the use of the respective parishes in the district.

"XIX. That all canvassing for Members of Parliament, as well as for Returning Officers, is hereby declared to be illegal, and meetings for that purpose during the balloting on the day of election, are hereby also declared to be illegal. *See Penalties.*

"DURATION OF PARLIAMENT.

"I. Be it enacted, that the Members of the House of Commons, chosen as aforesaid, shall meet on the first Monday in June in each year, and continue their sittings from time to time as they may deem it convenient, till the first Monday in June following, when the next new Parliament shall be chosen; they shall be eligible to be re-elected.

"II. That, during an adjournment, they be liable to be called together by the Executive in cases of emergency.

"III. That a register be kept of the daily attendance of each member, which, at the close of the session, shall be printed as a sessional paper, showing how the members have attended.

"PAYMENT OF MEMBERS.

"I. Be it enacted, that every Member of the House of Commons be entitled, at the close of the session, to a writ of expenses on the Treasury, for his legislative duties in the public service, and shall be paid   per annum.*

"PENALTIES.

"I. Be it enacted, that if any person cause himself to be registered in more than one electoral district, and vote in more than one such district, upon conviction thereof before any two

*The Committee understand that the *daily payment* of Members of Parliament has operated beneficially in Canada; but they fear that such mode of payment holds out a motive for lengthening the sessions unnecessarily; and if the time of sitting is limited by law, it may lead to too hasty legislations, both of which evils are obviated by an annual payment.

justices of the peace within either of such districts, he shall incur for the first offence the penalty of three months' imprisonment, and for the second offence twelve months' imprisonment.

"II. That any person who shall be convicted as aforesaid of wilfully neglecting to fill up his or her notice within the proper time, or of leaving out the name of any inmate in his or her notice, shall for the first offence incur the penalty of one pound for every name omitted; and for the second offence incur the penalty of three months' imprisonment, and be deprived of his electoral rights for three years.

" III. That any person who shall be convicted as aforesaid of forging any name, age, or time of residence, on any notice, shall for the first offence incur the penalty of three months' imprisonment, and for the second offence three months' imprisonment, and be deprived of his elective rights for three years.

"IV. That any person who shall be convicted as aforesaid, of having in any manner obtained the certificate of an elector other than his own, and of having voted or attempted to vote by means of such false certificate, shall for the first offence incur the penalty of three months' imprisonment, and for the second offence three months' imprisonment, and be deprived of his elective rights for three years.

" V. That any person who shall be convicted as aforesaid, of having forged a voter's certificate, or of having forged the name of any person to any certificate ; or having voted or attempted to vote on such forged certificate ; knowing such to have been forged, shall for the first offence incur the penalty of three months' imprisonment, and for the second offence three months' imprisonment, and be deprived of his elective rights for three years.

"VI. That any person who shall be convicted as aforesaid, of having forged, or caused to be forged, the names of any voters to a requisition nominating a Member of Parliament or a Returning Officer, shall for the first offence incur the penalty of three months' imprisonment, and for the second offence three months' imprisonment, and to be deprived of his elective rights for three years.

"VII. That any person who shall be convicted as aforesaid of bribery, in order to secure his election, shall be subject for the first offence to incur the penalty of two years' imprisonment, and for the second offence shall be imprisoned two years, and be deprived of his elective rights for five years.

"VIII. That any Agent of any Candidate, or any other person, who shall be convicted as aforesaid, of bribery at any election, shall be subject for the first offence to incur the penalty of twelve months' imprisonment, and for the second offence twelve months' imprisonment, and be deprived of his elective rights for five years.

" IX. That any person who shall be convicted as aforesaid, of going from house to house, or place to place, to solicit in any way votes in favour of any candidate for Parliament or Returning Officer, after the nomination as aforesaid, shall for the first offence incur the penalty of one month's imprisonment, and for the second offence two months.

"X. That any person who shall be convicted as aforesaid of calling together, or causing an election meeting to be held in any district during the day of election, shall for the first offence incur the penalty of three months' imprisonment, and for the second offence six months.

" XI. That any person who shall be convicted as aforesaid, of interrupting the balloting, or the business of the election, shall incur the penalty of three months' imprisonment for the first offence, and six months for the second.

" XII. That if any messenger, who may be sent with the state of the ballot to the returning officer, or with any other notice, shall wilfully delay the same, or in any way by his consent or conduct cause the same to be delayed, on conviction as aforesaid, shall incur the penalty of six months' imprisonment.

" XIII. That any Returning Officer who shall be convicted as aforesaid, of having neglected to appoint proper officers as directed by this Act, to see that proper balloting places and balloting-boxes are provided, and to give the notices and perform the duties herein required of him, shall forfeit for each case of neglect the sum of £20.

"XIV. That if any Returning Officer be found guilty of bribery or corrupt practices in the execution of the duties herein assigned to him, he shall incur the penalty of twelve months' imprisonment, and be deprived of his elective rights for five years.

"XV. That if any Deputy Returning Officer be convicted as aforesaid of having neglected to perform any of the duties herein assigned him, he shall forfeit for such neglect three pounds.

"XVI. That if any Deputy Returning Officer be convicted as aforesaid of bribery and corrupt practices in the execution of the duties of his office he shall incur the penalty of six months' imprisonment, and the deprivation of his elective rights for three years.

"XVII. That if any Registration Clerk be convicted as

aforesaid of having neglected to perform any of the duties herein assigned him, he shall forfeit for each such neglect five pounds.

"XVIII. That if any Registration Clerk be convicted as aforesaid of bribery and corrupt practices in the execution of the duties of his office, he shall incur the penalty of six month's imprisonment, and the deprivation of his elective rights for three years.

"XIX. That if the Parochial Officers in any parish neglect or refuse to comply with any of the provisions of this Act, they shall forfeit for every such neglect the sum of £50, or in default of payment, twelve months' imprisonment.

"XX. That all fines and penalties incurred under the provisions of this Act be recoverable before any two justices of the peace, within the district where the offence shall have been committed, and in default of payment, the said justices shall issue their warrant of distress against the goods and chattels of the offender; or in default of sufficent distress, he shall be imprisoned according to the provisions of this Act.

"That all Acts and parts of Acts relating to registration, nominations, or elections of Members of Parliament, as well as the duration of Parliament and sittings of members, are hereby repealed."

APPENDIX C.

THE LANCASTER TRIALS.

LIST OF PRISONERS FOUND GUILTY ON THE FOURTH AND
FIFTH COUNTS, AND OF THOSE ACQUITTED.

FOURTH COUNT.

F. A. Taylor
Robert Brook
George Candelet
James Fenton
P. M. M'Douall
Bernard McCartney

James Arthur
John Campbell
John Durham
James Leach
James Mooney

J. R. H. Bairstow
Thomas Cooper
C. Doyle
John Leach
David Morrison

FIFTH COUNT.

William Aitkin
A. Challenger
John Hoyle
Richard Otley
Robert Ramsden

John Arran
G. J. Harney
John Norman
Samuel Parkes
James Skevington

William Beesley
William Hill
Feargus O'Connor
Thomas Railton
Wm. Woodruffe

ACQUITTED BY CONSENT.

John Atlinson
William Scholefield
Thomas Pitt

James Cartledge
John Thornton

George Johnson
John Wilde

NOT GUILTY.

Patrick Broply
John Crossley
Thomas Mahon
Thomas Storah
James Grassby
James Scholefield
Thomas Browne Smith

J. Chippendale
Thomas Fraser
David Ross
William Booth
John Massey
Wm. Stephenson

Joseph Clarke
John Lomax
Albert Wolfenden
John Fletcher
Richard Pilling
James Taylor

LIST OF WORKS CONSULTED AS REFERENCES IN WRITING THE
FOREGOING HISTORY.

Northern Star ; Northern Liberator ; National Reformer
(1st and 2nd series) ; M'Douall's Chartist and Republican
Journal ; English Chartist Circular ; Scottish Chartist Circular ;
National Vindicator ; Lloyd's Weekly Newspaper ; Trials of
Feargus O'Connor and fifty-eight others (published by Feargus
O'Connor) ; O'Brien's Vindication of his conduct at the Sturge
Conference ; The Nonconformist ; The Evening Star ; The
Leicestershire Mercury ; The Reformer ; The Power of the
Pence ; Reynolds's Newspaper ; Reynolds's Political Instructor ;
The Progressionist ; Barker's People ; Notes to the People (by
Ernest Jones) ; Harney's Democratic Review ; Harney's Red
Republican, and Friend of the People ; Political Examiner ;
Leader ; People's Paper ; Northern Tribune ; Life of H.
Hetherington ; Star of Freedom ; The Felon Newspaper ; The
United Irishman ; The Nation ; The National Instructor (by
Feargus O'Connor) ; Howitt's Journal ; a Brief Enquiry into
the Natural Rights of Man. Besides these sources of infor-
mation, the author stands largely indebted to his own
experience, and the conversations he has at various times held
with leading men in the Chartist movement.

INDEX.